The 2012 BRD

BASEBALL RULE DIFFERENCES

BY CARL CHILDRESS

The only complete reference
to all differences: National Federation,
NCAA, NAIA,
and Official Rules.

29th EDITION

ACKNOWLEDGMENTS

This book supplements rather than supplants the rulebooks and case books published by the National Federation of State High School Associations (NFHS), the National Collegiate Athletic Association (NCAA), the National Association of Intercollegiate Athletics (NAIA), and the *Official Baseball Rules* (used in professional games and most youth leagues) as published by *Triumph Books*. The BRD is a source for rule differences only among those four codes. If a rule is not covered in this book, all books treat the situation the same.

My sincere thanks go also to the NFHS, particularly Kyle McNeely, NCAA, NAIA, and the Professional Baseball Umpire Corp for their invaluable assistance in providing interpretations, advice, and guidance. Thanks also are in order for Referee Enterprises, Inc., who published this book from 1989 through 1996. My special gratitude goes to Tom Hammill, who first saw the need to publish my book, and to Scott Ehret, who edited it during those eight years at *Referee*. It was Scott and Gerry Davis Umpire Education who convinced me to bring the BRD back to life. The task was picked up by Bradley Batt at Officiating.com, and the book is now independently published.

Let me also thank my readers (and critics) from previous years. If you are a "repeat offender," thanks for coming back. But if this is your first time with the BRD, let me thank you in advance. I know you will be educated, pleased, possibly amazed – perhaps even entertained.

Finally: Interpretations listed without specific attribution, including those suggestions styled as "BRD recommends," are mine – and mine alone – unless I claim support from a recognized authority.

INTRODUCTION

Please read the important announcement on page 11.

1 **ORIGIN.** Baseball and chess, so they say, have the most stable rules of any games. "They say" never followed the National Federation (yearly) or the NCAA (bi-yearly) rule changes. Even the OBR has come to the party, with major changes in 2007 and 2010. The last change before that was 1987! As a result of the growing separation among the various playing codes, to help amateur umpires find their way through the maze of differences, and because I kicked a pitching rule in a college game, I first offered *The Rules of Baseball: A Comparison* in 1982. Since 1992 it has been called *Baseball Rule Differences*, or "The BRD." This edition contains all changes for 2010 and 2011.

2 **PURPOSE.** The book, however, is much more than an encyclopedia of obscure rules and interpretations. The BRD organizes and lists the differences, examines the diverging philosophies behind them, explains and illustrates them, and advises you how best to cope with them when – if – they arise in your games. This book is an unparalleled guide for practical umpires. The BRD will quickly become your most valuable baseball book.

3 **ORGANIZATION.** The book is arranged alphabetically rather than by rule number. The ALPHABETICAL INDEX (page 339) simplifies your search for a major baseball category. This edition contains more than 3400 bibliographic references and rule citations as well as 1334 cross references. The CITATION INDEX is like a reverse telephone directory, one that leads you from the rulebook to the BRD section where the import of that statute is discussed.

4 **ABBREVIATIONS.**

AL: American League.

AO: Authoritative opinion.

AR: An Approved Ruling in NCAA or OBR rules.

CMT: A comment contained in the FED or OBR case books.

Note: The OBR case book is the italicized portion of their rulebook.

DBT: Dead-ball territory.

ED: Edition.

EX: Exception. (used only for rules citations)

FED: National Federation of State High Schools.

MLB: Major league baseball.

MLU: Major league umpire.
NAIA: National Association of Intercollegiate Athletics.
NCAA: National Collegiate Athletic Association.
NFHS: See FED.
NL: National League.
OBR: *Official Baseball Rules.*

OFF INTERP: This indicates a ruling made by one of the official rules interpreters, identified in Section 5 by an asterisk (*). **THIS EDITION CONTAINS 430 CURRENT OFFICIAL INTERPRETATIONS. *(ADDED)* THAT'S MORE THAN 60 NEW OFF INTERPS, MOST OF THEM PROVIDED BY JIM PARONTO, THE RULES INTERPRETER FOR THE NCAA.** Each OFF INTERP is enclosed by a box, as is this paragraph. Appendix B is a listing of the OFF INTERPS in this edition.

PEN: Penalty. (used only for rule citations)
§ : The BRD symbol for "section."
***REF*:** *Referee* magazine.
UIC: Umpire-in-chief or plate umpire.
URC: Umpire Resource Center bulletin board (www.umpire.org).

5 AUTHORITIES.

An arrow (➜) signifies a source of official interpretations. An asterisk (*) identifies someone whose opinion is authoritative though it does not yet rise to the level of "black-letter law," defined as specific language directly in the rulebook.

BOOTH: Jim Booth, OBR and LL on-line umpire for eTeamz.com Message Board.
* **BREMIGAN:** The late Nick Bremigan, AL umpire.
* **BRINKMAN:** Joe Brinkman, former AL umpire.
CC: Carl Childress.
➜ **DEARY:** The late Barney Deary, former director of PBUC (*q.v.*), known before as BUD (Baseball Umpire Development).
* **EVANS:** Jim Evans, former AL umpire and owner of the Academy of Professional Umpiring.
➜ **FETCHIET:** Rich Fetchiet, former secretary / editor of the NCAA rulebook.
➜ **FITZPATRICK:** Mike Fitzpatrick, former director of PBUC.
FORUM: Message Board – http://www.officialforum.com/forum/2 (hosted by Officiating.com).
➜ **HOPKINS:** B. Elliot Hopkins, current rules interpreter for the FED.
* **JEA:** *Official Baseball Rules Annotated* by Jim Evans, so dubbed by Jim Porter of Officiating.com. The JEA is considered the foremost

repository of "authoritative opinion" for OBR. Evans includes many official interpretations as well. Citations are: Chapter: Page [*e.g.*, (7:35)].

→ **JONES:** Cris Jones of PBUC, who supplied a few official interpretations via the eTeamz.com OBR Message Board.

→ **LEPPERD:** Tom Lepperd, Director of Umpire Administration for MLB.

→ **McNEELY:** Kyle McNeely, permanent chairman of the NFHS Rules Committee.

→ **MLBUM:** Major League Baseball Umpires Manual, containing instructions to umpires. That book is not generally available to amateur officials or clinicians. The BRD references many of those interpretations to the appropriate pages in the ***(EDITED)*** Wendelstedt manual. Also, I have swapped MLBUM language and citations for identical rulings in the PBUC Manual.

MTG: A clinic for FED or NCAA, with information given by a national interpreter.

NEWS: The *National Federation News*, a publication containing official rulings for high school baseball. At the time of this edition of the BRD, current interpretations may be viewed at the FED Website: http://www.nfhs.org

→ **PARONTO:** Jim Paronto, editor of the NCAA rulebook.

→ **PBUC UMPIRE MANUAL:** The umpire manual from the Professional Baseball Umpires Corp, a book containing official interpretations for all affiliated minor leagues. It is pronounced PEA-BUCK. The manual was greatly expanded in 2004, incorporating many additional rulings from the MLBUM. It will be cited simply as **PBUC**.

→ **PBUC STAFF:** The umpires employed by the Professional Baseball Umpires Corp. A few interpretations come from the winter meetings of the staff in Dallas, December 2000, and Boston, 2001.

PI: Professional interpretation, taken from the JEA.

→ **RUMBLE:** Brad Rumble, former rules interpreter for FED.

SE: Scott Ehret, former editor of *Referee* magazine.

STEVENS: Tim Stevens, Director of Baseball and NFHS rules interpreter, Washington state.

TH: Tom Hammill, former editor of *Referee* magazine.

→ **THURSTON:** Bill Thurston, former secretary / editor of the NCAA rulebook.

* **WENDELSTEDT:** Hunter Wendelstedt, NL umpire and co-owner of Wendelstedt Umpire School. A major improvement: The BRD has replaced the Jaksa/Roder manual (J/R) with the authoritative opinions

and official interpretations of Hunter and his staff. Their *Rules and Interpretations Manual* (2010 ed) is the most recent compilation of OBR plays and rulings available to the amateur umpire. You will find 400 OBR plays in that book! Email admin@umpireschool.com. Hunter's citation formats in the BRD include: HW/page# and P#/page #. (The "P" stands for "play.")

YEAST: Dave Yeast, former director of umpires and chief clinician for the NCAA.

6 SECTION FORMAT. (539 SECTIONS)

A When a section is revised for this edition, the heading is preceded by this symbol (★). Those revisions might include: (1) adding or dropping a note; (2) adding a new (or newly discovered) OFF INTERP; (3) recommending a different procedure; (4) explaining an editorial revision that clarifies the rule; (5) correcting a mistake from an earlier edition; or (6) adding amended rules' language. Additionally, to make it simpler to scroll through the headings, every section is identified by this symbol: ✪

To aid returning users of the BRD, I have marked all significant changes from the last edition as follows:

(NEW): The section has been created for this edition. It sometimes includes previous BRD material, collected from other sections; but it can also include a rule just added to baseball. See, for example, § 539.

(CHANGED):The section text, with the significant alteration generally underlined, includes changes made by a rules committee or by an official interpreter in a **PUBLISHED** ruling.

> "Quotation marks" and / or underlining identify exact rulebook language. The changed paragraph is bordered and shaded, like this one.

(REVISED): An OFF INTERP, play ruling, or rule explication is different from last year because of a rule change or inadvertent error.

(ADDED): The material is new to the BRD but not to the baseball lexicon. It also indicates plays, authoritative opinions, and notes that are new to this edition.

(EDITED): The text or format is changed for clarity or accuracy.

B I have referenced the NFHS and NCAA Points of Emphasis since 1982, the year the BRD was first printed. That will be a continuing practice, so new umpires can look back and track the issues that were "hot" in any given year. The Point of Emphasis will look like this: **POE 2008**.

C Sections tagged with an infinity symbol (∞) identify "different" rules that should be officiated alike, regardless of the level: That is, the rule is essentially the same at all levels, or – more often – a current interpretation, rather than exact rulebook language, harmonizes the codes. A reader might ask: "If we're supposed to call it the same at all levels, why do you cover it in your book of 'differences.'? Doesn't that just confuse umpires?" My response: When the official language of the codes is harmonized, only then will I delete the text that had outlined the previous deviations. If the harmony is created by an "authoritative opinion" or by an "official interpretation," I'll keep the explanation and discussion for two reasons: (1) Some umpire readers may not have seen the most recent rulings; and, more importantly, (2) official interpretations are subject to change, sometimes within the course of a season.

D When the national rulebook omits coverage:
(1) For those text paragraphs marked "**Point not covered**," rules language does not exist, but an official interpreter has decided how the play situation should be handled at that level.
(2) For those text paragraphs marked "No provision," neither rules language nor official interpretation exists. Each umpire must decide for himself the proper ruling. Officials encountering unexplored territory generally use as their guide any rule or precedent available from other levels, which is another benefit accruing from the BRD. (See ¶ 4 below.)
(3) Occasionally, following "No provisions," you will find the BRD recommendation for the umpire's proper course; for example, "Treat as in NCAA." Remember, though, it is only a recommendation.

(4) OFF INTERP 1-D4: **FETCHIET:** If no NCAA rule or interpretation exists to cover the situation, the umpire should adopt the OBR rule or interpretation. (phone call to cc, 11/27/01) ✠

(5) Often, one book has the same rule as another. For example, I might mark the NCAA content "Same as FED." We include the citation of the book being used as the model: "Same as FED 8-4-1c" but only if there is more than one provision in the model. The purpose

is to separate the exact provision that is the "same as" from others in that section; *i.e.*, an **ALSO** or OFF INTERP.

(6) While BRD still uses the same sources for official interpretations, in 2001 I added "authoritative opinion."

As I pointed out above, the views of those experts do not rise to the level of "official," but amateur umpires would do well to consider their opinions, regardless of the level being officiated.

E Shorthand explanation:

(1) The numbering style for plays is: A runner who begins the play on third is always R3; on second, R2; on first, R1. The batter or batter-runner is always B1 until play stops after his batted ball. Each defensive player is designated as in the scorebook: F6 is the shortstop, F1 is the pitcher, etc. Important note: I no longer limit the play rulings to one book [*e.g.*, FED only] unless the play is designed to illustrate a statute unique to that code.

(2) A penalty of "ball / balk" means the penalty depends on whether a runner is on base.

(3) A penalty of "warning / ejection" means that when the individual who was warned commits an identical infraction, he will be ejected. A penalty of "warning / illegal pitch" means that when the individual who was warned commits an identical infraction, the umpire shall charge him with a "ball."

(4) A penalty of "team warning / ejection" means that because of one team member's infraction, his entire team is warned. The next offender from that team guilty of the same offense is ejected without warning. As defined in the BRD, the term refers to a procedure in FED only.

(5) If the phrase is "runners return TOP" or "return to their original bases," they go back to the bases occupied at the time of the pitch.

(6) If the phrase is "award from TOT," the awards are measured from the bases occupied at the time of the throw.

(7) If the phrase is "runners remain TOI," they keep (or return to) the bases occupied at the time of the interference.

(8) Unless otherwise indicated, an "overthrow" means the ball became dead after the throw.

(9) Federation and NCAA rule references are separated by hyphens (8-1 refers to rule eight, section one); OBR references, by a decimal point (8.01 refers to rule eight, section one). To differentiate rulebook from case book citations, the Federation separates case book references by decimal points. (8.1.1a refers to a play dealing with rule

8-1-1.) Unless otherwise noted, Federation case book citations are from the 2012 edition and from the NFHS 2012 Website.

Readers sometimes ask why I include so many references from past years. The answer is simple: None of the rulings I cite have ever been rescinded. The Federation case book has a finite number of pages. A ruling dropped from their book – to make room for new situations – does not mean umpires should stop enforcing the missing provision. In 2001 the FED changed its citation form to 1.1.1 SITUATION A. The BRD retains the old style. All citations from the PBUC manual (formerly known as NAPBL) are identified by page numbers between braces { } and are from the 2012 edition.

F A "Note" is information that is only rarely paraphrased or quoted from the rule; rather, it generally contains additional data: history, interpretation, explanation, personal opinion, perhaps even a war story or two. For easy reference, I also numbered *Notes* consecutively throughout the manuscript This edition contains 510 notes. Notes are always printed in this type face and indicated by this symbol; ❀ ***(ADDED)*** When a Note is followed by a section number (e.g., Note 34-37 on p. 39), that is a reminder to the author and editor (me) NOT to erase the Note since there are references to it in other sections.

G All Plays are indicated by this symbol: ✲. When a Play is NOT indented, the material applies to all three levels. *Notes* that discuss a Play ruling are indented but not separated from the play. You'll find 274 plays in this edition.

> Plays fully indented, as is this paragraph, apply only to the code covered in the section text immediately above or to the codes identified in the Play.

H The various books often emphasize words, phrases, or clauses. For editorial ease, all ORIGINAL EMPHASIS WILL APPEAR IN THIS TYPE FACE, known as SMALL CAPS. Material I have highlighted is signaled by **THIS TYPE FACE.** I use this to direct your careful attention to selected portions of either the directly-quoted rules, opinion text, or general BRD text.

I Any text within brackets inside quotes is explanatory material I have added. Example: "Runners return [to their original bases] unless forced to advance."

J "Unmarked change" indicates the rules committee did not shade the rule revision. "Unannounced change" indicates the rules committee did not mention that the rule had been amended.

K Sometimes I need to cross-reference two sections where the material is of importance to all three rulebooks. When that happens, I have added a single reference following the section title.

L For editorial convenience I have numbered OFF INTERPs (*e.g.*, 46-34, which refers to OFF INTERP 46 in § 34); Plays (*e.g.*, 44-48, which refers to Play 44 in § 48); and AOs (*e.g.*, 24-436, which refers to AO 24 in § 436). Some rules include ancillary clauses, marked in the BRD as **ALSO**. They are numbered sequentially throughout the book, which makes for ease of reference when a section contains several different clauses. Also, to make the author's life easy, the BRD now indicates the language of an OFF INTERP with this symbol: ✠

M The OBR in 2007 lettered the OBR case book comments when they are attached to a subsection. For example, there's 6.02b CMT. Subsequent paragraphs in such material will be numbered here to make it easy to find the language being referenced. The *second* paragraph at that citation begins "Appeals on a half swing ..." and is labeled in the BRD as CMT ¶ 2. There are nine paragraphs.

N When the black-letter law matches in all three books, the text of the "difference" is deleted; but I retain the section title. Because of rule or interpretation changes, occasionally a "deleted" section springs back to life. That is marked ***(REVIVED)***.

O A friend of mine pointed out I wasn't consistent with some spellings: "Sometimes you write 'warm up' and sometimes you write 'warm-up.'" In case that bothers someone else, let me point out that "warm-up" is the adjective: a warm-up toss. "Warm up" is the verb: He needs to warm up. Likewise: first base (noun); first-base coach, (adjective). And so it goes ....

7 GENDER-NEUTRAL. For years I have argued against the "him / her" nonsense of these PC times. For 1500 years, the neutral pronouns in English were "he, him, his." I was taught – and millions of others as well – to say: "Everybody should raise his hand." Today, PC has forced us into horrible grammatical blunders: "Everybody [singular] should raise their [plural] hand." Alas! But now I have help. There are other intelligent beings on the planet: "Any reference in these *Official Baseball Rules* to 'he,' 'him,' or 'his' shall be deemed to be a reference to 'she,' 'her,' or 'hers,' as the case may be, when the person is female." (Note to Rule 2.00) Bravo!

8 NON-PROFESSIONAL PLAY. The *Official Baseball Rules* are based on the rules codified and first published in 1845 by Alexander Cartwright for the Knickerbocker Base Ball Club. They evolved into the professional statutes of today. Amateur leagues using that code often enact their own safety rules or adopt certain playing provisions to suit their players' ages and physical development. Where I suspect significant local departures exist, I point that out by referencing this paragraph: *See ¶ 8.* The flag means: Be certain you check with the supervisor of your league before enforcing the straight OBR rule outlined in that clause.

9 APPENDICES. ***(EDITED)*** Appendix A is a listing of the NAIA modifications to the NCAA Baseball Playing Rules. There are five modifications. For convenience, I've numbered the various clauses in those provisions, but those numbers have no official standing with the NAIA. Appendix B is a listing of all OFF INTERPs.

IMPORTANT ANNOUNCEMENT

In response to hundreds of requests, I decided last year to offer a PDF version of the BRD. I am repeating the EBRD for the 2012 edition. It includes hot links. For example, in this book if you go to § 10 [appeal missed base], you'll find four references: See § 112 [appeal runner who overran first], 250 [appeal after force out, continuing action], 253 [force removal affects appeal], and 430 [accidental appeal on a force play]. To follow that paper trail in the printed copy, you have to turn pages, leafing back and forth. Using the electronic version, you will simply click the link and be instantly transported there.

The electronic version (EBRD) sells for $15 — plus an email copy of your purchase receipt of this book. That is, you must buy the printed version to be eligible to receive the EBRD. Contact me: carl@bluezebrasports.com. After I get your email, I will instruct you how to make your payment to my PayPal account. If you don't have a PayPal account, you may send a money order. It will just take longer. Notice: Implied by your purchase of the EBRD is your agreement NOT to share the copy with your umpire buddies. BTW: There is also no shipping and handling charge for the PDF version. (grin)

Your research of the rules has just been made a whole lot easier!

Email me, whether you buy the EBRD or not, and I'll send you via snail mail a signed and dated "Thank You" card for this book.

Finally: Please feel free to post reviews of the book: good, indifferent, bad, on Amazon.com.
(http://www.amazon.com/2012-BRD-Baseball-Rule-Differences/dp/1468141082/ref=sr_1_4?s=books&ie=UTF8&qid=1328779751&sr=1-4)

If you have suggestions, complaints, corrections: Whatever. I welcome your feedback.

★ 1 APPEALS: DEFENSE: SHOWS INTENT ✪

FED: During a live ball the defense must make a verbal appeal unless "a play by its very nature is imminent and obvious to the offense." (8-2 Pen Nt) **EXCEPT:** If the action is continuing and the tagged base is a "force" base, the defense makes the appeal merely by "stepping on the missed base." (8.2.3, 2009 ed; 8.2.6e)

NCAA: POE 1990, 1992 [balk]: Point not covered.

> ***(ADDED)*** OFF INTERP 2-1: **PARONTO:** The defense may appeal verbally or by any act that unmistakably indicates an appeal. (email to cc, 12/5/11) ✠

OBR: ***(EDITED)*** Same as NCAA OFF INTERP 2 above.
1. ALSO: "A player, inadvertently stepping on the base with a ball in hand, would not constitute an appeal." (7.10d CMT ¶ 2)

✻ *Play 1-1:* B1 beats out an infield hit but misses the base. F3 takes the throw and "casually steps on first." *Ruling:* In FED, since the defense was making a "force" play "as a result of continuing action," B1 is out. The "casual" step was an appeal. In NCAA and PRO, the appeal must be unmistakable.

✻ *Play 2-1:* R1 is off with the pitch, which B1 slaps deep to centerfield. R1, certain the ball will fall in, continues toward third. His coach frantically signals him to return. He touches second and is sliding into first when the throw beats him. *Ruling:* Throwing the ball to first is an unmistakable appeal play: R1 is out at all levels.

2 APPEALS: DEFENSE: TAGS WRONG BASE DURING LIVE ACTION
ALL CODES NOW AGREE: TEXT DELETED, 1994.

★ 3 APPEALS: GAIN ADVANTAGEOUS FOURTH OUT: DURING : LIVE ACTION ✪

FED: Point not covered.

> OFF INTERP 3-3: **HOPKINS:** If the defense gains a third out during play but the batter-runner has not yet reached first at the time of the out, the defense may play on him at first for an advantageous fourth out. (email to Stevens, 5/11/01) (See 9-1-1 Ex d.)✠

NCAA: Point not covered.

> OFF INTERP 4-3: **FETCHIET:** Same as FED OFF INTERP 3-3. (Website 4/18/01, 8-6a) (See 8-6b-7.) ✠

OBR: Point not covered.

(CHANGED) OFF INTERP 5-3: **WENDELSTEDT:** [Play 3 below] "does not qualify to become an 'advantageous fourth out.' It is made on a runner who has not yet reached a base, not one who has missed a base, or not properly tagged up for one." (HW/fn[193]/214) (See 7.10.) ✠

⁂ *Play 3-3:* R3, R2, 2 outs. B1 singles to the outfield but injures himself coming out of the box; he cannot continue. R3 scores easily, but R2 is thrown out at home: 3 outs. The catcher then fires to F3, who tags first in advance of B1. *Ruling:* FED and NCAA: Cancel R3's run. ***(REVISED)*** OBR: The run scores.

❀ Note 1: Of all the interpretations I've encountered over the years, this is the most non-intuitive. We've always known the defense may gain an advantageous out by **APPEALING A BASERUNNING ERROR.** But who ever knew an out was available simply because the batter-runner was slow? I discovered that in 2001. I hope it never happens in one of my games. Or yours. ***(ADDED)*** I am pleased to report that in OBR games (summer leagues) when it happens — it didn't happen. Thank Hunter Wendelstedt.

★ ∞ 4 APPEALS: LAST TIME BY ✪

FED: "If a runner correctly touches a base that was missed (either advancing or returning), the last time he was by the base, that final touch corrects any previous baserunning infraction." (8-2-6L; 8.2.6h)

NCAA: Same as FED. (2-51)

❀ Note 2: "Last time by" has been a staple of the baseball blogs for years. For further information: Read the OBR OFF INTERPs and study Plays 4 and 5 below.

OBR: Point not covered.

OFF INTERP 6-4: **PBUC:** A runner who has missed a base either advancing or retreating but who touches it following an award, may correct that error "on the theory that touching the base 'the last time by' corrects **ANY** previous error." {6.12-4} ✠

EXCEPT: OFF INTERP 7-4: **FITZPATRICK:** "Last time by" does not apply to a runner who makes a travesty of the game, deliberately ignoring the baserunning rules. (phone call to cc, 11/8/01) ✠

⁂ *Play 4-4:* R3, R1 moving on the pitch, 1 out. B1 slaps a fly deep to center. R1 is convinced the ball will not be caught, but R3 tags properly and scores after the catch. R1 misses second on his way to third, but when he realizes the ball was caught, he touches second on his return and makes it safely to first. The defense then appeals that R1 missed second "while advancing." *Ruling:* The runner touched second his "last time by" the base. That cured his earlier mistake. The appeal is denied.

⁎ *Play 5-4:* R1 leaves too soon on a fly ball. He touches second and advances near third when he realizes he must return and does so by running directly across the diamond toward first. The ball gets by F3, and R1, after retouching first, makes it safely to second. The defense appeals that he missed second, the base on which he now stands, on his return to first. *Ruling:* The umpire will uphold the appeal. "Last time by" applies to situations where the runner could have touched the base but missed it by less than his body's length.

❀ Note 3: "Last time by" is among the more difficult concepts for many amateur umpires since they have been indoctrinated with the idea that whenever a runner misses a base, he must **CORRECT IT IN THE WAY HE MISSED IT** or be subject to appeal. In Play 4 above, some untutored umpires would allow the appeal: R1 missed second when "advancing." But if that was the case, when R1 tried to return to first, to be in "full compliance" he would have to: (● 1) retreat beyond second toward first; (● 2) touch second while returning toward third; and (● 3) retouch second on his way back to first. The runner would resemble the revolving target bear at the 1940s arcades with the electric eye on his shoulder. Simply: Since R1 wound up on his original base, the only base he advanced beyond was second, and he touched it, albeit on the way back.

2. ALSO: OFF INTERP 8-4: **PBUC STAFF:** A runner who left a base too soon and missed a subsequent base when returning would still be permitted to retouch – in order – both bases when accepting his award.
(email to cc, 12/15/00) (See § 434.) ✠

⁎ *Play 6-4:* R1 moving on the pitch. B1 flies deep to center, and R1 believes the ball will not be caught. He touches second and heads for third, where he learns the ball was caught. Trying to hustle back to first, he misses second. The ball is thrown to DBT, and the umpire awards R1 third. *Ruling:* If R1 touches first, second, and third in order, he is not in jeopardy of an out on appeal. He corrected his error on his "last time by."

❀ Note 4: Play 5 first appeared in the BRD in 2002. Play 6 entered in 2001. Now, those two plays have wound up on the NFHS Website 2011, #17 and #16. The BRD is flattered.

★ 5 APPEALS: LOSS OF: DEFENSE: ERRS ON APPEAL ✪

FED: Because an appeal is not a play, the defense may still appeal after erring on its first appeal. (8-2 Pen; 2.29.6b) (See § 15.)

NCAA: The defense has only one chance to appeal. In the case of multiple appeals, if the defense throws the ball to DBT on its first

appeal, or if any runner advances, the defense loses its right to appeal at any base. (8-6b-3; 8-6b-5b) After the ball is overthrown, the appeal will be allowed if: (• 1) The ball remains alive; and (• 2) the ball is returned immediately to the base being appealed. (8-6b-5; 8-6b-5a)
3. ALSO: If the defense announces – before making its first appeal – that it intends to appeal multiple infractions, a throwing error will cancel only the first appeal if, on the throwing error, the ball remains in live-ball territory. (8-6b-6 AR) (See § 8; 9; 11; 13.)

OBR: The appeal is canceled only when the defense throws the ball to DBT. Runners advancing have no impact. (7.10)
(See § 11 and 361.)

> **4. ALSO:** OFF INTERP 9-5: **MLBUM:** If the pitcher or any member of the defensive team throws the ball out of play when making an appeal, such act shall be considered an attempted pl ay. **NO FURTHER APPEAL WILL BE ALLOWED ON ANY RUNNER AT ANY BASE.** (5.2-3) ✠

(ADDED) ❀ Note 5: Wendelstedt **CORRECTLY** points out that MLBUM OFF INTERP 9 above contradicts black-letter law at 7.10. (HWfn[200]/216)

∞ 6 APPEALS: LOSS OF: DEFENSE: FIELDER IN FOUL GROUND: CONTINUING PLAY OVER ✪ (See § 245.)

FED: No provision.

❀ Note 6: The FED has no comment about what happens **DURING** an appeal. That's because they provide for a dead-ball appeal. Their philosophy is: Who cares where the players are during a dead ball? (See § 8 and 10.) But what if the team appeals in the old fashioned way ...?

NCAA: All players, except the catcher, must be in fair territory "to start an appeal" after the ball has become dead. The umpire should not put the ball in play if a fielder is in foul territory, but if he does, there is no penalty, and the defense may still appeal the same runner. "A fielder may go into foul territory to back up an appeal play after the ball has been put into play." (5-4; 5-4c; 5-4c Pen)

OBR: Same as NCAA 5-4 and 5-4c Pen. (4.03c)

> **5. ALSO:** OFF INTERP 10-6: **MLBUM:** If a fielder (other than the catcher) is in foul territory, the umpire should not put the ball in play. If the umpire inadvertently does so, there is no penalty (specifically, this is not a balk), nor would such action nullify a subsequent appeal attempt on the same runner once the ball is properly put back in play. A fielder may go onto foul territory to back up an appeal play after the ball has been put in play. (5.2-7) ✠

❀ Note 7: In your NCAA game, a fielder may now back up an appeal play after the ball is alive. In your Legion game (OBR), that's also legal. In FED, it's not necessary — which seems the smartest course of all. BTW: Be sure your OBR league knows about OFF INTERP 10 above. As the players say: "Hey, you never know."

∞ 7 APPEALS: LOSS OF: DEFENSE: IMPROPER PROCEDURE ✪

FED: No provision Treat as in OBR.

NCAA: No provision Treat as in OBR.

❀ Note 8: The Lepperd ruling below, OFF INTERP 11, deals with the defense trying to execute an appeal on ONE runner but not knowing how. NCAA has no rules provision. But they do provide a penalty for a team that cannot correctly execute an appeal where TWO runners are involved. (See § 11.)

OBR: Point not covered.

> OFF INTERP 11-7: **LEPPERD:** If the defense does not follow correct appeal procedure, that does not preclude a second or third appeal on the same runner at the same base. (Booth, eTeamz, 12/11/01) (See § 5.) ✠

⁎ *Play 7-7*: R1 stealing. B1 flies to the outfield. R1 has touched and rounded second when he realizes the ball was caught and he must return. He misses second on the way back and barely beats the throw to first. The umpire signals safe. Now F3, with the ball, tags first base *again* with his foot and says: "I appeal that he missed second coming back." *Ruling:* The umpire will not call out R1, but he will / may explain that the defense appealed improperly. (At all levels the defense must tag the runner or second base.)

❀ Note 9: Umpires have argued that the defense could not again appeal R1 for the same infraction: "Successive appeals may not be made on a runner at the same base." They are wrong. See OFF INTERP • 12 below.

> **6. ALSO:** OFF INTERP 12-7: **LEPPERD:** "The 'successive appeal' provision [of 7.10] refers to the defense throwing the ball out of play in an appeal attempt." (Booth, eTeamz, 12/11/01) ✠

⁎ *Play 8-7:* 2 outs, B1 triples. The defense announces it will appeal that B1 missed second. The pitcher from the rubber (legal) throws to third for a tag of the runner, but the ball gets away from the third baseman and B1 scores. The ball does not go out of play. The third baseman retrieves the ball and throws to F4, who steps on second: "I appeal that guy missed this base." *Ruling:* In FED, the appeal is allowed: Errors on appeal attempts have no bearing on the appeal procedure. In NCAA, a runner advanced, so the defense may not appeal again. In OBR, the appeal at third is not a "successive appeal" since the ball remained in play: It's a legal appeal.

8 APPEALS: LOSS OF: DEFENSE: INITIATES PLAY ✪

FED: A play initiated by the **DEFENSE** cancels any right to appeal. (8-2 Pen) (See § 9.)

NCAA: Same as FED. (8-6b-4) (See § 5.)

OBR: The right to appeal is canceled if **EITHER TEAM** initiates a play. (7.10) (See § 5 and 15.)

⁜ *Play 9-8:* R2. The runner scores on B1's single. The defense announces it will appeal that R2 missed third. As the pitcher toes the pitcher's plate in the set position, he sees that B1 has taken a long lead off first. But F1's pickoff throw is not in time. The first baseman then fires to F5, who appeals R2. *Ruling:* In FED, the defense may still appeal. (See OFF INTERP• 13-9.) In NCAA / OBR, it is too late to appeal. (See Play 10-9 and § 11.)

9 APPEALS: LOSS OF: OFFENSE: INITIATES PLAY ✪

FED: A play initiated by the **OFFENSE** does not cancel any right to appeal. (8-2 Pen) (See § 8.)

> **7. ALSO:** OFF INTERP 13-9: **HOPKINS:** If the defense plays on a runner who has taken an "inordinate lead," the play is **INITIATED** by the offense. (Website 2003, #12) ✠

NCAA: A play initiated by the **OFFENSE** does not cancel any right to appeal. (8-6b-4) (See § 8.) Same as FED except for OFF INTERP • 13 above.

OBR: The right to appeal is canceled if **EITHER TEAM** initiates a play. (7.10) (See § 15.)

⁜ *Play 10-9:* R2. The runner scores on B1's single. The defense announces it will appeal that R2 missed third. With a live ball the pitcher prepares to make his appeal when B1, who has stopped on first, breaks for second. The pitcher's throw is in time to retire B1. *Ruling:* In FED / NCAA, the defense may appeal R2 since the impetus for the play came from B1's attempt to take second. In OBR, the appeal opportunity is lost. (See Play 9-8.)

❀ Note 10: In FED / NCAA, even if the pitcher's throw to second is wild and B1 makes it safely to second or third, the appeal would still be allowed. (See § 5.)

10 APPEALS: MISSED BASE: RUNNER OR BASE TAGGED ON FORCE: PLAY CONTINUING ✪

FED: When a runner overslides but misses the base, he is out when tagged. If it is a force play, or if he has touched a succeeding base, he is out when he or the base is tagged. (8-4-2i)

NCAA: Same as FED. **EXCEPT:** The defense may obtain an out by tagging the base only on a force play. (8-1a Pen)
(See § 250 and 430.)

OBR: (● 1) In a force situation when a runner overslides or overruns and misses the base, if the force is removed because a following runner is put out – the rule says "forced out" – the runner is out only when tagged. (See § 253.) **EXCEPT:** If he advances to the next base, when he retreats toward the previous force base (which he missed), he is also out when the base is tagged for a live-ball appeal. (7.08e) (See § 112.) (● 2) In a non-force situation a runner is also out on appeal if "while advancing or RETURNING to a base, he fails to touch each base in order before he, or a MISSED base, is tagged." (7.10b and d)

❀ Note 11: The committee intended the material quoted above to cover a runner who left too soon on a caught fly ball. The ambiguity of the language forced the interpreters to "revise" the ruling via OFF INTERP • 14 below.

> **EXCEPT:** OFF INTERP 14-10: **PBUC STAFF:** Use 7.10d for all missed bases, not just home. If the ball and the runner are in the vicinity of the base, when the runner tries to return, he must be tagged to be out. Do not allow an "appeal" (no matter how obvious) of the missed base during that "unrelaxed" action. But if it was a force base, the defense may subsequently appeal to gain an advantageous fourth out. (email to cc, 12/15/00) ✠

✻ *Play 11-10:* R1. The runner, moving on the pitch, scores on B1's extra base hit but misses third. After he crosses the plate, his coach screams that he should return to third. He retouches home and, just after the ball arrives to F5 standing on third, R1 slides untagged into the bag. *Ruling:* In FED, R1 is out. In NCAA / OBR, R1 stays on third.

✻ *Play 12-10:* R1 moving on the pitch, R3, 2 out. B1 punches the pitch to short. F6's only play is at second, not in time. But R1 slides around the base without touching it. As he tries to scramble back, F4 tags him out. Meanwhile, R3's run scores. *Ruling:* In FED, the tag of R1 is a force out: The run does not count. In NCAA / OBR: (a) If the defense does not appeal, R3's run scores. (b) If it appeals, R1 becomes a force out for the "fourth" out, and the run does not count.

✻ *Play 13-10:* Same as Play 12-10, but the defense wishes to appeal that R1 missed second base, hoping to get a force out – an advantageous fourth out – to negate the run. *Ruling:* The appeal is allowed.

11 APPEALS: NO RUNNER OR WRONG RUNNER IDENTIFIED ✪

FED: No provision.

NCAA: If the defense wishes to appeal an alleged baserunning infraction where more than one runner might have committed the infraction, the defense must indicate which runner is being appealed. If it does not so indicate, the umpire is to give no sign. If the defense appeals the wrong runner, the umpire will give the "safe" sign, and no further appeal is allowed on any runner **AT THAT BASE.** (8-6b-6) (See § 341 for more information on **MECHANICS** as part of the rules.)

OBR: The defense may appeal each runner at each base. (7.10)

> **EXCEPT:** OFF INTERP 15-11: **PBUC:** If the defense "errs" (throws the ball to DBT during its first appeal attempt), its right to appeal any runner **AT ANY BASE** is lost. {6.4-6} ✠

⁎ *Play 14-11:* Bases loaded, 2 outs. B1 triples. The defense appeals that R1 missed second. The umpire denies the appeal. Next the defense announces it will appeal that B1 missed second. That appeal is also denied. The defense then announces it will appeal that R1 missed third. *Ruling:* The appeals are all legal. The defense could make eight appeals on this play: R1, R2, R3 at home; R1 and R2 at third; R1 and B1 at second; and B1 at first.

⁎ *Play 15-11:* R1, R3. Both runners retouch and advance when B1 flies out to center. The defense intends to appeal that both R3 and R1 left too soon. After the ball is made alive, the pitcher, while off the rubber, tries to throw to third but the ball goes into DBT. The defense then announces it: (a) wishes to appeal third again, or (b) wishes to appeal that R1 left first too soon. *Ruling:* In (a) and (b) in FED, the defense may still appeal. In (a) in NCAA, the defense may not appeal third now since it "erred" on its first attempt. In (b) in NCAA, there is no later appeal (for an infraction that may have been committed during R1's original advance) unless the defense announced before the bad throw that it intended to make an additional appeal. In (a) and (b) in OBR, cancel all further appeals. (See § 5.)

> **8. ALSO:** OFF INTERP 16-11: **PBUC STAFF:** (1) A player may make an out during play and an out on appeal. (2) After being called out on appeal at one base, the same player may not be appealed for a second out at a different base. (email to cc, 12/15/00) ✠

❀ Note 12: "For a second out" means one player may not make two of the three outs needed to end a half inning. A player may be called out more than once.

⁎ *Play 16-11:* Bases loaded, 2 outs. B1 hits for extra bases. He tries for third and is thrown out: 3 outs, 3 runs in. The defense then appeals that R1 missed third, and the umpire calls him out: 4 outs, and 2 runs in. The defense then appeals that either: (a) R1 missed second; or (b) B1 missed first. *Ruling:* The umpire will allow either appeal, either of which, if upheld, will be an advantageous FIFTH out, canceling the two remaining runs.

★ 12 APPEALS: ORDER OF ✪

FED: Point not covered.

OFF INTERP 17-12: **HOPKINS:** If the defense will make multiple appeals: When a force play situation is in effect, the appeals must be made in the proper order. (Website 2003, #4; affirmed, 2006, #12 and #13.) ✠

NCAA: No provision Treat as in OBR.

OBR: Point not covered.

OFF INTERP 18-12: ***(ADDED)*** **WENDELSTEDT:** Same as FED OFF INTERP 17 [this section]. (HW/fn[193]/214) ✠

⁎ *Play 17-12:* R3, R2, 1 out. B1 lines into the gap. R3 scores, R2 misses third. B1 reaches second, but he misses first. When action is over, the defense appeals that B1 missed first and then appeals that R2 missed third. *Ruling:* B1 is the SECOND out at first; R2, the third out, is not a force. R3's run counts.

⁎ *Play 18-12:* Same scenario as Play 17-12, **EXCEPT:** The defense appeals that R2 missed third (second out) and then B1 missed first (third out). R3's run does not count.

13 APPEALS: PITCHER THROWS FROM PITCHER'S PLATE ✪

FED: No provision. Treat as in NCAA.

NCAA: It is not a balk if the pitcher from the rubber throws to a base for an appeal. (8-6b-10)

OBR: Point not covered.

OFF INTERP 19-13: **PBUC:** Same as NCAA. {8.7} ✠

14 APPEALS: PROCEDURE FOR BASERUNNING ERRORS ✪

FED: POE 2002, 2003: The defense must appeal all baserunning infractions with a live ball before the next pitch to a batter of either team, a play, or an attempted play. **EXCEPT:** (● 1) During a dead ball the coach or any player (with or without the ball) may appeal a baserunning infraction. (8-2 Pen) During a live ball the defense (but not the coach) may appeal. (8.2.5c) (● 2) The appeal opportunity is canceled: (a) after an intentional walk; (b) when the pitcher and all infielders leave fair territory when a half inning is ending; or (c) when the umpires leave the field if the game is over. (8-2 Pen; 8.2.2j)

9. ALSO: The defense may not appeal a runner who is attempting to return to a missed base or one he had left too soon unless the base is a force base. (8.2.2e)

> **10. ALSO:** OFF INTERP 20-14: **HOPKINS:** The defense committing an error (throwing the ball to DBT] has no effect on the right of the defense to appeal. (Website 2002, #18) (See § 5.) ✠

> ✻ *Play 19-14:* **FED only**. R1, 2 outs. R1 steals. B1 hits for extra bases, misses second, and heads for third. The ball comes in and just before R1 touches the plate, the second baseman tags second and appeals that B1 missed the base. *Ruling:* The "live ball" appeal of a force base FOR A THIRD OUT cancels the run.

❀ Note 13: That appeal is not possible in OBR or NCAA.

> ✻ *Play 20-14:* **FED only.** R1, 2 outs. B1 hits for extra bases but is thrown out at third to end the half inning. The defensive players all rush off the field except for the catcher, who is in foul territory. He turns to the plate umpire and says: "I appeal that R1 missed the plate." *Ruling:* The appeal is legal: (a) The catcher is an infielder in FED play (2-13-3); (b) he is in foul territory, but for purposes of the rule he has not "left" the field since he is still in the vicinity of his position.

✻ *Play 21-14:* R1, 1 out. B1 doubles, with R1 scoring. With a live ball the defense touches second and appeals that R1 missed the base. The second baseman then touches B1 and appeals that he missed first. *Ruling:* All codes: Both appeals are legal: (a) live ball; (b) touch the missed base: (c) touch the runner who missed a base; (d) multiple appeals without making a travesty of the game.

✻ *Play 22-14:* R1, R2. B1 doubles, with R2 scoring and R1 stopping at third. F1 requests time, which the base umpire grants. The pitcher or the coach then says: "I appeal that R2 missed third." *Ruling:* In FED, it's a legal appeal. In NCAA / OBR, the appeal would be illegal. The ball must be alive.

❀ Note 14: In an OBR game, when the ball was made alive for the appeal, the runner at third could break for home. If the defense played on him, they could no longer appeal R1. (See § 8.)

NCAA: The defense must appeal all baserunning infractions with a live ball (8-6b-1a) before the next pitch to a batter of either team, a play, or an attempted play. (8-6b)
(For full particulars see § 5; 8; 9; 11; 15.)

OBR: Same as NCAA. (7.10) "Time is not out when an appeal is being made." (7.10 CMT ¶ 2) (See § 4; 5; 8; 9; 12; 13; 15 for more details.)

★ 15 APPEALS: TIME TO INITIATE AFTER: BASERUNNING INFRACTION ✪

FED: The defense must appeal before a legal or illegal pitch, an intentional walk (8.2.5b), a play or attempted play (during a half inning and NOT INITIATED BY THE OFFENSE [8.2.5d]), the pitcher and infielders leave fair territory (at the end of a half inning), or the umpires leave the field (at the end of the game). (8-2 Pen) Rumble ruled that a balk is an illegal pitch, so that would also cancel the right to appeal. (See OFF INTERP 21-16. See OFF INTERP • 37-29 for the FED definition of a "play or attempted play.")

NCAA: The appeal must be made before a pitch, play or attempted play, or before the PITCHER AND ALL FIELDERS leave the infield when a half inning or the game has ended. (8-6b) (See § 267.)
11. ALSO: A balk cancels all appeals. (8-6b-2 Ex)

OBR: The appeal must be made before a pitch ***(EDITED)*** to a batter of either team, play or attempted play, or before the defensive team leaves the field. (6.07b) "Defensive team leaving the field" is defined as the PITCHER AND ALL INFIELDERS leaving fair territory. (7.10) ***(EDITED)*** As in the NCAA, a balk is a play and cancels further appeals. (7.10 CMT ¶ 2) (See § 8 and 9.)

(ADDED) ❀ Note 15: In NCAA and OBR, the appeal must come before the next pitch to a batter of EITHER TEAM. FED doesn't allow for that so the appeal is canceled when the defensive team leaves the field.

❀ Note 16: Have you ever had a team appeal after the half inning has ended? Me, either. (grin)

SEE ESPECIALLY **OFF INTERP 300-361,** WHICH EXPLAINS HOW PROCEEDING "WITHOUT REFERENCE TO THE BALK" **(8.05** PEN) DOESN'T REALLY MEAN THE UMPIRE IGNORES THE BALK WHEN IT COMES TO APPEALS.

❀ Note 17: At all levels, an appeal is not a play.

❀ Note 18: In NCAA / OBR, black-letter law states that a balk during an appeal cancels the appeal, so Rumble's OFF INTERP 21-16 harmonizes all three codes. See the next two plays.

✻ *Play 23-15:* R1, R2, B1 doubles. R2 scores and R1 winds up on third. The defense calls time. Then, the coach yells that F1 should appeal that R1 missed second. The pitcher steps onto the rubber, and the umpire makes the ball alive. Without stepping toward third, the pitcher while on the rubber simply flips the ball to F5. The umpire yells: "That's a balk!" *Ruling:* The balk is a play (an "illegal pitch" in FED, according to OFF INTERP 21-16). Appeals are not legal after a play.

✻ *Play 24-15:* Same play: R1, R2, B1 doubles. R2 scores and R1 winds up on third. The defense calls time. Then, the coach yells that F1 should appeal that R1 missed second. The pitcher steps onto the rubber, and the umpire makes the ball alive. F1 steps toward third and throws. F5 appeals, and the umpire says: "Safe!" Now the defensive coach says: "Appeal B1. He missed first." The offensive coach argues: "It's too late to appeal. They already made a play." *Ruling:* An appeal is not a play or attempted play. The appeal attempt is granted.

16 APPEALS: TIME TO INITIATE AFTER: BATTING OUT OF ORDER INFRACTION ✪

FED: The standard appeal time frame (§ 15) also applies to the appeal of an improper batter. (7-1-2 Pen 2)

> **12. ALSO:** OFF INTERP 21-16: **RUMBLE:** A "balk is also an illegal pitch," so a balk would cancel the right of the defense to appeal. (*News* #3, 3/98; confirmed, Website 2003, #6) ✠

NCAA: The appeal must be made before the next pitch to a batter of either team, a play, or an attempted play. (7-11a-2)

OBR: Same as NCAA. (6.07b; 7.10) (See § 8 and 9.)

★ 17 APPEALS: TIME TO INITIATE AFTER: USE OF ILLEGAL EQUIPMENT ✪

FED: If the defense wishes to appeal an illegal glove, the appeal must be made before the next pitch. (1.5.7) An appeal of an illegal bat must be made before the next pitch following the turn at bat of the player who used the illegal bat. (7-4-1a) (See § 16, 82 and 83.) (See § 127 for the penalty for using an illegal glove.)

NCAA: The appeal must be made before a pitch, play or attempted play, or before the pitcher and all infielders leave fair territory on the way to the dugout ***(EDITED)*** if it is an inning- or game-ending play. (8-6b)

OBR: Same as NCAA. (6.07b; 7.10) (See § 8 and 9.)

∞ 18 AWARDS TO: BATTER-RUNNER: BATTED BALL: BOUNCES OVER FENCE ✪

FED: A fair ball bounding over a fence is a two-base award for all runners. (8-3-3c; OFF INTERP #3, 2008 Website)

> **13. ALSO:** OFF INTERP 22-18: **RUMBLE:** A bouncing fair batted ball that hits the foul pole above the top of the outfield fence and rebounds onto the playing field results in a two-base award. (*News* #8, 3/91) ✠

> **14. ALSO:** OFF INTERP 23-18: **HOPKINS:** "A fly ball hit deep to right field along the foul line hits the right fielder on the head. The ball then bounces off his head and, in flight, goes over the outfield fence, but does so on the foul side of the foul pole. Is this a home run? Ruling: No, this is a ground-rule double. A home run is a fair ball that goes over a fence in flight in fair territory." (Website 2008, #3) ✠

NCAA: UNLESS LOCAL GROUND RULES STIPULATE OTHERWISE, a fair ball bounding over or passing through a fence results in a two-base award. (8-3o-1) (See § 20 and 413.)

OBR: Same as FED. (7.05f)

★ ∞ 19 AWARDS TO: BATTER-RUNNER: BATTED BALL: DEFLECTED OVER FENCE ✪

FED: ***(EDITED)*** If a batted ball is deflected over the fence in fair territory, award two bases. (8.3.3h)

> **15. ALSO:** OFF INTERP 24-19: **RUMBLE:** The umpire should award a home run if a batted ball, even though carried several steps by the fielder, is subsequently "deflected" over the fence. (*News* #27, 4/88; confirmed, #17, 3/89) (See also § 28 and 8.3.3h.) ✠

In foul territory: same as in NCAA. (See OFF INTERP 22-18.)

NCAA: If fair territory: **Point not covered.**

> *(ADDED)* OFF INTERP 25-19: **PARONTO:** Same as FED OFF INTERP • 24 [this section]. (email to cc, 12/5/11) ✠

16. ALSO: Award two bases if a fair ball is deflected over the fence into foul ground. (8-3o-2) (See also § 21.)

OBR: In fair territory: **Point not covered.**

> OFF INTERP 26-19: **PBUC STAFF:** Same as FED OFF INTERP • 24 [this section]. Fitzpatrick: "The ball hit nothing but the fielder, so we consider it cleared the fence in flight." (phone call from Fitzpatrick to cc, 12/26/01) ✠

17. ALSO: In foul territory: Treat as in NCAA. (7.05f)

⁕ *Play 25-19:* A fielder gains possession of B1's batted ball, but his momentum carries him away from the plate and toward the fence. He is unable to reverse himself and eventually bangs into the fence; the ball pops out of his glove and over the fence in fair territory. *Ruling:* Award B1 a home run at all levels.

⁕ *Play 26-19:* A fielder chases a deep drive toward the centerfield fence, but as he reaches for the batted ball, it deflects off his glove over the fence. *Ruling:* The hit is a home run.

20 AWARDS TO: BATTER-RUNNER: BATTED BALL: HIT OVER SHORT FENCE ✪

FED: No provision.

NCAA: No provision. (See § 18.)

OBR: A batter whose fair ball goes over a fence at fewer than 250 feet from home is awarded two bases. (6.09d) (See § 232.) *See ¶ 8.*

★ ∞ 21 AWARDS TO: BATTER-RUNNER: BATTED BALL: HITS TOP OF FENCE AND GOES OVER ✪

FED: Point not covered.

> OFF INTERP 27-21: **RUMBLE:** It is a home run if a batted ball hits on top of the outfield fence and then bounds over in fair territory. (*News* #18, 3/85) (See § 19 and 8.3.3h.) ✠

NCAA: Same as FED OFF INTERP 27 [this section]. (7-6 AR 2)

OBR: Point not covered.

> OFF INTERP 28-21: **DEARY:** Same as FED OFF INTERP • 27 [this section]. (REF 7/84) ✠

★ 22 AWARDS TO: BATTER-RUNNER: BATTED BALL: LODGES IN: FIELDER'S GLOVE ✪ (See § 23.)

FED: A batted ball is immediately dead if it lodges in a player's equipment, such as a glove. (5-1-1f-5; 5.1.1q and r) **PENALTY:** The ball is dead, and the umpire awards each runner one base in advance of the last legally acquired base if, in the judgment of the umpire, the runner was attempting to advance. "If the lodged ball occurred when the batter-runner was trying for first, he shall be awarded one base. Preceding runners will be awarded bases needed to complete the award." (8-3-3f)

(ADDED) **18. ALSO:** A ball that is "temporarily stuck" is not "lodged." (5.1.1s)

❀ Note 19: The FED case book plays make it clear: If the fielder feels he must throw the ball / glove combo to another fielder, the ball is lodged and dead. That may be an example of ruling by compromise. A sizable number of umpires said that two bases were too many; an equal number seemed to say the fielder should throw the ball / glove for an out. When the rule was revised in 2006, FED lost the out but reduced the award.

NCAA: Point not covered.

> ***(ADDED)*** OFF INTERP 29-22: **PARONTO:** A ball stuck in a fielder's glove remains alive. If the fielder tosses the glove / ball combination to another fielder in time to complete a tag of a base or runner in advance of a base, and the ball / glove is held securely by the receiving fielder so that the fielder can demonstrate complete control, the runner or batter-runner is out. (email to cc, 12/5/11) ✠

OBR: Point not covered.

> OFF INTERP 30-22: **MLBUM:** A ball stuck in a fielder's glove is not to be considered out of play; the ball remains alive. It is legal for one fielder to throw the glove with a live ball stuck in it to another fielder. A fielder who possesses the ball / glove combination in his own hand or glove can complete a tag of a runner or base, just as if he were holding only the ball. (5.10) ✠

✻ *Play 27-22:* B1 hits a sharp, one-hop come-backer to the mound. F1 gloves the ball instinctively, then discovers the ball is lodged tightly between the fingers of his glove. As B1 hustles down the line, F1 removes his glove and throws it, with the ball still lodged, to F3 in

time to retire B1. *Ruling:* In FED, the ball is dead when "it becomes apparent that the ball [is] lodged." (5.1.1r) Award B1 first.
In NCAA / OBR, B1 is out.

★ 23 AWARDS TO: BATTER-RUNNER: BATTED BALL: LODGES IN: FIELDER'S UNIFORM ✪ (See § 22 and 39.)

FED: A batted ball is immediately dead if it lodges in a player's uniform. (5-1-1f-5) **PENALTY:** The umpire awards each runner two bases. (8-3-3c) (See § 24.)

NCAA: When a batted or thrown ball lodges in a player's uniform, the ball is dead and the umpire awards bases at his discretion. (8-3L)

OBR: Point not covered.

> OFF INTERP 31-23: **PBUC:** If a batted ball inadvertently goes into a player's or coach's uniform, the ball is dead. "The umpire will, using common sense and fair play, place all runners in such a manner that will nullify the action of the ball going out of play. ***(EDITED)*** ANY OUTS RECORDED PRIOR TO THE BALL GOING INTO THE PLAYER'S OR COACH'S UNIFORM (OR LODGING IN THE CATCHER'S FACE MASK OR PARAPHERNALIA) WILL STAND."{6.10} ✠

★ 24 AWARDS TO: BATTER-RUNNER: BATTED BALL: LODGES WITH: UMPIRE ✪

FED: If a fair batted ball lodges in an umpire's equipment, the ball is dead and the umpire awards each runner two bases. (5-1-1g-4; 8-3-3c) (See § 23.)

NCAA: Point not covered.

> ***(ADDED)*** OFF INTERP 32-24: **PARONTO:** If a fair batted ball lodges in an umpire's equipment or uniform, the ball is dead. Two bases are awarded (email to cc, 12/29/11) ✠

OBR: No provision. ***(REVISED)*** Treat as in NCAA.

★ ∞ 25 AWARDS TO: BATTER-RUNNER: IMPOSSIBLE TO AWARD TWO BASES ✪

FED: If a two-base award to a following runner would result in a preceding runner advancing three bases, the following runner will be awarded only one base. (8-3-3c-3; 8.3.5d)

NCAA: Point not covered.

(ADDED) OFF INTERP 33-25: **PARONTO:** Same as FED. (email to cc, 12/5/11) ✠

OBR: Same as FED. (7.05g CMT)

✲ *Play 28-25:* R1. B1 lofts a fly to the outfield. R1, thinking the ball may be caught, holds between first and second. The ball is not caught, and both R1 and B1 are between first and second when the outfielder overthrows first. *Ruling:* Award R1 third; B1, second.

26 AWARDS TO: RUNNER: ADVANCES BEYOND MERITED BASE
ALL CODES NOW AGREE: TEXT DELETED, 1996.

★ 27 AWARDS TO: RUNNER: BATTED BALL: CARRIED INTO DEAD-BALL TERRITORY AFTER CATCH ✪

(See § 28.)

FED: The ball is dead if a fielder with a batted ball caught in flight steps with both feet (or falls) into a dead-ball area. (5-1-1i) **PENALTY:** Each runner is awarded one base. (8-3-3d; 8.3.3a CMT [2000 ed]; Website 2001, #4) (See § 37, 123 and 125.)

❀ Note 20: If the defensive player fields a fair ball on the bounce and then steps with both feet into DBT – an unlikely but not impossible occurrence – the award would be two bases from the time the ball goes dead. (See Play 29-28.)

NCAA: The ball remains alive when a fielder enters DBT unless he falls or loses body control. (6-1d)
19. ALSO: If in making a catch a fielder slides intentionally, "he has not lost body control." (6-1d AR 2)
20. ALSO: If a fielder after a legal catch falls into the stands, into the dugout, or falls while in the dugout, the ball is dead and runners advance one base. (8-3m)
21. ALSO: If a fielder tries for a catch near the dugout and members of either team keep him from falling, the ruling is the player did not fall and the ball remains alive. (6-1d-2) (See OFF INTERP • 103-124 for very important limitations.)
22. ALSO: If a fielder after making a catch goes over or through the **OUTFIELD FENCE**, the ball is dead, even if the fielder lands on his feet. Runners advance one base. (6-1d-3; 8-3m) If a runner drops a fair ball outside the fence, it is a home run. (8-3m)

OBR: If a fielder after making a catch enters DBT, the ball remains alive unless the fielder falls down, when the ball becomes dead and runners are awarded one base. (5.10f; 7.04c; 7.04c CMT)

23. ALSO: If a fielder makes a catch and members of either team keep him from falling, it is a catch and a live ball. (2.00 Catch) (See § 125.)

24. ALSO: OFF INTERP 34-27: **PBUC:** If a fielder makes a catch and then drops the ball in DBT (or if the ball then goes into dead-ball territory), the award is two bases measured from the time of the drop. {6.8} ✠

25. ALSO: OFF INTERP 35-27: ***(EDITED)*** **PBUC:** If a fielder, in making a catch, enters a spectator area due to his momentum, the ball is dead and all runners are awarded one base, regardless of whether the fielder has fallen or remains standing. {6.5-5} ✠

❀ Note 21: If the umpire judges the fielder deliberately entered DBT, he should kill the ball and award all runners two bases measured from the time of the intentional act.

∞ 28 AWARDS TO: RUNNER: BATTED OR THROWN BALL: INTENTIONALLY DEFLECTED TO DEAD-BALL AREA ✪ (See § 27.)

FED: If any ball (other than a pitch, a throw by the pitcher from the pitcher's plate, or a batted ball caught in flight) is intentionally thrown, carried, or deflected into a dead-ball area, the ball is dead. The umpire awards each runner two bases measured from TOT or deflection. (8.3.3a CMT [2000 ed]; 8.3.3j; 8.3.3k) (See § 19.) (See § 37 for rules regarding a pitch deflected to dead-ball area.) (Study especially§ 42 and 434.)

❀ Note 22: Though the book does not mention an "intentional" deflection of a batted or thrown ball, the FED philosophy is clearly outlined in 8.3.3k, which I explain in § 37.

NCAA: If a fielder intentionally kicks or deflects a thrown or batted ball into DBT, each runner is awarded two bases measured from the time of the intentional act. (8-3o-5)

OBR: Point not covered.

OFF INTERP 36-28: **PBUC:** Same as NCAA. {6.8} ✠

⁎ *Play 29-28:* R1, R2. B1's short fly is maybe fair, maybe foul. The right fielder is charging hard as the runners go halfway. F9 cannot make the catch, and the ball deflects off his glove. Finally he gains possession of the ball and intentionally steps with both feet into DBT. At the time he enters dead-ball territory, each runner and B1 have advanced one base. *Ruling:* Both runners score and B1 goes to third.

❀ Note 23: If a batted or thrown ball is **UNINTENTIONALLY** deflected into DBT, the award is the same at all levels: two bases measured from TOP (batted ball) or TOT (thrown ball).

❀ Note 24: If a pitch is **UNINTENTIONALLY** deflected into dead ball territory, the award is the same at all levels: one base measured from TOP.

★ ∞ 29 AWARDS TO: RUNNER: FIRST PLAY BY INFIELDER: FAKED OR FEINTED THROW ✪

FED: Point not covered.

> OFF INTERP 37-29: **HOPKINS:** A fielder with the ball walking a few steps toward a runner constitutes a play. (Website 2003, #7) A pitcher steps off the pitcher's plate and turns "abruptly" toward an occupied base. That is a play. (Website 2003, #11) A faked or feinted throw also constitutes a play. (Website 2003, #10) ✠

EXCEPT: A feint is not considered a throw. (8.3.5h)

NCAA: Same as OBR OFF INTERP • 38 [this section]. (8-3o-3 AR 2)

OBR: Point not covered.

> OFF INTERP 38-29: **PBUC:** "A PLAY OR ATTEMPTED PLAY ... shall be interpreted as a legitimate effort by a defensive player who has possession of the ball to actually retire a runner. This may include an actual attempt to tag a runner, a fielder running toward a base with the ball in an attempt to force or tag a runner, or actually throwing to another defensive player in an attempt to retire a runner. A fake or a feint to throw shall not be deemed a play or an attempted play. (The fact that the runner is not out is not relevant.)" {6.1} ✠

⁎ *Play 30-29:* R2. B1 slaps a grounder to the shortstop, who runs a few steps toward second as R2 retreats. F6 then overthrows first. At TOT, B1 had already touched first. *Ruling:* In FED, R2 scores, and B1 goes to third (second play). In NCAA / OBR, B1 stops at second: The throw by F6 was the first play by an infielder.

❀ Note 25: NCAA / OBR: If F6 had tagged R2, or attempted a tag, that would have been his "first play," and B1 would be awarded third. Observe that the runner at second did not advance on the play, so NCAA 8-3o AR 1 and the Approved Ruling at OBR 7.05g AR do not apply.

∞ 30 AWARDS TO: RUNNER: FIRST PLAY BY INFIELDER: FIELDING BATTED BALL ✪

FED: For purposes of measuring awards, the act of fielding is not a "play." (8-3-5; 8.3.5f and g) (See § 29.)

NCAA: Same as FED. (8-3o-3 AR 2)

OBR: Same as FED. (See OFF INTERP • 38-29)

★ ∞ 31 AWARDS TO: RUNNER; FORCED TO ADVANCE FOLLOWING BALK ✪

FED: A balk "entitles" each runner to advance one base. (2-3)

> **26. ALSO:** OFF INTERP 39-31: **HOPKINS:** A runner is forced to accept the awarded base. (Website 2007, #6) ❀

NCAA: Following a balk, each runner "must" advance one base. (9-3 Pen)

OBR: A balk is a penalty "entitling" (2.00 Balk) runners to a base; or they "advance" (5.09c); or they "may" advance; (7.04a) or they ***(EDITED)*** "shall" advance (8.05 Pen).

32 AWARDS TO: RUNNER: FORCED TO ADVANCE FOLLOWING: BASE ON BALLS ✪

FED: Even in a game-ending situation, as on a walk to a batter with the bases loaded in the bottom of the last inning of a tied game, all runners forced to advance on an award must advance and touch the next base or be liable to appeal. (8-2-1; 9-1-1 Nt 2) (See § 474.)

NCAA: Same as FED. (8-1a; 8-1a AR)

OBR: In such a game-ending situation, only the runner from third and the batter-runner are required to touch the next base. (4.09b)

✻ *Play 31-32:* In the home half of the final inning of the conference championship game, the score is tied and the bases are loaded with 2 outs when B1 receives ball four. He hurries to first and R3 crosses the plate, but R1 and R2 immediately join the victory celebration. *Ruling:* In FED / NCAA, on appeal either R1 or R2 is out (both failed to touch the next base). Since it is a force out, the run is canceled and play continues into extra innings. In OBR, the game is over.

❀ Note 26: OBR does not provide a time frame for the advance; simply, you wait around until B1 and R3 decide to touch the bases, when the game ends. Many umpires, myself included, would "remind" the runners to advance.

❀ Note 27: **Concerning § 33 and 34:** FED deals with "obstruction." NCAA divides it into two types: 1 and 2. PRO calls those same types: a and b. On 1 / a, the ball is immediately dead: The defense is playing on the runner. There's a big problem with that, according to most experts. On 2 / b, the ball remains alive regardless. That's the FED way, the smart way, the easy way for umpires because there's no decision to make. Obstruction in FED? Wait 'til the play is over and then ....

★ 33 AWARDS TO: RUNNER: OBSTRUCTION: BASE TO MEASURE FROM: MINIMUM AWARD: RUNNER NOT PLAYED ON (TYPE 2 / B) ✪ (See § 34, 349 and 350.)

FED: The umpire awards an obstructed runner, whether played on or not, at least one base beyond his **POSITION** on base at the time of the obstruction.) If the runner achieves the base he was "attempting to acquire," the obstruction is ignored. (8-3-2) **EXCEPT:**

OFF INTERP 40-33: **HOPKINS:** If the runner is not attempting to advance or the fielder did not change the pattern of play, the obstruction is ignored. (Website 2008 #14) ✠

❀ Note 28: OFF INTERP • 40 above is a significant departure from the traditional FED interpretation of obstruction. On this point, at least, the NFHS joins its colleagues. Bravo!

EXCEPT: OFF INTERP 41-33: **STEVENS:** If the batter-runner is obstructed following his fly ball, when the ball is caught, he is out, and the obstruction is ignored. (phone call to cc, 12/8/04) ✠

✻ *Play 32-33*: B1 pops up to the first baseman near the foul line. The pitcher also goes to catch the fly and obstructs B1. The first baseman catches the ball. *Ruling:* B1 is out.

NCAA: POE 1993, 1994, 2001, 2002, 2003. 2004 [obstruction]: Type 2: Same as OBR. (2-54; 6-3c; 8-3e-1 Pen) (See **27. ALSO** below.)

❀ Note 29: ***(EDITED)*** Jim Paronto, the secretary of the NCAA rules committee, writes about the 2011 change like this: "The committee believes this rule [and its application] are second nature to most in baseball!" Ha! Here's a renowned baseball expert, Jim Evans, writing about this Type a / 1 obstruction: "This rule is not clearly written and can be easily misinterpreted if not studied carefully. ... What constitutes 'a play being made on him'? The umpire must determine whether the fielder is making a play on a batted ball, a thrown ball, or is actually in the act of trying to retire an advancing runner. The runner must be making a legitimate effort to advance." (7:37) Etc., etc., etc.

27. ALSO: Special provisions exist for dealing with obstruction of the batter-runner before he touches first: (● 1) On a ground ball, the ball is dead, and the batter-runner receives first; (● 2) on an infield line drive or pop-up, the ball remains alive: If the ball is caught, the play stands; if not, the umpire awards bases as "justified"; (● 3) on a ball hit to the outfield, play continues until all play has stopped, and the umpire will then award any bases that are justified.
(6-3d 1-3; 8-3e 1 through 2 and Pen)

OBR: Type (b): The umpire will award any bases that will "nullify the act of obstruction." The ball is delayed dead. (7.06b) If an obstructed runner advances beyond the base he would have received, "he does so at his own peril." (7.06b CMT)

28. ALSO: OFF INTERP 42-33: **PBUC:** Special provisions exist for dealing with obstruction of the batter-runner before he reaches first: (1) On balls hit in the infield, same as NCAA. (2) On a ball hit to the outfield, a catch results in an out but a fair, uncaught ball results in awarded bases; the batter-runner receives at least first. {7.29}
(See § 362 for comment on the OBR notion of "delayed dead ball.") ✠

29. ALSO: OFF INTERP 43-33: **LEPPERD:** Type (b) obstruction DOES NOT carry an AUTOMATIC minimum award of one base. The umpire may use his judgment. (Booth, eTeamz, 12/11/01) ✠

30. ALSO: OFF INTERP 44-33: **PBUC:** "[Following obstruction] if there is any doubt in the minds of the umpires about where the runner or runners shall be placed, the umpires shall confer." {7.26} (See § 508.) ✠

⁂ *Play 33-33*: **OBR only.** R2, 2 outs. Speedy B1 singles deep to center. As R2 rounds third, F5 obstructs him. Before R2 touches the plate, B1 is out trying to stretch his hit. *Ruling:* Lepperd: "It would be judgment by the umpire as to whether the obstruction caused the runner to touch home plate AFTER the third out." (Booth, eTeamz, 12/11/01)

⁂ *Play 34-33:* R1. B1 singles to right. Both the ball and R1 are headed for third when the first baseman "accidentally" trips B1, who – after touching first – is on his way back to the base. There is no subsequent throw to first, and speedy R1 beats the throw to third. *Ruling:* In FED, the umpire ignores the obstruction since it did not change the pattern of play. (See OFF INTERP • 40 [this section]). In NCAA / OBR, B1 also remains on first: no minimum award.

⁂ *Play 35-33:* 2 outs. B1 flies to medium center field. The pitcher, believing the half inning is over, sprints for his first-base dugout and obstructs B1 before the batter-runner has touched first. The fly ball is then (a) caught or (b) dropped, with B1 being thrown out sliding into second. *Ruling:* In (a), B1 is out. In (b), the umpire awards B1 second.

⁂ *Play 36-33:* 4 Oct, 2003: Boston hosts Oakland in Game 3 of the ALDS. Athletics batting. Miguel Tejada (see Play 41-34) is on second. Ramon Hernandez bounces one toward Nomar Garciaparra, who misses the tough chance: The scorer from Boston ruled it an error! The outfielder rushes to grab the ball as Tejada tries to round third. Third baseman Bill Mueller gets in his way. Umpire Bill Welke points and yells: "That's obstruction!" Tejada then begins to jog home, whereupon the catcher Jason Varitek tags him, whereupon Umpire Paul Emmel says: "He's out!" *Ruling:* The umpires consult (see OFF INTERP • 44 [this section]) and decide that Tejada would certainly not have reached the plate safely. On Type b / 2, obstruction, the ball remains alive. Tejada tried to advance beyond his protected base (third). Therefore, the out stands. It's the same ruling in FED / NCAA.

AO 2-33: EVANS: When Type b Obstruction occurs, the umpire must make an "initial decision" to which base he will protect the runner. That is determined by the position of the runner, the speed of the runner, the position of the fielder, and the location of the ball at the very instant the obstruction occurs.
That "initial decision" may change based on subsequent events; *e.g.*, ball eludes a fielder or ball is dropped by a fielder.

Teaching Points:
Emphasize principle of "watch the ball / glance at runner."

Emphasize that the umpire must acknowledge the obstruction immediately by pointing to the obstruction and verbally stating "That's obstruction!" without calling Time. Compare [that] to football and basketball where flags are thrown and whistles are blown but play continues in many cases.

Emphasize that this is one of the acceptable times for crews to consult for proper placement of runners. (email to cc, 10/26/04)

> ⁂ *Play 37-33:* **OBR only.** Game 5 of the NLCS, 14 Oct, 2002: Benito Santiago (San Francisco) is on first with 2 outs in a scoreless game. David Bell hits for extra bases. Santiago makes third, rounds the bag, and runs into the third baseman, Miguel Cairo (St. Louis). "That's obstruction!" yells the third-base umpire, Jeff Nelson. Santiago stops his advance and returns safely to third. *Ruling:* Santiago is "awarded" third, which is the base he made on his own.

❀ Note 30: That outcome sets, for the time being, the philosophy of MLB in regard to protecting a runner to an advance base during type b obstruction. The criterion to apply, according to Nelson and his supervisor Steve Palermo, is this: THE UMPIRE MUST BE CERTAIN THE RUNNER WOULD HAVE ACHIEVED HIS ADVANCE BASE or he will protect him only to the retreat base.

Nelson: "The throw came in and I knew what it had to be. I was positive that Santiago was not going to make home plate on the play. I have to be 100% sure that he's going to get home before I can give it to him. **SO I PLACED HIM ON THIRD BASE.**"

Thus, the current state of obstruction in OBR is: (● 1) When in doubt, call it obstruction. (● 2) If it's Type b, when the runner returns after the obstruction, leave him on his retreat base. You might not be right, but you will be popular. (See also Obstruction Table, § 34.)

34 AWARDS TO: RUNNER: OBSTRUCTION: BASE TO MEASURE FROM: MINIUM AWARD: RUNNER PLAYED ON (TYPE 1 / A) ✪ (See § 33 and 349.)

IMPORTANT: SEE § 350 FOR HOW TO RULE WHEN A FIELDER BLOCKS THE BASE WHILE FIELDING THE BALL, I.E., WAITING TO RECEIVE A THROW.

FED: The umpire awards an obstructed runner, whether played on or not, at least one base beyond his **POSITION** on base at the time of the obstruction. (8-3-2) (See § 351.) If the runner achieves the base he was "attempting to acquire," the obstruction is ignored. **EXCEPT:** If the runner is not attempting to advance or the fielder did not change the pattern of play, the obstruction is ignored. (Website 2008 #14) (See OFF INTERP • 40-33.)

31. ALSO: OFF INTERP 45-34: **HOPKINS:** If an obstructed runner commits interference, penalize the infractions in order. (Website 2009, #15) ✠

✻ *Play 38-34:* R1, R2, B1 singles. R2 is obstructed after he has rounded third. He then interferes with the catcher' s attempt to play on R1 at third. *Ruling:* At all levels: R2 is awarded home. R1 is out because of the interference. B1 returns TOI. But in FED and NCAA, if the contact between R2 and F2 was malicious, then R2 would be out (rather than receiving home) and ejected.

NCAA: An obstructed runner on whom the defense plays is awarded at least one base beyond the base "last touched legally." The ball is **IMMEDIATELY** dead. (2-54; 8-3e-1 Pen)

32. ALSO: "All runners shall be awarded bases they would have received had there been no obstruction." (2-54)

33. ALSO: OFF INTERP 46-34: **PARONTO:** An obstructed runner who then commits interference causes the runner on whom the defense (would have) played to be out. (San Antonio MTG, 1/4/04)
(Same as FED OFF INTERP 45 [this section].) ✠

✻ *Play 39-34:* R1, R3. R3 is trapped in a rundown and obstructed by the pitcher as he tries for the plate. He sees F2 about to play on R1, heading for second, and knocks the ball out of his hand. R1 makes it safely to third. *Ruling (status of the ball):* In FED, the ball is delayed dead on the obstruction but immediately dead on the interference. In NCAA / OBR, the ball is immediately dead on the obstruction, so the interference never happened. *Ruling (scope of the award):* In FED, R3 scores on the obstruction; R1 is out. In FED, if the interference was malicious, R3 would also be out and ejected. In NCAA / OBR, R3 scores on the obstruction; R1 returns to the base occupied at the time of the obstruction, which could be a *succeeding* base. (See AO 3 [this section].)

OBR: An obstructed runner (one on whom the defense plays or the batter-runner before he touches first) is awarded a minimum of one base from the base "he last legally touched." The ball is immediately dead. (7.06a)

AO 3-34: EVANS: Following obstruction, a trailing runner is awarded the next base if he is at least halfway to that base at the time of the obstruction. (7:39)

AO 4-34: EVANS: This rule is not clearly written and can be easily misinterpreted if not studied carefully. ...What constitutes "a play being made on him"? The umpire must determine whether the fielder is making a play on a batted ball, a thrown ball, or is actually in the act of trying to retire an advancing runner. The runner must be making a legitimate effort to advance."

34. ALSO: OFF INTERP 47-34: **FITZPATRICK:** For the purpose of an obstruction award, a runner guilty of missing a base or leaving a base too soon is considered to have touched or left the base legally. After the award, if the runner fails to correct his infraction, he will be declared out on proper appeal. (email to cc, 11/15/00) (See § 352.) ✠

❀ Note 31: OFF INTERP 47 above is important because it harmonizes the way umpires should officiate all three codes. But don't forget § 354.

❀ Note 32: Here's a table that shows obstruction awards in the major codes:

-

OBSTRUCTION TABLE		
FED	RUNNER: played on, not played on	delayed dead, 1 base minimum if the pattern of play is affected
NCAA	RUNNER: played on — Type 1	immediately dead, 1 base minimum (Same as OBR)
	RUNNER: not played on — Type 2	delayed dead, bases as "justified" (Same as OBR)
OBR	RUNNER: played on — Type (a)	immediately dead, 1 base minimum
	RUNNER: not played on — Type (b)	delayed dead, bases to "nullify" obstruction

⁕ *Play 40-34:* Following a single B1 misses first, tries to return, and is obstructed by the first baseman, who tags him out. *Ruling:* At all levels the umpire awards B1 second.

⁕ *Play 41 -34*: 4 Oct, 2003. Boston hosts Oakland in Game 33 of the ALDS. Red Sox batting. Damian Jackson grounds to Eric Chavez, who traps Jason Varitek off third. During the rundown, Ramon Hernandez chases Varitek back toward third, intending to throw to Miguel Tejada. (See Play 36-33) Chavez, in the base path without the ball and not making a play, contacts Varitek. *Ruling:* NCAA and OBR: Umpire Bill Welke calls "Time! That's obstruction." He awards Varitek home on the Type a obstruction, one base in advance of the base last legally touched. The batter-runner is allowed to advance to second. In FED, the ball remains alive. If the defense plays on the batter-runner, for example, what you see is what you get. Any advance he makes is also a WYSIWYG. After play has stopped, the umpire awards R3 home, which is the mandatory one-base award for all obstructed runners on whom the defense is playing.

❀ Note 33: "Last legally touched" is an absolute fiction, totally meaningless in baseball. Awards for obstruction are invariably measured from the runner's **POSITION** on base at the time of the obstruction. If you're in doubt, see Bogus Play A next.

Bogus Play A-34: NCAA and OBR only. Bubba smashes one in the gap and is thinking of third from the moment he leaves the batter's box. In his haste he does not touch second. He is obstructed by the shortstop and thrown out at third. *Ruling:* According to the language of the book, the umpire awards Bubba second! Why? The last base he touched was first; one base in advance of that is second. Ergo, he gets a double.

Note 33 continued: Don't try to sell that ruling in any of your games where the players bathe themselves. Naturally, you will put Bubba on third, and everyone will be happy. They won't know you kicked the "black-letter law." As a life-long iconoclast, I contend Bubba **SHOULD GET ONLY SECOND** because he, too, violated the rules. He was cheating on his way to third; he ought to pay some price. BTW: If Bubba doesn't return to touch second, he is subject to appeal.

On the other hand, there is this: A runner who passes the base he would have reached on an award and misses that base shall be considered as having advanced to that base. He is out when he or the base is tagged. (6.08c CMT; 7.04d) (See § 10 for a very important caveat concerning "tagging the base.") One could argue, then, that Bubba has "touched" second in a metaphorical sense. Do you suppose Bill Klem worried about figures of speech?

35 AWARDS TO: RUNNER: OVERTHROW: BASES RECEIVED
ALL CODES NOW AGREE: TEXT DELETED, 2011)

36 AWARDS TO: RUNNER: PENALTY IGNORED
ALL CODES NOW AGREE: TEXT DELETED, 1997.

∞ 37 AWARDS TO: RUNNER: PITCH: DEFLECTED INTENTIONALLY TO DEAD-BALL TERRITORY ✪

FED: When a pitch eludes the catcher and is intentionally deflected into a dead-ball area by a fielder: (● 1) If the ball would have gone dead without the deflection, runners are awarded one base; (● 2) if the deflection *caused* the ball to become dead, runners receive a two-base award, measured from the time of the deflection. (8.3.3k) (See § 27 and 28. See especially § 356.)

NCAA: No provision. (See Note 34 [this section].)

OBR: Point not covered.

OFF INTERP 48-37: **PBUC STAFF:** A pitch is intentionally deflected to DBT: Treat the pitch as a throw and award two bases from the bases occupied at the time of the intentional act. (email to cc, 12/15/00) ✽

❀ Note 34-37: Both NCAA and OBR cover **BATTED OR THROWN BALLS** that are intentionally deflected into DBT. (See § 28, where NCAA by rule and OBR by interpretation award two bases from the time of the intentional act.) Each book also covers what should occur when a **PITCH IS ACCIDENTALLY DEFLECTED:** Award two bases measured from the bases occupied at TOP. (NCAA 8-3o-4; OBR 7.05h AR) In NCAA, BRD recommends: Treat a "pitch" as a "throw" and award two bases measured from the time of the intentional act.

⁂ *Play 42-37:* R1, R2. F1's wild pitch is bouncing around in live territory near the dugout. The catcher goes for the ball, which has almost stopped rolling, looks over his shoulder at the runners, and then kicks the ball into the dugout. At the time F2 kicks the ball, R2 has already touched third and R1 has rounded second. The umpire determines the kick was intentional. *Ruling:* In NCAA (BRD recommendation) and OBR (official ruling), both runners score: two bases from the time of the intentional act. In FED, you will decide: If you believe the pitch would have gone dead anyway, award R2 third and R1 second, which is where they were before the ball went dead. If F2's kick sent the ball into the dugout, both runners score, as in NCAA / OBR.

❀ Note 35: To the FED, the fielder's intent is not relevant; what counts is the impetus that caused the ball to go dead.

38 AWARDS TO: RUNNER: PITCH: DEFLECTED UNINTENTIONALLY TO DEAD-BALL TERRITORY ✪

FED: Point not covered.

OFF INTERP 49-38: With R1 on first, a pitch hits the catcher's shin guards and is deflected toward the dugout. R1 had left first base headed for second as F1 released the pitch and is standing on second base when the deflected pitch rolls into the dugout. R1's head coach argues that R1 should be awarded third base. RULING: R1 is awarded one base from where he was at the time of the pitch. R1's award is second base and he will remain at second, and not be advanced to third base. (Website 2010, #18}✠

NCAA: If a fielder trying to field a wild pitch, passed ball, or wild pick-off throw deflects the ball to DBT, two bases are awarded from TOP. (8-3o-4)

35. ALSO: "If the pitch has stopped rolling, or it is clear the ball will not roll into dead ball territory, and a new impetus is applied to the ball by a defensive player, the awards are two bases from the time of the act." (8-3o-4 AR)

OBR: If a pitch is deflected, the award is two bases measured from TOP. (7.05h AR)

∞ 39 AWARDS TO: RUNNER: PITCH: LODGES WITH: CATCHER ✪ (See § 23 and 40.)

FED: When a pitch lodges in the catcher's equipment, the ball is dead. (5-1-1g-4; 5.2.1b) **PENALTY:** The umpire awards each runner one base. (8-3-3d)

❀ Note 36: Don't forget to check out § 23. That situation is much less likely to occur but far more likely to create excitement.

NCAA: If a pitch or throw by the pitcher from the pitcher's plate lodges in the catcher's equipment **OTHER THAN HIS GLOVE** and becomes unplayable (6-4d), the ball is dead. **PENALTY:** Runners advance one base. (8-3k)

OBR: Same as NCAA. (5.09g) (See OFF INTERP • 31-23.)

★ ∞ 40 AWARDS TO: RUNNER: PITCH: LODGES WITH: UMPIRE ✪ (See also § 39.)

FED: If a pitch or throw by the pitcher from the pitcher's plate lodges in an umpire's equipment, the ball is dead. (5-1-1g-4) **PENALTY:** Runners advance one base. (8-3-3d)

❀ Note 37: The Baserunning Awards Table (2012 FED rulebook, p. 49) allows the batter one base when a pitch lodges in an umpire's uniform or equipment on ball four. But there is no rulebook justification for that! And on strike three? For that, you have to return to those golden days of yesteryear (1990!) and read 5.1.1n. ***(ADDED)*** Let me point out if there were fewer than two out and first base was occupied, the 1990 umpire would call out the batter, but the living runners would advance one base.

NCAA: Same as FED. (8-3k) (See § 41.)

OBR: If a pitch passes the catcher, lodges in the umpire's equipment, and **REMAINS OUT OF PLAY**, runners advance one base. (5.09g) On a third strike ***(ADDED)*** or ball four the batter is awarded first. (5.09g CMT ¶ 3) (See § 41.)

∞ 41 AWARDS TO: RUNNER: THROW LODGES WITH: UMPIRE ✪

FED: If a fielder's throw lodges in an umpire's equipment, award each runner two bases. (8-3-3c) (See § 40.)

NCAA: Same as FED. (8-3o-3) (See § 40.)

OBR: Point not covered.

OFF INTERP 50-41: **FITZPATRICK:** Same as FED. (email to cc, 12/15/00) ✠

42 AWARDS TO: RUNNER: THROW / PITCH CARRIED TO DEAD-BALL TERRITORY ✪

FED: The rules provide for an award when a throw – not by the pitcher from the pitcher's plate – is carried to DBT.
(8.3.3 CMT [2002 ed]; 8.3.3h) (See § 28.)

❀ Note 38: BRD recommends: Treat a pitch the same as a throw.

NCAA: When a pitch or throw is carried into the bench, dugout, or other DBT, if the fielder does not fall, the ball remains alive and in play. If he falls, all runners advance one base measured from the base occupied at the TIME OF THE FALL. (6-1e)

OBR: No provision. (See Note 39 [this section].)

AO 5-42: EVANS *Play:* The batter drills a hot grounder toward second. The catcher advances toward the first base dugout to back up the throw to first. He positions himself in the dugout on the second step. The throw eludes the first baseman and bounces directly to a perfectly positioned catcher. The batter-runner is unable to advance. Is this a heads-up play by the catcher? *Ruling:* The catcher was not thinking. He put himself in an out of play area to field a thrown ball. The ball is considered "in the dugout" and the batter-runner is awarded second. If he had secured possession while on the playing field and then stepped into dead ball territory without falling, this would have been legal. (7-26)

⁜ *Play 43-42:* **OBR only.** R1. B1 singles to right, and R1 heads for third. The right fielder guns the ball directly to third. At the time of the throw R1 is nearing third, and B1 has not yet touched second. The ball skips past the third baseman, where it is grabbed by the pitcher, backing up the base. F1 is off balance and falls into the dugout. At the time of the fall, R1 has touched third and B1 has touched second. *Ruling:* R1 scores; B1 stops at third. (The pitcher was not injured.)

❀ Note 39-42: The OBR tells us what to do if a fielder, after catching a fly ball, falls into DBT. It tells us what to do if a pitch or throw by the pitcher from the rubber goes into dead ball territory. IT DOES NOT TELL US what happens when a fielder gloves a throw and falls into DBT. The BRD recommends treat as in Evans AO 7[this section].

43 BATTER: BALLS AND STRIKES ARGUED ✪ (See § 75.)

FED: Any umpire's decision involving judgment, such as the call of a ball or strike, is final. (10-1-4) (See § 421.)

❀ Note 40: The difference between FED and the other books is this: Umpires at other levels have specific language that prohibits game participants from arguing balls and strikes. FED quietly sanctions such objections — as long as they are sportsmanlike. Question: "A player or coach who questions a ball or strike shall be ejected. True or False?" Answer: "False. (3-3-1 Pen)" (Question and answer are from the 1993 FED Baseball Rules Exam, Part II, #60.) If the player or coach questions in an unsportsmanlike manner, warning / ejection is the ticket. (3-3-1g)

NCAA: **POE 2000**: Game participants may not argue balls and strikes. **PENALTY:** warning / ejection. (3-6f AR 1) (See § 75.)
36. ALSO: A coach may argue that a decision is contrary to the rules. But "coaches are not entitled to a second opinion because they dispute a call." (3-6e) Once the umpires confer, their decision is final. "If a call is reversed, the coach is entitled to an explanation." (3-6e AR)
37. ALSO: A coach or manager who leaves his position to argue balls and strikes or a checked swing may be "ejected without warning." (3-6f-AR 2)

OBR: No person connected with the game may **LEAVE HIS POSITION** on the field, the coaching box, or the bench to argue balls and strikes. **PENALTY:** warning / ejection. (9.02a CMT) (See § 75. See also § 358, which explores another subject the skipper can't argue.)

❀ Note 41: If you're not sure whether umpires enforce the penalty, ask Mike Hargrove, former manager of the Cleveland Indians. He took a hike in the second game of the 1998 AL Division Series. Joe Brinkman tossed him after just three pitches! Of course, Ron Luciano once dumped Earl Weaver during the pregame meeting, but that was in the International League and hardly counts.

★ 44 BATTER: BATTER'S BOX: DELAYS ENTERING: PENALTY STRIKE ✪

FED: ***(EDITED)*** The batter must take his place promptly in the box. (7-3-1) **PENALTY:** If he delays for 20 seconds after the pitcher has the ball, the umpire shall call an automatic strike. The umpire should caution the batter that he has x-amount of seconds left.

(7.3.1a) "The pitcher need not pitch, and the ball remains live." (7-3-1 Pen)

(MOVED FROM 2011 § 333) ❀ Note 42: The quote from the FED book above – "the ball remains live" – makes this the perfect time and place for my annual bashing of the affected use of a **DESCRIPTIVE** adjective in place of a **PREDICATE** adjective. (● 1) It's a live ball. [correct] (● 2) The ball is alive. [correct] But to use "live" in the second locution shows a lamentable and total ignorance not only of grammar but of history. Below is a summary of the use of "live" and "alive" in the OBR:

Word	Function	Times used
live	descriptive adjective "With a live ball, the fielder....	3
	predicate adjective (a grammatical monstrosity) "And the ball is live."	0
alive	descriptive adjective (a grammatical monstrosity) "It's an alive ball."	0
	predicate adjective "The ball is alive."	10

Mrs. Lois Smith Douglas Murray, my freshman English teacher at Baylor University back in 1955, may rest assured: I will never write such a foolish sentence as "It is an alive ball." Equally foolish – and equally ugly – is "The ball is live." A professional umpire chastised me: "You know the ball is an inanimate object. It can't be **ALIVE**." I replied: "Well, then, it damn sure can't be **DEAD**, either."

38. ALSO: If both the batter and the pitcher violate the 20-second count, the umpire will assess the batter with a strike. (7.3.1c) (See § 46.)

❀ Note 43: Case book play 7.3.1c is exactly how they handle that at the NBC World Series. But in Wichita the 20-second clock is not in the umpire's head; it's on the scoreboard!

NCAA: Other than the start of a half inning as the 90-second clock is winding down (see **39. ALSO** below): When the batter delays entering the batter's box, the umpire shall call a strike. The ball remains alive. On the third strike the batter is out. The pitcher does not have to deliver. (7-1b-2; 7-4g) (See particularly § 518 for the new NCAA method of handling delays by the **PITCHER.**)

❀ Note 44: The NCAA is much tougher on the recalcitrant batter than the FED. A high school umpire must wait 20 seconds; his college brother, just a heartbeat.

39. ALSO: At the start of a half inning, with the 90-second clock running, "a strike results if the batter is not in the box ready to take the pitch with five seconds or less showing on the clock and time expires." The umpire may, but is not required to grant time. Only unusual circumstances would justify "Time." The batter does not receive a warning that the clock is about to expire. (Appendix F)

40. ALSO: After a warning, if anyone argues "any penalty or timing procedure," the offender is subject to immediate ejection. The head coach may point out a clock malfunction. (Appendix F)

41. ALSO: If the batter's box penalty (§ 45) is applied and the batter then refuses to re-enter the batter's box, the umpire shall award an additional strike. The pitcher shall not pitch, but the ball is alive. (7-1d)

OBR: Same as NCAA. **EXCEPT:** The ball is dead. (6.02c)

> **42. ALSO:** OFF INTERP 51-44: **PBUC:** When the batter refuses to enter the box after being warned, "the proper mechanic is for the umpire to call 'Time' and then signal 'Strike.'" {3.21} ✠

43. ALSO: The umpire shall give the batter "a reasonable opportunity" to get into the box before calling a second (or third) penalty strike. (6.02c CMT)

44. ALSO: The umpire should "encourage" the on-deck batter to get into the box after the previous batter has reached base or made an out. (6.02d CMT ¶ 2)

★ 45 BATTER: BATTER'S BOX: LEAVES: BETWEEN PITCHES ✪

FED: POE 1996, 1997, 2009: Once the batter enters the batter's box, he must keep one foot inside unless:

(● 1) he swings at a pitch;

(● 2) he is forced out of the box by a pitch;
(See Note 46 [this section].)
(● 3) the batter attempts a drag bunt;
(● 4) the catcher or pitcher feints or attempts a play at any base;
(● 5) the pitcher with the ball leaves the dirt portion of the mound or positions himself on the mound farther than five feet from the pitcher's plate;
(● 6) a member of either team requests and is granted time;
(● 7) the catcher does not catch the pitch; or
(● 8) the catcher leaves his box to give defensive signals or adjust his equipment. (7-3-1; 7-3-1 a through h; 7.3.1f through j)
PENALTY: The umpire shall call a strike, and the ball remains alive. (The defense could attempt a play, for example.) (7-3-1 Pen)

❀ Note 45: My students find it easier to memorize when the batter **CANNOT** step out: after a called "strike" or a called "ball" that didn't force the batter from the box.

POE 2009, 2012: Pace of the game. (See NCAA [this section].)
45. ALSO: When a batter checks his swing but hears "Strike!" and steps out, the umpire "shall not" call a penalty strike because the pitch was in the zone rather than a swinging strike, as the batter surmised. (7.3.1n, 1999 ed)
46. ALSO: The umpire will assess a penalty strike only if the batter begins to delay the game and take advantage of the spirit of the rule. (7-3-1)

NCAA: POE 1994, 1995, 1996, 1997, 2001, 2002, 2004, 2009, 2011: Once the batter enters the batter's box, he must keep one foot within the lines of the box unless:
(● 1) he swings at a pitch;
(● 2) he is forced out of the box by a pitch;

❀ Note 46: Thurston [and Rumble for FED] define "forced out of the box" as occurring whenever the pitch causes the batter to step out. An inside pitch is an obvious instance, but the interpreters also include those times when the batter is off balance after leaning forward to take an outside pitch.

(● 3) a member of either team requests and is granted time;
(● 4) a defensive player attempts a play on a runner at any base;
(● 5) a batter feints a bunt;
(● 6) there is a wild pitch or a passed ball;
(● 7) the pitcher leaves the dirt portion of the pitching mound after receiving the ball; or

(● 8) the catcher leaves his position to give defensive signals. (7-1c-1 a through h) **PENALTY:** Same as FED. (7-1c-1 Pen)

47. ALSO: The batter may not leave the **DIRT PORTION OF THE PLATE AREA** unless: (● 1) a substitution occurs; or (● 2) time is granted for an offensive or defensive conference. (7-1c-2a, -2b and -2c)

❀ Note 47: The committee believes umpires across the country do not consistently apply the batter's box rule and "instructs umpires to strictly enforce" this provision. (**POE 2011**)

48. ALSO: The umpire shall "encourage" the on-deck batter to take his place promptly in the box after the previous hitter has reached base or made an out. (7-1d Nt)

❀ Note 48: Concerning the "batter's-box-rule": Observe two major differences. (● 1) A high school batter who legally leaves the box may go onto the grass. A college batter must stay on the dirt except in two instances. (● 2) A high school batter leaves when the catcher or pitcher attempts a play. The college batter as well can step out when the shortstop breaks for second, whether the pitcher wheels or not.

49. ALSO: POE 2008. 2009: The committee is concerned about the pace of the game. Umpires should pay careful attention to: the batter's box rule (§ 45), conferences (§ 150), and speeding the time between innings and pitching changes. (See § 368.)

OBR: ***(ADDED)*** The batter shall not leave his box after the pitcher "comes to Set Position or starts his windup." (6.02b) **PENALTY:** The umpire shall call a ball or strike "as the case may be." (6.02b Pen)

(ADDED) ❀ Note 49: Point one: They are, of course, "kidding" when they say there is a penalty. Point two: Umpires through the years have generally expanded the zone in such instances. Point three: The MLB rules committee doesn't really mean what they say. What they intended to say was the batter could not leave his box after the pitcher "comes to the stop in Set Position." If he does, the umpire might call a strike, but only if the pitcher pitches one. Amazing!

50. ALSO: Major league rule: The batter shall not be permitted to leave the box without good reason. He may not, for example, claim he needs pine tar for his bat, etc. **PENALTY:** ejection. (6.02b CMT ¶ 2)

❀ Note 50: "Leaves the box" in MLB means the batter heads back to his bench or dugout area. At the professional level, only if the batter can prove his bat is broken will he be allowed to return to his dugout.

51. ALSO: National Association rule: Same as NCAA 7-1c-1. (6.02d-1)

52. ALSO: National Association rule: The batter may leave the box and the dirt area of the plate during a substitution or conference for either team. (6.02d-2)

❀ Note 51: Check with your youth league, which may have adopted these minor league rules.

46 BATTER: BATTER'S BOX: LEAVES: DURING PITCH ✪

FED: When the pitcher delivers the ball as the batter, without being granted time, steps out of the box with ONE FOOT: (● 1) if the pitcher hesitates in his delivery, there is no penalty to either player; but (● 2) if the pitcher legally delivers, the umpire shall call the pitch a strike (no matter the location of the pitch) and the ball remains alive. (6-2-4d-1)

53. ALSO: If the batter steps out of the box with TWO FEET as the pitcher begins his pitching motion: (● 1) if the pitcher hesitates, the umpire shall call a penalty strike for leaving the box; or (● 2) if the pitcher delivers legally, the umpire shall call **TWO STRIKES**, one for the pitch (no matter the location) and one for leaving the box. (6-2-4d-1; 6.2.4i)

54. ALSO: When the batter holds up his hand to REQUEST TIME: (● 1) if the pitcher hesitates, there is no penalty to either player; but (● 2) if the pitcher delivers legally, the umpire shall call the pitch a strike (no matter the location). (6.2.4h)

55. ALSO: Whether time is granted (resulting in no strike) is umpire judgment. (5.2.1a) (See § 44.)

56. ALSO: If the umpire determines that the batter's actions are designed to create a balk, he will eject the batter. (3-3-1o Pen) (See § 359.)

NCAA: If a batter leaves the box when the pitcher is delivering, the pitch is a ball or strike, as the case may be. The ball remains alive. (7-1b-1 Pen) (See § 359.)

OBR: Same as NCAA. (6.02b Pen)

47 BATTER: BATTER'S BOX: STANDS WITHIN ✪

FED: The batter must stand completely in the batter's box; *i.e.*, "not touching the ground outside the batter's box." (2-7-2;7.3.2a; 7.3.2c CMT) The umpire shall direct the batter to stand "so neither foot is outside the lines of the batter's box." (7.3.2b)

❀ Note 52: It is legal for a batter to assume a position with the heel or toe of his foot (feet) on the line of the box as long as the remaining portion of his foot (feet) is not touching the ground outside the box.

NCAA: The batter must have both feet in the box."at the time of the pitch." (1-3a; 7-1e)
57. ALSO: Umpires are to enforce the rule "as written." **PENALTY:** If the lines are erased, the umpire will require the batter to stand with both feet at least six inches from the plate. (7-1e; 7-1e AR; 7-1e Pen)

OBR: Same as FED. (6.03; 6.03 AR)

58. ALSO: OFF INTERP 52-47: **PBUC:** The umpire shall instruct the batter to remain within the lines of the box "if [the infraction is] brought to the attention of the umpire." Failure to comply subjects the offender to ejection. {3.19} ✠

★ 48 BATTER: BATTER'S BOX: STEPS: ON PLATE / OUTSIDE BOX: HITS FAIR OR FOUL OR FOUL TIP ✪

FED: The batter is out and the ball is dead if he hits fair or foul while either foot or knee "is touching the ground completely outside the lines of the batter's box or touching home plate."
(7-3-2; 7-3-2 Pen)

59. ALSO: OFF INTERP 53-48: **HOPKINS:** If the batter hits a foul tip while touching the plate or outside the lines of the batter's box: The ball is dead and the batter is out. (Website 2003, #2) ✠

NCAA: The batter is out if he hits fair or foul while touching the plate or with one foot on the ground completely outside the lines of the batter's box. (7-10a; 7-10a Pen)
60. ALSO: If the batter hits a "foul tip" while not "within the lines of the batter's box," it is not a foul tip but a foul ball. He is out. (7-8) (See § 73.)

OBR: If the batter hits fair or foul with one foot on the ground completely outside the batter's box: Same as FED / NCAA. (6.06a) If the batter steps on the plate and hits fair or foul:
Point not covered.

OFF INTERP 54-48: ***(EDITED)*** **WENDELSTEDT:** Unless the batter's foot is COMPLETELY outside the lines of the box when he steps on the plate, he is not out when he hits the pitched ball fair or foul. (HW/154) (See § 83.) ✠

61. ALSO: OFF INTERP 55-48: **PBUC:** The batter is out if he hits a foul tip with one foot completely outside the batter's box. {3.19} ✠

⁜ *Play 44-48:* B1 is in the front of the batter's box to hit the curve before it breaks. He takes a mighty swing and foul tips the pitch, which the catcher catches. The umpire notices the batter has one foot on the ground outside the batter's box. *Ruling:* In FED, the batter is out. [Website interpretation] In NCAA, the batter is out. [black-letter law] In OBR, the batter is out. [PBUC interpretation]

★ ∞ 49 BATTER: DEFINITION ✪

FED: The batter is the player of the offensive team who is "entitled to occupy either of the two batters' boxes." (2-7-1)

❀ Note 53: The implications of the definition match the official language of the NCAA.

NCAA: A player on-deck is a "batter" when the previous batter is put out or reaches a base: "The new batter does not have to enter the batter's box to be considered the batter." (9-4a AR 3)

OBR: The batter is "an offensive player who takes his position in the batter's box." (2.00 Batter)

62. ALSO: OFF INTERP 56-49: **PBUC:** ***(EDITED)*** A batter's time at bat begins when the preceding batter is put out or becomes a runner. {8.12} ✠

❀ Note 54: The definition affects balks at all levels. Question: Can a pitcher balk when a batter is not in the box? Answer: Yes. In NCAA / OBR, the definition also has impact on a coach or manager making a second trip to the mound while the "same batter" is at bat. (See § 152.)

DESIGNATED HITTER

❀ Note 55: The NCAA DH rule is the most intricate rule in baseball — and the most difficult to master. No official can hope to umpire games for both high school and college without a thorough knowledge of the DH rule differences. The summary comparison that follows will help you understand the various differences in the NCAA DH rule as they pertain to FED and OBR. (The numbers in parentheses refer to the appropriate sections in this book.)

NCAA DESIGNATED HITTER RULE

POE 1990, 1992, 1993, 1994, 1995, 1996, 2001, 2002

SUMMARY

● 1. The DH bats only for the pitcher. (OBR is the same.)
FED: The DH bats for any defensive player and all subsequent substitutes for that player. (§ 51)

● 2. If no DH is listed, the pitcher is automatically the DH.
FED / OBR: In such a case no DH is allowed. (§ 52)

● 3. If the DH plays defense, the pitcher bats for the replaced defensive player, unless multiple substitutions are made, when the coach may designate their spots in the lineup. (OBR is the same.)
FED: The DH and the player for whom he bats (or has batted) are "locked" into a single position in the batting order. The DH and that player (or players) may not play defense at the same time since they occupy the same spot in the lineup. (§ 64)

CAUSES FOR TERMINATION OF THE DH

● 1. The DH plays defense. (FED / OBR are the same.) (§ 64)

❀ Note 56: In NCAA, the DH may pitch without terminating the role of the DH; that's not so in FED / PRO.

● 2. A defensive player becomes the pitcher. (OBR is the same.)
FED: That move would not terminate the DH. (§ 65)

● 3. The pitcher plays defense. (OBR is the same.)
FED: That move would not terminate the DH. (§ 66)

❀ Note 57: In OBR, the DH is always terminated if the game pitcher pinch hits for the DH (§ 68). A similar move also might terminate the FED DH, but for a different reason: In any FED game where the DH hits for the pitcher, when that game pitcher pinch hits for the DH, the role of the DH is terminated, not because it was the **PITCHER** who was pinch hitting but because the player entering to hit was one for whom the DH had batted.

● 4. A pinch hitter bats for anyone other than the pitcher and then the pinch hitter becomes the pitcher. (OBR is the same.)
FED: That move would not terminate the DH. (§ 67)

ILLEGAL LINEUP CHANGES

● 1. The DH may not pinch run for any **OTHER** player in the lineup. (OBR is the same.)
FED: The DH may re-enter to pinch run for a player (or subsequent substitutes for that player) who earlier replaced the DH. (§ 71)

• 2. Once a player leaves the offensive lineup, he may not return offensively. The DH may not re-enter. (OBR is the same.)
FED: The DH (or any starter) may re-enter once. (§ 62 and 63)

• 3. If the DH replaces the pitcher, the pitcher may become the DH at that time but not later in the game.
FED / OBR: Such a switch may not be made. (§ 56)

• 4. If the pitcher becomes the DH, he may not re-enter on defense in any capacity.
FED / OBR: Such a change cannot be made. (§ 57)

• 5. If the P/DH is replaced as the DH, he may continue to pitch, but he may not later move to defense or return as the DH. (§ 52 and 57)
FED / OBR: The situation is not applicable. (§ 60)

• 6. If the pitcher (who is not also the DH) enters to play defense and a new pitcher goes to the mound, those "two" substitutions alone do not constitute multiple substitutions. (But see § 64 for an important exception.)

OBR: The two substitutions would be enough. (§ 66)
FED: The situation is not applicable.

❀ Note 58: The object is to juggle the batting order legally so that the pitcher does not automatically bat in the spot vacated by the defensive player (whom the DH is replacing). (See Play 53-66.)

LEGAL NCAA LINEUP CHANGES

• 1. The DH and the pitcher may swap positions. [The lineup remains at 10 players.] (§ 56 and 57)

• 2. The P/DH may be replaced as the DH but remain as the pitcher. [The lineup lists 9 players and increases to 10.] (§ 60)
❀ Note 59: He cannot return as DH.

• 3. The P/DH may be replaced as pitcher but remain as DH. A subsequent substitute may pinch hit for the DH and become the DH. [The lineup lists 9 players, increases to 10, but cannot return to 9.] (§ 61)
❀ Note 60: Once a P/DH is relieved, neither he nor any **SUBSEQUENT DH** may become the pitcher or enter on defense.

• 4. The DH may become the P/DH and later be replaced as the pitcher but remain as the DH. [The lineup lists 10 players, reduces to 9, and then returns to 10.] (§ 58)

● 5. The pitcher may become the P/DH and later be replaced as the DH but remain as the pitcher. [The lineup lists 10 players, reduces to 9, and then returns to 10.] (§ 59 and 68)

1. PRELIMINARIES

★ 50 BATTER: DH: DH BATS: AT LEAST ONCE ✪

FED: No provision.

NCAA: No provision.

NAIA: ***(CHANGED)*** DH rule: Same as NCAA.
Last edition: Same as NCAA.

OBR: The DH must bat at least once unless the opposing club changes pitchers. (6.10b-2) **PENALTY: Point not covered.**

OFF INTERP 57-50: **FITZPATRICK:** If the DH has not batted once, the pinch hitter batting for the DH is out if at bat or on base. Whenever discovered, he is disqualified. The original DH is out of the game, but the role of the DH remains. (phone call to cc, 11/8/01; (See OFF INTERP 59-69.) ✠

❀ Note 61: Mike Fitzpatrick labeled this truly a 9.01c infraction:

✻ *Play 45-50:* **OBR only.** Jackson is the DH, batting ninth. In the third inning it is Jackson's turn to bat for the first time, but Kelly bats and singles. Before a pitch or a play the defense appeals. *Ruling:* Kelly is out and disqualified. Jackson is also removed from the game, but the role of the DH remains.

❀ Note 62: ***(EDITED)*** The designated hitter is one of nine major rules or interpretations **WHERE EACH LEVEL TREATS THE SITUATION DIFFERENTLY.** The other eight are: § 83 (use illegal bat); § 124 (throw from dead-ball area); § 144 (conferences); § 245 (positions occupied at time of pitch or play); § 246 (fighting); § 266 (improperly declared infield fly); § 378 (hidden ball play); § 488 (illegal substitutes).

51 BATTER: DH: DH BATS: FOR PITCHER OR PLAYER ✪

FED: The DH may bat for any starter and all substitutes for that starter. (3-1-4) (See Play 52-64.)

NCAA: The DH bats only for the pitcher and his substitutes. (7-2a)

OBR: Same as NCAA. (6.10b-1)

63. ALSO: "The DH may not sit in the bullpen unless he is serving as the catcher in the bullpen." (6.10b-15)

52 BATTER: DH: DH LISTED BEFORE GAME ✪

FED: A team may have a DH only if he is listed before the lineup becomes official. (3-1-4) (See § 415.)

NCAA: If no DH is listed, the pitcher is automatically the DH and will be considered as two players. Such a dual player is known as the pitcher / designated hitter or P/DH. (7-2b)

OBR: Same as FED 3-1-4. (6.10b-1) (See § 415.) **EXCEPT:** If the DH is not identified on the lineup card, when discovered after both teams have played the field, the pitcher must replace the player who did not assume a fielding position. The replaced player has been substituted for. (6.10b-11i)
64. ALSO: In the top of the first inning, if the home team manager has not identified the DH, he shall put his pitcher's name into one of the nine spots in the batting order. The replaced player has been substituted for. (6.10b-11ii)
65. ALSO: When the pitcher must become the DH, the replaced player has been substituted for and is removed from the game. Any plays that occurred before the error was discovered shall count. (6.10-11)

★ 53 BATTER: DH: DH POSITION IN LINEUP ✪

FED: POE 1983, 1984, 1990: The DH should be listed below or ***(EDITED)*** to the right of the player for whom he bats. (POE [1990 ed])

NCAA: No provision.

(ADDED) ❀ Note 63-53: The practice in situations where the DH may be the pitcher (9-man lineup) is simply to put the pitcher into the slot where he will bat.

OBR: No provision.

(ADDED) ❀ Note 64: Straight OBR lineups are simple with a DH: Batting slots 1 through 9. The pitcher is listed below the ninth hitter. Often, umpires leave a blank line between the batters and the pitchers. Remember, though, your OBR leagues may allow the DH since that increases participation.

54 BATTER: DH: DH SUBSTITUTE ANNOUNCED✪

FED: No provision.

NCAA: No provision.

OBR: A substitute for the DH does not have to be announced until it is his turn to bat. (6.10b-13)

2. NCAA PITCHER-AND-DH SHUFFLE

55 BATTER: DH: DH AND PITCHER SWAP POSITIONS ✪

FED: Not applicable.

NCAA: If the DH is not the pitcher and the DH replaces the pitcher, at the time of that substitution the pitcher may replace the DH. (7-2c-5a) **PENALTY:** Once the coach reaches the dugout, he may no longer move the replaced pitcher to defense or DH. (7-2c-5 Pen)

OBR: Not applicable.

56 BATTER: DH: DH BECOMES PITCHER ✪

FED: If the DH (Able) re-enters as the **PITCHER** after being removed for a pinch hitter (Baker), the "new" DH (Baker) must leave the game. The "old" DH (Able) has moved to **DEFENSE**, thus ending the role of the designated hitter. The pinch hitter (Baker) is simply ineligible to participate further. (3-1-4)

NCAA: If a substitute pinch hits or pinch runs for the DH, the replaced DH may become the pitcher; but that substitution must be announced at the time of the pinch hitter's / runner's entry. (7-2c-7a)

❀ Note 65: The "old" DH (now pitcher) may not later move to a defensive position because that would require him to return offensively. (7-2c-3c) (See § 59; 60; 63; 497.)

❀ Note 66: It's easy to remember the coach must announce at the moment he pinch hits for the DH that the DH will become the pitcher in the next half inning. If he doesn't, then the DH has been removed from the game — and may not re-enter. (See § 62.)

⁎ *Play 46-56:* **NCAA only.** Able is the DH. In the fourth, Baker pinch hits for Able. The coach comes to announce that Able will replace Charles as the pitcher in the next half inning. *Ruling:* Legal. **BUT:** *Play:* In the seventh the coach returns to say that Able will now move to first base, and the first baseman (David) will become the pitcher. *Ruling:* "No can do!" you tell the coach. Reason: Once a player is removed from the offensive lineup, he may not return. (See § 63.) If Able is permitted to play first base, Baker – the DH – is lost. Able must then hit where Baker is hitting; ergo, Able would return to the offensive lineup.

OBR: Such a substitution would be illegal since the replaced "old" DH may not re-enter. (3.03)

57 BATTER: DH: PITCHER BECOMES DH ✪

FED: Not applicable.

NCAA: If the game pitcher is not the DH, when he is replaced as the pitcher, he may be immediately inserted as the DH. The pitcher may not re-enter in any capacity. (7-2c-2a; 7-2c-2b; 7-2c-5a)

66. ALSO: Anytime before the pitcher is removed as the pitcher, he may pinch hit or pinch run **ONLY** for the DH and become the DH. This change must be announced at the time the pitcher is removed. (7-2c-2 AR)

67. ALSO: Anytime the pitcher is replaced, he may move to a defensive position and bat for the replaced defensive player. The DH is terminated, and the new pitcher will hit in the DH spot. (7-2c-2b) (See § 66.)

68. ALSO: There is no loss of the DH, but the player may not re-enter the game in any other capacity, "*i.e.*, as the pitcher." (7-2c-2b-2)

> ✻ *Play 47-57:* **NCAA only.** Able is the P/DH. Jackson pinch hits for him in the fourth and becomes the DH. In the seventh the coach announces that Jackson is going to become the P/DH. *Ruling:* Illegal. Whether the change is made on defense or offense is irrelevant. Jackson may not re-enter as pitcher.

OBR: Not applicable.

3. P/DH: TWO PLAYERS IN ONE

58 BATTER: DH: DH BECOMES P/DH ✪

FED: Not applicable.

NCAA: The DH may enter to pitch, becoming the P/DH, and subsequently be relieved as the pitcher but remain as the DH. (7-2c-3 AR)

> ❀ Note 67: The reason: He has not left the offensive lineup. (See § 63.)

OBR: Not applicable.

★ 59 BATTER: DH: PITCHER BECOMES P/DH ✪

FED: Not applicable.

NCAA: The pitcher may ***(EDITED)*** bat or run **ONLY** for the DH and become the P/DH. He may then be replaced as the DH but stay as the pitcher. (7-2c-10) He could not later play defense, which would require him to return offensively. The pitcher may bat only for the DH. **PENALTY:** The pitcher is ejected. (7-2c-10 Pen) If the pitcher leaves as pitcher but remains as the DH, that change must be announced to the UIC at the time of the pitcher's replacement. (5-5c AR; 7-2c-1b) (See § 56, especially Play 46.)

OBR: Not applicable. (But see § 68.)

60 BATTER: DH: P/DH REPLACED AS DH ✪

FED: Not applicable.

NCAA: If the P/DH is replaced as the DH, he may remain as the pitcher but may not later be moved to a defensive position or return as the DH. (7-2c-4a and b)

❀ Note 68: The reason: If he later moved to defense, he would also return on offense since he is no longer the pitcher. (See § 56, 59 and 63.)

⁎ *Play 48-60:* **NCAA only.** The visiting Clerics begin the game with Adams pitching and Baker as the DH [10-player lineup]. In the fifth, substitute Charles pinch hits for Baker and enters to pitch. He is now the P/DH [9-player lineup]. In the top of the eighth, Charles singles. The coach arrives to report that Davis will now pinch run for Charles (replacing him offensively), but Charles will return to pitch in the bottom of the eighth. [10-player lineup] (7-2c-7a) *Ruling:* Legal. The lineup went from 10 to 9 to 10: "When the P/DH ... is replaced as the DH, the individual may remain in the game as a pitcher."(7-2c-4; 7-2c-7a) Davis, the pinch runner, is now the DH. (7-2c-7)

OBR: Not applicable.

61 BATTER: DH: P/DH REPLACED AS PITCHER ✪

FED: Not applicable.

NCAA: If the P/DH is replaced as pitcher, he may remain as the DH or play defense. If he stays as the DH, neither he nor any subsequent DH may later enter in any other role. (See § 57.) If the P/DH goes to defense, terminating the role of DH, he may return as pitcher once in the game (9-4e) since he was considered two players. (7-2c-5a; 7-2c-5b-4)

⁂ *Play 49-61:* **NCAA only.** Kelly is the P/DH. In the fifth, he is moved to shortstop with Landry coming to pitch and Martin being announced as the DH for Landry. *Ruling:* Not legal: When Kelly goes on defense, the DH is terminated. Landry will hit in the spot vacated by the replaced shortstop. But in the ninth, the coach wants to bring Kelly back to the mound and move Landry to second. Legal.

OBR: Not applicable.

4. DH AND REENTRY

62 BATTER: DH: RE-ENTERS ✪

FED: A DH may re-enter in the role of the DH. (3-1-3)

NCAA: A replaced DH may not re-enter in any capacity. (7-2c-9) (See § 57.)

OBR: Same as NCAA. (6.10b-4) (See § 498.)

63 BATTER: DH: PLAYER RETURNS OFFENSIVELY ✪

FED: A player may leave the lineup and return offensively and / or defensively under the reentry rule. (3-1-3)

NCAA: Once a player leaves the **OFFENSIVE** lineup, he may not return offensively. He might, however, remain as the pitcher. If he does remain as the pitcher, he may not move to any other position. (7-2c-3a and c) (See § 56.)

❀ Note 69: He may not play anywhere except pitcher because that would also require his return offensively.

⁂ *Play 50-63:* **NCAA only.** Able is the P/DH, batting third. In the fourth, Baker pinch hits for Able, and the coach informs the umpire that Able will remain as pitcher, with Baker now the DH. In the eighth, the coach sends Baker to play first base, readily acknowledging that the move will terminate the position of DH. *Ruling:* If you're the umpire, you also hope he will "readily acknowledge" that Able must leave the game. The coach will initially argue that Able will now hit in the slot occupied by the removed first baseman. You will point out that Able was originally in the offensive lineup and cannot return.

OBR: Once withdrawn, no player may re-enter. (3.03; 6.10b-4) (See § 119 and 498.)

5. CAUSE FOR TERMINATION

64 BATTER: DH: DH PLAYS DEFENSE ✪

FED: A DH may play defense; that terminates the DH position and, when he does not replace the player for whom he bats, that defensive player must also leave the game. (If any previous DH plays defense, that also terminates the role of the DH.) (3-1-4; 3.1.4b and d)

❀ Note 70: The DH is locked into his position in the batting order at all levels. But **ONLY FED** locks the person for whom the DH hits into a specific batting-order slot.

> **69. ALSO:** OFF INTERP 58-64: **RUMBLE:** When a DH enters the game on defense and the defensive player **REMAINS IN THE GAME**, the DH would be an illegal substitute and ejected when discovered. (*News* #8, 3/89) ✠

NCAA: When the DH plays defense, the DH position is terminated. (7-2c-1a) The change may be made anytime. (7-2c-1) **EXCEPT:** When the DH becomes the pitcher, the DH is not automatically terminated. (7-2c-3b)

70. ALSO: The pitcher (or a substitute for the pitcher) will bat in place of the replaced defensive player, unless multiple substitutions are made, when the coach may designate their spots in the lineup. (7-2c-1b; 7-2c 1c AR 2) (See § 66.)

71. ALSO: "When the designated hitter and the pitcher both enter on defense at the same time, the coach must designate the positions in the batting order of the new pitcher and the previous pitcher." (7-2c-1c AR 3)

❀ Note 71: AR 3 was added to the book because of an error discovered by your "humble" writer. See BRD 2006, § 64.

⁂ *Play 51-64:* **NCAA and OBR only.** Able is the pitcher, Baker is the DH, batting third. The coach sends the pitcher to first and the DH to second. There are two new players entering the offensive lineup, including the pitcher moving to defense. *Ruling:* The role of the DH is terminated. Baker, the former DH, continues to bat third. The old pitcher (Able) and the new pitcher (Sub) may fill either of the open slots (F3 or F4). In NCAA, ordinarily the umpire will not consider those substitutions to be a multiple swap: "Multiple substitution, used for the purpose of changing the batting order, does not occur unless two new players **(NOT INCLUDING THE PITCHER GOING TO A DEFENSIVE POSITION)** are brought into the game." (7-2c-1c AR 1) But when the DH and the departing pitcher both move to defense at the same time: Treat as in OBR, *i.e.*, two substitutions constitute "multiple subs."

❀ Note 72: In FED, Able and Baker cannot play defense at the same time.

OBR: When the DH plays defense, the role of the DH is terminated. (6.10b-12) The pitcher must bat in the spot of the replaced defensive player unless multiple substitutions are made, when the manager may designated their spots in the lineup. (6.10b-5)
72. ALSO: Unlike NCAA, two substitutes constitute "multiple subs."

⁂ *Play 52-64:* Two innings before regulation play ends, the skipper sends his DH to play center field. *Ruling:* Assume in FED the DH has been hitting for the third baseman. The center fielder, of course, must move — either out of the lineup or to a new defensive position. Additionally, the third baseman must leave the game since he occupies the same spot in the batting order as the DH. If the old center fielder leaves the game, the new third baseman will bat in the spot vacated by the old center fielder. If the old center fielder becomes the new third baseman, all is well. Of course, the FED coach could move his old center fielder to yet another defensive position, which would force still another player to leave the lineup. In short: In FED when the DH plays defense, two players must **ALWAYS** leave: The player for whom the DH batted and the replaced defensive player.

In NCAA and OBR, where the DH has been hitting for the pitcher, the pitcher must now bat in the spot previously occupied by the center fielder. But the center fielder's slot is the lead-off spot for the next half inning, and the pitcher is a weak hitter. With that in mind, the manager also inserts a new right fielder, whose spot in the lineup does not come up until eight hitters have batted. Since two players entered, the manager may stipulate where the players bat. That means his pitcher may now hit for the replaced right fielder, last in the list of upcoming batters, and he might not have to bat at all. The new right fielder, of course, hits in the spot formerly occupied by the removed center fielder. Did you get all that?

65 BATTER: DH: DEFENSIVE PLAYER BECOMES PITCHER ✪

FED: Not applicable.

NCAA: If a defensive player becomes the pitcher, the DH is terminated. The DH may take the defensive player's position, or a substitute may play the defensive position vacated by the new pitcher and bat in the DH's spot. (7-2c-6)

OBR: Same as NCAA. (6.10b-14)

66 BATTER: DH: GAME PITCHER PLAYS DEFENSE ✪

FED: No effect.

NCAA: Once the game pitcher moves to defense, the DH is terminated. (7-2c-1a) For purposes of that clause, "pitcher" is not a defensive position. (7-2b Nt) Multiple substitution is defined as **THREE** new players, if the pitcher (who is not also the designated hitter) is one of the players moving to defense. (5-5e AR; 7-2c-1 AR 1) (But see Play 52-64.) The change must be made when the team is on defense. Thus, the pitcher may not "pinch hit" for a defensive player though he may do so for the DH and then assume a defensive position. (See § 64.)

> * *Play 53-66:* **NCAA only.** Abel, the pitcher (who is not also the DH), moves to play second, and Baker from the bench comes to pitch. *Ruling:* That is not a multiple substitution: Baker (the new pitcher) will bat in the DH's spot while Abel (the old pitcher) will bat in place of the second baseman.

> * *Play 54-66:* **NCAA only.** Abel, the pitcher (who is not also the DH), moves to play second, Baker from the bench comes to pitch, and Charles from the bench enters to play first. *Ruling:* That is a multiple substitution: Now the coach has three open slots, and he may fill them as he chooses.

OBR: Same as NCAA. **EXCEPT:** "Pitcher" is considered a defensive position. Therefore, when the pitcher goes to defense, one other substitute constitutes a multiple substitution. (6.10b-8) (See Play 52-64.)

67 BATTER: DH: PINCH HITTER BECOMES PITCHER ✪

FED: Not applicable.

NCAA: If a pinch hitter bats for any player and then becomes the pitcher, the DH is terminated. (7-2c-8)

> ❀ Note 73: The reason: The DH bats only for the pitcher, but the new pitcher is already entered into the offensive lineup.

OBR: Same as NCAA. (6.10b-9)

68 BATTER: DH: PINCH HITTER / RUNNER FOR DH ✪

FED: A pinch hitter or pinch runner for the DH becomes the DH. (3-1-4; 3.1.4b) **EXCEPT:** The DH is terminated if the player for whom the DH currently hits (or any player for whom he has batted), pinch hits or pinch runs for him. (3.1.4a and c)

NCAA: A pinch hitter or pinch runner for the DH becomes the DH. (7-2c-7)

73. ALSO: If any change involving the pitcher and the DH is made while on offense, that is, if the pitcher bats or pinch runs for the DH, the pitcher may become the P/DH. (7-2c-10)

❀ Note 74: The DH is the only player for whom the pitcher may pinch hit or pinch run. (See § 59.)

OBR: A pinch hitter or pinch runner for the DH becomes the DH. (6.10b-4; 6.10b-6) **EXCEPT:** If the game pitcher bats for the DH, the role of the DH is ended. (6.10b-10) (See § 69.)

69 BATTER: DH: PITCHER PINCH HITS FOR DH ONLY ✪

FED: Not applicable.

❀ Note 75: Since the DH may hit for anyone, the pitcher and the DH are not bound together in the same way they are in NCAA or OBR. But if the DH is hitting for the pitcher Garza, they share the same spot in the batting order, so Garza would have to hit only in the **DH SLOT**. Any other pitcher would be free to bat for any other position player. (3-1-4)

NCAA: The pitcher may pinch hit or pinch run for the DH only. (7-2c-10) **PENALTY:** If the pitcher bats for someone other than the DH, the pitcher is ejected on discovery. (7-2c-10 Pen)

OBR: The pitcher may pinch hit only for the DH. (6.10b-10) **PENALTY: Point not covered.**

OFF INTERP 59-69: **FITZPATRICK:** If the pitcher bats for anyone other than the DH: When appealed properly, the pitcher is an improper batter. The proper batter is out and removed from the game. The pitcher will continue to bat in the spot of the replaced player, and the new defensive player hits in the DH spot. The role of the DH is terminated whenever the infraction is discovered. (phone call to cc, 11/8/01) ✠

⁎ *Play 55-69:* **NCAA and OBR only.** 2 outs. Able should bat but the pitcher Jackson reports as a pinch hitter. The umpire does not discover the error. After Jackson walks, the defense appeals. *Ruling:* In NCAA, the pitcher is ejected and replaced with a pinch runner. The role of the DH is not affected. In OBR, Able is out and removed from the game. Baker will lead off the next half inning. The role of the DH is terminated, whenever discovered. The player replacing Able will hit in the DH spot.

❀ Note 76: Some internet "experts" on the newsgroup rec.sport.officiating went to great lengths to prove that Fitzpatrick's interpretation was wrong. Mike might not be right, but he **CANNOT** be wrong. LOL.

∞ 70 BATTER: DH: DH EJECTED ✪

FED: Point not covered.

> OFF INTERP 60-70: **RUMBLE:** When a DH is disqualified, the ejection has no effect on the position of DH. (*News* #11, 3/83; #21, 3/85; #17, 3/87) ✠

NCAA: Ejection of a DH has no effect on the "position" of the DH. (7-2c-11)

74. ALSO: If the ejected DH is a P/DH, he may be replaced by two players. (7-2c-11 AR)

OBR: No provision. Treat as in NCAA 7-2c-11.

71 BATTER: DH: DH PINCH RUNS ✪

FED: The DH may pinch run if he is re-entering and running for a player who earlier replaced him. (3-1-4)

NCAA: The DH may not be a pinch runner. (7-2c-7b)

OBR: Same as NCAA. (6.10b-6)

❀ Note 77: Some readers are confused by the statutes in § 68 and 71. Example: Able pinch hits or pinch runs for the DH. Able is merely an entering substitute. When he takes his position in the box or on base, he is now the DH. Two innings later the fat first baseman walks, and the coach would like Able to pinch run. The umpire won't permit that. Reason: Able is hitting in the DH spot, but if he pinch runs for another player, he would be hitting in that spot as well. Oops!

ONE FINAL NOTE ON THE DH: Out of well over 1900 words written in four books about this rule, **ONLY ONE PROVISION IS COMMONLY SHARED:** The DH is locked into the batting order; no multiple substitutions can change the spot where the DH hits.

THAT CONCLUDES THE DISCUSSION OF THE DESIGNATED HITTER

∞ 72 BATTER: FIELDER DISTRACTS ✪

FED: No provision. Treat as in NCAA. (See § 118.)

❀ Note 78: Though FED has no language that prohibits a fielder from deliberately distracting a batter, such actions fall within the bounds of the "fair play" statute. (See 3-3-1g-4.)

NCAA: A fielder shall not station himself in the batter's line of vision and deliberately attempt to distract him. (5-15a-3)
PENALTY: ejection. (5-15a-3 Pen)

OBR: Same as NCAA. (4.06b; 4.06 Pen)

★ ∞ 73 BATTER: FOUL TIP: DEFINITION ✪

FED: Any batted ball that goes directly to the catcher's hands or mitt and is subsequently caught "**BY THE CATCHER**" is a foul tip. (2-16-2; 2.16.2b and c)

NCAA: "A foul tip is a ball batted by the batter **WHILE STANDING WITHIN THE LINES OF THE BATTER'S BOX** that travels directly from the bat to the catcher's hands and is caught legally by the catcher." (2-36; 7-8)

OBR: "A foul tip [is any batted ball] that goes sharp and direct from the bat to the catcher's hands and is legally caught." (2.00 Foul Tip; 6.05b CMT ¶ 1)

EXCEPT: OFF INTERP 61-73: **PBUC:** ***(EDITED)*** A foul must be caught by the CATCHER unassisted. {9.3} ✠

(ADDED) AO 6-73: **HW:** If a pitched ball bounces in the dirt and then is hit sharp and direct to the catcher's glove or hand, and is then caught, this shall be a foul tip. (HW ¶ 7.4/153)

74 BATTER: HALF-SWING CALL: APPEALED ✪

FED: The appeal of the call of "ball" on a half swing is not automatic; the UIC **MAY** ask for help if he wishes. (10-1-4a) (See § 76.)

NCAA: When a **PLAYER OR COACH** appeals the call of "ball" on a half swing, the umpire **MUST** ask for help. (3-6f) (See § 76 and 93.)

OBR: If the **CATCHER OR MANAGER** asks the UIC to get help on a half swing, the appeal must be granted. The field umpire's decision "shall prevail." (9.02c CMT ¶ 2)

75. ALSO: OFF INTERP 62-74: **PBUC:** With two strikes on the batter, when he checks his swing – if a pitch is a passed ball or wild pitch – the plate umpire shall "ask the base umpire for help immediately (while the catcher is retrieving the ball) without waiting for an appeal request from the defense." {9.8} (See 341.) ✠

76. ALSO: OFF INTERP 63-74: **PBUC:** After an appeal of a half swing, the plate umpire in a three-man crew shall ask the umpire "on the foul line, regardless of whether the batter is right- or left-handed." {9.8} ✠

★ 75 BATTER: HALF-SWING CALL: ARGUED ✪

FED: No provision.

NCAA: ***(ADDED)*** Balls, strikes, and checked swings may not be argued by players or coaches. **PENALTY:** First offense: The umpire shall record a warning. Second offense: Ejection without warning. (3-6f AR 1)

> ***(ADDED)*** ❀ Note 79: Paronto: "If a coach leaves the dugout or his position to argue balls or strikes, including a half swing, he is subject to ejection without warning." (email to cc, 12/ 06/11)

OBR: Managers and players may not protest the call of a ball or a strike on the pretense that they are asking for information about a half swing. (9.02c CMT)

★ 76 BATTER: HALF-SWING CALL: GUIDELINES FOR JUDGING ✪

FED: On a half swing if the batter carries the barrel of the bat past his body, the umpire may call a strike. (7.2.1b; 10.1.3) The final decision is based on "whether the batter struck at the ball." (10-1-4a) (See § 74.)

NCAA: The definition now speaks of a "half swing," which is "an attempt by the batter to stop his forward motion of the bat on the swing," and that puts "himself in jeopardy of a strike being called." Such a swing is a strike if the barrel head of the bat passes the batter's front hip. (2-38)

> ❀ Note 80: Pitching coaches are happy that "the front edge of home plate" no longer has any bearing on a strike call. That's simply because a batter standing deep in the box can swing past his hip **WITHOUT** the ":barrel head of the bat" passing the plate. Mark well this change: Baseball doesn't often modify rules to benefit the defense. Runs, that what they want. Runs!

77. ALSO: The criterion listed above does not apply to an attempted bunt. (2-38 AR) (See OFF INTERP 64 below for two other exemptions from the Half-Swing guidelines.)

> **78. ALSO:** OFF INTERP 64-76: **THURSTON:** The Half-Swing guidelines do not apply to: (1) a batter who pivots in the box with his arms close to his body (as opposed to extended); or (2) a batter who stands in the front part of the box. (phone call to se,12/20/93) ✠

OBR: No provision.

The BRD recommends: At any level of play, when the batter leaves his bat in the strike zone, if the batter does not attempt to bunt the ball, a pitch out of the strike zone is just that — out of the zone: "Ball!" is the call.

AO 7-76: EVANS: The umpire's decision on a checked swing shall be based entirely on his judgment as to whether or not the batter struck at the pitch. A strike is **NOT** automatically ruled if the barrel of the bat breaks the plane of the plate. (Appendix A-28)

77 BATTER: HALF-SWING CALL: REVERSED ✪

FED: If the call on a half swing is reversed and the umpires determine the changed call placed either team at a disadvantage, the UIC may "rectify" any claimed injustice. (10-2-3L; 10.2.3 h and I)

❀ Note 81: You are particularly referred to Play 269-506.

NCAA: Point not covered.

> OFF INTERP 65-77: **THURSTON:** In a half-swing situation both teams should be alert that a runner may steal a base or be thrown out. (phone call to se, 12/20/93) ✠

OBR: Same as NCAA OFF INTERP 65 above. (9.02c CMT ¶ 4)

⁎ *Play 56-77:* With a 2-2 count the batter appears to check his swing, and the plate ump calls: "Ball. No, he didn't go!" The pitch gets away from the catcher, but he retrieves it quickly and asks the ump to appeal his call. The field umpire reverses the decision and rules a strike. The defense tags B1 before he can reach first. *Ruling:* In FED, you have the authority to determine whether the defense would have retired the batter-runner if the pitch had originally been ruled a strike. In other words, did the reversal of the "ball" call place B1 in jeopardy? Your decision determines whether the out stands or B1 is awarded first. In NCAA / OBR, B1 is out.

❀ Note 82: There is a breakdown in mechanics here. Since the half swing occurred in a situation where the batter could become a batter-runner, the field umpire should announce a decision without waiting for an appeal. (See OFF INTERP 63-74.)

78 BATTER: HELMET: MANDATORY ✪

FED: The batter must wear a protective helmet with double ear flaps. (1-5-1)

NCAA: Same as FED. (1-15a)

OBR: The batter must wear a single or double ear flap helmet. (1.16a) (See § 427.) *See ¶ 8.*

79 BATTER: HELMET: PLAYER REFUSES TO WEAR: PENALTY
ALL NOW AGREE: TEXT DELETED,1995.

★ 80 BATTER: HIT BY PITCH: DEFINITION ✪

FED: A batter is hit by the pitch if the pitch touches him or his clothing when it is "reasonably well-fitted." (2-40a; 8-1-1d)
79. ALSO: If the pitch touches a batter's loose clothing, such as a shirt that is not worn properly, the batter is not entitled to first. (8-1-1d-2.)

NCAA: POE 1990, 1992, 1993. 1996, 1997 [batter hit by pitch]: A batter is hit by the pitch if it touches him or his clothing when he is in a "legal batting position." (6-4c)

OBR: Same as NCAA 6-4c. (5.09a; 6.08b)

(ADDED) **AO 8-80: HW:** The umpire does not award the batter first if he is hit by a pitch in the strike zone if the pitch bounced first. Reason: It could no longer be a called strike.(P231/168)

> ⁕ *Play 57-80:* **OBR only.** A slow curve his B1's arm in front of the plate. B1 makes no attempt to avoid the pitch. *Ruling:* If in the umpire's judgment the pitch would have been a strike, it is called as such. B1 is not awarded first.

80. ALSO: Assuming the batter attempts to avoid the pitch, if it "touches the ground" and then hits him, he shall be awarded first base (HBP). (2.00 Ball CMT)

❀ Note 83: At all levels, of course, the ball is dead when the batter is hit by a pitch, regardless whether he goes to first or stays in the box.

★ 81 BATTER: HIT BY PITCH: PENALTY ✪

FED: POE 2005, 2008: A batter must not "permit a pitched ball to touch him." If he does or if the pitch is a strike, the umpire does not

award the batter first.
(7-3-4; 7-3-4 Pen; 7.3.4d; 8-1-1d; 8-1-1d-1; 8.1.1d)

81. ALSO: OFF INTERP 66-81: **HOPKINS:**: With a count of 3-2, the batter permits a pitch that is a ball to hit him. He will be awarded first base since it was ball four. (Website 2009, #7) ✠

82. ALSO: OFF INTERP 67 -81: **McNEELY:** The batter will be awarded first unless he tries to get hit by the pitch. He may not permit the pitch to hit him, but: "Movement to avoid the pitch may or may not be such an indication." (TASO MTG, 1/15/10) ✠

(EDITED) ❀ Note 84: In an email exchange between the BRD and Kyle McNeely on 18 / 19 January, 2011, I pointed out that 8.1.1d. stated the batter will not be awarded first if "he does not attempt to avoid being hit." That, I said, contradicts 7.3.4d. In the 2011 BRD I published Kyle's "workaround." In 2012, the editor removed the offending sentence from 8.1.1d. Score one for us.

NCAA: A batter hit by a pitch is awarded first unless the pitch is a strike. (8-2d) **EXCEPT:** The umpire should not award first to a batter "who intentionally gets touched by moving or rolling" into the pitch. The ball is dead and ruled a strike or ball as the case may be. Runners may not advance. (8-2d AR)
(EDITED) **83. ALSO:** If a batter freezes and is hit by a pitch that is "clearly" inside the vertical lines of the batter's box, the ball is dead and he is awarded first. (8-2d-2 AR)

OBR: The batter must make an attempt to avoid the pitch. (5.09a; 6.08b)

★ 82 BATTER: w/ILLEGAL BAT: ATTEMPTS TO USE ✪

(See § 182 and 218.)

FED: ***(EDITED)*** A batter may not step into the batter's box with an **ILLEGAL** bat , as opposed to a **DEFECTIVE** bat. (See § 182).
PENALTY: The ball is dead (5-1-1c) and he is out. (7-4-1a)

84. ALSO: PENALTY: In addition to the batter always being out: First offense: His head coach is restricted. Second offense, same team: his head coach is ejected. Third offense, same team: The adult designated as the head coach is ejected. (4-1-3a; 1.3.2g)
Last edition: No provision.

(ADDED) ❀ Note 85: If there is a fourth offense, ask the administrator at the field to convene a meeting among the special education coordinator, the athletic department, and the umpire association president.

❀ Note 86: We now have two categories of impermissible bats: (● 1) **ILLEGAL**, which (a) are altered or (b) do not meet the specifications of the rules: A batter who enters the box with or uses such a bat is out when discovered; (● 2) **DEFECTIVE**, which (a) are broken, (b) are cracked, (c) discolor the ball, or (d) are dented. Those bats when discovered are simply removed with no additional penalty. (See § 182.)

85. ALSO: The illegal bat may be detected by the umpire or by the defense. The case book speaks of a "tacky" bat caused by adding some substance (pine tar) more than 18 inches from the knob end. (1.3.5a) (See Play 60-83 and § 15; 180, 181; 183; 185.) (See § 206 for provisions dealing with a tacky glove.)

NCAA: If an altered or flattened bat is detected before the first pitch, it shall be removed from the game. "If detected after the first pitch, [legal or illegal: see Note 87 this section] the batter is out and runners may not advance. (1-12a and b Pen) Other illegal bats are removed from the game, No one may be called out for those other bats, except as provided in OFF INTERP 68 [this section]. (See § 83.)

❀ Note 87-82: The "legal or illegal" became the NCAA official position when I emailed Jim Paronto, rules interpreter for the NCAA. "If I say," he wrote, "that it's after a pitch, legal or illegal, will I be opening a can of worms?" I assured him the can would stay tightly shut. So he emailed: "Big Papa: Let's go with 'a pitch, legal or illegal' and then if I (we) have to make a clarification, we can do that." **EXCEPT:** "Legal or illegal" never made it into the book. Oh, well ....

⁕ *Play 58-82:* **NCAA only.** Bubba steps into the box with a bat altered to increase the distance factor. The pitcher, miffed because Bubba had homered in his last at bat, winds up and delivers without getting on the rubber. The base umpire says: "That's an illegal pitch!" The defensive coach says: "That's an illegal bat." The plate umpire says: "I agree. Bubba is out." The offensive coach says: "That wasn't a pitch. He wasn't on the rubber." *Ruling:* The plate umpire settles things with: "It was an **ILLEGAL** pitch. Bubba is still out."

86. ALSO: OFF INTERP 68-82: **THURSTON:** If a batter tries to use a bat that is illegally bent, dented, or flattened, the umpire will order him to obtain a legal bat. If the batter refuses, he is declared out. (phone call to se, 11/9/89) (See § 218.) ✠

OBR: A batter who attempts to use an altered bat (as opposed to merely illegal) is out, ejected, and may be subject to additional penalties. *See ¶ 8.* Other bats are simply removed. (6.06d) (See § 83.) A batter is "deemed" to be attempting to use an illegal bat if he steps into the box with such a bat. (6.06d CMT)

87. ALSO: OFF INTERP 69-82: **PBUC:** The umpire should stop a batter from attempting to use an "obviously illegal bat." {3.10} ✠

88. ALSO: OFF INTERP 70-82: **PBUC:** A manager may claim that an opposing player is using an altered bat only once per game, and only [immediately] before or after the player is at-bat. {3.10} ✠

★ 83 BATTER: w/ILLEGAL BAT: USES ✪ (See § 182.)

FED: A batter may not use an **ILLEGAL** bat (as opposed to defective: see § 182). **PENALTY:** If the infraction is discovered by the umpire or the defense before the next pitch to a batter of either team, the defense may elect the penalty (batter out, runners return TOP) or the result of the play. (7-4-1a; 7.4.1d) (See § 17; 48; 82; 180; 181; 183; 185; 218.) (See also coach verifies legal equipment.)

(ADDED) ❀ Note 88: Plays 1.3.5d and e are illuminating. In d, the bat has a crack in it. Since the coach has verified that all his bats are legal, the batter is out and the coach is restricted. If the crack is not discovered until after the batter has batted – in the case book play, he homers – the home run counts. In e, an illegal bat is discovered while the batter is circling the bases following his home run. The batter is out, no run scores (there were already two out), and the head coach is restricted. The bottom line for 2012 *et. seq.*: Use a legal bat!

NCAA: If the batter uses an altered bat, he is out; runners return TOP. (1-12a and b; 1-12a Pen; 7-10b Pen) (edited) A bat may not have a loose knob, or be dented or bent, or lack a safety knob. ***(ADDED)*** **PENALTY:** The defective bat is removed. (1-12c; 1-12c Pen) (See § 82.)

OBR: If the batter uses an altered bat, he is out, ejected, and in MLB possibly subject to additional penalties. Runners must return TOP though any outs made on the play will stand. (5.09d; 6.06d)

(See § 7. See OFF INTERP 70-82 for how many times a manager may question a batter's bat in one game.)

❀ Note 89: Neither NCAA nor OBR gives a time frame for the appeal. NCAA says "after hitting"; OBR says, "He uses." BRD recommends: Do not allow an appeal after the next pitch to a batter of either team.

✻ *Play 59-83:* Bases loaded, 1 out. B1 singles. R3 and R2 score, but tremendous defensive work gets R1 out going for third and B1 out trying to sneak into second. Three outs, two runs in. The sides change, and the pitcher prepares to pitch when the team now at bat appeals that B1 used an illegal bat altered to increase the distance factor. After inspecting the bat, the umpire agrees. *Ruling:* In FED, the coach may accept the play (if he wants the inning over), or he may send the runners back and take his chances with two outs. In NCAA, no runs are in: The bases are loaded, now with two outs. In OBR, B1 is out and ejected. The out made by R1 also stands, so there are three outs and no runs in.

❀ Note 90: This play has been in the BRD since 1999. Over the years, several people emailed to ask why the runs didn't count. "It's a time play," Randy from Arizona wrote. "If there's no force play, runs that score before the third out count." We're so accustomed to the batter making a "real out" that it's hard to equate a technical out with the rules. The runs don't score because the batter-runner (B1) did not make first safely.

✻ *Play 60-83:* B1 steps into the box with a bat altered to increase the distance factor and homers. Next, B2, the on-deck batter who is holding the same bat, marches into the box. At that moment the defense appeals the illegal bat. *Ruling:* In NCAA, the defense has blundered: B1 simply gets a legal bat, while giving the opponents the raspberries. In FED and OBR, the defense has obtained a double play: B1 is out for using an altered bat; B2, for trying to use such a bat.

❀ Note 91: ***(EDITED)*** Using an illegal bat is one of nine major rules or interpretations **WHERE EACH LEVEL TREATS THE SITUATION DIFFERENTLY**. The other eight are: § 50-71 (designated hitter); § 124 (throw from dead-ball area); § 144 (conferences); § 245 (positions occupied at time of pitch or play); § 246 (fighting); § 266 (improperly declared infield fly); § 378 (hidden ball play); § 488 (illegal substitutes).

84 BATTER: IMPROPER BATTER: RECOGNIZED BY: DEFENSE ✪

(See § 16 for the time frame to appeal batting out of order.)

FED: POE 1999: After a legal appeal of an improper batter, the proper batter is out; "any outs made on the play stand." An out for batting out of order supersedes an out made by the improper batter.

Unless they advanced because of a stolen base, balk, wild pitch, or passed ball (7-1-1), other runners return TOP (7-1-1 Pen 2) (See also § 86.)

⁂ *Play 61-84:* R3, 2 out. Able should bat but Baker bats and singles. R3 scores, but B1 had rounded first and is thrown out trying to return. The teams change sides. Before the first pitch, the team on defense in the previous half-inning appeals that Baker was an improper batter. The umpire agrees. *Ruling:* Able is out, not Baker. R3's run does not count.

> **89. ALSO:** OFF INTERP 71-84: **RUMBLE:** The defensive coach may appeal a batting-out-of-order violation, regardless of how he learned of it. (*News* #11, 3/99) ✠

NCAA: After a legal appeal, the proper batter is out and "**ALL RUNNERS**" return to bases occupied before the action of the improper batter. (7-11a-2)

❀ Note 92: "All runners" clearly implies that even runners who were out will be returned.

OBR: After a legal appeal the proper batter is out (6.07b-1), and the umpire will "nullify any advance or score" made as a result of actions by the improper batter. (6.07b-2) (See § 465.)

> **90. ALSO:** OFF INTERP 72-84: **PBUC:** When an improper batter's action causes a runner to be out (a force out or double play, for example), if the batting-out-of-order appeal is upheld, only the proper batter is out; any other outs are canceled. {4.3} ✠

⁂ *Play 62-84:* R1, 0 out. Able should bat but Baker steps in and hits into a 6-4-3 double play. The umpire recognizes the appeal of the defense. *Ruling:* In FED, R1 remains out, Able is out, and Baker bats with the bases empty. In NCAA / OBR, R1 returns to first, Able is out, and Baker is the next batter.

⁂ *Play 63-84:* R2 (Hale), R1 (Irwin), 0 out. Abel should bat but Baker bats instead. On the first pitch the offense attempts the double steal, with Hale thrown out at third and Irwin safe at second. On the next pitch Baker triples. The defense then appeals that Baker is an improper batter. *Ruling:* Hale remains out while Irwin returns to second; Abel is out, with Baker removed from third and batting now in his proper turn.

⁂ *Play 64-84:* R2 (Hale), R1 (Irwin).Abel should bat but Baker hits instead, slapping into a rare 6-5-4 double play — with the second baseman's throw to first not in time to nip Baker for a triple play. The defense then appeals that Baker is an improper batter *Ruling:* In FED, the defense gets the triple killing anyway: Hale and

Irwin remain out on the play; Abel is out on appeal, with Baker now due up first in the next inning. In NCAA / OBR, Hale and Irwin are returned to second and first, Abel is out, and Baker, removed from first, bats.

★ ∞ 85 BATTER: IMPROPER BATTER: RECOGNIZED BY: OFFENSE ✪

FED: POE 1999: An improper batter may be "discovered" by either team. (7.1.1b) After the improper batter has completed his at-bat, only the defense may "appeal" the infraction. (7-1-1) (See § 84 and 488.)

❀ Note 93: Before the improper batter completes his at-bat, his coach may say, "Hey, that's the wrong batter," and the proper batter will step in, assuming the count. After the at bat, if the offense "discovers" the infraction, the umpires will ignore it unless the defense appeals. But see § 86 for circumstances under which the UMPIRE will himself "discover" the improper batter.

NCAA: Same as FED. (7-11a) (See § 84.)

OBR: Improper batters are out "on appeal." (6.07a)

⁎ *Play 65-85*: **NCAA and OBR only.** Bases loaded, 1 out. Able should bat but Baker bats and hits into a double play. The coach immediately appeals that his own batter was improper! *Ruling:* The umpire does not recognize the appeal. Unless the defense complains – which it won't because a run would score – the half inning is over.

❀ Note 94: In the old days if such a play had happened, an untutored umpire might feel obliged to call out Able, return the runners to their bases, and let Baker, who is now the proper batter, hit again. In FED, of course, the outs stand, even if the defense appeals.

86 BATTER: IMPROPER BATTER: RECOGNIZED BY: UMPIRE ✪

FED: POE 1999: If the umpire recognizes an ILLEGAL SUBSTITUTE batting-out-of-order, he shall call attention to it if the improper batter (illegal sub) is still at bat. (3.1.1c) (See § 488 and 499.)

91. ALSO: OFF INTERP 73-86: **RUMBLE:** If the umpire detects a STARTING PLAYER batting out of order, he should wait for an appeal. (*News* #35, 4/87; confirmed, Points of Emphasis, 1993 ed) ✠

⁎ *Play 66-86:* **FED only.** After one strike, the umpire realizes that illegal substitute S1 is at bat though B4 is due up.

Ruling: S1 is out and restricted to the dugout. Though B4 has been removed from the game, he may return if he has reentry privileges remaining. In either case, the next batter who steps up does so with a count of 0 and 1.

❀ Note 95: The FED ruling at 3.1.1c stops short of resolving the entire situation: Who is the next batter — B4 or B5? Since the penalty for the illegal sub supersedes the penalty for batting out of order, **THE OFFENSE DID NOT BAT OUT OF ORDER.** B4 (or his legal substitute) is now the proper batter because — B4 was always the proper batter.

NCAA: The umpire, official scorer, and the public address announcer are forbidden to point out the presence of an improper batter in the box. **PENALTY:** The umpire shall warn the official scorer or announcer that on the next violation he will be removed from his position. (7-11a AR)

OBR: The umpire shall not direct the attention of any person to the presence of an improper batter in the batter's box: "This rule is designed to require constant vigilance by the players and managers of both teams." (6.07d CMT)

87 BATTER: IMPROPER BATTER: SUBSTITUTE REPORTS / ENTERS FOR WRONG BATTER ✪

FED: No provision Treat as in OBR.

NCAA: No provision Treat as in OBR.

OBR: Point not covered.

OFF INTERP 74-87: **FITZPATRICK:** A substitute cannot bat out of order, for he is replacing whoever should be at the plate. There is no penalty when the substitute reports for the wrong player if the batting order is not affected. (phone call to cc, 11/8/01) (But see OFF INTERP • 59-69 for important information that affects the pitcher batting for someone other than the DH in NCAA / OBR.) ✠

⁂ *Play 67-87:* Able should bat. Substitute Jackson arrives at the plate and tells the UIC: "I'm Jackson [he got that right], batting for Baker [he got that wrong]." The umpire pencils in the change but does not catch the error. Jackson singles. Now Baker bats and singles. Before a pitch or a play, the defense appeals.
Ruling: No penalty. The substitute reported for the wrong player, but the batting order continued without interruption.

❀ Note 96: Jackson must be pretty dumb since he ought to see Baker (whom he thinks he is replacing) warming up in the on-deck circle.

88 BATTER: ON DECK: HELMET MANDATORY ✪

FED: The on-deck batter must wear a helmet with flaps over both ears. (1-5-1) **PENALTY:** The umpire shall require him to obtain one; also, team warning / ejection. (1.1.5c, 1992 ed) (See § 428.)

NCAA: Same as FED 1-5-1. (1-15a) **EXCEPT:** **PENALTY:** Ejection for failure to comply with the umpire's order to obtain a proper helmet. It is not a team warning. (1-15a Pen)

OBR: Point not covered. (See also § 78.)

> OFF INTERP 75-88: **FITZPATRICK:** In the minor leagues helmets are not required for a player in the on-deck circle. (phone call to cc, 11/8/01) *See ¶ 8.* ✠

❀ Note 97: In your adult games you would be well advised to require the on-deck batter to wear a helmet. Use the elastic clause 9.01c as your authority.

★ ∞ 89 BATTER: ON DECK: NUMBER OF PLAYERS ALLOWED ✪

FED: Only one on-deck batter is allowed. (3-3-1j) **PENALTY:** warning or ejection. (3-3-1j Pen) (See § 90.)

NCAA: Same as FED 3-3-1j. (5-2c)

(ADDED) ❀ Note 98: NCAA allowed two on-deck batters until 2008!

NAIA: A batter **MUST** be on-deck when it is his turn to bat. (Modification 2-6.2)

OBR: Point not covered.

> OFF INTERP 76-89: **PBUC:** "The next batter up must be in the on-deck circle, and this is the only player who should be there (*i.e.*, not more than one player at a time). This shall be strictly enforced. No other player of the side at bat will be permitted on the field except the batter, base runners and coaches." {3.5} (See also § 91.) ✠

★ 90 BATTER: ON DECK: TIMES WARM-UP PITCHES ✪

FED: No team member or coach shall enter the area behind the catcher when he and the pitcher are in their positions. (3-3-1h; 3-3-3; 3.3.3) **PENALTY:** warning / ejection. (3-3-1h Pen; 3-3-3 Pen) (See § 89 and 91.)

❀ Note 99: The intent of the rule is to prevent players from being there when the pitcher is warming up between half innings or delivering to the batter. **POE 1993, 1994, 1995**: Safety is the primary motivation.

NCAA: No **UNIFORMED** team member or coach shall be near or behind the plate while the pitcher is warming up or delivering. ***(ADDED)*** The on-deck batter shall be in the "vicinity"of his dugout. (5-2e) **PENALTY:** warning / ejection. (5-2e Pen)

OBR: Concerning players in the stands behind the plate during warm-up: No provisions. Concerning a batter timing pitches: **Point not covered.**

OFF INTERP 77-90: **FITZPATRICK:** The on-deck batter must remain in his circle until beckoned to the batter's box (at the start of a half inning) or the previous batter has completed his turn at bat. (phone call to cc, 11/8/01) ✠

★ 91 BATTER: ON DECK: USES ON-DECK CIRCLE ✪

FED: The on-deck circle need not be occupied, but if a batter wishes to warm up, he must use his team's on-deck circle — provided it is located a safe distance from home plate. (1-2-3) (See § 240.)
92. ALSO: An on-deck batter must remain in the "area" of his on-deck circle while the pitcher is warming up. (3-3-3)
PENALTY: team warning / ejection. (3-3-3 Pen)
93. ALSO: A player may not occupy the opposing team's on-deck circle. (1-2-3) (See § 90.)

NCAA: The on-deck batter may not be inside a triangle created by an extension of the first- and third-base lines. "The on-deck position should be in the ***(ADDED)*** near vicinity of the dugout." (1-5e) **PENALTY:** warning / ejection. (5-2e Pen)

OBR: ***(EDITED)*** **Point not covered.**

(ADDED) OFF INTERP 78-91: **PBUC:** OFF INTERP76-89 applies. ✠

★ 92 BATTER: STRIKE: DEFINITION OF ZONE ✪

FED: POE 1987, 1988, 1989, 1990, 1991, 1992: The strike zone is measured from the knees to a spot halfway between the batter's shoulders and his waistline. (2-35; 2.35.1; 7.2.1a) It is based on the batter's normal or natural stance, not his stance as he prepares to swing at a pitch, which is the OBR guideline. "The height of the strike zone is determined by the batter's normal batting stance. If he crouches or leans over to make the shoulder line lower, the umpire determines height by what would be the batter's normal stance." (2.35.1; 2.35.1 CMT)

❀ Note 100: FED 7.2.1a concerns a coach coming to the plate to ask: "What's the strike zone?" According to the case book: "The umpire informs the coach that ...." I suspect whoever wrote that sentence never umpired in any game where the players shaved. A regular partner of mine from the 1950s had an interesting answer. Whenever a coach who didn't know him asked that question, he would say: "I haven't decided yet."

94. ALSO: If the batter leaves his bat in the strike zone during a bunt, when the ball passes through the zone, it is not a strike unless the batter moves the bat: "The mere holding of the bat in the strike zone is not an attempt to bunt." (7.2.1b)

NCAA: POE 1990,1992, 1993, 1994, 1996, 1997, 1998, 1999, 2000, 2002, 2003, 2004, 2006, 2007: The strike zone is from the "bottom of the kneecaps" to the "midpoint between the top of the shoulders and the top of the uniform pants" when the batter assumes his "natural" position. (2-72; 7-4b)

95. ALSO: The rule urges the umpire to call the strike based on the position of the ball when it crosses the plate, not on where F2 catches it. (7-4b AR 1)

OBR: The strike zone is measured from the "midpoint between the top of the shoulders and the top of the uniform pants" down to the "hollow beneath the kneecap." The zone is determined from the batter's stance when he prepares to swing at a pitch. (2.00 Strike Zone)

(ADDED) AO 9-92: **WENDELSTEDT:** "In general, the top of the strike zone is approximately 2 ½ to 3 baseball widths above a batter's belt." Thus, "the top of the strike zone is usually in line with a batter's front elbow and forearm in a normal swing." (HW/4)

(ADDED) ❀ Note 101: Neither NCAA nor OBR have any official interpretation dealing with a batter who leaves his bat in the strike zone. BRD recommends: Treat as in FED 7.2.1b.

❀ Note 102: The BRD believes that the strike zone definitions in NCAA / OBR are now technically the same, and they are **LOWER** than the high school zone. But see Note 104 below for the *de facto* definition at all levels.

❀ Note 103: Little League for the 2011 season changed their rules to mandate that the umpire call a strike when the batter holds the bat in the strike zone when the pitch is delivered, even if the batter does not "offer" at the pitch. This applies only to the softball divisions. Can baseball be far behind? ***(ADDED)*** The rule change did not make it for baseball divisions in 2012, so I am optimistic. But I also claimed A. J. Burnett would someday become a pitcher of note.

❀ Note 104-92: Former AL umpire Rich Garcia gave the best definition of the strike zone: "A strike is where I call it and they don't bitch!"

★ 93 BATTER: STRIKE: SIGNALED BY UMPIRE ✪

FED: The umpire should use his left hand to show "balls" **FOLLOWED BY** the number of strikes on his right. (Signal chart) (See § 341.)

NCAA: The UIC must give a clear visual and oral indication of all strikes. (3-7b)

OBR: ***(EDITED)*** The UIC must "call and count" balls and strikes. (9.04a-2)

★ 94 BATTER: THROWS BAT CARELESSLY ✪

FED: POE 1984, 1985, 1986: A player may not carelessly throw his bat. (3.3.1v; 3.3.1w, 2006 ed) **PENALTY:** team warning / ejection. (3-3-1c Pen) (See § 95.)

> **96. ALSO:** OFF INTERP 79-94: **RUMBLE:** If a batter throws his bat toward a pitch, that constitutes a carelessly thrown bat with all attendant penalties. (*News* #19, 3/87) ❀

❀ Note 105: The bat need not touch anyone for the umpire to invoke the penalty. Furthermore, the player endangered by the carelessly thrown bat may be a teammate of the offender, and whether the "perp" is on offense or defense is irrelevant.

⁜ *Play 68-94:* **FED only.** Bubba flies out to center field and carelessly flips his bat, which cracks into the catcher's left ankle. The umpire issues a team warning. Two innings later Bubba's teammate, Ricardo, is catching. With a runner on second B1 strokes a single and throws his bat down in the third-base line. In his haste to clear the base path of the dangerous object, Ricardo grabs the bat and throws it toward the on-deck circle, where it strikes (or narrowly misses) an offensive player. *Ruling:* After the play is over, the umpire will eject Ricardo. The ruling would have been the same if the bat had hit (or just missed) one of Ricardo's teammates. (See § 168.)

⁜ *Play 69-94:* **FED only.** R1. Left-handed B1 attempts to sacrifice. The defense detects the play and pitches out. B1, attempting to protect the runner, throws his bat at the pitch. The bat sails very near F5, charging in for the play. *Ruling:* B1 is guilty of carelessly throwing a bat.

NCAA: Point not covered.

> ***(ADDED)*** OFF INTERP 80-94: **PARONTO:** "The umpire should address carelessly thrown bats with the appropriate head coach. There is no official warning." (email to cc, 12/29/11) ✠

OBR: No provision. *See ¶ 8.*

★ 95 BATTER: THROWS BAT OR HELMET DELIBERATELY ✪

FED: Players may not deliberately throw "a bat, helmet, etc." to show their disgust. (3-3-1m; 3.3.1v)
PENALTY: ejection. (3-3-1m Pen) (See § 94.)

NCAA: Point not covered.

> ***(ADDED)*** OFF INTERP 81-95: **PARONTO:** A player may be immediately ejected for intentionally throwing his bat or helmet because of his displeasure at an umpire's call or because of his disgust with himself. (email to cc, 12/5/11) ✠

OBR: Point not covered.

> OFF INTERP 82-95: **MLBUM:** "Any player throwing equipment in disgust of an umpire's call shall be reported and subject to fine, and if flagrant, to ejection. The offender is to be notified that he is being reported for an equipment violation." (2.19) *See ¶ 8.* ✠

96 BATTER-RUNNER: ADVANCES TO FIRST AFTER: BASE ON BALLS ✪

FED: A runner awarded first is out if he is not on base before the time of the next pitch, he reaches his bench or dugout, or the infielders have left the diamond. (8.1.1b)

NCAA: No provision.

OBR: If, after being forced, a runner refuses to proceed to home or a batter entitled to first refuses to advance, he shall be declared out. If two are out, no run may score; if fewer than two are out, the reluctant player is out and the run scores, provided the runner on third does advance to the plate. (4.09b Pen)

★ ∞ 97 BATTER-RUNNER: ADVANCES TO FIRST AFTER: BASE ON BALLS: TIME NOT CALLED ✪

FED: If a batter receives ball four, the umpire shall not grant time until the batter reaches first. (2-4-2; 2.4.2) (See § 99.)

NCAA: Same as FED 2-4-2. (6-1a AR)

OBR: Point not covered.

> OFF INTERP 83-97: **FITZPATRICK:** Same as FED 2-4-2. (phone call to cc, 11/8/01) ✠

★ 98 BATTER-RUNNER: ADVANCES TO FIRST AFTER: DROPPED THIRD STRIKE ✪

FED: On a dropped third strike with fewer than two out ***(EDITED)*** and first base unoccupied, the batter may try for first until the time of the next pitch or until he "reaches his bench or other dead-ball area." (2.20.2; 8.1.1b) With two out, the batter may try for first until the infielders have left the diamond or until he "gives up" by reaching his bench or dugout area. (8-4-1i; 7.4.1a and b; *News* #5, 3/97) (See § 279.)

97. ALSO: If the batter-runner is not entitled to run, the umpire "shall forcefully announce" that he is out. The ball remains alive. (8.4.1k, 2006 ed) (See § 341.)

NCAA: The batter is out if he does not try for first before he "leaves the dirt area surrounding home plate heading toward his dugout." (7-11u)

OBR: Same as NCAA 7-11u. (6.09b CMT) **EXCEPT:**

> OFF INTERP 84-98: **PBUC:** A batter who, after a third strike not caught in flight, "lingers" at home plate (for example, removing his shin guard) shall be called out. {6.15} ✠

⁂ *Play 70-98:* 2 outs.B1 swings and misses for strike three. The catcher drops the ball; but instead of tagging B1 or throwing to first, F2 rolls it back to the mound. B1 is near his third-base dugout when he realizes he is not yet out. He streaks directly across the diamond, crosses the pitcher's mound, and reaches first before the infielders realize what's happening. *Ruling:* In FED, B1 is safe if he begins his streak before all infielders have left the diamond. When B1 decides to run, his base path is a direct line to first from his initial spot on the field. In NCAA / OBR, B1 is out. (See § 426.)

99 BATTER-RUNNER: ADVANCES TO FIRST AFTER: INTENTIONAL BASE ON BALLS: BALL IS DEAD ✪

(See § 100.)

FED: If the umpire grants an intentional walk, the ball is immediately dead. (2-4-3; 5-1-3; 2.4.2) (See § 97.)

NCAA: Not applicable. (See § 97.)

NAIA: No provision.

❀ Note 106: Since the umpire may grant an intentional walk without any pitches in NAIA, the BRD recommends killing the ball to make the award.

OBR: Not applicable.

★ 100 BATTER-RUNNER: ADVANCES TO FIRST AFTER: INTENTIONAL BASE ON BALLS: NO PITCHES ✪ (See § 99.)

FED: The coach or the catcher may request that the umpire grant an intentional walk, when no pitches need be delivered. The walk may be granted on any ball and strike count. (2-4-3) (See § 97.)

NCAA: The pitcher must deliver four pitches. (8-2b) (See § 97.)

NAIA: Same as FED 2-4-3. (Modification 2-6.1) (See § 100.)

OBR: Same as NCAA 8-2b. (6.08a) *See ¶ 8.*

∞ 101 BATTER-RUNNER: BATTED BALL / PITCH HITS: ANIMAL OR BIRD ✪

FED: No provision. Treat as in NCAA.

NCAA: If a throw, pitch, or batted ball hits an animal, the ball is alive if it remains in live-ball territory. (6-1h)
98. ALSO: The umpire may call time when an animal hinders the normal progress of the game. (6-5c)

OBR: Point not covered.

OFF INTERP 85-101: **PBUC** If a batted or thrown ball strikes a bird in flight or an animal on the playing field, the ball is alive and in play the same as if it had not touched the bird or animal." {7.21} (See § 105.) ❀

* *Play 71-101:* A batted ball hits a guy wire or sea gull in left field. *Ruling:* The ball is fair or foul depending on the position of the ball WHEN IT HITS THE GROUND OR THE FIELDER. Such a ball may be caught for an out.

99. ALSO: OFF INTERP 86-101: **PBUC:** A pitch that touches an animal or bird is immediately dead, and the umpire orders a do-over. {7.21} ✠

∞ 102 BATTER-RUNNER: BATTED BALL HITS: BAT OR BATTER TWICE IN BOX ✪

FED: If a batted ball ACCIDENTALLY hits the bat a second time while the batter is still holding the bat and still in his batter's box, the ball is foul. (8-4-1d-2; 8.4.1a) (See Note 126-103 for an important distinction between FED on the one hand, and NCAA / OBR on the other.)
100. ALSO: If the batted ball hits the batter while he has no foot entirely outside the batter's box, the ball is foul UNLESS THE UMPIRE JUDGES THE BATTER INTERFERED DELIBERATELY. (8.4.1b)

NCAA: It is a foul ball if a "legally batted ball" hits the dirt or home plate and then hits the batter or his bat, which is in the hands of the batter, while he is in the batter's box. In effect: Same as FED. (7-7e)

OBR: If a batted ball hits the batter or his bat while the batter is in his legal position, it is a foul ball. (6.05g)
101. ALSO: A "legal position" is defined as a batter with both feet in the batter's box. (6.03) Thus, if the batter has one foot outside the box when he is hit, he is out. (6.05h)

⁕ *Play 72-102:* B1 bunts and heads for first. Because of back spin, the ball bounces up and strikes B1 or the bat while it is still in his hand. *Ruling:* If the ball is over foul ground when it hits B1 or his bat, it is a foul ball.

❀ Note 107: The point of the OBR change at 6.05g and 6.05h is to codify what umpires have always done; that is, call a ball foul even though it might hit the plate and bounce up to touch the batter or the bat in fair territory. A batted ball that hits the batter in foul territory is still foul. as exemplified in the play above.

103 BATTER-RUNNER: BATTED BALL HITS: BAT TWICE IN FAIR TERRITORY ✪

FED: If the batter DELIBERATELY hits a fair batted ball in FAIR OR FOUL TERRITORY, the ball is dead and the batter is out. (5-1-1b; 8-4-1d; 2.5.1e; 8.4.1a) (See § 102 and 281.)

❀ Note 108-103: The FED rule is NOT THE SAME as NCAA or OBR, whose rules apply only in fair territory. Before 1981 the FED rule read: "[The batter-runner is out if] HIS BAT HITS THE BALL A SECOND

TIME and the act is intentional or the bat is carelessly dropped or thrown in such a way as to strike the ball and deflect its course. ... If it is clearly accidental and the **BALL ROLLS INTO THE BAT**, it is not interference." Now **THAT** language is the same as NCAA / OBR. The 1981 FED revision was caused by concern about judgment problems for umpires, so the batter was out in either case. Still, the intent of the current rule, adopted in 1994, was to penalize only for **DELIBERATE** interference.

NCAA: If the batter drops the bat and the ball accidentally hits the bat again in **FAIR TERRITORY**, the ball remains alive. (7-11m)

OBR: Same as NCAA. (6.05h)

⁜ *Play 73-103:* B1 bunts down the first-base line and carelessly tosses down his bat. The ball reverses and rolls into his bat in fair territory. *Ruling:* No interference: The ball remains alive.

∞ 104 BATTER-RUNNER: BATTED BALL HITS: BEYOND IMAGINARY LINE ✪

FED: A batted ball hitting beyond an imaginary line running between first and third is a fair ball, regardless of where the ball might first settle. (2-5-1b)

NCAA: No provision.

OBR: No provision.

∞ 105 BATTER-RUNNER: BATTED BALL HITS: FOREIGN OBJECT IN FAIR TERRITORY ✪

FED: No provision. Treat as in NCAA.

NCAA: Subject to local ground rules, a batted ball that strikes "a power line, tree limb or other overhead object" in the playing field is a live ball. (6-1j)

OBR: Point not covered.

OFF INTERP 87-105: **FITZPATRICK:** Same as NCAA 6-1j. (email to cc, 11/15/00) (See § 101.) ✠

❀ Note 109: At all levels, unless there are local ground rules to the contrary: If a batted ball strikes a tree's limbs that hang out over fair territory, the ball remains alive. If the fielder makes the catch, the batter is out; if not, the runner is entitled to any bases he can get. If the ball hits the tree over foul territory, it is a foul ball and dead. If the ball lodges in the tree over fair territory, the umpire awards two bases.

★ ∞ 106 BATTER-RUNNER: BATTED BALL HITS: PITCHER'S PLATE ✪

FED: Point not covered.

> OFF INTERP 88-106: **HOPKINS:** A batted ball hitting the pitcher's plate and rebounding to foul ground between home and first or home and third **WITHOUT TOUCHING A FIELDER** is a foul ball as it did not hit beyond the imaginary line in the infield. (Website 2003, #13) (See § 104.) ✠

NCAA: Same as FED. (7-7f)

OBR: ***(EDITED)*** Same as FED. (2.00 Foul Ball CMT)

∞ 107 BATTER-RUNNER: BATTED BALL HITS: UMPIRE IN FOUL GROUND ✪

FED: No provision. Treat as in NCAA.

NCAA: The ball remains in play if a fair ball strikes an umpire in foul ground. (8-2f)

OBR: No provision. Treat as in NCAA.

∞ 108 BATTER-RUNNER: BATTED BALL INTENTIONALLY DROPPED: BUNT ✪

FED: With fewer than two out and at least first occupied, the ball is dead and the batter is out if an infielder intentionally drops a bunted fair ball. The ball is dead, and runners return. (5-1-1j; 8-4-1c; 8.4.1f)

102. ALSO: A fielder gently knocks down a batted ball with the back of his glove. That is an intentional drop: "Manipulating the ball to the ground is prohibited." (8.4.1g)

NCAA: Same as FED 8-4-1c. (7-11q)

OBR: The rules specify an out for line drives and fly balls only. (6.05L) **EXCEPT:**

> OFF INTERP 89-108: **FITZPATRICK:** Same as FED 8-4-1c. (email to cc, 11/15/00) ✠

✻ Play 74-108: R1, R2, 1 out. B1 bunts the ball directly to the first baseman charging in. F3 grabs the ball in flight, deliberately drops it, and then fires to the shortstop covering third. The throw is wild, and the ball rolls into left field. Before it is returned to the infield,

R2 has scored, R1 is on third, and B1 has taken second.
Ruling: The ball is immediately dead when F3 intentionally drops it. The batter is out, and runners return TOP.

❀ Note 110: At all levels, a bunt may not result in a declared infield fly.

109 BATTER-RUNNER: BATTED BALL INTENTIONALLY DROPPED: LINE DRIVE OR FLY BALL TO THE INFIELD
ALL CODES NOW AGREE: TEXT DELETED 1994.

110 BATTER-RUNNER: OVERRUNS FIRST: ON AWARD✪

FED: A batter awarded first on a base on balls may not overrun the base. If he does, he is in peril of an out regardless of whether he feints or attempts an advance. (8-2-7; 5.1.4b)

❀ Note 111: Of course, if the base on balls is intentional, the ball is dead: B1 may step off first with impunity. (See § 97, 100 and 111.)

NCAA: The batter-runner may overrun first if he returns immediately and does not make an attempt to go to second. (8-5b; 8-5i Ex) (See § 111 and 112.)

OBR: Same as NCAA. (7.08j)

⁂ *Play 75-110:* B1 takes ball four. The pitch: (a) is gloved by the catcher, or (b) goes to the screen. In each case B1 runs through the bag at first, but he makes no attempt (or feint: FED only) to advance to second. *Ruling:* In FED, when tagged off the base the batter-runner is out in both (a) and (b). In NCAA / OBR, he cannot be tagged out in either (a) or (b).

★ *(EDITED HEADING)* 111 BATTER-RUNNER: OVERRUNS FIRST ON: BATTED BALL: ATTEMPTS OR FEINTS AN ADVANCE OR TURNS INTO FAIR TERRITORY ✪

FED: After a batted ball, a batter-runner may overrun first without peril of an out provided he does not attempt, **NOR FEINT AN ATTEMPT,** to go to second. (8-2-7) (See § 110 and 112.)
103. ALSO: Concerning which direction the batter-runner must turn after passing the bag: No provision.
Adopt OFF INTERP 90 [this section].

NCAA: The batter-runner is in jeopardy of an out only on an attempt (not a feint) to go to second. (8-5i Ex)
104. ALSO: Concerning which direction the batter-runner must turn after passing the bag: No provision.
Adopt OFF INTERP 90 [this section].

OBR: Same as NCAA. (7.08j)

105. ALSO: OFF INTERP 90-111: ***(EDITED)*** **EVANS:** "Simply turning toward 2nd base shall not be interpreted as making an attempt to run to 2nd. This is a judgment call by the umpire. However, a single step or head feint may be interpreted as an attempt to advance (umpire's judgment). The umpire must be convinced that the runner made SOME MOVEMENT which indicated that he might try to advance to 2nd. (7:72) ✠

❀ Note 112: I am always amazed that certain "rules" hang on long after they've been changed. Here, from MLB umpire Billy Evans' *Simplified Baseball Rulebook* (**1922 edition!**) is his take on the subject: "**YEARS AGO** when a baserunner crossed first base, it was necessary that he turn to the right after so doing. Otherwise he made himself liable to be put out. Many baseball fans are still confused on this rule. They cling to the old version. That is why you often hear someone yell, 'He turned wrong,' when a baserunner after crossing first base turns to his left. A baserunner after over running first base has the right to turn to the right or left to return to that base."

★ 112 BATTER-RUNNER: OVERRUNS FIRST: TIME TO RETURN ✪

FED: After overrunning first, the batter-runner must return immediately. (8-2-7) (See § 111.)

NCAA: Same as FED 8-2-7. (8-5i Ex) (See § 110.)

OBR: If the batter-runner fails to return at once to first after overrunning the bag, he is out on appeal (7.08j) or when he or the base is tagged. (7.10c) (See § 10.)

AO 10-112: EVANS: The stipulation requiring the runner to "return at once" is a provision that appeared in the late 1800s and was designed to expedite play. In that same era, runners were required to "run" back to their original bases when foul, fly bails were not caught. These rules are not strictly enforced in today's game as they were intended by the early rulesmakers.

(ADDED) **106. ALSO:** OFF INTERP 91-112: **WENDELSTEDT:** "A batter-runner who reaches first base but returns to the home plate side while the ball is alive is in jeopardy of being put out if tagged." (HWfn[182]/199) ✠

⁎ *Play 76-112:* B1 hits to third. F5's throw to first is off-line, and B1 slides under a swipe tag by the first baseman. B1 stands up to dust off the dirt and is tagged off the base on the home plate side of the bag. *Ruling:* B1 is out.

(ADDED) ❀ Note 113: Close examination of the text of these three statutes convinces me there is no difference among the books. This text will disappear in the 2013 edition.

113 BATTER-RUNNER: RETREATS TOWARD PLATE TO EVADE TAG✪

FED: A batter-runner may legally retreat toward the plate to avoid a tag unless he touches or runs beyond the plate or leaves the baseline to avoid a tag, when he will be called out. The ball remains alive. (8.1.1a)

> **107. ALSO:** OFF INTERP 92-113: **RUMBLE:** When a batter is retreating toward the plate, the umpire will **ALWAYS** call obstruction if B1 "collides" with the catcher who neither has the ball nor is making a play. (*News* #17, 3/94) (See OFF INTERP • 94 [this section] for a contrasting view.) ✠

NCAA: Same as FED. (7-11p AR 3) **EXCEPT:** The rule does not mention the status of the ball, and no OFF INTERP exists to deal with obstruction.

OBR: Point not covered.

> OFF INTERP 93-113: **PBUC:** A batter-runner retreating toward the plate is out if he touches or runs beyond the plate. {7.30 Nt} ✠

> **108. ALSO:** OFF INTERP 94-113: **PBUC:** When a batter is retreating toward the plate, the umpire rules obstruction only when he judges it is INTENTIONAL. {7.30 Play 1} (See OFF INTERP • 92 [this section] for a contrasting view.) ✠

114 BATTING PRACTICE ✪

FED: Point not covered.

OFF INTERP 95-114: **RUMBLE:** The umpire may not require the home team to provide time for the visitors to take batting practice in a batting cage or tunnel during the game: "The umpire has no jurisdiction over the use of equipment or facilities **OUTSIDE THE CONFINES OF THE FIELD.**" But if the ping of the bats is distracting, the umpire may prohibit further use of the tunnel by the home team. (Website 2001, #1) ✠

❀ Note 114: Three other infractions are listed as occurring outside the "confines of the field": illegal warm-up device (§ 187), use of tobacco (§ 503), and wearing a bandanna (§ 521). FED does not allow the umpires to police those illegal activities until they have jurisdiction by going inside the confines of the field. (See Note 416-419.) **EXCEPT:** Umpires must ensure that a player warming up the pitcher **ANYWHERE** is wearing the prescribed protective gear. (See § 194.)

NCAA: If batting practice is scheduled, the visiting team must also be allowed 30 minutes of batting practice. (4-3a) A batting cage is recommended. (4-3c) (See Note 418-419.)

OBR: Point not covered.

OFF INTERP 96-114: **FITZPATRICK:** A batting tunnel is outside the field fence but inside the stadium fence. The visitors want the UIC to give them equal use of the tunnel. The umpire has no control outside the field. Thus, the home team may use the tunnel; the visitors may not. (phone call to cc, 11/8/01) ✠

115 BENCH: AUTHORIZED PERSONNEL ✪

FED: Only "bench personnel" may occupy the bench or be in the dugout. (3-3-1j) **PENALTY:** Non-coach: warning / ejection; coach: restriction or ejection. For failure to comply, coach or player: forfeit. (3-3-1jPen)

❀ Note 115: FED does not define "bench personnel." Barring an ejection or other problems, that is anyone the head coach wants on the bench.

NCAA: Only eligible players in uniform, coaches, managers, athletic trainers, physicians, scorekeepers, and bat persons shall occupy a team's dugout or bullpen. (1-16c) (See § 116.)

OBR: "Players, substitutes, managers, coaches, trainers and bat boys" may occupy the bench. (3.17) (See § 119.)

★ 116 BENCH: PLAYERS MUST OCCUPY ✪

FED: POE 1995, 1996, 1997, 1998, 1999, 2000, 2001, 2005, 2008, 2009: All personnel must be inside the designated bench or dugout area unless the rules require them to be elsewhere: on base, in the bullpen, in the field, etc. (3-3-1j) (See § 231 for the "extended" dugout.) **PENALTY:** Non-coach: warning / ejection.
Coach: restriction / ejection. For failure to comply [with the ejection order], coach or player: forfeit. (3-3-1j Pen) (See § 138 and 309.)
EXCEPT: If team members are loosening up where a fence or "other structure" offers no protection – as in a pitcher warming up "in the bullpen" in dead ball territory – a team member "with a glove" must be stationed between them and home plate. "No one is to interfere with a live ball." (3-3-4)

❀ Note 116: Assigning a sub to protect a pitcher / catcher warming up down the foul line has been common practice on ball fields since I started umpiring over 55 years ago. Now the FED – only – has given it rules stature. Bravo! But I can't figure out how the protector can do his job if he can't "interfere" with that fair ball slicing directly for the catcher's back. I suppose they mean interfere with a thrown ball.

109. ALSO: Both teams must occupy their benches or the bullpen during the opposing team's infield practice (3-3-1g5; 3.3.1h, I, and j) and the pregame conference between coaches and umpires. (2-10-2)

NCAA: POE1998, 2007: Umpires and coaches shall "require" coaches and all personnel to remain in the dugout or DBT while the ball is in play. No coach or team personnel shall leave the dugout until the ball is dead. (1-16a; 3-8d) (See § 115.) If dugouts are small, a "clearly visible" line should identify the DBT that will serve as an extended bench. (1-16b) **PENALTY** for not being in authorized area: warning / ejection. (3-8d Pen) (See § 164 and 309.)

OBR: Team members and coaches shall be in their bench area. (3.17) **PENALTY** for not being in authorized area: Same as NCAA. (3.17 Pen) (See 164.)
(ADDED) **110. ALSO:** Players on the disabled list may occupy the bench during the game. (3.17 CMT) (See § 115.)

(ADDED) ❀ Note 117: It may seem far-fetched that an umpire should know disabled players are allowed on the bench since we have no "lists" for amateur games. Still, injured players do attend the games, they do sit on the bench — and they are expressly forbidden to engage in bench jockeying in your adult OBR leagues and – by extension – FED and NCAA venues. (See § 119.)

∞ 117 BENCH: UMPIRE CLEARS ✪

FED: The umpire may clear the bench. (10-2-3c)

NCAA: The umpire may clear the bench, which is defined as requiring "affected participants" to leave the dugout. (3-7i)
111. ALSO: Eligible players and coaches cleared from the bench remain eligible to participate in the game. (3-7i)

OBR: Same as NCAA. (4.08; 4.08 Pen)

AO 11-117: EVANS: A stern warning to the manager informing him of the impending consequences should always be given prior to taking this drastic action [clearing the bench]. The starting lineup, trainer, and coaches are generally allowed to remain on the bench unless the umpire feels that they have contributed to the protest. Known violators may be singled out and ejected and cannot be recalled. (4-26)

118 BENCH JOCKEYING: FAIR PLAY REQUIRED ✪

FED: POE 1992, 1993, 1994, 1995, 2004: No person connected with either team shall exhibit behavior inconsistent with the spirit of fair play. (3-3-1g-4) **PENALTY:** warning or ejection. (3-3-1g Pen) (See § 72.)

NCAA: Umpires may warn or eject participants for "unsportsmanlike behavior." (3-6d; 3-6d AR 1; Code of Ethics #6)
112. ALSO: After a team member is ejected for unsportsmanlike behavior, if the verbal abuse continues, the umpire will eject the head coach along with subsequent offenders. (5-17 Pen)
113. ALSO: "Any orchestrated activities by dugout personnel designed to distract, intimidate, or disconcert the opposing team or reflect poor sportsmanship shall not be allowed." (5-17)
114. ALSO: A participant ejected for violating this rule is also suspended for one game. (3-6d Pen) (See § 118, 141 and 246.)

OBR: No provision. (See § 119.) *See ¶ 8.*

119 BENCH JOCKEYING: REMARKS TO OPPONENTS PROHIBITED ✪

FED: POE 1994, 1995, 2003, 2008, 2009: No person connected with either team shall make any intimidating remarks to anyone connected with the other team. (3-3-1g-2)
PENALTY: warning or ejection. (3-3-1g Pen; 3.3.1j) (See § 118.)

115. ALSO: Ejection for "intimidating remarks" can be immediate [no prior warning], and the **EJECTION SERVES AS A TEAM WARNING.** (3.3.1jj) (See § 517.)

116. ALSO: A **POE 2011** calls for coaches to exercise more control over activities occurring outside the field.

117. ALSO: "The NFHS disapproves of any form of taunting that is intended or designed to embarrass, ridicule or demean others under circumstances including race, religion, gender, or national origin." (3-3-1g-2)

> ❀ Note 118: In straight language, "intimidation" is called "taunting"; in the street language of the 90s and beyond, it's "trash talk." Bad behavior by any other name is still bad behavior. Talk is cheap, they say. So some teams replaced talk with the intimidating **STARE** and waving of bats menacingly while their opponents warmed up during infield practice. FED outlawed that nonsense in 2004. (See § 116.)

NCAA: Umpires may warn a team or individuals or eject participants for bench jockeying, "which would include personal and malicious remarks, cursing and obscene language toward opponents, umpires or spectators." (3-6d; 3-6d AR 1; Code of Ethics #5)

118. ALSO: After a team member is ejected for "bench jockeying," if the verbal abuse continues, the umpire will eject the head coach along with subsequent offenders. (5-17 Pen)

119. ALSO: A participant ejected for violating this rule is also suspended for one game. (3-6d Pen) (See § 118 141 and 246.)

OBR: "Bench jockeying" is specifically mentioned (and thus sanctioned) in the code. Players on the disabled list and **INELIGIBLE SUBSTITUTES** are expressly forbidden to address comments to the opposing team or the umpires. (3.06 CMT; 3.17 CMT) *See ¶ 8.*

120. ALSO: No team member shall use language that will "refer to" or "reflect upon" opposing players. (4.06a-2)

★ *(EDITED HEADING)* 120 BLEEDING / CONCUSSION ✪

FED: BLEEDING: A player or coach who is bleeding or has an open wound is prohibited from further participation until he receives "appropriate" treatment. Bleeding must be stopped, and the injured person must change ***(ADDED)*** "or clean" his uniform if "there is **ANY** amount of blood on his uniform." The game may be delayed for a "reasonable" time, after which the umpire shall require the injured party to withdraw from the game. (3.1.6a; Communicable Disease Procedures) "Every effort should be made to allow the player to participate." (3.1.6b) Normal reentry rules apply. (3-1-6; 4.4.1d, 2006 ed; Website 2012, # 5 and 6)
Last edition: The uniform had to changed if the garment was "blood-soaked."

(ADDED) OFF INTERP 97-120: **HOPKINS:** A player whose uniform has blood on it must change before he participates. He may use a teammate's jersey (the number change will be reported), a jersey from the freshman or junior varsity team, or even a tee shirt with his number put on it. (Website 2012, #6) ✠

❀ Note 119: ***(EDITED)*** The rule is now much more restrictive than in years past. (It entered the book in 1994.). Surely we've all continued after a bloody nose dripped some blood onto a player's uniform. Not any more. Be sure your state association conveys the importance of this change to your local coaches.

CONCUSSION: ***(MOVED HERE FROM 2011 § 488)*** **121. ALSO:** Any player who exhibits signs consistent with a concussion "shall be immediately removed from the game and shall not return to play until cleared by an **APPROPRIATE HEALTH-CARE PROFESSIONAL**." Symptoms include loss of consciousness, headache, dizziness, confusion, loss of balance problems. (3-1-5; 10-2 3k; 3.1.5a and b) (See § 120.)

❀ Note 120: On the one hand, FED called heightened attention to concussions, but on the other, significantly eased a coach's problem of re-entering an injured player. "Appropriate health care professional" ain't the same as a "physician." At least they didn't say "licensed athletic trainer."

⁂ *Play 77-120:* ***(EXPANDED)*** **FED and NCAA.** During pregame practice the home team's center fielder is knocked unconscious. After some moments he comes to his senses and informs his coach he is OK. The coach puts him into the lineup, which act the visiting coach protests at the pregame meeting. *Ruling:* The player may participate since the officials were not yet in charge when F8 was rendered unconscious. (See § 419.)

NCAA: BLEEDING: As soon as possible, time shall be called when any game participant has an open wound that is oozing or bleeding.

(● 1) During practice, the player should not return to the field unless cleared by "medical personnel." (● 2) During a game, if the wound can be treated "without undue delay, play shall be stopped until the athlete has received treatment and is cleared to play by medical personnel." (3-9) "In a situation where a player is bleeding, a decision to substitute for the player must be made within 10 minutes from the time play is stopped. A substitute player must begin warming up immediately when the blood rule is in effect." (3-9 AR; 9-4a AR 5) (See § 498.)

122. ALSO: An athletic trainer may use "a substance" to stop bleeding if it dries before play resumes. (9-2e AR 2)

❀ Note 121: "Medical personnel" does not necessarily mean a licensed physician or nurse. A certified team trainer will suffice.

CONCUSSION: ***(ADDED)*** **123. ALSO:** An athlete who exhibits signs, symptoms or behaviors consistent with a concussion, either at rest or during exertion, should be REMOVED IMMEDIATELY FROM PRACTICE OR COMPETITION and should not return to play until cleared by an appropriate health care professional. Sports have injury timeouts and player substitutions so that student-athletes can get checked. (NCAA rules, Appendix G)

OBR: BLEEDING: Point not covered.

OFF INTERP 98-120: **PBUC:** "It is important for all umpires to know that some precautions will be taken that may cause brief delays in a game. For example, if a garment(s) is penetrated by blood or other potentially infectious materials, the garment(s) shall be removed immediately or as soon as feasible." Most often, the problem should be resolved between half innings, but "there may be cases when the situation must be acted upon immediately." {9.19} ✠

CONCUSSION: ***(ADDED)*** MLB and the players' union announced a new set of protocols that took effect on opening day, 2011, to deal with concussions, including the creation of the new, seven-day disabled list that should give team doctors and the injured players more flexibility to address head injuries.

124. ALSO: Each team will have to designate a specialist who deals with mild brain injuries to evaluate players and umpires when needed and be required send its medical reports to Dr. Gary Green, MLB's medical director, for approval before the injured player is cleared to return to the field. (See Note 122 below.) Last edition: No provision. *See ¶8.*

(ADDED) ❀ Note 122: These rules were adopted in March, 2011, too late for last year's BRD. Here's a URL where you can read further details about the new policy:

http://msn.foxsports.com/mlb/story/Major-League-Baseball-adds-disabled-list-for-concussions-32911
Of course, your local OBR leagues will not have reached the MLB stage of dealing with concussions or unconsciousness. Be certain, though, you are conversant with those Leagues' regulations.

121 CAPTAIN OF THE TEAM ✪

FED: The coach MUST designate one player as captain. (1-1-1) (See § 418.) The captain may inform the umpire if his team will accept the penalty for use of an illegal glove. (1-5-7)

NCAA: No provision.

OBR: The umpire-in-chief may point out obvious errors in the lineup to the captain or manager. (4.01e CMT)

∞ 122 CATCH: CATCHER USES PROTECTOR TO SMOTHER FOUL TIP ✪

FED: No provision. Treat as in OBR.

NCAA: No provision. Treat as in OBR.

OBR: If the catcher catches a foul tip by smothering the ball with his mitt against his body protector, that shall be a catch if the "ball touched the catcher's hand or mitt first." (6.05b CMT ¶ 2) (See § 126.)

123 CATCH: DEAD-BALL TERRITORY: INSIDE BENCH OR DUGOUT ✪

FED: No provision. (See § 125.)

NCAA: A fielder cannot make a catch while touching the bench or dugout area with any part of his body. (6-1d; 6-1d-1) (See § 125.)

OBR: Same as NCAA. (6.05a CMT)

> OFF INTERP 99-123: **PBUC:** A fielder is "in the dugout" if he has "one or both feet on the surface inside the dugout" or has dived into the dugout with "neither foot on or above the playing surface." {3.5} ✠

> OFF INTERP 100-123: **PBUC:** The lip of the dugout, the top of the dugout that is even with the playing surface, is considered outside the dugout. {6.5} ✠

OFF INTERP 101-123: **PBUC:** A ball striking equipment on the lip of the dugout is dead. {6.5} ✠

125. ALSO: OFF INTERP 102-123: **DEARY:** A fielder may not go onto the top of the dugout to catch the ball. (*REF* 8/83) ✠

126. ALSO: A player may climb onto a roll of canvas or a railing to make a catch. (2.00 Catch CMT)

★ 124 CATCH: DEAD-BALL AREA: THROW FROM ✪

FED: If a fielder has one foot in dead-ball territory, he may throw. If he steps with both feet into that area, the ball is dead. (5-1-1i) (See § 27 and 42.)

NCAA: The ball remains "in play" if a fielder with the ball steps into dead-ball territory unless he falls down or loses body control. (6-1d) If a fielder slides "intentionally, he has **NOT** lost body control." (6-1d AR 2)

EXCEPT: Unless ground rules dictate otherwise, a fielder **MAY NOT THROW** from DBT. (6-1d-1a and b)

❀ Note 123: Apparently some umpires believe the effect of 6-1d-1a/b is to allow a fielder to throw from DBT unless ground rules stipulate otherwise. That's not an issue for readers of the BRD, which pointed out in 1996: "Thurston ruled that the general procedure is: A fielder may not throw from DBT." (phone call to se, 12/2/93) The ball is alive while the fielder is in DBT, and runners may advance at their own risk. But the fielder, unless the ground rules allow it, must not throw until he steps with both feet into live-ball territory.

127. ALSO: OFF INTERP 103-124: **THURSTON:** Here is his proposed ground rule covering dead-ball areas: "If a fielder makes a catch and then enters a dead-ball area with the ball, the ball is dead and runners **DO NOT ADVANCE**. If the fielder **INTENTIONALLY** carries the ball into a dead-ball area, the ball is dead and runners advance one base from the time the ball becomes dead." (phone call to se, 12/20/93) (See § 413.) ✠

128. ALSO: **PENALTY** for an unauthorized throw from DBT: The ball is dead, and the umpire awards all runners one base. (6-1d-1b Pen)

OBR: Unless he falls down or loses body control, the fielder may throw from any dead-ball area. (5.10f; 7.04c CMT)

AO 12-124: EVANS: "The critical factor in this ruling is the definition of FALLS. A player may stumble, lean on a dugout wall, be supported by players from either team, and teeter on a fence railing without actually falling. This is a judgment call and the umpire must be alert and in position to judge the player's status after catching a fly ball." (5:35; 7:10)

⁑ *Play 78-124:* Near shallow right field a marked line curves around the unprotected bullpen. A fielder in DBT has a clear view of the field and would throw across the bullpen when trying to prevent a runner's advance. In the fourth inning with none out, R2 retouches at second as F9 catches B1's high flu ball. The fielder's momentum carries him across the line, where he: (a) throws to F4, his cutoff man; or (b) runs into live-ball area before throwing; or (c) falls down attempting to throw. *Ruling:* In FED, the ball is dead in all cases; award R2 third. In NCAA, the result depends on the pregame conference. If an exception was not adopted: In (a) and (c), the ball is dead and R2 is awarded third. In (b), the ball remains alive: R2 advances at his own risk. (See Play 79 [this section] for what happens when Thurston's ground rule is adopted.) **OR:** During the pregame conference, the coaches may have agreed that dead-ball areas would be treated as in 6-1d. In that instance, NCAA is exactly like OBR, which is: In (a) and (b), the ball remains alive. In (c), the ball is dead. The umpire awards R2 third.

> ⁑ *Play 79 -124:* **NCAA only.** The dead-ball area described in Play 78 above has been discussed at the pregame meeting and Thurston's ground rule adopted. In the fourth inning with none out, R2 retouches at second as F9 makes the catch and then: (a) runs several steps to cross into the dead-ball area; or (b) is carried by his momentum completely across the line, where he: (1) throws to his cutoff man; or (2) runs back to live-ball territory before throwing; or (3) stops and walks slowly back toward the diamond with the ball. *Ruling:* In all cases the ball is dead. Then: In (a) and (b-1), R2 gets third. In (b-2) and (b-3) R2 remains on second.

❀ Note 124: Thurston's ground rule specifies that the ball becomes immediately dead when F9 steps into DBT; the fielder is prevented from making a play, as in (b-2) above. In the absence of Thurston's or some similar ground rule, though, unless the fielder falls down or loses body control, he may always return to live-ball territory before throwing.

❀ Note 125: ***(EDITED)*** Throwing from a dead-ball area is one of nine major rules or interpretations WHERE EACH LEVEL TREATS THE SITUATION DIFFERENTLY. The other eight are: § 50-71 (designated hitter); § 83 (use illegal bat); § 144 (conferences / trips to the mound); § 245 (positions occupied at time of pitch or play);§ 246 (fighting); § 266 (improperly declared infield fly); § 378 (hidden ball play); § 488 (illegal substitutes).

★ 125 CATCH: DEAD-BALL AREA: TOUCH DURING ✪

FED: If a fielder has **ESTABLISHED HIS POSITION** with at least one foot in live-ball territory, he will make a "legal catch" when he gains control of the ball. The line marking the division between the two areas is live territory. (2.9.1c CMT; 5.1.1L) (See § 123.)

> **129. ALSO:** OFF INTERP 104-125: **RUMBLE:** A fielder who has touched dead-ball territory with both feet may, before touching the ball, reestablish himself for a legal catch by putting one foot back onto live-ball territory. (FED MTG, 1/17/91) ✠

❀ Note 126: A player may leave the ground and – while in the air – make a legal catch. The point: He is not actually required by the rule to have one foot **TOUCHING** live-ball territory.

130. ALSO: A fielder must be **COMPLETELY** in dead-ball territory before the ball becomes dead: "As long as any part of [a fielder's] body is touching the designated dead-ball line, the ball remains live." (5.1.1p)

NCAA: The fielder must catch ["have secure possession of"] the ball before he touches the dead-ball area with any part of his body. (2-15e; 6-1d-1) (See § 123 and 124.)

131. ALSO: A fielder may make a legal catch after entering DBT as long as he completely returns to live-ball territory at the time of the catch.(6-1d-1 AR)

❀ Note 127: A player could be touching the line and make a legal catch. But if any part of his foot extended across the line, the catch would not be allowed. Try to officiate **THAT** with an imaginary line.

OBR: ***(ADDED)*** Same as NCAA 2-15 e. (6.05a CMT)

❀ Note 128: Enforce FED OFF INTERP 104 [this section] in your NCAA / OBR games: Always allow a fielder to return to live-ball territory, with both feet, to make a catch. See also § 123.

✻ *Play 80-125:* R2, 1 out. R2 retouches on B1's short pop fly to foul right field. The right fielder finally makes the catch. When he grabs the ball, he is straddling a line dividing live-ball from dead-ball territory. F9's momentum then causes him to step with both feet into DBT though he does not fall down. R2 tries for third and is thrown out. *Ruling:* In FED, it is a catch and a dead ball when F9 steps into dead-ball ground with both feet; the umpire awards the runner third. In NCAA / OBR, it is simply a foul ball.

★ 126 CATCH: DEFINITION ✪

FED: POE 1982, 1984, 1985: After gaining possession of a batted ball in flight, the fielder is not credited with a catch if he drops the ball when he falls down (2.9.1c) or runs into a wall or another fielder. (2-9-1; 2.9.1c CMT)

132. ALSO: OFF INTERP 105-126: **HOPKINS:** A sharp line drive knocks the glove from the second baseman's hand, and it falls to the ground with the ball still in the pocket. Is this a catch? Ruling: No. (Website 2008, #2) ✠

133. ALSO: A fielder's attempt to regain his balance is considered part of the catch of a throw. During that attempt, if the ball comes free, it is not a catch. A catch is not complete until the ball is secured by the bare or glove hand. (2.9.1a and b)
134. ALSO: If a speeding fielder gloves a ball and his momentum carries him several more yards, when he drops the ball, that is not a catch. (2-9-1)

NCAA: Same as FED. (2-15; 6-1d-1) **EXCEPT:** If a player makes a catch in front of a flexible, wind-screen fence, it is not a catch if he is "stepping on, over, or against the fence." He may touch or lean up against the fence. (1-2c AR)
135. ALSO: In establishing a catch, "the fielder shall demonstrate complete control and that the release of the ball is voluntary and intentional." (2-15)

OBR: Same as FED. (2.00 Catch) (See § 122.)

❀ Note 129: Baseball tradition is unambiguous. Establishing a catch means: (● 1) The fielder, after gaining control of the ball, has reversed his direction and started to run the ball toward the infield [The MLBUM defines that as "when the momentum of the catch is completed" (8.1)]; or (● 2) the fielder is reaching for the ball to make a throw. [The FED rule is the same. (2-9-1)] When a fielder drops a ball, those are the only two circumstances that you may interpret as creating a "voluntary and intentional" release.

❀ Note 130: When a player makes a "catch" as he dives to the ground or slams into a barrier: If he hangs on to the ball until a teammate removes it from his hand or glove, the "voluntary and intentional release" test is met. Rule it a catch.

127 CATCH: ILLEGAL GLOVE: STATUS OF BALL / PENALTY ✪

FED: When a fielder touches a batted or thrown ball with an illegal glove or mitt, the ball is delayed dead. (5-1-2g) (See § 17.) **136. ALSO:** When the umpire recognizes an illegal glove, it is removed. If the offense appeals before the next pitch, it may accept the play or the penalty. (1-5-7; 1.5.7) **PENALTY:** Each runner receives: four bases, if the illegal glove prevented the ball from becoming a home run and three bases, if a fielder touched a batted ball (other than a possible home run). The award is two bases if a pitched or thrown ball is touched by the illegal glove. (8-3-3a , b and c; 1.4.3, 1991 ed) (See § 203; 204; 205; 206.)

> **137. ALSO:** OFF INTERP 106-127: **HOPKINS:** If the fielder catches a foul ball with an illegal glove, the ball is simply foul unless the offense elects to take the result of the play. (1-5-7; Website 2008, #18) ✠

❀ Note 131: Please understand that a pitcher's multicolored glove is illegal, but the penalty is not so Draconian; merely, remove the glove as soon as it is detected. (See § 207.)

NCAA: If a fielder makes a catch with an illegal glove, on proper appeal the offense may take the play or replay the pitch. Follow the regular appeal procedure at 8-6b. (1-13c Pen 2)

OBR: The dimensions for fielder's gloves are spelled out in 1.14. (See § 204.) **PENALTY: Point not covered.**

> OFF INTERP 107-127: **PBUC STAFF:** Any catch made with an illegal glove is a legal catch. (email to cc, 12/15/00) ✠

❀ Note 132: OBR treats an illegal glove like an illegal substitute: They chunk the sub but keep his plays.

AO 13-127: EVANS: The penalty [for an illegal glove] is temporary confiscation of the illegal glove. No play or game action shall be nullified because of such an equipment violation. Players who fail to cooperate with an umpire's order may be ejected. (1:37)

✻ *Play 81-127:* While wearing a glove whose dimensions are not legal, F7 makes a spectacular catch in foul territory, after which R3 retouches and scores. The offense appeals properly, and the illegal glove is recognized by the umpire. *Ruling:* In FED, the offense may have the penalty (foul ball, runners return) or the play (batter-runner out, one run in). In NCAA, the offensive coach may also take the penalty (runner returns to third, replay the pitch) or the play (batter-runner out, one run in). In OBR, the play stands. At all levels, the glove is removed.

⁎ *Play 82-127:* B1's hard smash ricochets off the pitcher's glove and bounces to F4, who can make no play: B1 is safe at first. It is then discovered that F1 is wearing a glove whose dimensions are not legal. *Ruling:* In FED, the umpire awards B1 third. In NCAA, the play stands but only because no catch was made. In OBR, the play also stands. At all levels, the glove is removed.

128 COACH: ADDRESSES PLAYERS ✪

FED: A base coach may address only the **BATTER OR RUNNERS.** (3-2-1)

NCAA: The coach may address only his **TEAM MEMBERS.** (3-3c)

OBR: No provision. Treat as in NCAA. *See ¶8.*

129 COACH: ASSISTANT: APPEALS UMPIRE DECISIONS ✪

FED: No member of the coaching staff who is not the head coach may leave "the vicinity" of the bench or coaching box to "**DISPUTE**" an umpire's judgment call. (3-3-1g-6) **PENALTY:** Both the head coach and the offender shall be restricted to the dugout. "If the offense is judged severe enough, the umpire may eject the assistant and restrict the head coach." (3-3-1g-6 Pen)

NCAA: No assistant coach may leave his position anywhere (box, dugout, bullpen) to "**APPEAL**" an umpire's decision. (3-2) **PENALTY:** Warning / ejection. (3-2 Pen) (See § 507.) *See ¶8.*

❀ Note 133: The FED / NCAA are in harmony except for the Penalty. The NCAA doesn't provide for restrictions, so the only one who gets the ax is the offender.

OBR: A coach may not "object" to an umpire's decision based on judgment. (9.02a)

❀ Note 134: If a "coach" may not object to a judgment call, the inference is plain: He **MAY** protest (appeal) other decisions. (See § 7.) But the OBR specifically gives the "manager" the right to appeal a decision he believes is in conflict with the rules. (9.02b) In 2009, NCAA also codified the right of the head coach to complain about rules enforcement. (See § 43.)

130 COACH: ASSISTANT: ROSTER PLAYER ✪

FED: No provision.

NCAA: An assistant coach is not eligible to participate as a player. (3-2)

OBR: No provision.

★ 131 COACH: COACHING BOX: ELIGIBLE PLAYER ✪

FED: Any "member of the team at bat" may occupy the coaching box except one ejected for "unsportsmanlike conduct." (3-2-1) (See § 132 and 135.)

(ADDED) ❀ Note 135: Let's face it: In a project as complicated as the BRD, mistakes will occur. Sometimes I am to blame; sometimes, the editors of a book are at fault. Here's a passage (3-2-1) from the **2007 NFHS** rulebook:

"One player or coach may occupy each coach's box while his team is at bat. A coach or player occupying the coaches' boxes shall remain in the box upon the batter entering the box until the release of the ball by the pitcher if requested by the opposing coach. Once this request is made, it applies to both teams for the remainder of the game. A coach who is not in the uniform of the team shall be restricted to the bench / dugout. However, a coach may leave the bench / dugout to attend to a player who becomes ill or injured. He may address base runners [sic] or the batter. Coaches may wear prostheses and use mobility devices. Any member of the team at bat, who has not been ejected for unsportsmanlike conduct, may occupy a coach's box. PENALTY: At the end of playing action, regardless of who violates the rule, the head coach will be restricted to the bench/dugout."

Now, here is 3-2-1 as it appears in the **2008 NFHS** book:

"One player or coach may occupy each coach's box while his team is at bat. ~~A coach or player occupying the coaches' boxes shall remain in the box upon the batter entering the box until the release of the ball by the pitcher if requested by the opposing coach. Once the this request is made, it applies to both teams for the remainder of the game.~~ A coach who is not in the uniform of the team shall be restricted to the bench/dugout. However, a coach may leave the bench/dugout to attend to a player who becomes ill or injured. He may address base runners [sic] or the batter. Coaches may wear prostheses and use mobility devices. Any member of the team at bat, who has not been ejected for unsportsmanlike conduct, may occupy a coach's box."~~PENALTY: At the end of playing action, regardless of who violates the rule, the head coach will be restricted to the bench/dugout.~~

THOSE DELETIONS WERE UNANNOUNCED AND UNMARKED CHANGES!

Consequently, all BRD editions from 2008-2011 erroneously indicated a Penalty for those who violated 3-2-1.

My mistake: Trusting the FED editor too much.

My pledge: **IT WILL NOT HAPPEN AGAIN.**

NCAA: Any **ELIGIBLE SUBSTITUTE** or team member may coach. (3-3) **EXCEPT:** A withdrawn player, who is not an eligible substitute, may be a base coach. (5-5i)

OBR: The coach must be a "team member in uniform." (2.00 Coach) (See § 135.)

> **138. ALSO:** OFF INTERP 108-131: **PBUC:** ***(EDITED)*** "Players removed from the game (other than by an umpire) may ... act as base coaches." {3.2} (See § 488.) ✠

★ 132 COACH: COACHING BOX: HELMET MANDATORY ✪

FED: Players or other students in the coaches' boxes must wear protective helmets. (1-5-1) (See § 131 and 135.) **PENALTY:** team warning / ejection. (1-5-1 Pen; 1.5.1c)

> **139. ALSO:** OFF INTERP 109-132: **HOPKINS:** With the bases empty, the visiting team is at bat and the assistant coach in the first base coach's box is wearing a dual flap helmet while the head coach in the third base coach's box is wearing a hard liner under his team cap. The home team coach complains to the umpire-in-chief that both coaches must wear the same type of protective helmet in accordance with MLB rules. Ruling: The NFHS has not mandated that adult coaches shall wear protective head gear while occupying a coach's box. It is the prerogative of the respective coach to wear such protective equipment. The NFHS is conducting research to determine if protective head gear should be required and, if so, which type (hard liner, flapless, one-flap, dual flap) would be most effective. (Website 2008, #20) ✠

NCAA: Base coaches must wear a helmet. The committee recommends the helmet meet NOCSAE standards.
PENALTY: The umpire will not continue play until the offending coach complies with the rule. (1-14g)

OBR: First- and third-base coaches will wear helmets in the box. (1.16e)

(ADDED) ❀ Note 136: The helmets in NCAA and OBR games need not have dual earflaps.

★ 133 COACH: COACHING BOX: OBJECTS OTHER THAN SCOREBOOK ✪

FED: POE 1990: While in the coaching box, a coach may not have any object other than a rulebook, a "Personal Digital Assistant

(PDA) or comparable electronic score-recording device," stopwatch, or a scorebook for keeping score. (3-3-1i) [radar gun, portable laptop computer? no; (3.3.1k) cell phone? no] (3.3.1l) ***(ADDED)*** [electronic score-recording device? yes.] (3-3-1i) **PENALTY:** restriction or ejection. (3-3-1i Pen) (See § 219.)

NCAA: Point not covered.

> ***(ADDED)*** OFF INTERP 110-133: **PARONTO:** A coach may not have any electronic object(s) or a scorebook on the field of play. (email to cc, 12/5/11) (See § 219.) ✠

OBR: No provision. (But see § 219.)

★ 134 COACH: COACHING BOX: STATIONED INSIDE WHEN ON OFFENSE ✪

FED: A coach **MAY** occupy each coaching box. (3-2-1)

> **140. ALSO:** OFF INTERP 111-134: **HOPKINS:** The defense calls the umpire's attention to a coach not in his box. The umpire determines he is not gaining any advantage or "causing any problems." The coach's actions are legal. (Website 2008, #19) ✠

NCAA: A coach **SHALL** occupy each box. (5-2b)

141. ALSO: At the time of the pitch, the base coach must "remain" in the coach's box. He may be positioned farther away from home plate than the "boundaries of the coaches' box." (1-3c)

❀ Note 137: In 2009 the NCAA added the very rule the FED adopted in 2007 — and dropped after only one year. Hopkins: "The rule was virtually impossible to enforce...." The *raison d'etre* for the edict is unclear. Is it to prevent coaches from stealing the catcher's signs? If that was the reason, they would have said he must be in the box when the pitcher is getting his sign from the catcher. Is it for safety purposes? Hardly: That extra 20 feet (the length of the box) is not likely to give a coach a significant advantage in avoiding a line drive headed straight for his helmet. Whatever the purpose of the rule, the enforcement will be brutally difficult, as the FED noted. To a coach screaming that the batter is out of the batter's box, the umpire may ask: "Hey, you want me to watch the pitch or his feet?" No one knows what the reply should be to: "Blue, he's out of the coach's box."

OBR: Same as NCAA 5-2b. (4.05a) **EXCEPT:** ***(ADDED)*** If one team complains that a coach is not remaining inside the box, the umpire will "strictly enforce the rule and require "all coaches on both teams to remain in the coach's box at all times." (4.05b CMT)

> **142. ALSO:** OFF INTERP 112-134: **PBUC:** An umpire may not begin a half inning until both coaches have reached the boxes. {3.6} ✠

(ADDED) **143. ALSO:** Same as NCAA 1-3c. (4.05a CMT)

★ 135 COACH: COACHING BOX: UNIFORM ✪

FED: POE 1990, 1991: A coach in the box must be in team uniform. If he is not, he is restricted to the bench. He may still go onto the field to attend a player. (3-2-1; 3.2.1d) State associations are free to adopt guidelines that would allow coaches to dress in attire "consistent with the team uniform." (3.2.1e)

NCAA: A coach in the box must be in uniform identical to the players. If a team jacket or windshirt is worn, "it must include the team's official logo and be consistent with the team's uniform color and apparel. If both coaches opt to wear a jacket, the jackets must be uniform." (1-14f; 3-3a) (See OFF INTERP 113 [this section].) (See also § 519 and 520.)
144. ALSO: A coach, like a position player, may wear a jacket under his jersey as long as it is the same color as the undershirt. The coach must wear a game jersey when he is in the coaching box. (1-14e)

> **EXCEPT**: OFF INTERP 113-135: **PARONTO:** The crew chief will make a determination at the plate conference, depending on the weather, whether to allow base coaches to wear a heavy parka-type jacket while coaching the bases. (email to cc, 11/11/04, detailing an interpretation from early 2004) ✠

OBR: A base coach must be a team member in uniform. (2.00 Base Coach; 4.05b-1)
145. ALSO: The manager is not required to wear a uniform. (2.00 Manager)

> **146. ALSO:** OFF INTERP 114-135: ***(EDITED)*** **WENDELSTEDT:** A base coach may not wear a jacket. (HW/3.2.6c/35) ✠

136 COACH: COACHING BOX: USES CRUTCHES / WHEELCHAIR ✪

FED: Coaches may wear prostheses and use mobility devices. (3-2-1; 3.2.1a, b and c) (See § 510 for the complete list of dangerous items an umpire **MAY WEAR / USE.**)

❀ Note 138: How times change! A FED **POINT OF EMPHASIS** in 1990 read: "Umpires should not allow an injured coach, whose movement is dependent on crutches, a cane, or motorized or manually operated wheelchair to occupy a coach's box." Ah ... for the good ol' days.

NCAA: No provision

OBR: Point not covered.

> OFF INTERP 115-136: **FITZPATRICK:** Each league should adopt its own policy regarding how to deal with the Americans with Disabilities Act. (phone call to cc, 11/8/01) ✠

★ 137 COACH: GUARANTEES LEGALITY OF EQUIPMENT ✪

FED: POE 1987: ***(EDITED)*** The game may not begin until both head coaches have informed the UIC that all players are equipped legally. That official will resolve all questions. (2-10-2; 1-5-10; 4-1-3b; 4.1.3a) **PENALTY:** ***(ADDED)*** First offense: head coach is restricted. Second offense: head coach is ejected. Third offense: designated head coach is ejected. (See especially § 417.)

> ✻ *Play 83-137:* **FED only.** As personnel are attending to an injured catcher, his coach informs the UIC that the young man was not wearing a protective cup: "I knew it, but I didn't think it was necessary," says the coach. *Ruling:* The act is flagrantly unsportsmanlike, and the umpire must **RESTRICT** the coach.

NCAA: ***(REVISED)*** At the pregame meeting the umpire shall "receive confirmation from the head coach or his representative that playing equipment meets NCAA rules and regulations." (4-4c)

OBR: No provision.

138 COACH: INFIELD PRACTICE BEFORE / DURING GAME ✪

FED: POE 2005: Before the game begins: During either team's infield practice, the opponents may not be anywhere in live ball territory except their bullpen. (3-3-1g-5) After the game begins, coaches may not conduct infield or outfield practice. (3-3-1e; 10.2.3b) **PENALTY:** warning / ejection. (3-3-1e Pen) (See § 116.)
147. ALSO: During a charged conference a coach may not throw balls to a substitute outfielder. (3.3.1dd)

NCAA: No provision.

OBR: Point not covered.

> OFF INTERP 116-138: **DEARY:** After the game begins, coaches may not conduct infield or outfield practice. (*REF* 9/82) ✠

139 COACH: TIME CALLED PROMISCUOUSLY ✪

FED: No provision.

NCAA: The umpires shall prohibit the "promiscuous" calling of time by coaches and players when it is an obvious tactic to delay the game. (6-1a Nt 1)

OBR: No provision.

★ 140 COACH: UNSPORTSMANLIKE BEHAVIOR: DEFINED ✪

FED: Coaches shall not exhibit behavior inconsistent with the spirit of fair play. (3-3-1g-4) **PENALTY:** warning/ejection. (3-3-1g Pen)

NCAA: POE 1992, 1993, 1994, 2006: Coaches shall not engage in any "misconduct," defined as "any act of dishonesty, unsportsmanlike conduct or unprofessional behavior that discredits the contest, the institutions or intercollegiate athletics." (2-53) (See § 166 and 246.)
148. ALSO: POE 1994: A coach may not remove his team from the field or refuse to continue play because of a dispute with umpires. (5-15b) **PENALTY:** The coach shall be suspended from his team's next two scheduled contests. (5-15b-Pen)
149. ALSO: The UIC shall report the incident to the athletic director of the offending school, the conference commissioner – if applicable – and the secretary-editor of the NCAA rulebook. (5-15b Pen) (See § 258.)
150. ALSO: Conferences may adopt more stringent penalties. (5-15b)

OBR: The game is forfeited if a team refuses ***(ADDED)*** or is unable to continue play. (4.17) (See § 259.) *See ¶8.*

141 COACH: UNSPORTSMANLIKE BEHAVIOR: EJECTED FOR PLAYER INFRACTION ✪

FED: No provision.

NCAA: Following a warning to both teams, if a pitcher is disqualified for throwing at a batter, the umpire will eject the head coach as well. (9-2g Pen)
151. ALSO: Having ejected a participant for "bench jockeying," if the umpire ejects another member of that team, the head coach is also ejected. (5-17 Pen) (See § 118; 119; 246.)

OBR: Following a warning to both teams, if a pitcher is disqualified for throwing at a batter, his head coach is also ejected. (8.02d-2) (See § 405.)

> **152. ALSO:** OFF INTERP 117-141: **MLBUM:** If a pitcher is ejected for throwing at a batter, the replacement pitcher shall be given sufficient time to warm up. (7.4) ✠

★ 142 COACH: UNSPORTSMANLIKE BEHAVIOR: RESTRICTED TO DUGOUT ✪

FED: POE 2000, 2001, 2002: The umpire may restrict a coach to his dugout for various infractions. (3-3-1g through L; 3.3.1i through m) Following restriction, the coach may come onto the field only to attend an injured player. (3-3-1g through L Pen) If ejected, the coach may return to attend an injured player only "when requested" [by the umpire]. (3-3-2; 3.3.2a, b and c) (See § 163 and 164.)
153. ALSO: PENALTY: A coach who is available but who skips the pregame meeting will be restricted to the dugout. (3-2-4; Website 2008, #15)

> **154. ALSO:** OFF INTERP 118-142: **HOPKINS:** A head coach who is late because he was caught in traffic is not in violation of the rule requiring him to attend the pregame meeting. (Website 2008, #16) ✠

155. ALSO: Restriction is not required as a first step toward ejection: If the umpire judges the infraction serious, he may eject immediately. (3.3.1m)
156. ALSO: The umpire may eject a restricted coach for further misconduct. (3.3.1m)

> **157. ALSO:** OFF INTERP 119-142: **RUMBLE:** A restricted coach may bring players to the dugout for a charged conference. (*News* #14, 3/89) (See § 149, 155 and 156.) ✠

Play 84-142: **FED only.** The coach of the Bobcats is restricted to the dugout. He calls time and brings F1 and F2 to the bench for a charged conference. *Ruling:* Legal.

NCAA: Ejection is the umpire's only resort. (3-6d)

OBR: Same as NCAA 3-6d. (9.01d) ***(ADDED)*** (See § 168, which explains when ejections take effect.) *See ¶8.*

143 COACH: USES AMPLIFIER ✪

FED: A coach may not use an amplifier or bullhorn to communicate with his players during games. (3-3-1L) **PENALTY:** warning or ejection. (3-3-1L Pen)

NCAA: No provision.

OBR: No provision.

★ 144 CONFERENCES: ACCUMULATE ✪

FED: Conferences do not accumulate for use in extra innings. (3-4-1; 3.4.1a) (See § 151 and 155.)

NCAA: ***(EDITED)*** Defensive conferences accumulate. (9-4a AR2) ***(ADDED)*** Unused offensive conferences may be used in extra innings. (6-5f-3) (See § 154 and 155.)

OBR: Not applicable.

❀ Note 139: ***(EDITED)*** Conferences (trips to the mound) are one of nine major rules or interpretations **WHERE EACH LEVEL TREATS THE SITUATION DIFFERENTLY.** The other eight are: § 50 (designated hitter); § 83 (use illegal bat); § 124 (throw from dead-ball area); § 245 (positions occupied at time of pitch or play); § 246 (fighting); § 266 (improperly declared infield fly); § 378 (hidden ball play); § 488 (illegal substitutes).

★ 145 CONFERENCES: CHARGED TO DEFENSE: BETWEEN HALF INNINGS ✪

FED: The coach may stand with his pitcher at the mound between half innings. If his presence creates a delay: **PENALTY:** The umpire "may" charge a conference. (3.4.1h)

NCAA: Point not covered.

> ***(ADDED)*** OFF INTERP 120-145: **PARONTO:** This is now covered with the timed, 90-second count between each half-inning. When the 90- second (or 108-second count for televised contests) expires, a penalty of one ball will be charged to the pitcher. As long as the "conference" does not delay the start of the half-inning, the meeting is allowed. (email to cc, 12/5/11) ✠

OBR: Point not covered.

OFF INTERP 121-145: **DEARY:** Same as FED 3.4.1h. (*REF* 12/85) ✠

PENALTY: OFF INTERP 122-145: **DEARY:** If such a "conference" delays the game: Following the first delay, the umpire should warn the coach that on the next delay he will be charged with a trip to the mound. A team must be warned once per game before the penalty is invoked. (*REF* 12/85) ✠

146 CONFERENCES: CHARGED TO DEFENSE: MULTIPLE: COACHES INSIDE DIAMOND ✪

FED: Coaches or their non-playing representatives may confer with a defensive player or players during a charged conference. (2-10-1; 3-4-1; Website 2007, #4)

158. ALSO: If a defensive coach attends an injured player on the field, the other defensive coach "is free to have a conference" with the pitcher. (3.4.1 e and f)

❀ Note 140: The case book ruling indicates that if the umpire believes a player is faking an injury so that confidential information can be given to anyone in the field, the official may prohibit additional conferences from "taking place at that time."

NCAA: Point not covered.

OFF INTERP 123-146: **FETCHIET:** If two coaches go onto the field during the same conference, each is charged with a conference. (Website 4/20/01) ✠

OBR: Point not covered.

OFF INTERP 124-146: **FITZPATRICK:** Allow only one coach inside the diamond per trip. Do not permit a second conference while the same batter is at bat. (phone call to cc, 11/8/01) ✠

159. ALSO: OFF INTERP 125-146: **FITZPATRICK:** If a pitching change is made, the coach may not then huddle with his defensive players after leaving the mound as that is prohibited by 8.06c). (phone call to cc, 11/8/01) ✠

❊ *Play 85-146:* A pitching coach makes a change. After he leaves the mound, the head coach calls his defense to the foul line to chat while the new pitcher is warming up. *Ruling:* In FED, the conference is legal. In NCAA, charge the defense with two conferences. In OBR, warn the coach he must not engage in that discussion. If he insists on the conference, eject him. When the hitter finishes his at-bat, eject the pitcher as well.

❀ Note 141: Umpires at all levels should make sure that a visit to an "injured" player is not simply a ploy to get confidential information to the mound or infield. If the skipper does begin to "coach" (disregarding the "injury"), charge the defense with a conference or a trip.

147 CONFERENCES: CHARGED TO DEFENSE: MULTIPLE: TRIPS DURING ONE CONFERENCE ✪

FED: Point not covered.

OFF INTERP 126-147: **RUMBLE:** A coach may request time for a conference, confer with one player in one part of the field, and then move to meet with another player as part of the same charged conference. (*News* #41, 4/89) ✠

❀ Note 142: The OFF INTERP isn't needed, though, because of the NFHS provisions outlined in § 150 [when conferences end].

NCAA: No provision

OBR: One coach or manager is permitted during each trip. (8.06a) (See § 150.)

148 CONFERENCES: CIRCUMVENTION BY DEFENSE ✪

FED: Point not covered.

OFF INTERP 127-148: **RUMBLE:** An umpire may charge a conference when the coach approaches the foul line to shout instructions to the defense if the official believes the coach is "conferring" with his players. (*News* #32, 4/86) ✠

160. ALSO: A coach who yells defensive instructions from the dugout is not charged with a conference. (3.4.1i)

NCAA: A coach may not circumvent the charged conference rules, such as but not limited to going near the foul line to confer with the pitcher or a defensive player. (9-4a-2) If a coach talks to a defensive player, that shall be "considered a trip whether the player goes to the mound or not." (9-4a-2 AR 1)

OBR: When a coach or manager confers with a defensive player, a trip is charged only when – before a pitch or intervening play – the player goes to the mound or the pitcher comes to the player. (8.06 CMT) *See ¶8.*

149 CONFERENCES: DEFINITION ✪

FED: A charged conference is a meeting between the coach or his non-playing representative and a player or players. (2-10-1; 3-4-1; 3.4.1d) (See § 146. See also Play 84-142.)

❀ Note 143: **POE 2009**: This is a "pace of the game" problem: Umpires are "encouraged" to speed up these conferences.

NCAA: Same as FED 3-4-1. (6-5e AR)
161. ALSO: It is an "offensive trip" when two offensive coaches delay the game to confer. (6-5f) (See § 156.)

OBR: Not applicable.

❀ Note 144: In FED / NCAA, a defensive conference is not charged when the pitcher is removed. OBR is similar: A skipper who removes his pitcher still has a free trip that inning to the new pitcher. The "removal" visit, then, is not a trip. Moreover, if the manager goes to the mound, removes his pitcher, and remains to talk to the reliever, that is not considered a trip to the new pitcher. (MLBUM 7.12)

★ 150 CONFERENCES: END / BEGIN ✪

FED: (● 1) A defensive conference held in **FAIR TERRITORY** ends when the coach crosses the foul line on his way back to the bench; a defensive conference held in **FOUL TERRITORY** also ends when the coach first starts back to his bench (3-4-3; 3.4.3); (● 2) an offensive conference ends when the coach first starts back to his position (3-4-4; 3.4.4); (● 3) a conference between a restricted coach and a player or players ends when **ANY PLAYER** starts back to his position. The umpire shall allow a "reasonable" amount of time for any conference (3-4-4), but he may inform a coach that his "time is up." (3.4.3)

NCAA: A conference, which may include a meeting with infielders, begins when the coach crosses the foul line. It ends when the coach leaves the dirt circle or the pitcher begins his eight warm-up pitches. (9-4d)

❀ Note 145: The book gives no guidelines for what action ends an **OFFENSIVE** conference. BRD recommends: Use the FED regulation.

OBR: A trip to the mound ends when the coach leaves the 18-foot circle at the mound. (8.06) (See § 147.)

> **162. ALSO:** OFF INTERP 128-150: **PBUC:** When the manager or coach leaves the 18-foot circle surrounding the pitcher's plate, "he must keep going and not return to the mound." {8.12} ❀

❀ Note 146: Perhaps you remember the Don Mattingly incident when he stepped off the mound and returned to answer an infielder's question. His bad! The umpiring crew forced the Dodgers to replace the pitcher. Their bad!! You can read what should have been done by going to § 152 or MLBcenter.com.
http://www.mlbcenter.com/articles/2010-mlb/dodgers-giants-recp_072210.html

163. ALSO: OFF INTERP 129-150: ***(EDITED)*** **WENDELSTEDT:** "If the manager and pitcher attempt to confer while off the mound area, the umpire should instruct them to continue their conference within the 18-foot dirt circle. (HW/50) ✠

151 CONFERENCES: EXCESSIVE: PITCHER REMOVED FROM MOUND ✪

FED: (● 1) After three charged conferences during regulation play, the pitcher must be replaced as pitcher for the remainder of regulation play **EACH TIME** the coach confers with any defensive player. (● 2) On the second (and each successive) charged conference in any extra inning, the pitcher must be replaced as pitcher for the remainder of the game. (● 3) In either case, the pitcher may remain in the game. If he leaves, he may re-enter later at a non-pitching position if he has not previously left the game. (3-4-1; 3-4-1 Pen; 3.4.1c) (See § 158.)

NCAA: (● 1) After three charged conferences during regulation play: Same as FED 3-3-01 in regulation play. (9-4a) **EXCEPT:** (● 2) After the second charged conference in any half inning: Same as OBR 8.06b. (9-4b) **164. ALSO:** If extra innings are played, a team is entitled to one additional charged conference for the remainder of the game, regardless of how many innings (9-4a), but unused conferences from the regulation portion of the game **ACCUMULATE.** (9-4a AR2) (See § 155 and 158.)

❀ Note 147: BRD recommends: Warn a coach before he uses his "excessive" conference. After all, by rule the umpire is required to warn the coach when he has used his last **OFFENSIVE** conference. (6-5f-2)

✻ *Play 86-151* Part one: **FED and NCAA only.** Two simultaneous games are played on adjoining fields. At the end of regulation play, Coach Vasquez (FED) has used three conferences and Coach Neeley (NCAA) has used two. In the first extra inning each coach visits Bubba, the pitcher. Bubba stays in the game. In that same inning each coach visits the mound a second time. *Ruling:* In FED, Coach Vasquez must remove Bubba; he already used his free trip that inning. So Vasquez puts Scott on the mound. In NCAA, Bubba is also finished (because of the second trip in one inning), but it is only the third conference in the game for Coach Neeley, who also sends in Scott.

Part two: **FED and NCAA only**. In the same inning, both coaches visit the mound a third time. *Ruling:* In FED, Vasquez must remove Scott even though it is his first visit to that pitcher. (Vasquez has already used his free trip. He gets another free trip in the next inning.) In NCAA, Scott may stay. But every time Neeley visits the mound for the remainder of the game, his pitcher must be removed.

❀ Note 148: If Vasquez or Neeley was coaching in an OBR game, Scott would get to stay, for it would be the coach's first trip to that pitcher in that inning.

OBR: The pitcher must leave the mound when the manager makes a second trip in the same half inning. (8.06b) *See ¶8.*

> **165. ALSO:** OFF INTERP 130-151: **PBUC:** On the second trip in a half inning, the pitcher must be removed "FROM THE GAME." {8.12} *See ¶8.* ✠

> **166. ALSO:** OFF INTERP 131-151: **PBUC:** "If a rain delay occurs during a manager's or coach's trip to the mound (or after the trip but while the same batter is still at bat), a new pitcher may be substituted when the game is resumed following the rain delay." {8.12} ✠

❀ Note 149: Amateur coaches and players using OBR rules are sometimes unaware of OFF INTERP 130 [this section] though the interpretation should be the standard for all games played under OBR rules. BRD strongly recommends: Discuss the provision at the pregame meeting unless you are certain both teams understand the rule.

❊ *Play 87-151:* The coach sprints to the mound and – because of some rule – is required to remove his pitcher. *Ruling:* At all levels the pitcher is barred from returning to pitch. In FED / NCAA, he may remain as a fielder (or in NCAA as the DH). In OBR, the pitcher must leave the game. (Naturally, *See* ¶ *8.*)

❊ *Play 88-151:* **FED and NCAA only.** After the first pitch in the top of the seventh, the coach goes to the mound. It is discovered he is taking his fourth charged conference. *Ruling:* The pitcher is finished as pitcher in that game.

152 CONFERENCES: ILLEGAL: SAME BATTER ✪

FED: Not applicable.

NCAA: A coach may not make a second trip to the mound in the same half inning with the same player at bat. However, if a pinch-hitter enters the game after the coach's "free" trip, the coach may make a second trip but he must remove the pitcher from the mound. (9-4c) **EXCEPT:** If the pitcher has not faced one batter: When the offense pinch bats, the coach may go to the mound if he has a "free" trip available and if it is not his second trip to that pitcher. (9-4c) (See § 49; 147; 151; 153; 496.)

> ⁕ *Play 89-152:* **NCAA only.** Having been charged with no conferences, Coach Vasquez brings Parker to pitch in the sixth. Parker immediately walks the first batter he faces. Long-suffering Vasquez returns to the mound to discuss the falling NASDAQ. Bubba steps up to hit and promptly swings at two pitches over his head. The offensive coach next sends Scott to pinch hit — with two strikes. Coach Vasquez now wants to go back to the mound to replace Parker. *Ruling:* Vasquez may return because of the pinch hitter for Bubba. Parker may not return to pitch in that contest. (See Play 90-153.)

OBR: Same as NCAA. **EXCEPT:** The coach / manager has no "free" trips: On the second visit, the pitcher must leave the game. (8.06c) (See § 49; 147; 151; 153; 496.)

153 CONFERENCES: ILLEGAL: SUBSTITUTE PITCHER ✪

FED: The umpire will not allow a defensive conference if it causes the removal of a pitcher who has not complied with the pitching-substitution rule. (3-1-2) (See § 496.)

> ❀ Note 150: No penalty is listed for a coach who insists on illegally going to the mound. The umpire's only recourse would be restriction to the dugout or ejection.

NCAA: Point not covered.

OFF INTERP 132-153: **THURSTON:** Same as FED 3-1-2, with additions below. (phone call to se, 11/89) ✠

INTENTIONALLY ILLEGAL CONFERENCE: If the coach insists on making an illegal trip, he is ejected. When the current hitter completes his at bat, F1 is also ejected.

> ❀ Note 151: NCAA 9-4c-3 provides an identical penalty, but it is reserved for those times when the coach insists on a conference while the **SAME BATTER** is at the plate. (See § 49.)

OBR: Same as FED. (3.05c CMT) (See § 494 and 496.)

> ⁕ *Play 90-153:* **NCAA and OBR only.** Bubba gives up his fifth hit in a row, and his coach goes to the mound, later signaling for reliever Poe. Hemingway is scheduled to bat, but Faulkner is announced as a pinch hitter. *Ruling:* In NCAA, the coach may return unless he has already been charged with three

conferences, when the umpire will not allow the trip. If the skipper crosses the foul line in spite of a warning, he is ejected. Poe also will be history as soon as Faulkner completes his at bat. If all free trips have been used and the umpire erroneously allows the visit, Poe will pitch to Faulkner and then he is removed from the mound for the remainder of the game; the coach gets to stay. In OBR, since that is the coach / manager's first trip to Poe (the meeting when Bubba was relieved does not count as a trip) the visit is legal. (See Play 89-152.)

154 CONFERENCES: NOT CHARGED WHEN OPPONENTS CALL TIME ✪

FED: If one team calls time, during that conference the opposing coach, whether on offense or defense, may confer with his players without being charged a conference as long as the meeting ends about the same time as the other team's charged conference. (3-4-5; 3.4.1b)

> **167. ALSO:** OFF INTERP 133-154: **RUMBLE:** While the umpire is dusting the plate or the catcher meeting with the pitcher, if the offensive coach visits with a player without delaying the game, no conference is charged. (*REF* 10/85) (See § 156.) ✠

NCAA: If a **DEFENSIVE** coach requests time and is charged with a conference, the opposing team is not charged with an offensive conference unless they delay the game. (6-5f-4)

> **168. ALSO:** OFF INTERP 134-154: **THURSTON:** If the *defense* confers during a charged offensive conference, the defense is still charged with a conference. (phone call to se, 11/9/90) ✠

169. ALSO: During a "prolonged injury timeout," a meeting anywhere, even at the mound, between pitcher and coach is not a trip unless the meeting causes further delay. (9-4a AR 4)

OBR: Point not covered.

> OFF INTERP 135-154: **PBUC STAFF:** Same as NCAA OFF INTERP 134 [this section]. (email to cc, 12/15/00; affirmed, phone call to cc, 11/8/01) ✠

✻ *Play 91-154:* The third-base coach signals for time to talk to B1. As they meet between home and third, the defensive coach hustles out to chat **BRIEFLY** with his pitcher. The two conversations break up about the same time. *Ruling:* In FED, do not charge the defense with a conference; rather, the conference is charged to the offense. In NCAA / OBR, it is a charged defensive conference or trip to the mound. In NCAA, it is also an offensive trip: two for the price of one.

155 CONFERENCES: NUMBER ALLOWED: DEFENSE ✪

FED: A coach, without penalty, may have three charged conferences per game, with one per inning in an extra-inning contest. (3-4-1) (See § 144, 151 and 159.)

> **170. ALSO:** OFF INTERP 136-155: **RUMBLE:** After having batted, if a team huddles together before taking the field, the umpire should warn the team that on any subsequent "huddle," the coach will be charged with a conference. (*News*#32, 4/81) ✠

NCAA: The coach has three charged conferences plus one for the entire extra-inning period. (9-4a) (See § 144 and 151.)

OBR: Not applicable. *See ¶8.*

❀ Note 152: In games played under a time limit, such as USSSA youth games, BRD recommends using the FED OFF INTERP 136 [this section] to hurry the defense onto the field.

156 CONFERENCES: NUMBER ALLOWED: OFFENSE ✪

FED: The offense may have one charged conference per inning. The umpire will deny any subsequent request for a conference. (3-4-2) (See § 146.)

NCAA: The offense may have three free conferences per game, with one additional conference for the duration of any extra innings. Conferences accumulate. (See § 144.) An offensive "trip" is charged each time a coach delays the game or requests time to talk to offensive personnel, whether hitter, runner, on-deck batter, or another coach. (6-5f)

❀ Note 153: Bravo for the college half of Indianapolis. Defensive / offensive conferences are treated the same. Bravo, I say again!

171. ALSO: The umpire will warn a coach when he has completed his maximum number of offensive trips. (6-5f-2)

PENALTY: (● 1) If the coach persists in an illegal offensive conference, the player involved is ejected. (● 2) When two offensive coaches confer during an "excess" offensive trip, the assistant coach must be removed from the game. (6-5f-2 Pen) (See § 149; 154 and 159.)

❀ Note 154: BRD recommends: Warn the defensive coach before he uses his last visit.

> **172. ALSO:** OFF INTERP 137-156: **THURSTON:** If two players are involved in the same "excess" offensive trip, the coach will decide which one of the players must leave the game. (NCAA MTG, 11/8/92) ✠

173. ALSO: When an offensive substitute enters the game, do not charge an offensive trip even if team members confer. (6-5f-5)

OBR: No provision.

157 CONFERENCES: PLAYER-MANAGER OR PLAYER-COACH VISITS MOUND ✪

FED: Not applicable.

NCAA: Not applicable.

OBR: Point not covered.

OFF INTERP 138-157: **PBUC:** If a **PLAYER-MANAGER** goes to the mound, the umpire shall always charge a trip to the mound. {8.12} (See § 155.) ✠

174. ALSO: OFF INTERP 139-157: **PBUC:** If a **PLAYER-COACH** makes a trip to the mound, it is a trip by a **PLAYER** unless the umpire judges the player-coach is abusing that privilege, when he will inform the player-coach that the next visit will be charged as a trip to the mound. {8.12} ✠

158 CONFERENCES: PITCHER REMOVED WITHOUT CONFERENCE ✪

FED: A coach with three charged conferences may remove his pitcher without going to the mound. If no other rule impinges, such as a limitation of innings pitched or player being withdrawn a second time, the pitcher may return to the mound in that contest. (3.4.1g)

❀ Note 155: The case book ruling points out that "no conversation" between coach and players may occur during the switch. The purpose of the limitation of conferences is to prevent a team from unduly delaying the game. Whether the coach has his "fourth conference" on the mound or at home plate, it still results in delay. The NCAA/OBR sensibly treat a "trip" as a trip, wherever it takes place.

NCAA: After having been charged with a trip to the mound in an inning or having been charged with three trips in a non-extra-inning game, if the coach goes to the umpire to make a pitching change, that shall constitute an excessive trip, which shall be charged when the umpire enters it on the official lineup card. The pitcher, if he remains in the game, may not return to pitch in that contest. (9-4b AR 1)

❀ Note 156: One can only surmise that the purpose of charging the conference only after it is recorded is to give the coach time to change his mind.

OBR: Point not covered.

OFF INTERP 140-158: **FITZPATRICK:** The pitcher is removed from the game if the coach, conferring with the umpire, has already been once to the mound in that half inning. (phone call to CC, 11/9/00) ✠

159 CONFERENCES: UMPIRE RECORDS TRIPS ✪

FED: The umpire is required to keep a record of all charged defensive and offensive conferences and notify the coach each time a conference is charged. (10-2-3j) (See § 155.)

NCAA: The umpire is required to keep a record of "offensive" conferences and to notify the coach when each is charged. (6-5f-1)
175. ALSO: The umpire will record each free trip (defensive conference) and the inning it occurred. (9-4a Nt) (See § 155 and 156.)

OBR: Not applicable.

★ 160 DEAD BALL IMMEDIATE: BALL BECOMES ALIVE ✪

(See § 161.)

FED: After a dead ball, the ball becomes alive when: (• 1) the pitcher has it while assuming a legal pitching position on the pitcher's plate; (• 2) the batter and the catcher are in their proper positions; and (• 3) the umpire calls "Play" and gives the appropriate. (5-1-4)

NCAA: The ball is put in play hand signal when the pitcher has the ball on the pitcher's plate, the batter is in his box, and the umpire calls or signals "Play." (6-6)

OBR: The ball is put in play when the pitcher has a ball on the pitcher's plate and the plate umpire calls "Play." (5.11)
176. ALSO: The umpire shall call play "as soon as" the pitcher takes his place on the pitcher's plate with the ball. (5.11)

EXCEPT: OFF INTERP 141-160: **PBUC:** The umpire may not declare the ball alive unless a batter is in the box. {6.17} ✠

❀ Note 157: The "contradiction" above [ball alive when pitcher takes the mound or ball alive when batter is in the box] is one of those frequent occurrences in OBR rules where a **MODERN INTERPRETATION** has superseded an **OLDER RULE.** That event just drives some untutored umpires to drink. (And their choice of drink ain't Dr Pepper.) BRD recommends: Always adopt the most current, "official" ruling. The professional rules committee prefers not to deal with the players' union, which has the right to veto any rule change. So, instead of a change in language, the committee simply changes the instructions to the umpires. That's enough said about this.

★ 161 DEAD BALL IMMEDIATE: DO NOT PITCH SIGNAL ✪
(See § 160.)

FED: The FED book depicts a "Do not pitch" signal: right arm out, fingers pointing up, palm toward pitcher. The ball is dead. (5-1-1h; Signals A; casebook New Play 12, 1992 ed) (See § 341.)

NCAA: Same as FED 5-1-1h. (6-5h) (See § 160.)

OBR: Point not covered.

> OFF INTERP 142-161: **DEARY:** The ball is dead when the umpire raises his hand in the "Do not pitch" signal. (*REF* 2/88) ✠

> **177. ALSO:** OFF INTERP 143-161: **FITZPATRICK:** To make the ball alive, the procedure is the same as in NCAA. ✠ (email to cc, 11/15/00)

❀ Note 158: Knowing this AO might help you in a protest situation. R1: There has been a dead ball. The pitcher is ready, you are ready, and B1 is in the box — looking down with **HIS** hand raised. Suddenly the pitcher picks off R1. It's your decision whether R1 is back in the dugout or stays on the base.

162 DEAD BALL IMMEDIATE: HALF INNING CAUSES
ALL CODES NOW AGREE: TEXT DELETED, 1996.

★ 163 EJECTION: COACH ✪

FED: An ejected coach must leave the "vicinity of the playing area and is prohibited from further contact, direct or indirect, with his players." **EXCEPT:** He may return to attend an injured player "when requested [to do so by the umpire]." (3-3-2; 3.3.2a, b and c) (See § 142.)

❀ Note 159: State associations should have rules that supersede the FED to ensure high school players remain under adult supervision. (See OFF INTERP • 145-164.)

NCAA: Same as FED. (3-6d AR2) **EXCEPT:** May a coach return to care for an injured player? **Point not covered.**

> ***(ADDED)*** OFF INTERP 144-163: **PARONTO:** An ejected coach may take no further part in the game; *i.e.*, same as OBR. (email to cc, 12/19/11) ✠

OBR: An ejected coach / manager shall "leave the field and take no further part in that game." (4.07)

❀ Note 160: Interestingly enough, the book does not prohibit "communication."

★ 164 EJECTION: PLAYER PARTICIPANTS LEAVE FIELD AFTER ✪

FED: Ejected participants must leave the game. (3-3-1g through q Pen)

178. ALSO: POE 1989: They should remain "in the team's dugout or elsewhere under the direct personal supervision of the coach." (See § 116, 163 and 515.)

> **179. ALSO:** OFF INTERP 145-164: **RUMBLE:** State associations are responsible for setting guidelines that dictate where game participants go after ejection. (*News*#42, 4/88) ✠

❀ Note 161-164: The umpire may "restrict" a player to the dugout (3-3-1 g through L), but that is tantamount to ejection. If you live in a state where ejected players are suspended, you may want to restrict since it has the same "calming" effect. (But see Note 168-167.)

> **180. ALSO:** OFF INTERP 146-164: **RUMBLE:** A coach must immediately announce the name of a substitute for an ejected player. (*News*#4, 3/90) (See § 489.) ✠

❀ Note 162: The name of the team member replacing an ejected player is needed for forfeit purposes: Does the offending team have an eligible substitute? (See § 488.) Since teams may play with eight players (§ 259), it is important to obtain the substitute's name and thereby insure that the team is not continuing with **SEVEN** players, pending a late arrival..

NCAA: Ejected players "must be removed from sight and sound of the contest." (3-6d AR2) Sight and sound is defined as: The ejected participant cannot (● 1) view the contest; (● 2) communicate with his team; or (● 3) be where the umpires might hear him. "He must have left the confines of the playing field and the grandstands." (3-6d AR2) The ejected person may not "return to the dugout, field or grandstands until the umpiring crew has been escorted to its dressing area by security or game management." (3-6d AR 3) **PENALTY:** Failure to abide by the rules of ejection: The offender is suspended for one game. (3-6d AR 2/3 Pen)

(ADDED) **181. ALSO:** The game will be suspended until the "order of removal" is obeyed. (5-12f) (See § 116.)

❀ Note 163: You gotta love the NCAA. They are quite meticulous in the writing of their rules. They admit that after the ejected person is banished, "it may still be possible for [him] to be able to hear the sounds of the game." In other words, the umpire crew doesn't need to follow him to Elba to be sure he's so far away that he can't hear the base umpire scream: "That's a balk!"

182. ALSO: If game management cannot restore order, "the game will be suspended until order is restored." (3-6d AR 4 Pen)

183. ALSO: OFF INTERP 147-164: **THURSTON:** Ejected team members may not be in the dugout, bullpen, press box, or in any area near other team representatives. The prohibition includes any dead-ball area identified as an "extended dugout." (phone call to se, 11/9/89) (See § 231.) ✠

184. ALSO: If a person is ejected and suspended in the first game of a double-header, he must serve the suspension in the second game. (3-6d AR5 Pen)

OBR: Ejected participants may "take no further part in the game" nor may they wear uniforms while sitting in the stands, ***(EDITED)*** where "they must be well removed" from their teams' dugout or bullpen. (4.07) (See § 163 and 248.) *See ¶8.*

❀ Note 164: In NCAA, the umpire should require the name of a substitute for an ejected player as stipulated in FED OFF INTERP 146 [this section]. In OBR, the name is needed only if the team is on defense. (See § 259.)

★ 165 EJECTION: POST-GAME ✪

FED: No provision.

NCAA: (● 1) "If a situation occurs after the last out to end a game and this conduct would result in an ejection during the normal course of play, the umpire / crew chief will issue a postgame ejection." (● 2) "If the ejected person is an assistant coach, player or other team personnel, the umpire / crew chief is to inform the head coach personally or through the home team game management administrator on site." (● 3) "If the head coach is ejected, the umpire / crew chief is to inform the head coach and the home team game management administrator of the head coach's postgame ejection." ***(EDITED)*** ~~(● 4) "If a pitcher receives a post-game ejection for unsportsmanlike actions, the pitcher will receive a four-game suspension."~~ (● 4) The ejecting umpire shall file a suspension report with the conference administrator, coordinator and NCAA secretary-rules editor noting that the ejection shall be served in that team's next scheduled contest." (Appendix D) (See § 246 and 515.)

(ADDED) ❀ Note 165: The material crossed out above was deleted from Appendix D in 2007. I missed it even though it was an announced editorial change. As the players say: "My bad."

❀ Note 166: From the actions of the NCAA rules committee, one would think that NCAA baseball is like the Afghani war zone. Umpires now have the right to suspend participants from up-coming games. That's a throwback to the turn of the 19th century when professional umpires could also fine a player or manager. The NCAA's fight rule is **THREE TIMES AS LONG** as Cartwright's original rulebook that started the whole affair. There's Appendix D, quoted above, with just one main idea: How you should handle an ejection **AFTER** the game is over. As my grandson asks: "What up with that?"

OBR: No provision.

166 EJECTION: REASONS FOR ✪

FED: Umpires disqualify participants for: (● 1) objecting to decisions; (● 2) unsportsmanlike conduct; and (● 3) infractions where ejection is dictated by the rules. (10-1-6; 10-3-1) (See § 164.)

NCAA: Umpires eject participants for violations of the Coaches' and Players' Codes of Ethics. (3-6d) (See § 164 for the penalty provisions. (See also § 246.)
185. ALSO: Conferences may add additional penalties [beyond the simple ejection]. (3-6d)
186. ALSO: Umpires must file an ejection report with the offending team's athletic director. If the school involved is a member of a conference, the conference administrator must also be informed. (2-25) (See § 423.)
187. ALSO: If an ejection results in a suspension, the umpire must file a second report with the "conference administrator, coordinator and NCAA secretary-rules editor." (Appendix D-4)

OBR: Same as FED with the addition of "unsportsmanlike language" as cause for ejection. (9.01d)

167 EJECTION: SUSPENSION RESTRICTIONS ✪

FED: No provision.

NCAA: Suspended personnel may not (● 1) be dressed in game uniform; (● 2) interact with umpires; (● 3) communicate with teammates or work out with the team at the game site; or (● d) be in the stadium once pregame activities start. (Appendix D-4a-d) (See § 165.)

❀ Note 167: Though it is not the umpire's duty to enforce the above restrictions, if he doesn't know them, he can't take action when a suspended player violates them.

188. ALSO: If a player cannot serve a suspension during the current season, it shall be served at the beginning of the "official NCAA spring season." (2-73)

OBR: No provision.

❀ Note 168-167: Some states (FED) and youth leagues (OBR) have adopted rules concerning a one- or two-game suspension penalty for any ejected participant. That's administrative action, not connected with umpiring. Jon Bible agrees with my assessment: "If you gotta eject, don't worry about other consequences." (TASO meeting, 15 January, 2011.) (But see Note 161-164.)

168 EJECTION: TAKES EFFECT ONLY AFTER DEAD BALL ✪

FED: Ejections and warnings shall be made "at the end of playing action." (10-1-6; 3.3.1a; 3.3.1d)

NCAA: If conduct on the last play of a game warrants an ejection, the umpire may issue a "postgame ejection." He must inform the appropriate game management administrators as well as his assignor or supervisor. Conferences may adopt further penalties. (Appendix D) Concerning when an ejection takes effect: Treat as in FED.

OBR: Same as FED 10-1-6. **EXCEPT:** No provision exists for warnings since umpires do not officially warn in OBR play except when they suspect a beanball war (pitchers throwing at batters). (9.01d) (See § 405.)

★ 169 EQUIPMENT: BASEBALLS: APPROVED ✪

FED: Only baseballs with the NFHS "authenticating mark" are legal. (1-3-1) ***(ADDED)*** A list of all NFHS "authenticated products" is available at the FED Website, www.nfhs.org (See § 176 for a very important "difference.")

189. ALSO: OFF INTERP 148-169: **RUMBLE:** The umpire should play a scheduled game even if there are no authenticated baseballs available and then report the game to the state association. (*News* #20, 3/99) (See § 227, for another example of the FED's insistence that scheduled games go forward, regardless of illegalities.) ✠

NCAA: No provision. (See § 171.)

(ADDED) ❀ Note 169: From 1987-1999, the official ball for NCAA tournament play was the "raised-seam Wilson A1001." From 2000-2004 the official ball was the "raised-seam, Rawlings R1-

NCAA." Beginning in 2005, the music died; that is, the endorsements ran out.

OBR: No provision covers OFFICIAL baseballs. Specifications for any legal ball do exist. (1.09) (See § 171.)

∞ 170 EQUIPMENT: BASEBALLS: BALL COMES APART DURING PLAY ✪

FED: No provision. Treat as in NCAA.

NCAA: If a live ball partially comes apart during play, it remains alive "until action is completed." (6-1g)

OBR: Same as NCAA. (5.02 CMT)

★ 171 EQUIPMENT: BASEBALLS: COMPOSITION AND SIZE ✪

FED: The baseball ***(EDITED)*** shall be a sphere with yarn wound around a core of cork, rubber, or "similar material." The circumference must be 9 to 9¼ inches. The "coefficient of restitution" (COR) cannot exceed .555. (1-3-1)

NCAA: The baseball may be 9 to 9½ inches in circumference with yarn wound around a core of cork, rubber, or "combination of both." The coefficient of restitution (COR) cannot exceed .555. (1-11) (See § 169.)

❀ Note 170: The college baseball can be LARGER than the FED or OBR balls. In 1985 NCAA read "9¼" as did all baseball rulebooks. Since 1986 NCAA has read "9½." 'Fess up now: Did you know that? Something else you might not know: See § 204.

OBR: Same as FED 1.11. (1.09) ***(ADDED)*** **EXCEPT:** There is no provision concerning a coefficient of restitution. (1.09)

★ 172 EQUIPMENT: BASEBALLS: NUMBER REQUIRED FOR GAME ✪

FED: The home team, ***(ADDED)*** or home team management in tournaments, must provide at least 3 umpire-approved baseballs with which to start and no fewer than 2 to finish the game. (1-3-1; 1.3.1)

NCAA: The home team must provide at least 12 baseballs. (4-1b) Enough balls should be provided so that a "glossy" ball need never be used in the game. "Moistened river silt" is recommended as the rubbing compound. (1-11a)

OBR: The home team must provide 12 "reserve" baseballs. (3.01d)
190. ALSO: The umpire is responsible for inspecting the baseballs to ensure they are regulation and properly rubbed up. (3.01c)

173 EQUIPMENT: BASES: COMPOSITION AND SIZE ✪

FED: Bases, with or without tapered edges, may be of white canvas, synthetic material, or molded rubber, 2 to 5 inches thick. The material inside must be "soft." (1-2-9)

NCAA: Bases may be of white canvas or suitable rubberized material, 3 to 5 inches thick. (1-7)

OBR: Bases may be of white canvas or rubber-covered bags, 3 to 5 inches thick. (1.06)

174 EQUIPMENT: BASES: MAGNETIC ✪

FED: Magnetic, breakaway bases [bases designed to "disengage their anchor systems"] are legal. (1-2-9)

NCAA: Same as FED, but the base is called a "release-type base." (1-7a) If such a base is dislodged, the point nearest the engagement anchor is considered the base. (1-7 AR)

OBR: The breakaway base is not legal. (1.06) *See ¶8.*

★ 175 EQUIPMENT: BASES: SAFETY ✪

FED: By state association adoption only: The safe-base (a double-sized base, ***(EDITED)*** white with an orange extension into foul territory, may be used as first base. (1-2-9; 1.2.9a and b)

> **191. ALSO:** OFF INTERP 149-175: **RUMBLE:** State associations may set guidelines for using the safe-base. (*News* #2, 3/99)❀

❀ Note 171: Situation 1.2.9a and Suggested Double First Base Rules (following Speed-up Rules) offer some minimal guidelines for dealing with the safe-base, an innovation largely ignored by the baseball world.

NCAA: The "safe base" may be used during the "regular" season only. (1-7b)

OBR: The safe-base is not legal. (1.06) *See ¶8.*

176 EQUIPMENT: BATS: APPROVED ✪

FED: No provisions. (See § 169 and 184.)

NCAA: POE 1990 [bats - legal / illegal]: Bats, except those of one-piece solid wood must undergo the NCAA certification process. (1-12a) (See § 181 and 188.)

OBR: Point not covered.

> OFF INTERP 150-176: **PBUC:** The umpire will penalize a player using an unapproved bat as if it was illegal for pine tar; *i.e.*, the bat is removed but the batter is not out or ejected. {3.8; 3.9} ✠

177 EQUIPMENT: BATS: COLORED ✪

FED: No provision.

NCAA: No provision.

OBR: Colored bats are illegal unless approved by the rules committee. (1.10d)

★ 178 EQUIPMENT: BATS: CUPPED ✪

FED: Point not covered.

> ***(ADDED)*** OFF INTERP 151-178: **MCNEELY:** Cupped bats are legal. (email to cc, 1/22/12) ✠

NCAA: A wooden bat may be cupped to a maximum depth of 1 inch. (1-12a)

OBR: A bat cupped more than 1 inch deep and 2 inches wide, or less than 1 inch in diameter, is illegal. The indentation must be free of right angles with no foreign substance added. (1.10b)

179 EQUIPMENT: BATS: IDENTIFICATION MARK REQUIRED ✪

FED: No provision.

NCAA: An 18-inch identification mark is mandatory. (1-12a; 1-12c)

OBR: No provision.

★ 180 EQUIPMENT: BATS: ILLEGAL WRAPPING ✪

FED: Any wrapping that makes the bat handle flush with the knob end creates an illegal bat. (1-3-2b-1; 1.3.5a, 1990 ed) **PENALTY:** The batter is out if the bat is detected while he is in the box. If the batter hits with the bat, the defense on appeal may take the result of the play or the penalty (batter is out). (7-4-1a; 7.4.1d) (See § 82 and 83.)

NCAA: Point not covered.

> ***(ADDED)*** OFF INTERP 152-180: **PARONTO:** Any wrapping that makes the bat handle flush with the knob creates an illegal bat. **PENALTY:** (1) batter attempts to use: See § 82; (2) batter uses: See § 83. (email to cc, 12/19/11) ✠

OBR: No provision.

★ 181 EQUIPMENT: BATS: MATERIALS MADE OF ✪

FED: Bats may be wood, aluminum, or composite. (1-3-2a) All graphite-composite bats are approved for use. (1.3.2b) Graphite-Kevlar, graphite-ceramic, ***(ADDED)*** bamboo, and fiberglass-boron are listed as examples of legal composites as are titanium and cryogenic bats. (1.3.2c, 2011 ed) (See § 184.)

NCAA: ***(ADDED)*** To be legal, a bat must display the NCAA seal of approval. (1-12b-6)

(ADDED) ❀ Note 172: Paronto: "Because of 1-12b-6, there should be no need to list all types of materials used in non-wood bats." (email to cc, 12/19/11)

OBR: Not applicable.

★ 182 EQUIPMENT: BATS: NON-WOOD: ILLEGAL ✪

(See § 82 and 83.)

FED: ***(EDITED)*** Bats that are altered from the manufacturer's original design or that do not meet the rule specifications are illegal. **POE 2002, 2012**: Remove without penalty any broken, cracked, or dented bats as well as any that deface the ball. No foreign substance may be inserted into the bat. (1-3-5) Pine tar or other foreign substance may not be added to the bat farther than 18 inches from the knob end. (1-3-3)

> **192. ALSO:** ***(CHANGED)*** "No artificial or intentional means shall be used to control the temperature of the bat." (1-3-5; 1.3.5f; Website 2012 #3)
> Last edition: No provision.

(ADDED) ❀ Note 173: The performance of a non-wood bat deteriorates as the temperature drops. FED doesn't want someone sticking his bat into a hot bath when the temperature on the field is45 degrees.

193. ALSO: *(CHANGED)* A wood-composite bat is a non-wood bat and is therefore subject to the standards of BBCOR. BESR bats are no longer legal. (1.3.2d, 2011 ed)

> *(ADDED)* OFF INTERP 153-182: **HOPKINS:** A bat with both the BESR and BBCOR labels is legal. (Website 2012, #1) ✠

194. ALSO: Removing a bat from play because it appears to have smudged a ball is entirely within the purview of the UIC. If he does declare the bat illegal, there is no penalty. (1.3.5a 2010 ed.)

NCAA: Non-wood bats that are altered or do not display the approved certification mark are illegal. Bats that are not marked 18 inches from the knob or deface the ball are merely removed from the game without penalty. (1-12a and b Pen)

OBR: Not applicable. *See ¶8.*

183 EQUIPMENT: BATS: NON-WOOD: KNOBS / END CAPS ✪

FED: Knobs must be permanently and securely fastened. (1-3-2b-1) **PENALTY:** See § 180. (See § 82, 83 and 218.)

195. ALSO: "Molded" grips are legal, as are knobs that are lathed, welded, or permanently fastened. (1-3-2b-1) (See § 185.)

196. ALSO: The end cap is made of rubber, vinyl, plastic or other approved material. It must be securely fastened so that only the manufacturer can remove it without damaging or destroying it. By definition, a one-piece construction bat does not have an end cap. (1-3-2b-5)

NCAA: Knobs and end plugs must be firmly attached. (1-12b-4) **PENALTY:** None listed. (1-12 Pen)

197. ALSO: A bat with a loose handle is removed from the game. **PENALTY:** If use of the bat is continued, the batter currently using the bat is ejected. No one may be called out. (1-12c Pen) (See § 83.)

OBR: Not applicable.

★ 184 EQUIPMENT: BATS: NON-WOOD: LEGAL✪

FED: ***(CHANGED)***Non-wood (aluminum, bamboo, composite, fiberglass, titanium) bats are legal. (See § 181.) The maximum length is 36 inches; the maximum diameter, 2 ⅝ inches. The bat shall not weigh, numerically, more than 3 ounces less than the length of the bat. A 33-inch bat may not weigh less than 30 ounces. (1-3-2c-2 and 3; 1.3.2a, b and c; 1.3.5b)
Last edition: The underlined materials above were not in the rules.

198. ALSO: A bat with "manufactured holes or ridges in the taper of the bat" is legal." (1.3.2c) As of January 1, 2012, all bats "not made of a single piece of wood" must meet the Batted Ball Coefficient of Restitution (BBCOR). ***(ADDED)*** "No BBCOR label or sticker or decal will be accepted on any non-wood bat." The BBCOR standard must be signified by a "silkscreen or other permanent certification mark." (1-3-2d; 1.3.2f)

199. ALSO: The mark must be "rectangular, a minimum of one inch on each side and located on the barrel of the bat in any contrasting color to read: ***(CHANGED)*** 'BBCOR .50.'" (1-3-2d) Last edition: BBCOR .50 was not required on the label. **EXCEPT:**

(ADDED) OFF INTERP 154-184: **HOPKINS:** A BBCOR bat with a certification mark that measures 1¼ by ½ inch does not make the bat illegal. "The key point is that the bat is a legal BBCOR bat and does have a certification mark. (Website 2012, #2) ✠

200. ALSO: ***(CHANGED)*** The NFHS "will work with appropriate parties to research and develop a baseball bat tamper-evident protocol." It will be presented to the Committee in 2012, with any action to become the rule for bats manufactured at January 1, 2015." (1-3-2d Nt) Last edition: No provision.

201. ALSO: OFF INTERP 155-184: **RUMBLE:** The scandium and multiple wall bats are legal. (*News* #4 and #7, 3/99) (See § 82; 83; 181; 188; 218.) ✠

NCAA: Non-wood bats may be used. The entire bat must be round, with a constant radius at any point, and the hitting area must be smooth. (1-12b)

202. ALSO: The maximum length of a non-wood bat is 36 inches; diameter, 2 ⅝ inches; weight, no more than 3 units less than the length; for example, a 36-inch bat could not weigh less than 33 ounces. (1-12b-3; 1-12b-5) (See § 188 and 350.)

203. ALSO: A bat must have an approved coded certification mark on the barrel of the bat signifying the bat is legal for NCAA competition.

Thus, the list of certified bats is no longer necessary. (1-12b-6; NCAA 2011 video, Paronto)
PENALTY: Any bat that does not display the approved certification mark shall be removed from the game. The batter with such a bat, after stepping into the box or hitting, shall be declared out. (1-12-b Pen)
204. ALSO: Bat models must be approved by going through "the NCAA certification program." **NO BAT FROM A PREVIOUS YEAR IS LEGAL.** (NCAA 2011 video, Paronto.)

OBR: Only wooden bats are legal. (1.10a)

★ 185 EQUIPMENT: BATS: NON-WOOD: SAFETY GRIP ✪

FED: All non-wood bats must have a safety grip made of cork, tape, or commercially manufactured composition material extending 10 to 18 inches. Slippery, plastic "electrical" tape is not legal. Resin, pine tar, or any drying agent are permitted only on the grip. (1-3-2c-1)
PENALTY: See § 180. (7 4-1a) (See § 82, 83 and 188.)

NCAA: Aluminum bats, whether used in **PRACTICE OR A GAME**, must have a leather, rubber, or taped safety grip attached to the handle. (1-12d) ***(ADDED)*** If the bat handle comes loose: **PENALTY:** The bat is removed and the player warned. (1-12d Pen)

OBR: For up to 18 inches from the knob, the bat handle may be treated with any substance or material to improve the grip. (1.10c)
PENALTY: If the safety grip extends past 18 inches, the bat shall be removed. (1.10c)

> ❀ Note 174: Do not confuse this rule – bat removed – with the penalty for a bat altered to improve the distance factor – batter out and ejected. (See § 82 and 83.)

186 EQUIPMENT: BATS: NON-WOOD: STRAIGHT HANDLES ✪

FED: Point not covered.

OFF INTERP 156-186: **RUMBLE:** The softball zig-zag bat is legal (*News* #17, 3/82; #32, 4/85) ✠

> ❀ Note 175: In the 26 seasons since the zig-zag bat became legal, I have never seen a baseball player use one.

NCAA: All bats, both **WOOD** and **NON-WOOD**, must have a direct line from the center of the knob to the center of the large end, a rule that effectively outlaws zig-zag bats. (1-12b-2)

OBR: Not applicable.

★ 187 EQUIPMENT: BATS: USED TO LOOSEN UP ✪

FED: Only bats may be used for warmup. They may be weighted or have metal rings or blades securely attached. Iron bars and chains are illegal. (1-3-4; 1.3.4) **PENALTY:** team warning / ejection. (1.3.5e, 1992 ed)

> **205. ALSO:** OFF INTERP 157-187: **RUMBLE:** Umpires have no jurisdiction outside the "confines of the field" or "stadium," so players there could use non-approved devices to warm up. (*News* #2, 3/83; #20, 3/84; #5, 3/85; #27, 4/90) ✠

❀ Note 176: Three other infractions are listed as occurring outside the "confines of the field": batting practice during a game (§ 114), use of tobacco (§ 503), and wearing a bandanna (§ 521). Umpires may not police those illegal activities until they have jurisdiction when the offenders go "inside" the confines of the field. (See § 419.) **EXCEPT:** Umpires must ensure that a player warming up the pitcher **ANYWHERE** is wearing the prescribed protective gear (See § 194.)

NCAA: Point not covered.

> ***(ADDED)*** OFF INTERP 158-187: **PARONTO:** Same as FED 1-3-4. 7 (email to cc, 12/19/11) ✠

OBR: No provision. *See ¶ 8.*

★ 188 EQUIPMENT: BATS: WOODEN ✪ (See § 184.)

FED: A bat made of a single piece of wood shall be a smooth cylinder with a maximum length of 36 inches and a maximum diameter of 2¾ inches. (1-3-3; New Case Play 7, 1992 ed)

(ADDED) ❀ Note 177: Play 7 did not make it into the 1993 case book.

(EDITED) **206. ALSO:** The bat **MAY** be roughened or wound with tape or twine not more than 18 inches from the knob end. (1-3-3)

❀ Note 178: A safety grip is not required for wooden bats; it is mandatory on nonmetal bats. (See § 185.)

NCAA: The wooden bat must be a smooth, rounded stick (maximum length, 42 inches; maximum diameter, 2 ¾ inches) and must be of "one-piece solid wood unless "certified in accordance with the NCAA certification program." (1-12a) **PENALTY:** The batter, after using or attempting to use a non-legal bat, is out and runners return TOP. (1-12a Pen)

❀ Note 179: The college wooden bat may be up to six inches longer and ⅛-inch bigger around than the college non-wood bat. (added) The college bat is also .14 inches larger than the OBR. Any FED bat, metal or wood, could be 42 inches long until 1992.

OBR: The bat must a smooth, rounded stick no more than 2.61 inches ***(ADDED)*** (2 5/9ths) in diameter at its thickest part with a maximum length of 42 inches and may be made of solid wood. (1.10a) *See ¶8.*

207. ALSO: The bat handle for not more than 18" from its end may be "covered or treated with any material or substance to improve the grip. (1.10c)

208. ALSO: If a bat does not conform to 1.10c "during or after" the bat has been used, "it shall not be grounds for declaring our or ejecting the batter." (1.10c CMT)

(ADDED) OFF INTERP 159-188: **WENDELSTEDT:** The defense discovers a bat with strips of electrical tape wrapped around the barrel of the bat. *Ruling:* The batter is out and ejected." (P214/157) ✠

(ADDED) ❀ Note 180: HW says: "The only logical reasoning for the batter to have this around the barrel end of the batter is either to improve the distance factor or cause an unusual reaction on the ball." BRD says: The umpire should also confiscate the bat.

★ ∞ 189 EQUIPMENT: BATTING GLOVE UNDER FIELDING GLOVE: PITCHER WEARS ✪

FED: The pitcher may not wear sweatbands on his wrists or an exposed batting glove (not even a nondescript, gray batting glove) under his fielder's glove, if – in the judgment of the umpire – such items are distracting to the batter. (1.4.2, 2009 ed; Website 2004, #9)

NCAA: The pitcher may not wear ***(EDITED)*** "another" glove under his fielding glove. (9-2h)

(ADDED) ❀ Note 181: The 2011 BRD said the fielder couldn't wear a batting (golfing) glove. As we used to say: Same difference.

OBR: Point not covered.

OFF INTERP 160-189: **PBUC:** Treat as in NCAA 9-2h. {3.13} (See § 190.) ✠

★ 190 EQUIPMENT: BATTING GLOVE UNDER FIELDING GLOVE: PLAYER WEARS ✪

FED: No provision.

NCAA: Point not covered.

> ***(ADDED)*** OFF INTERP 161-190: **PARONTO:** Same as OBR OFF INTERP 162 [this section]. (email to cc, 11/19/11) ✠

OBR: Point not covered.

> OFF INTERP 162-190: **PBUC:** A defensive player may wear a batting glove, but he may not rub the ball on it. {3.13} ✠ (See § 189.)

★ 191 EQUIPMENT: CASTS / SPLINTS: PITCHER ✪

FED: A pitcher may wear a padded cast on his "nonpitching" arm. White or gray casts are illegal. (10.2.3d) (See § 192 for the dimensions and characteristics of padding [***CHANGED***] as well as for the power of the state association to permitting "exceptions to the NFHS playing rules.")

NCAA: A pitcher is prohibited from wearing a cast on his pitching hand or fingers, but he is specifically entitled to wear a cast on the "non-pitching hand" if it is "padded and covered" (not white and not distracting to the batter or umpire). (9-2e AR 1) (See § 192.)

OBR: Point not covered.

> OFF INTERP 163-191: **DEARY:** A player may not pitch if he has a cast on either arm. (*REF* 6/83, quiz question #4) ✠

★ 192 EQUIPMENT: CASTS / SPLINTS: PLAYER / COACH ✪

(See § 191.)

FED: By state association adoption: Game participants may use prostheses if they "are no more dangerous to players [and coaches] than the corresponding human body parts and do not place an opponent at a disadvantage." (1-5-8; 1.5.8e CMT) Casts and braces must be padded. "All hard and unyielding items must be padded with a closed-cell, slow-recovery foam padding no less than one-half-inch thick. Knee and ankle braces that are unaltered from the manufacturers's original design production do not require additional padding." (1.5.8a through g) (See 10.2.3d.) The umpire shall rule on the legality of casts or splints. Each official must decide for himself if the cast is "unreasonably" dangerous, hence illegal. (1-5-9) (See § 136 and 215.)

(CHANGED) 209. ALSO: Because of "applicable laws," each state association may "authorize exceptions" to the playing rules "to provide reasonable accommodations to individual participants with disabilities or special needs." The exceptions must not alter the sport, allow illegal equipment to put players in danger, or "place opponents at a disadvantage." (1-5-8)

(ADDED) ❀ Note 182: `ly decided that individual states have their own way of looking out for the safety of players. The umpire still has the final say, absent a directive from his state association.

NCAA: "Any hard cast must be padded and covered." (1-15f)

OBR: No provision.

193 EQUIPMENT: CATCHER: PROTECTIVE ✪

FED: The catcher must wear a head protector, shin guards, body protector, protective cup (if male), and a (**POE 1984, 1985, 1986, 1992**) mask with a throat protector. (1-5-3) The throat protector, which is either part of or attached to the mask, must "adequately" protect him. (1-5-4) (See § 211.)

210. ALSO: The helmet must have "full ear protection (dual ear flaps)." (1-5-4)

211. ALSO: The head, face, and throat protector(s) may be one piece or multi-piece. (1-5-4)

212. ALSO: POE 2002, 2003: The catcher's helmet must bear the NOCSAE seal of approval. (1-5-4) Hockey-style masks that meet NOCSAE standards are legal. (1.5.4b) A skull cap helmet-mask combination is illegal because it has no protection for the ears. (1.5.4a)

NCAA: When fielding his position, warming up the pitcher, or catching in the bullpen, the catcher must wear a protective helmet and mask with a built-in or attachable throat guard. (1-15c and d)
PENALTY: The player may not catch, but he is not ejected. (1-15 Pen c and d) (See § 194 and 211.)

213. ALSO: It is **RECOMMENDED** that the catcher's helmet bear the NOCSAE seal of approval. (1-15d AR)

OBR: The catcher must wear a helmet when fielding his position, but a throat guard is not mandatory. (1.16d) *See ¶8.*

★ 194 EQUIPMENT: CATCHER: WARMS UP PITCHER ✪

FED: Any player in a crouch who warms up a pitcher "at any location," inside or outside the "confines of the field," must wear a cup (if male), a mask with a throat protector, and a head protector. (1-5-4) Whether the umpires are in charge of the field is not relevant. (10.1.2a) (See § 419.)

***(ADDED)* 214. ALSO:** Regardless of how hard the pitcher throws, a player warming up a pitcher is not required to wear a helmet unless he crouches. (1.5.4c)

***(ADDED)* 215. ALSO:** A coach wants his catcher to use a hockey style mask and helmet combination that have not been tested together. The umpire-in-chief will not permit the equipment to be used unless the coach can provide documentation to the contrary. (1.5.4d)

> ❀ Note 183: Several other infractions are listed as occurring outside the "confines of the field": batting practice during a game (§ 114), illegal warm-up devices (§ 187), use of tobacco (§ 503), and wearing a bandanna (§ 521). FED does not allow the umpires to police any of those illegal activities until they have jurisdiction by going "inside" the confines of the field. (See § 419.) But FED feels strongly about the danger facing a player not wearing protective equipment while warming up a pitcher, thus the exception outlined above.

NCAA: All catchers must wear a protective helmet and face mask when fielding their positions or warming up the pitcher between half innings or in the bullpen. (1-15d) **PENALTY:** The player may not catch, but he is not ejected. (1-15d Pen) (See § 193.)

OBR: No provision.

195 EQUIPMENT: CLEATS
ALL CODES NOW AGREE: TEXT DELETED, 1991.

★ 196 EQUIPMENT: DISTRACTING ITEMS: PITCHER: ARMS / WRISTS ✪

FED: The pitcher may not wear items on his arms, wrists, or hands that in the judgment of the umpire are distracting to the batter. (1-4-2; 6-2-1f) **PENALTY:** The offending item must be removed before the next pitch. (6-2-1f Pen)

216. ALSO: Inherently legal items (such as ***[ADDED]*** an exposed gray batting glove, sweatbands on his wrists, white, therapeutic elastic sleeve) must also be removed if the umpire judges they are distracting to the batter. (1.4.2, 2009 ed)

NCAA: The pitcher may not wear items on his arms, wrists, or hands that in the JUDGMENT OF THE BATTER or umpire are distracting. (9-2h)

217. ALSO: Specifically mentioned as distracting (in addition to wrist bands) are jewelry (chains), or white logos. (9-2h)
PENALTY: The offending item will be removed, or the pitcher will be ejected. (9-2h Pen) (See § 189; 199; 200; 536.)

❀ Note 184: The tough part of this rule is a pitcher wearing an item that the batter (but not necessarily the umpire) finds distracting. According to Thurston, if the batter insists (and why wouldn't he?), the distracting item must be removed.

OBR: No provision. (See § 197.)

197 EQUIPMENT: DISTRACTING ITEMS: PITCHER: GLOVE ✪

FED: No provision.

❀ Note 185: But see § 196, which is ample authority to get the dangling laces on a high school pitcher's glove to — un-dangle.

NCAA: A glove with loose [dangling] lacing is prohibited. (9-2h)

OBR: The glove shall not be distracting in any manner. (1.15a)

> **218. ALSO:** OFF INTERP 164-197: **PBUC:** If the umpire judges that long lacing or strings on the glove are distracting, he may order the pitcher to cut the string or get a new glove. {3.11} ✠

198 EQUIPMENT: DISTRACTING ITEMS: PITCHER: HEAD ✪

FED: If the pitcher's cap continues to fall off during delivery, the umpire will warn the coach that because of the distraction to the batter (or delay of game) the cap must be securely fastened or the pitcher will be removed from the mound (but not the game). (10.2.3c)

NCAA: No provision.

OBR: No provision.

199 EQUIPMENT: DISTRACTING ITEMS: PITCHER: TAPE ✪

FED: The pitcher may not wear tape or bandages on the fingers or palm of his pitching hand. (6-2-1g; 6.2.1c) **PENALTY:** The infraction must be corrected before the next pitch. (6-2-1g Pen)

NCAA: The pitcher may not attach tape or other material of a color different from his uniform or glove to his glove, arms, or clothing. (9-2h) The pitcher may not wear a bandage or band-aid on his pitching fingers.

(9-2e AR 1) **PENALTY:** warning / ejection. (9-2e Pen; 9-2h Pen) (See § 162.)

OBR: The pitcher may not put on his glove any foreign substance that is a different color from his glove. (1.15b) **PENALTY:** None listed. (See § 167.)

❀ Note 186: Penalize as in NCAA, using 9.01c as your rule reference.

200 EQUIPMENT: DISTRACTING ITEMS: PLAYER: JEWELRY ✪

FED: POE 1987: Players participating in the game may not wear jewelry. (3-3-1d; 3.3.1gg) A player may wear a medical alert necklace or a religious medal; such items are not "jewelry." But the medical alert device must be securely taped to the player's body and may be visible. The religious medal must be taped and worn **UNDER** the uniform. (1-5-12; 1.5.12a and b) **PENALTY:** team warning / ejection. (3-3-1d Pen)

> **219. ALSO:** OFF INTERP 165-200: **RUMBLE:** A pitcher may not wear a medical alert bracelet on his pitching arm. (*News* #12, 3/86) ✠

> **220. ALSO:** OFF INTERP 166-200: **RUMBLE:** The prohibition against jewelry would not apply to non-adult coaches in the coaching box. (*News* #41, 4/83) ✠

NCAA: No provision prohibits jewelry on position players. Pitchers may not wear jewelry if the batter or umpire finds it distracting. (9-2h) (See § 163.) **PENALTY:** The umpire will order the distracting item removed; if the wearer refuses, he is ejected. (9-2h Pen)

OBR: Point not covered.

> OFF INTERP 167-200: **PBUC:** Players, especially pitchers, may not wear distracting jewelry. {3.16} *See ¶8.* ✠

201 EQUIPMENT: DISTRACTING ITEMS: PLAYER: TAPE ✪

FED: No provision. (See § 196.)

NCAA: No provision. (See § 199.)

OBR: No player may put tape of a different color from his uniform on his person. (1.11d)

❀ Note 187: The OBR 1.11d prohibition would also apply to pitchers. (See § 199.)

202 EQUIPMENT: ELBOW PADS✪

FED: No provision.

NCAA: A player may wear one elbow pad not longer than 10 inches and surrounded by a nylon pad. No player may wear an upper or lower arm protector unless he has: (● 1) proper identification describing who the player is and the nature of the injury; (● 2) a doctor's report diagnosing the injury; and (● 3) a physician's report of how long the equipment should be used. (1-15e)

OBR: Point not covered.

> OFF INTERP 168-202: **MLBUM:** An elbow pad may not exceed 10 inches in length when lying flat, and the shell of the pad must be surrounded by a nylon pad. (2.1) ✠

203 EQUIPMENT: GLOVES / MITTS: CATCHER'S MITT✪

FED: The size of the catcher's mitt is not limited. The catcher's mitt may be used only by catchers. (1-3-6) (See § 205.)

NCAA: POE 2002: Same as FED. (1-13a) **PENALTY** for refusal to secure proper equipment within a "reasonable" time: ejection. (1-13a Pen 1)

OBR: The catcher's mitt is limited to 38 inches in circumference and 15 ½ inches from top to bottom. (1.12)

> **221. ALSO:** OFF INTERP 169-203: **PBUC:** The catcher's mitt may have a vinyl fluorescent piece attached. {3.14} ✠

★ 204 EQUIPMENT: GLOVES / MITTS: FIELDER'S GLOVE: SIZE✪

FED: The maximum dimensions of any glove or mitt worn by a fielder other than the catcher are: 14 inches long and 8 inches wide with 5 ¾-inch webbing at the fingertip and a 5 ¾-inch webbing between the bottom of the thumb and the first finger. (1-3-6) (See § 127 and 205.) **PENALTY** for refusal to obtain a proper glove: ejection. (1-5-4 Pen)

NCAA: POE 2001, 2002: The glove may be 12 inches long, 8 inches wide, with webbing of 5 ¾ inches at the top and 3 ½ inches at the base. (1-13c; 1-13c AR 1) **PENALTY** for refusal to secure proper equipment within a "reasonable" time: ejection. (1-13c Pen 1) (See § 205.

❀ Note 188: The legal college glove is significantly smaller than the high school model. Tell the truth now: Do you measure the gloves in your freshman NCAA games? In **ANY** college games? Amazing! The ball may be larger (more to hit), the wooden bat is half a foot longer (more reach), and the glove must be smaller (more difficult to hold the ball). No wonder NCAA batting and earned run averages are sky high.

OBR: ***(EDITED)*** Each fielder, other than the first baseman, "may use or wear" a glove with these dimensions: 12 inches long, 7 ¾ inches wide with 5 ¾-inch webbing. (1.14) **PENALTY** for the use of an improper glove: The umpire shall "cause the illegal glove to be removed" (● 1) "on his own initiative," (● 2) "at the recommendation of another umpire," or (● 3) upon a merited complaint from the opposing manager. (1.15c)

222. ALSO: OFF INTERP 170-204: **PBUC:** "A player refusing to comply with an umpire's order to relinquish his glove may be ejected." {3.12} ✠

223. ALSO: OFF INTERP 171-204: **PBUC:** "Play that has occurred prior to the measurement of a glove found to be illegal will be allowed to stand." {3.12} ✠

(ADDED) **224. ALSO:** OFF INTERP 172-204: **PBUC:** "Each manager is limited to TWO requests per game" for the umpire to examine a glove. If a glove is found to be illegal, it should be removed from the game. {3.12} ✠

205 EQUIPMENT: GLOVES / MITTS: FIRST BASEMAN'S MITT ✪

FED: No distinction exists between a fielder's glove and a first baseman's mitt. Fielders may use either one at any position. (1-3-6; 1.3.6c; 1.4.3, 1991 ed) (See § 127 and 204.)

NCAA: **POE 2002**: The first baseman's mitt is limited: 12 inches long, 8 inches wide, 5 inches in the crotch area, with a 4 ½-inch width at the top narrowing to 3 ½ inches at the base. (1-13b AR) It may be used only by first basemen and catchers. (1-13c) (See § 204.) **PENALTY** for refusal to secure proper equipment within a "reasonable" time: ejection. (1-13c Pen 1)

OBR: Same as NCAA. (1.13; 1.14)

206 EQUIPMENT: GLOVES / MITTS: MANDATORY ✪

FED: Leather gloves or mitts "shall" be used by all fielders. (1-3-6) (See § 127.)

225. ALSO: A glove may not be altered to "create an adhesive, sticky, and / or tacky surface." "Glove conditioning lotion" is legal. (1-3-6; 1.3.6b) (See § 82 for a tacky bat.)

NCAA: Leather gloves or mitts "may" be worn. (1-13)

OBR: Same as NCAA. (1.14)

★ 207 EQUIPMENT: GLOVES / MITTS: PITCHER: COLOR✪

FED: A glove that "includes the colors white or gray shall be removed from the game upon discovery by either team and / or umpire." (1-3-6; 1.3.6e)

226. ALSO: A pitcher whose glove was removed may use it again if the white / gray is removed or covered up. (1.3.6e)

> ✻ *Play 92-207*: **FED only.** A pitcher makes a spectacular catch of a hard line drive. The offensive coach then calls the umpire's attention to a huge, white manufacturer's logo. *Ruling:* The catch is allowed, but the glove is removed. (Website 2008, #18)

❀ Note 189: A multicolored pitcher's glove is no longer an illegal glove. It's just not a legal glove. The point, of course, was to remove the "illegal-glove" penalty, assessed by some because a logo had some white threads. It's a case where the NFHS used common sense. (Don't even think of adding the words: "for a change.")

NCAA: ***(EDITED)*** The pitcher's glove must be black or brown. (1-13c AR2)

> ❀ Note 190: The rationale for the change says: "The overall color of the glove is important." The umpire may always remove a glove he feels is distracting. (See § 197.)

OBR: The pitcher's glove, EXCLUSIVE OF PIPING, may not be white or gray ***(ADDED)*** "nor in the judgment of an umpire, distracting in any manner." (1.15a)

227. ALSO: OFF INTERP 173-207: **PBUC:** "Any pitcher starting or entering the game wearing a colored glove must wear the same colored glove for the entire game." {3.11} **PENALTY:** None listed! ✠

228. ALSO: **PENALTY:** The umpire shall remove an illegal glove: (● 1) on his own initiative; (● 2) at the behest of another umpire; or (● 3) on a complaint from the opposing manager — if the umpire thinks the complaint has merit. (1.15c)

❀ Note 191: One would think something so simple as the color of a glove would allow the codes to achieve unanimity. One would think wrong.

✻ *Play 93-207:* B1's come-backer is grabbed by the pitcher, who throws to first for the out. The offensive coach now appeals that the pitcher's glove is illegal. The umpire examines the glove and discovers several white threads visible in the manufacturer's logo. *Ruling:* The glove is removed from play. No bases are awarded. The out stands.

★ 208 EQUIPMENT: HELMET: NON-ADULT BAT / BALL SHAGGERS ✪

FED: POE 2006, 2007, 2008: Non-adult bat / ball shaggers must wear protective helmets ***(EDITED)*** that meet the NOCSAE standard in any live-ball area, even when the ball is dead. (1-5-1, 1.5.1e and f) **PENALTY:** Warning to coach and individual; on the next infraction, the offender may "not be allowed on the field." (1-5-1) The warning is not considered a team warning. (Comments on Rule Changes, 1993 ed, at 1-1-5, p. 3) (See § 517.)

NCAA: It is recommended that all "bat handlers" wear helmets. (1-15b)

OBR: Bat boys and / or bat girls must wear a double ear flap helmet while on the field and performing their duties. (1.16f)

★ ∞ 209 EQUIPMENT: HELMET: PITCHER ✪

FED: The pitcher's helmet or face protector must have a "**NON-GLARE**" surface. (1-5-5)
229. ALSO: Any defensive player may wear a face / head protector; its outer covering must have a non-glare surface (1-5-5) and does not need dual earflaps. (1.5.5c)

NCAA: The pitcher's helmet must have a "**NONGLOSSY**" finish. (9-2h)

OBR: No provision.

★ 210 EQUIPMENT: HELMET: PROTECTIVE DEVICE ATTACHED / TAPE ✪

FED: POE 2004, 2005, 2006, 2007: Face protectors attached to batting helmets are now generally approved, but to qualify as legal equipment a face protector must be attached to the helmet: (● 1) at the time of manufacture; or (● 2) later, through a procedure approved by the manufacturer. The face mask must meet NOCSAE standards. (1-5-2; 1.5.2) (See § 214.)

NCAA: Point not covered.

> *(ADDED)* OFF INTERP 174-210: **PARONTO:** Same as FED 1-5-2. (email to cc, 12/19/11) ✠

EXCEPT: Any tape attached to a helmet must be removed before the helmet may be used. (1-15a AR 1)

OBR: No provision.

211 EQUIPMENT: HELMET: SEAL OF APPROVAL ✪

FED: Each batting helmet must bear the NOCSAE stamp of approval and an embossed or attached exterior warning label. (1-5-1; *News* #2, 3/86; 1.1.5e, 1990 ed)
230. ALSO: The NOCSAE seal is required on all catchers' helmets. (1-5-4; 1.5.4d; 1.1.5q [2002 ed])

> **231. ALSO:** OFF INTERP 175-211: **HOPKINS:** A helmet is not legal if the NOCSAE stamps "are not legible and cannot be read." (Website 2004, #2) ✠

Play 94-211: **FED only.** A batter appears wearing a helmet with the warning label but not the NOCSAE stamp. *Ruling:* The batter must obtain a legal helmet unless the coach can produce written verification that the helmet meets NOCSAE standards. (1.1.5i, 1989 ed)

NCAA: POE 1990 [illegal helmet]: The NOCSAE seal is required; the warning label is not. (1-15a AR 2)

OBR: No provision.

212 EQUIPMENT: KNEE BRACES
ALL CODES NOW AGREE: TEXT DELETED, 1995.

213 EQUIPMENT: LOOSE ON FIELD (SEE § 301.)

214 EQUIPMENT: NON-TRADITIONAL OR EXPERIMENTAL ✪

FED: Non-traditional equipment must be reviewed by the rules committee before it will be permitted. (1-5-11) (See § 210; 236; 532.)

NCAA: Same as FED. "Only equipment that meets specifications published in the NCAA Baseball Rules may be used in intercollegiate competition. The rules committee is responsible for interpretations of NCAA rules. (1-10)

OBR: Experimental bats may not be used in either championship or exhibition play without approval by the rules committee. (1.10a Nt)

215 EQUIPMENT: PROSTHESES ALLOWED ✪

FED: A player may wear an artificial limb [prosthesis]. The individual state associations are charged with setting the parameters. (1-5-8) (See § 133, 192 and 510.) **EXCEPT:** Even if a prosthesis is medically prescribed, if the state association has not approved it, it may not be worn. **PENALTY:** If the ball is touched with [an unapproved prosthesis], the offensive team has the choice of taking the penalty (8-3-3a, b an c) or the play. (1.5.8g)

❀ Note 192: The prosthesis in question was a "basket-shaped, glove-like" device worn by F3 on defense. I could have used something like that when I played.

NCAA: No provision.

OBR: No provision.

216 EQUIPMENT: SCREENS: FIRST BASE ✪

FED: No provision.

NCAA: During batting practice it is recommended that an eight- by six-foot protective screen be provided for the first-base area. (4-3d)

OBR: No provision.

217 EQUIPMENT: SCREENS: PITCHER ✪

FED: No provision.

NCAA: A six- by four-foot protective screen for the pitcher, provided by the home team, is **REQUIRED** during batting practice. If there will be no screen at the playing site, the visitors should be notified "in advance." (4-3b) (See Note 418-419.)

OBR: No provision.

★ 218 EQUIPMENT: UMPIRE INSPECTS ✪ (See § 82.)

FED: POE 1989, 2000, 2001, 2002, 2009: Before the game the UIC should inspect the ***(CHANGED)*** the condition of the field. ~~equipment [bats/helmets] of both teams and remove any that are illegal.~~ (10-2-3a) See § pregame meeting. Last edition: The umpires inspected equipment.

> ***(ADDED)*** ❀ Note 193: FED joined its big brother, the NCAA: Umpires no longer have to go inside the dugout before the game. The onus for proper compliance is placed directly on the head coach's shoulders. That does not mean you ignore the rules governing legal/illegal equipment. You will have to decide when someone appeals that a piece of equipment is illegal.

232. ALSO: Broken, cracked, or dented bats are illegal. **PENALTY:** The bat is removed from the game. (1.3.5b)

233. ALSO: POE 2009: Bats that deface the ball, have been altered to increase the distance factor, fail to meet rule specifications, or have been rejected by the umpire but used in the game anyway are also illegal. (1-3-5) **PENALTY:** The batter is out for using or attempting to use such bats. (7-4-1a Pen) (See Note 104-82 and § 83.)

234. ALSO: "The NFHS does not perform scientific tests on any specific items of equipment to determine if the equipment poses undue risks to student-athletes, coaches, officials or spectators. Such determinations are the responsibility of equipment manufacturers." (Note before 1-1.)

NCAA: Umpires will no longer inspect equipment in the dugout before the game. Rather, each head coach at the pregame meeting will certify his team's equipment meets "all NCAA rule requirements." (4-1a; 4-4c) **PENALTY:** If the field dimensions, equipment, and facilities are illegal, the game is subject to forfeit if conditions are not corrected in a reasonable length of time. (4-1a Pen) **PENALTY:** For use of an illegal bat: The batter is out. (7-10b Pen) (See § 83.)

> ❀ Note 194: Justification for the change: "The committee's reasoning is two fold. First, the committee does not believe having umpires enter both dugouts to check bats and helmets for legality starts the relationship in the right way between coaches and umpires. Secondly, since all NCAA bats are certified, very few bats are deemed illegal. Additionally, teams do not always make all bats and helmets available to umpires during pregame activities. Coaches currently have the right to challenge a bat as illegal and they continue to have this right."

OBR: Before the game the umpire shall require "strict observance of all rules governing implements of play and equipment of players." (3.01a)

219 EQUIPMENT: VIDEO: COACH USES✪

FED: The use of video equipment for coaching purposes during a game is prohibited. (3-3-1f; 3.3.1hh; 3.3.1ii)
PENALTY: warning / ejection. (3-3-1f Pen)

❀ Note 195: FED comments make it clear: The rule prohibits non-media personnel with video equipment from being in the vicinity of the bench, dugout, or bullpen. Media personnel would be relocated if their equipment was used for coaching purposes.

> **235. ALSO:** OFF INTERP 176-219: **HOPKINS:** Information gathered from a radar gun may not be communicated to a coach during the game. (Website 2002, #10) (See § 133.)✠

NCAA: "Nonuniformed team personnel" may be in the stands to chart pitches, use radar guns, or videotape play, but the tape may not be used during the game. Features of the rule:
(● 1) Scouting information may not be relayed to the field or team personnel.
(● 2) "Games and individuals shall not be videotaped from the dugout."
(● 3) Teams may videotape themselves but not other teams.
(● 4) The video equipment is limited to the area behind home plate stretching from the cutout at first to the cutout at third.
(● 5) Cameras may not tape / film from beyond the outfield fence except for televising a game.
(● 6) Monitors for viewing tape or film during a game are prohibited in the dugout or adjacent areas. (5-2f)

❀ Note 196: The rule also prohibits any team from recording any game in which it does not participate.

236. ALSO: Electronic equipment shall not be used to transmit information among team personnel. (5-2f AR 1)
237. ALSO: "In-stadium, pitch-speed monitors may be used in all games." (5-2f AR 4)
238. ALSO: The prohibition against electronic equipment does not apply to telephones, cell phones, walkie talkies, etc., used to communicate between a team's dugout and its bullpen. (5-2f AR 2)
239. ALSO: Televisions and internet streaming must be turned off in the dugout and clubhouse during the game. (5-2f AR 3)

OBR: Point not covered.

> OFF INTERP 177-219: **PBUC:** The use of cellular phones, walkie-talkies, pagers, or any other portable communication devices during the game is prohibited. Laptop computers are not allowed in the dugout. {3.25} ✠

> **240. ALSO:** OFF INTERP 178-219: **MLBUM:** Reference to a video replay during an argument by a manager, coach, or player will result in an immediate ejection. (2.22) ✠

220 EQUIPMENT: VIDEO: UMPIRE USES ✪

FED: No game official may use video equipment as an aid in making a decision: Instant replay, therefore, is prohibited. (10-1-5; 10.1.4) (See § 421 for an additional prohibition.)

NCAA: Umpires should consult video evidence, if available, to identify players involved in a fight. "The review should occur immediately after the incident." (5-16c-4)

❀ Note 197: Since players involved in the fight will be suspended from the next game, it is important to identify them accurately.

OBR: Point not covered.

> OFF INTERP 179-220: **MLBUM:** Umpires may not employ electronic media to revise or assist in any decision other than those allowed by rule. (2.23) (See § 505.) ✠

★ 221 FAIR BALL: BALL BREAKS PLANE OF FOUL LINE ✪

FED: Point not covered.

> OFF INTERP 180-221: **HOPKINS:** A fielder's blowing on the ball is the same as touching it. The umpire will rule fair/foul based on where the ball was when the fielder committed the act. (Website 2008, #1) ✠

NCAA: Point not covered.

> OFF INTERP 181-221: **FETCHIET:** A batted ball comes to rest not touching the foul line, "but a portion of the ball is breaking the plane of the foul line." Ruling: Fair ball. (Website 4/20/01, 2-Fair Ball) ✠

OBR: Point not covered.

> OFF INTERP 182-221: ***(EDITED)*** **WENDELSTEDT:** Same as NCAA OFF INTERP 181 above. (HW/4/MLBUM 6.19) ✠

∞222 FEINT: DEFINITION ✪ (See § 372 and 375.)

FED: A feint is any movement that "simulates the start of a pitch or a throw to a base." It is used to deceive a runner. (2-28-5) Arm motion is not required. (See OFF INTERP • 311-375.) (See § 373 and 374.)

NCAA: A feint does not require arm motion. (9-3b AR-3)

OBR: Point not covered.

OFF INTERP 183-222: **PBUC:** Same as NCAA. {8.5g Nt} ✠

223 FIELD: BATTER'S BOX LINED ✪

FED: No provision.

NCAA: POE 1998: It is "mandatory" that all four sides of the batters' boxes be lined. (1-3a) (See § 81 and 225.)

OBR: No provision.

224 FIELD: BULLPEN ✪

FED: No provision.

NCAA: All college baseball facilities shall have a regulation bullpen for both teams constructed to the exact measurements of the mound on the playing field: "Each bullpen must be large enough to allow two pitchers to warm up at the same time." A pitcher warming up in the bullpen should be throwing in the same direction as he would be if he was on the mound. (1-5c; 4-3e) (See § 364 and 409.)

OBR: No provision.

225 FIELD: CATCHER'S BOX: SIZE ✪

FED: The catcher's box is 43 inches by 8 feet, measured from the point of the plate. (1-2-1 Diagram; 2-9-3)

NCAA: POE 2000: The box is 48 inches by 6 feet, measured from the back line of the batter's box. (1-3a; Diagram 1)
241. ALSO: It is mandatory that the catcher's box be lined as shown in Diagram 1. (1-3b) (See § 223.)

OBR: Same as FED. (1.04 Diagram 2)
❀ Note 198: The area of the NCAA catcher's box is 36 square feet. That's about 27 percent larger than the FED/OBR box and surely gives any college catcher enough room to glove (for a strike) that cut fastball breaking about six inches off the plate.

★ 226 FIELD: CHALK LINES: ERASED ✪

FED: No provision.

NCAA: Players, coaches, and umpires may not deliberately erase chalk lines. (3-6j) **PENALTY: Point not covered.**

> ***(ADDED)*** OFF INTERP 184-226: **PARONTO:** "The umpire has full power to require the batter to move to a proper position. He may require the grounds crew to reline the box. He may eject participants for repeatedly refusing to obey a lawful order." (email to cc, 12/20/11) ✠

(ADDED) ❀ Note 199: Mr. Paronto assumed – correctly – that most problems with chalk lines occur in the batter's boxes. The rule also applies to the coaches' boxes but not to that part of the running-lane line that intersects with the foul line. There, umpires may erase a couple of inches with impunity. (grin)

OBR: No provision.

227 FIELD: CHALK LINES: WIDTH / COLOR ✪

FED: The recommended width of the "foul" line is 2 ½ inches. (1-2-5) "All non-permanent lines should be white." (1-2-2)
242. ALSO: Permanent lines painted the school colors, a maroon fire hose, or painted, wooden 2x4s are legal. (1.2.2a)
243. ALSO: "If the foul lines are not legal, the game will be played anyway." The state association should be informed. (1.2.2b) (See § 169.)

NCAA: The "chalk" lines shall be 2 to 3 inches wide. (1-3)

OBR: No provision.

228 FIELD: COACHING BOX: SIZE ✪

FED: The coaching box shall be 20 feet by 5 feet, located 15 feet from the foul line. (1-2-1 Diagram 2)

NCAA: Same as FED. (1-3c)

OBR: The box is 20 by 10 feet, located 15 feet from the foul line. (1.04 Diagram 1)
244. ALSO: The lines in front and back of the box may be a minimum of 1 foot; a maximum of 10. (104 Diagram 1)

229 FIELD: CROWD CONTROL: UNRULY SPECTATORS ✪

FED: The umpire may eject a spectator(s). (5-2-1c)

❀ Note 200note: BRD recommends: Direct the home game administrator or someone from the host team to take care of any disruptive fans. (See § 117)

NCAA: The onus for crowd control rests on the home team athletic director or his designated representative. (See § 485.) The responsible person should be ready to use the public address system to warn the crowd about unseemly behavior, such as profanity, racial remarks, etc. (4-9) **PENALTY:** Offenders "may" be removed from the game site. (4-9) (See § 117.)

❀ Note 201: If the AD is not present and has not designated a game administrator, by default the representative is the head coach.

OBR: Umpires may eject spectators "from the field." (9.01e-2) (See § 260.)

★ 230 FIELD: DEFINITION ✪

FED: The playing field includes both foul and fair territory but not DBT, which is "beyond the playing field." (2-42)

NCAA: Point not covered.

(ADDED) OFF INTERP 185-230: **PARONTO:** Same as FED 2-42. (email to cc, 12/20/11) ✠

OBR: No provision.

231 FIELD: DUGOUT ✪

FED: If the dugout is to be temporarily extended, it shall extend toward the outfield away from home plate and parallel to the foul line. (1-2-4) Both dugouts must be equally extended. (1.2.4 a through d) (See § 115.)

❀ Note 202: The restriction applies only to temporary extensions (chalk lines, for example.) If the school wishes to make permanent alterations, they may do so "in any direction that works best for the particular field." (McNeely, TASO Austin MTG, 1/15/10)

NCAA: An extended dugout may not be on the home plate side of the bench. (1-16b AR 1) No "extra," on-deck batter may swing a bat in the extension. (1-16b AR 2) Any dead-ball area used for bat boys / girls may not be used by any uniformed player. (1-16b AR 3)
(See OFF INTERP 147-164.)

OBR: No provision

x232 FIELD: FENCE: DISTANCE FROM HOME PLATE ✪

FED: The recommended distances to the outfield fence are at least 300 feet down the foul lines and 350 feet to deepest center field. (1-2-5)

NCAA: The recommended distances are: 330 from home to each foul pole; 375 feet to left- and right-center; and 400 to deepest center field. If the distance to the foul pole is less than 330 feet, the other measurements should be rounded out to the recommended distances. (1-2b)

OBR: The minimum allowable distance to the fence is 250 feet. New distances (for parks built since 1958) are 325 to 400 feet. (1.04 Nt a and b) (See § 20.)

> ❀ Note 203: Several ball parks violate the 325-foot distance. Fenway Park is exempted, but AT&T Park (Giants) and Yankee Stadium are well short of the minimum. BTW: Many complain about the "short porch" (314) in right in New York. But it's only 310 to the rightfield fence at the Pesky Pole in Boston. Amazing!

233 FIELD: FENCE: HEIGHT ✪

FED: No provision.

NCAA: The outfield fence should be at least six- and preferably eight-feet high. (1-2c) (See § 126.)

OBR: No provision.

★ ∞ 234 FIELD: LIGHTS CALLED FOR ✪

FED: Whenever possible, the UIC shall see that lights are turned on at the beginning of an inning. (10-2-3n)

NCAA: Same as FED. (3-7f)

OBR: The umpire shall order the lights turned on whenever he believes darkness has made further play hazardous. (4.14)

> **245. ALSO:** OFF INTERP 186-234: **PBUC:** ***(EDITED)*** The umpire should call for the lights at the beginning of an inning UNLESS SOME UNUSUAL CIRCUMSTANCE (SUCH AS AN ABNORMALLY LONG HALF INNING) FORCES HIM TO DO OTHERWISE. {5.1} ✠

(NEW) 235 FIELD: LIGHTS FAIL ✪

FED: If darkness interferes with play, the umpire shall call "Time" and suspend play. (4-2-3)

246. ALSO: If lights fail during a play: No provision. Treat as in OBR OFF INTERP 187-235.

NCAA: A game may be stopped because of "inclement weather, darkness, light failure or curfew" (5-9a) or "crowd behavior." (5-8c)
247. ALSO: If lights fail during a play: No provision. Treat as in OBR OFF INTERP 187-235.

OBR: The umpire shall suspend play when light failure "makes it difficult or impossible for the umpires to follow the play. (5.10b)
248. ALSO: A league may adopt its own regulations governing games interrupted by light failure." (5.10b Nt)

249. ALSO: OFF INTERP 187-235: **WENDELSTEDT:** If lights fail: (● 1) "After a ball has been put in play and before the play is over, the batter will return to bat and all runners will return to their original bases. The entire play is "nullified. (● 2) If the batter and / or runners were awarded bases prior to the light failure, they should be allowed to advance to their awards when play resumes." ✠

⁜ *Play 95-235*: R3. B1 lays down a perfect sacrifice bunt just to the right of and beyond the mound. As F4 tries valiantly to field the ball, all field lights go off. The base umpire is certain that B1 would have been safe at first and R3 would have scored easily. *Ruling:* Too bad for the offense. The play is void. When the game resumes, B1 will be back in the box with the count he had before the bunt, and R3 will be "ahuggin'" third.

⁜ *Play 96-235:* With the bases loaded, B1 homes over the left-field fence. As he goes into his home run trot, all lights fail. *Ruling:* When play resumes, all runners will be allowed to advance around the bases according to baserunning rules.

★ 236 FIELD: MOUND: ARTIFICIAL ✪

FED: A mound created with synthetic materials is legal. (1-2-7; 1.2.7) (See § 214.)

NCAA: No provision.
(ADDED) ❀ Note 204: Paronto: "Only mounds that meet the requirements of 1-10 are legal." (email to cc, 12/20/11)

OBR: No provision.

★ 237 FIELD: MOUND: PORTABLE ✪

FED: Point not covered.

OFF INTERP 188-237: **RUMBLE:** A portable pitcher's mound is not legal. (*News* #27, 4/89; confirmed, #30, 4/90 and #17, 3/91) ✠

❀ Note 205: Obviously, portable mounds are "legal" in stadiums configured for both football and baseball, such as the New Orleans Superdome. Equally obvious: Some high schools around the country play on fields used also for Youth Leagues, fields where the pitching distance varies, hence the need for portable mounds.

NCAA: Point not covered.

(ADDED) OFF INTERP 189-237: **PARONTO:** "Portable mounds are legal, but when they are to be used, both teams must agree on their use before the visitors arrive at the game site." (email to cc, 12/28/11) (See § 236.) ✠

(ADDED) ❀ Note 206: Paronto: "Umpires should check the condition of the field and all equipment (4-1a Pen) to determine if the facilities are legal and will not be hazardous to the safety of the student athlete." (email to cc, 12/28/11)

OBR: No provision.

238 FIELD: MOUND: SPECIFICATIONS
ALL CODES NOW AGREE: TEXT DELETED, 1991.

239 FIELD: NON-REGULATION ✪

FED: No protests concerning a non-regulation field shall be accepted after the game has started. (1-2-12; 1.2.12) (See § 420 and 421.)

NCAA: A field found to be illegal must be made legal within a "reasonable" time, or the home team is subject to forfeit. (4-1a Pen)

OBR: No provision. (See § 421.)

240 FIELD: ON-DECK CIRCLE ✪

FED: The on-deck circle should be 37 feet from the plate. If there is not sufficient room, the circle should be a "safe distance" from home plate. (1-2-1 Diagram 2; 2-23; 1.2.1, 1990 ed)

NCAA: Where space is available, the circle must be a minimum of 30 feet from the plate. The recommended distance is 37 feet. (1-5e) **250. ALSO:** The on-deck circle may not be located within the triangle created when the first- and third-base lines are extended: "The on-deck position should be in NEAR VICINITY of the dugout." (1-2a Diagram 2; 1-5e)

OBR: The on-deck circle must be 37 feet from the plate. (1.04 Diagram 1) *See ¶8.*

★ 241 FIELD: SCOREBOARD ✪

FED: No provision.

NCAA: A scoreboard is recommended. ***(ADDED)*** "It shall not be placed in line with the batter's background sector of vision." (1-17) (See § 485.)

OBR: No provision.

242 FIELD: START OF GAME: FIELD UNPLAYABLE ✪

FED: The home coach shall decide whether conditions are suitable for starting the game. (4-1-1)

NCAA: The coach and the AD shall decide if the field is playable. (4-2a)

OBR: The home team shall decide if conditions warrant play. (3.10a)

❀ Note 207: In 1870, the home team captain decided whether to start. By 1950, the captain or manager could decide. Now it's the "home team," meaning the general manager.

243 FIELD: SUSPENSION OF GAME: FIELD UNPLAYABLE ✪

(See § 509.)

FED: After the umpire calls "Play," the "umpires" are the sole judges of when to suspend play. (4-1-1) **EXCEPT:** The UIC has sole authority to stop the game if "conditions become unfit for play." (10-2-3e)

NCAA: Only the UIC may suspend play. But the UIC must consult with the game administrator "to determine suspension, resumption or termination of play." The administrator and the UIC "shall follow lightning guidelines in the appendix section." (4-2b; Appendix C) (See § 229 and 485.)

OBR: Same as NCAA concerning who suspends play. (3.10c)

> **EXCEPT:** OFF INTERP 190-243: **PBUC:** Before the UIC calls the game, he and his crew must consult in full view of the stands: "The consultation adds support to the decision." {5.3} ✠

❀ Note 208: "Consulting" is the current buzz word in umpiring circles. You'll remember the long "consultation" among the umpires in the 2003 ALDS after Miguel Tejada was tagged out jogging to the plate following an obstruction call at third.

(See Play 36-33. See also § 509, which covers consultation between/among umpires.)

244 FIELD: WARNING TRACK ✪

FED: No provision.

NCAA: It is recommended that a warning track (15-feet wide minimum) be constructed in front of the outfield fence, backstop, and dugout areas. (1-5a) (See § 309.)

OBR: No provision.

★ 245 FIELDER: POSITIONS OCCUPIED AT TIME OF PITCH/PLAY ✪ (See § 6.)

FED: Except the catcher, all fielders must be in fair territory at TOP. ***(EDITED)*** A fielder is in fair territory if he has **ONE** foot touching fair ground. (1-1-4) **PENALTY:** ball/balk. (1-1-4 Pen) **EXCEPT:** A fielder **WITHOUT PENALTY** may go onto foul ground to take a throw from a pitcher on the pitcher's plate. (1.1.4)

NCAA: Except the catcher, all fielders must be in fair territory when the ball is put in play. A fielder is in fair ground if he has **ONE** foot in fair territory. (5-4) **PENALTY:** A play is nullified if the defense benefits. (5-4c Pen) (See § 6 for how this affects an appeal.)

✻ *Play 97-245:* ***(EDITED)*** **FED and NCAA only.** R1, R3, 1 out. The umpire points to the pitcher, signifying a live ball. F9 sneaks up the line in foul territory, readying himself to back up a throw to ensure that R3 cannot score on a wild throw. Just before the pitcher delivers, the right fielder jumps back into fair ground. B1 smashes a drive off the first baseman's glove, and F9, because of his proximity to the base, makes a miraculous catch. He throws to F3 to double up the runner. *Ruling:* In FED, the play stands: F9 was in fair ground at the time of the pitch. In NCAA, the play is nullified: When the UIC put the ball in play, F9 was in foul ground.

> **251. ALSO:** OFF INTERP 191-245: **THURSTON:** If a fielder moves into foul territory (perhaps expecting an appeal) before the pitcher delivers a pitch that is not a batted ball, there is no advantage to the defense, and the pitch will stand whether it is a ball or strike. (phone call to se, 2/13/95) ✠

(ADDED) ✻ *Play 98-245*: **FED and NCAA only.** R1, R3, 1 out, 2-2 count. The umpire signals a live ball. The pitcher is peering in for his sign while F9 sneaks up in foul territory behind first. The pitcher delivers. B1 swings and misses for strike three. The coach at first base s points out to U1 that the right fielder is still in foul territory. *Ruling:* In FED, it's a balk. R3 scores, R1 goes to second. In NCAA, the play stands: The pitch did not result in a batted ball.

OBR: Except the catcher, all fielders must be in fair territory when the ball is put in play ***(EDITED)*** "at the start of" or "during a game." (4.03)

AO 14-245: EVANS: In the major leagues the first baseman is not required to have both feet in fair territory. (4:9)

> **252. ALSO:** OFF INTERP 192-245: **PBUC:** Umpires should not insist a first baseman have both feet in fair territory unless one team complains, but thereafter the umpire will require fielders to have both feet in fair ground: "Enforce the rule as written." {3.18} ✠

AO 15-245: EVANS: "No inning shall commence with less than nine defensive players on the field. If an inning is started inadvertently with less than nine players, all action which takes place under these conditions shall be nullified." (4:72)

❀ Note 209: Evans' "Customs and Usage" ruling is identical to Wendelstedt's OFF INTERP below.

> **253. ALSO:** OFF INTERP 193-245: ***(EDITED)*** **WENDELSTEDT:** PENALTY: Any play is nullified when a fielder is not in fair territory. (HW/72) ✠

(ADDED) ❀ Note 210: Here is a the summary of the differences:

IF WE ASSUME A FIELDER IS NOT IN FAIR GROUND

> **FED:** At the time of the pitch: PENALTY: ball/balk.
> **NCAA:** At the time the ball becomes alive: PENALTY: Play stands if the defense does not benefit.
> **OBR:** At the time the ball becomes alive: PENALTY: All action is nullified.

(ADDED) ✻ *Play 99-245:* 0 on, 0 outs, 0 count. The lead-off batter of the inning homers. As the BR is touching third base, the right fielder comes sprinting out of his dugout. He had been in the restroom between innings and was not on the field for the pitch. *Ruling:* In FED, the home run is nullified. B1 returns to bat with a count of 0-1. In NCAA, the play stands. In OBR, the play is nullified. B1 re turns to bat with a count of 0-0.

(ADDED) ❀ Note 211: The play is adapted from Wendelstedt, P61/73.

✻ *Play 100-245:* Able singles to lead off the seventh. Baker doubles. With two men on, the UIC discovers the right fielder is missing. It is determined F9 was not on the field during the two at bats. *Ruling:* ***(EXPANDED)*** In FED, balk: Both runners advance. In NCAA, the play stands. In OBR, the inning begins again.

✻ *Play 101-245:* R3: The manager goes to the mound, and F7 stands in the bullpen. When the trip is over, F7 starts toward his third-base dugout. The third baseman plays well away from the bag, so R3 takes a big lead. F1 then steps to third as the left fielder and third baseman both race for the bag. F7 takes the throw, but his tag of R3 is not in time. *Ruling:* In FED, the play stands. In NCAA / OBR, the play is nullified.

✲ *Play 102-245:* R3. B1 flies deep to left. The umpire realizes F7 was not in fair territory at the time of the pitch. F7 catches the ball, R3 retouches, and he is out at the plate. *Ruling:* In FED, it's a balk: R3 scores, B1 bats again. In NCAA, the play is nullified unless the umpire determines the left fielder gained no advantage. In OBR, the play is nullified.

✲ *Play 103-245:* R1, R3. The pitcher (on the pitcher's plate) attempts to pick off R3, but his throw goes into the stands. Before the attempt, the left fielder had moved onto foul ground to take the throw.
Ruling: ***(REVISED)*** In FED / NCAA, the overthrow stands: Award each runner one base, so R3 scores and R1 goes to second. In OBR, you will nullify the play.

❀ Note 212: The play stands in FED: It was legal because the pitcher did not deliver; if he had pitched, it would have been a balk. In NCAA, the play stands because the defense did not benefit. In OBR, nothing happened because the left fielder was in foul ground when the play began.

✲ *Play 104-245:* R1, R3. The pitcher from the set delivers for a called strike one. The right fielder, thinking a play was on, had sneaked into foul territory behind R1. *Ruling:* In FED, enforce the balk penalty: No pitch, both runners advance. In NCAA, the strike stands. In OBR, the umpire nullifies the pitch.

❀ Note 213: Remember, though, in FED if the pitcher had tried to pick off R1, the right fielder would have occupied a legal position.

✲ *Play 105-245:* R1, R3. The pitcher's pick-off throw rolls down the right-field line. At TOT, the right fielder had sneaked into foul territory behind R1. R3 scores, but R1 is thrown out trying for third. *Ruling:* In FED, the play stands: F9 was in legal position. In NCAA, the offensive coach has an option: one run in and one man out, or a "do-over" with runners still at the corners. In OBR, the play is nullified.

❀ Note 214: The umpire has no business trying to decide if the college team benefitted from the play. Let the skipper choose.

❀ Note 215: ***(EDITED)*** Position occupied at time of pitch or play is one of nine major rules or interpretations **WHERE EACH LEVEL TREATS THE SITUATION DIFFERENTLY**. The other eight are: § 50-71 (designated hitter); § 83 (use illegal bat); § 124 (throw from dead-ball area); § 144 (conferences); § 246 (fighting); § 266 (improperly declared infield fly); § 378 (hidden ball play); § 488 (illegal substitutes).

★ 246 FIGHT RULE: CHARGING OR ABUSING AN OFFICIAL OR OPPONENT ✪

FED: No game participant may charge an umpire. (3-3-1k)
PENALTY: warning or ejection. (3-3-1k Pen)

***(CHANGED)* 254. ALSO:** "Confronting or directing unsportsmanlike conduct" to an umpire after the game or until he leaves the field is forbidden. (3-3-1g-7) **PENALTY:** The state association shall determine appropriate action." (3-3-1g7 Pen) Last edition: No provision.

***(CHANGED)* 255. ALSO:** "The game officials retain clerical authority over the contest through the completion of any reports ... that are responsive to actions occurring while the umpires had jurisdiction." (10-1-2; Website 2012, #8 and 9) Last edition: No provision.

256. ALSO: No game participant may leave his position or bench to engage in "fighting or physical confrontation." (3-3-1q) **PENALTY:** Ejection. (3-3-1q Pen) A coach who attempts to stop the fight is not in violation. (3-3-1q Pen; 3.3.1pp, qq, and rr)

(ADDED) OFF INTERP 194-246: **HOPKINS:** After a confrontation between a runner and the shortstop, several players leave the dugout and advance to the foul line. "THEY DO NOT ENGAGE IN ANY CONFRONTATIONAL ACTIVITY." *Ruling:* "Players who leave their positions on the field or the bench during a fight or physical confrontation are to be ejected. (Website 2012, #10) ✠

NCAA: POE 1990, 1992, 1993, 1994, 1995, 1996, 1997, 1998, 1999, 2000 [fight rule penalty]: No player, coach, or team representative may physically abuse or fight with an official or opposing player. (5-16) (See § 247 and 248.)
(See § 405 for BEANBALL information.)

☹ **POE 1999**: PHYSICAL ABUSE OF: OFFICIAL: Physical abuse is defined as "any THREAT of physical intimidation or harm to include pushing, shoving, kicking, intentionally spitting, spewing, throwing at or ATTEMPTING TO MAKE PHYSICAL CONTACT." (5-16b)

257. ALSO: For a violent attack on ("punching or kicking") or fight with an official or opposing coach, the suspension **PENALTY:** Next five games, even for first offense. (5-16b Ex) (See PARTICIPANTS LEAVE POSITIONS [this section] for the definition of a fight.)

258. ALSO: Umpires should immediately consult video evidence, if available, to identify players involved in a fight. (5-16c-4) (See § 220.)

259. ALSO: If multiple suspensions would create a "difficulty in fielding a team for its next game or games," the institution may request staggered suspensions from its conference. Independent teams should work with the secretary-rules editor. (5-16 AR2)

☹ PHYSICAL ABUSE OF: PLAYER: Physical abuse is defined as an attempt to "strike with the arms, hands, legs, feet or equipment in a combative manner or intentionally spitting at an opponent." (5-16a)

260. ALSO: The penalties are in effect for fall ball and carry over into spring competition, from the regular season to the post season, and from the post season to the upcoming season. (5-16)

261. ALSO: Conferences may adopt more stringent penalties. (5-16a and b Pen 4g) **PENALTY:** The offender(s) is immediately ejected. He must leave the field, he may not communicate with any team personnel, and he must change out of his uniform if he remains at the site. (5-16a and b Pen 4a and 4b) (See § 164.) Additionally:

(● 1) for first offense: three-game suspension; (5-16a and b Pen 1)

(● 2) for second offense in the same season: five-game suspension; (5-16a and b Pen 2)

(● 3) for third offense in the same season: suspension for the remainder of the season, including postseason play. If the ejection comes in the last game of a season, a one-game penalty is assessed for the first contest in the following spring season. (5-16a and b Pen 3)

EXCEPT: The suspensions meted out under the fight rule **DO NOT APPLY** to participants ejected for verbal abuse or arguing (5-17 Pen AR) though any participant ejected for a violation of the Code of Ethics is suspended for one game. (3-6d Pen) (See § 119, 247 and 248.)

262. ALSO: Suspensions are served for the "team's next previously scheduled and completed contest(s)." Halted or suspended games "against the originally scheduled opponent" shall count as "regularly scheduled contests." Games may not be added after the incident to satisfy the penalty. (5-16 AR 1)

263. ALSO: Suspended participants must serve their suspensions at once: "There shall be no appeal of the penalty." (5-16a and b Pen 4h)

> * *Play 106-246:* **NCAA only.** Players from Baylor and Texas A&M duke it out in the final game of a series, and umpires suspend two players from each team. The University of Texas is coming to College Station, and the first game will be completion of a previous game halted in the top of the ninth inning with A&M leading 9-0. The two suspended Aggies are withheld from the game (inning). *Ruling:* The players have NOT served their suspension: Although the game was "previously scheduled," it was not "completed."

264. ALSO: Players suspended for infractions of the Fight Rule "shall be prohibited from any communication or contact, direct or indirect, with the team, coaches and/or bench personnel from the start of the contest to its completion — including all extra innings." (5-16)

☹ **POE 1995, 1996**: PARTICIPANTS LEAVE POSITIONS: Team personnel (players, coaches, trainers, managers) shall not leave their positions to participate in a fight, which is defined as a confrontation marked by "pushing, shoving or bumping." (5-16c) An individual's "position" is determined by where he is at the time a confrontation occurs. (5-16c)

PENALTY: (● 1) All team members who participate in a fight after leaving their positions shall receive a three-game penalty for a first offense.

(● 2) A batter or runner who starts a fight by charging the pitcher is suspended for three games.

(● 3) A pitcher who leaves the mound to start a fight is suspended for three games.

❀ Note 216: One might think the rules committee is stacked with former pitchers. A 3-game suspension for a player amounts to 3 games. Three games for a pitcher? He won't even miss a start. Amazing!

(● 4) If players involved in action join a fight, they are ejected and suspended for three games.

(● 5) Second offenders are suspended for the remainder of the season, including postseason competition. (5-16c Pen 1 through 5)

☺ PENALTY FOR STOPPING FIGHTS: (● 1) Any player involved in a fight who has remained at his position and is judged to be merely defending himself shall not be ejected or suspended. (5-16c Pen AR 1) (● 2) A player or coach who makes physical contact with another player "in an obvious attempt to prevent a fight or confrontation shall not be ejected or suspended." (5-16c Pen AR 2)

☺ UMPIRES' JURISDICTION: An umpire has jurisdiction to impose penalties for fighting "from the beginning of the game until the umpires have left the playing area (stadium) after the final game of the day." (5-16a and b Pen 4e) (See § 419.)

265. ALSO: POE 1998, 1999, 2000: The "ejecting" umpire must file a "suspension report" with the athletic director of the offending team, the secretary-editor of the NCAA rulebook, and – if appropriate – a conference administrator. (5-16a and b Pen 4f)

☺ENFORCEMENT: The institution's head baseball coach and athletic director are responsible for enforcing the penalties. (5-16a and b Pen 4c)

OBR: No game participant may make intentional contact with an umpire. (4.06a-4) **PENALTY:** ejection. (9.01d)

266. ALSO: OFF INTERP 195-246: **PBUC:** Any member of the offensive team who charges the pitcher will be automatically ejected if he "moves a reasonable distance toward the pitcher with the intention of fighting." {3.24} ✠

❀ Note 217: ***(EDITED)*** Fighting is one of nine major rules or interpretations **WHERE EACH LEVEL TREATS THE SITUATION DIFFERENTLY.** The other eight are: § 50-71 (designated hitter); § 83 (use illegal bat); § 124 (throw from dead-ball area); § 144 (conferences / trips to the mound); § 245 (positions occupied at time of pitch or play); § 266 (improperly declared infield fly); § 378 (hidden ball play); §488 (illegal substitutes).

247 FIGHT RULE: SUSPENDED PLAYER: CAUSES FORFEIT ✪

FED: No provision.

❀ Note 218: Some state associations, conferences, or districts have rules regarding players participating after suspension. Check with your supervisor.

NCAA: If a player or coach suspended under the provisions of the "Fight Rule" (§ 246) participates in a game, it will be forfeited when the infraction is discovered. (5-16a and b Pen 4c) (See § 248.)

OBR: No provision. (See § 119 and 248.) *See ¶8.*

248 FIGHT RULE: SUSPENDED PLAYER: IN UNIFORM / DUGOUT ✪

FED: No provision.

NCAA: Personnel suspended for fighting shall not be in uniform, allowed in any team area, or perform any team duty while serving their suspension. (5-16b-Pen 4a and b) (See § 164, 246 and 247.)

OBR: Suspended players, coaches, or managers may not be in the dugout or the press box. (4.07 CMT)

249 FLY BALL: DEFINITION ✪

FED: A fly ball is a batted ball that rises an "appreciable height above the ground." (2-6-2)

267. ALSO: OFF INTERP 196-249: **RUMBLE:** "Appreciable height" means the batted ball must rise above the batter's head before it can be caught for an out. (*News* #33, 4/87) ✠

NCAA: A fly ball is a batted ball that goes "high" in the air "directly off the bat." (2-31)

OBR: A fly ball is a batted ball that goes high in the air "in flight." (2.00 Fly Ball)

★ 250 FORCE PLAY: NOT REMOVED FOR APPEAL OF BASERUNNING ERROR ✪

FED: A force in effect at the time of the pitch remains in effect for the entire play only if a baserunning error occurs **BEFORE** a following runner is put out. (8-2 Pen; 9-1-1b; 9.1.1k) (See § 253.)

NCAA: If a runner is put out during live action, his out does not remove the force on any preceding runner who might later be called out for a baserunning infraction. (8-5j Ex)

OBR: Point not covered.

OFF INTERP 197-250: **FITZPATRICK:** Same as FED 8-2 Pen. (email to cc, 11/15/00) ✠

❊ *Play 107-250:* Bases loaded, 1 out. B1 slaps an apparent extra-base hit, but he is thrown out trying for second (2 outs). On appeal, R2 is called out for missing third (3 outs). *Ruling:* R3's run does not count — but for different reasons at different levels. In NCAA, the run is canceled because the force remained in effect throughout the play. In FED and OBR, the force in effect at the time of the pitch remained throughout the play because the running error occurred **BEFORE** the out at second. (Study Play 108 next.)

❊ *Play 108-250:* Bases loaded, 0 out. B1 hits into a 6-4-3 double play. R3 scores easily. R2, running hard, tries for home and is safe on a close play. On appeal, R2 is then declared out for missing third: 3 outs. *Ruling:* In NCAA, even though two following runners were put out first, R3's run is canceled: R2 was forced to third at the time of the pitch — and never legally made it. In FED and OBR, because the baserunning error occurred after the out at second, the force on R2 was removed and R3's run counts.

251 FORCE PLAY: REINSTATED
ALL CODES NOW AGREE: TEXT DELETED, 1991.

252 FORCE PLAY REMOVED: ADVANCING RUNNER MISSES BASE
THIS SECTION WAS REINSTATED AS § 10.

★ ∞ 253 FORCE PLAY REMOVED: FOLLOWING RUNNER IS PUT OUT ✪

FED: For any given runner, a force is removed whenever a "following runner is **PUT OUT** at a previous base." (2-29-3) (See § 250.)

NCAA: Same as FED. (8-5j Ex)

OBR: A force is removed whenever a following runner is "put out on a **FORCE PLAY**." (7.08e) (See § 10.)

★ 254 FORFEIT: DOUBLE ✪

FED: No provision.

NCAA: **POE 1999**: The umpires will declare a double forfeit if: (● 1) Both teams are at fault and the situation is "so out of control" that continuing the game is unsafe; or (● 2) following ejections and suspensions neither team has enough eligible players. (5-12h) **PENALTY:** Following ejections for fighting: If a team does not have sufficient players to continue, it will forfeit the next **THREE** contests. (5-12h Pen)

> ***(ADDED)*** ❀ Note 219-254: "A game shall be forfeited only as a **LAST RESORT**" says the NCAA rule. (5-12) That applies to the double forfeit discussed here and to § 255, 256, 257, 258, and 260. Regardless of black-letter law, though, if a forfeit situation arises and one team cannot resolve its problem, the UIC "SHOULD" forfeit. (BRD recommendation)
> BRD omitted § 259 from the "may/may not" forfeit list because when a team has just eight players, it **CANNOT** continue. "Forfeit" is the only option.

OBR: No provision.

255 FORFEIT: FAILURE TO APPEAR: FIRST GAME ✪

FED: A team **"SHALL"** forfeit if it "is late in appearing or beginning after the umpire calls 'Play.'" (4-4-1a) State associations must set guidelines for forfeits when one team is late in appearing. (4.4.1f)

NCAA: Unless the delay is unavoidable, after a team arrives at the game site, it **MAY** forfeit that game for failure "to appear upon the field or,

being upon the field, refuses to begin" a regularly scheduled game within five minutes after the umpire calls, "Play."
(5-12a) (See Note 219-254 and § 457.)

OBR: Same as NCAA. (4.15a)

❀ Note 220-255: I am indebted to Jim Evans for enlightening me on the difference between "shall forfeit" (OBR 4.16 [groundskeepers won't do their jobs] and OBR 4.17 [insufficient players] and "may forfeit" (OBR 4.15, which includes all those offenses that so upset amateur umpires). (JEA 4:70) On the other hand, the NCAA lists all forfeit offenses as possibilities: "a game **MAY** be forfeited...." Obviously, they don't mean that literally in all situations; for example, a team has only eight eligible players. No one can guess what would happen if an umpire, reading (literally) from the 2011 NCAA book, says: "Well, let's play on with eight."On the third hand, FED, wisely, does not offer the UIC any leeway; that is, there is no "may forfeit" language in that book. See ya! In short: FED – all must; NCAA – all may; OBR – some must, some may. I LOVE THIS GAME!

★ ∞256 FORFEIT: FAILURE TO APPEAR: SECOND GAME ✪

FED: No provision.

NCAA: Point not covered.

> ***(ADDED)*** OFF INTERP 198-256: **PARONTO:** Same as OBR 4.15g. (email to cc, 12/20/11) (See Note 219-254.) ✠

OBR: If a team fails to appear for the second game of a double-header within 20 minutes after the end of the previous game, the game may be forfeited unless the time has been extended by the UIC of the first game. (4.15g) *See ¶8.*

★ 257 FORFEIT: FIELD NOT MADE READY ✪

FED: The home team shall forfeit if it "fails to comply with the umpire's order" to make the field ready for play. (4-4-1g) (See § 239.)

NCAA: Point not covered.

> ***(ADDED)*** OFF INTERP 199-257: **PARONTO:** After the umpire calls "Play," he 6is in charge of the grounds crew. (email to cc, 12/20/11) (See § 239.) (See also Note 219-254) ✠

OBR: Same as FED. (4.16) (See Note 220-255 and § 514.)
268. ALSO: The UIC is in charge of groundskeepers to make the field ready between games of a double-header or whenever the game is suspended because the field is unfit. (3.11)

258 FORFEIT: GAME NOT RESUMED ✪

FED: After a "reasonable time," the game shall be forfeited if one team refuses to continue play following the start of the contest. (4-4-1c)

NCAA: A team may forfeit if it does not resume play within one minute after the umpire's order. (5-12c) (See § 140.)
(See also Note 219-254.)

OBR: Same as NCAA. (4.15d) (See Note 220-255 and § 514.)

★ 259 FORFEIT: INSUFFICIENT PLAYERS ✪

FED: When no eligible substitute is available, a team may finish the game with eight (but not fewer than eight) players. **PENALTY:** For fewer than eight players: The short-handed team shall forfeit the game. (4-4-1f) (See § 164 and 488.)
269. ALSO: If a player must leave the game after reaching base and the team has no eligible substitute, the most recent batter not on base may run for the incapacitated or ejected player. The "emergency substitute" runs until he is put out, scores, or the half inning ends; but the "missing" player is thereafter called out each time his turn comes to bat.
(4-4-1f Nt 1; 7-4-1g; 4.4.1b)

> **270. ALSO:** OFF INTERP 200-259: **HOPKINS:** If a player at bat (B1) must be replaced because of illness, injury, or ejection, when there is no eligible substitute, the batter is declared out. B2 is the next batter. (Website 2010, #12) ✠

⁎ *Play 109-259:* **FED only.** With 0 out, B1 has a count of 0-1 when his nose begins to bleed. He must be removed, but the team has no eligible substitutes. *Ruling:* B1 is out. B2 now bats with 1 out.

271. ALSO: A team reduced to eight players may return to nine. (4-4-1f Nt 2; 4.4.1 c and d) (See § 498 to learn who can be in the starting lineup.)

272. ALSO: A short-handed team is not required to return to nine players. (4.4.1c CMT; confirmed, Website 2007, #17)

❀ Note 221: There was a problem with the 2010 case book. Situation 4.4.1a concerned a team with an ejected player and no eligible substitutes. The ruling: "The team may play with eight and it must finish with eight." Contrast that with Situation 4.4.1d, referenced above, where a short-handed team may return to nine. The editor caught the error: Both plays now have the same ruling.

NCAA: A team **MAY** forfeit when it no longer has nine eligible players. (5-12g) (See § 164 and Note 219-255.)

❀ Note 222: Here's a quote from the NCAA book: ***(EDITED)*** "A game **MAY** be forfeited by the umpire-in-chief, **AFTER CONSULTATION WITH**

THE UMPIRING CREW" for eight reasons, one of which is a team remains with insufficient players. (See Note 220-255.)

OBR: ***(EDITED)*** A team SHALL forfeit when it cannot – or refuses to – put nine eligible players ON THE FIELD. (4.17) (See § 140. See also § 245 for what happens when the defense INADVERTENTLY does not put nine men on the field.)

273. ALSO: OFF INTERP 201-259: **FITZPATRICK:** If a team does not have nine eligible players remaining, the game is forfeited when the short-handed team: (1) on defense, is on or must take the field; or (2) on offense, reaches a vacant position in the batting order. (email to cc, 11/15/00) ✠

❀ Note 223: At all levels, teams must begin the game with nine players.

⁜ *Play 110-259:* R1, R2, 1 out. The home team, behind one run in the last inning, is at bat. B1 singles. R3 crosses the plate to tie the score, but R2 is thrown out trying to tally the winning run. He heatedly protests the umpire's decision and is ejected. His team has no eligible substitute, and the ejection leaves the coach with only eight players.
Ruling: In FED, the game continues. In NCAA, the short-handed team "may" forfeit. In OBR, the game continues: The winning run is on first with 2 outs. If R1 scores, the home team will win; if the defense records a third out, the home team forfeits.

⁜ *Play 111-259:* The same action occurs as in Play 110 above, but this time the player objecting is the on-deck batter. He is ejected, leaving the team with only eight eligible players. *Ruling:* In FED, an out is registered because the "missing" player is due to bat. The game moves into extra innings. In NCAA, the contest "may" be forfeited. In OBR, since the team has no substitute available and a vacant spot has been reached in the lineup, the team must forfeit.

★ 260 FORFEIT: POLICE PROTECTION INADEQUATE ✪

FED: No provision.

NCAA: Point not covered.

(ADDED) OFF INTERP 202-260: **PARONTO:** It is the home team's Game Management responsibility to provide adequate security for the protection of spectators, participants, and umpires throughout the contest and until the umpires have left the game site. (email to cc, 12/20/11) ✠ (See also Note 219-254.) (See § 229.)

OBR: The game may be forfeited if, after 15 minutes, the home team has not provided sufficient police protection to clear the field of spectators. (3.18 Pen) (See § 229.)

261 FORFEIT: REPORT SUBMITTED ✪

FED: No provision.

❀ Note 224: Check league, district, or conference rules for the correct forfeit procedures.

NCAA: POE 1998, 1999: If a game is forfeited, the UIC shall submit a written report to the athletic directors involved as well as the conference office (if applicable), and the secretary-rules editor of the NCAA Rules Committee. (5-12 Nt)

OBR: The written forfeit report is submitted to the league president. (4.18) *See ¶8.*

❀ Note 225: Funny how that is still in the book when there isn't a league president anymore. Bud Selig abolished the position in 1999. According to *Baseball Digest*, he did it to "unify the leagues."

★ 262 FORFEIT: UMPIRES CONSULT ✪ (See § 509.)

FED: The UIC has "sole authority to forfeit a game." (10-2-2)

NCAA: Forfeit is a "last resort." The UIC after consultation with the "umpiring crew" may forfeit a game. (5-12)

❀ Note 226: "Consultation" is a vague term, but it does mean everybody must get together in full view of the teams and fans. In a three-man crew, will they take a vote? (See § 423.)

OBR: Same as FED. (9.04a-6; 9.04b-3) **EXCEPT:**

> ***(ADDED)*** OFF INTERP 203-262: **PBUC:** Before declaring a game forfeited, the crew shall consult with the league office. {5.15} *See ¶8.* ✠

★ 263 FRATERNIZATION ✪

FED: No provision.

NCAA: Point not covered.

> ***(ADDED)*** OFF INTERP 204-263: **PARONTO:** Same as OBR. (email to cc, 12/20/11) ✠

OBR: Umpires shall prohibit fraternization among uniformed members of different teams ***(ADDED)***. or "mingle with spectators." (3.09)

∞264 INFIELD FLY: DEFINITION ✪ (See § 265.)

FED: The umpire will declare an infield fly if it can be handled with ordinary effort by an infielder. The rule "does not preclude" an outfielder from making the catch. (2-19) (See § 266.)

NCAA: The umpire will declare an infield fly if it can be handled by an infielder, the battery, or an **OUTFIELDER STATIONED IN THE INFIELD.** (2-47)

❀ Note 227: Here's more evidence that the catcher is not an infielder. (See § 267.)

OBR: Same as NCAA. (2.00 Infield Fly) (See § 317.)
274. ALSO: The umpire will declare an infield fly if it can be handled by an **OUTFIELDER NOT STATIONED IN THE INFIELD** when the official judges an infielder could as easily have handled the ball. (2.00 Infield Fly CMT) (See § 267.)

> OFF INTERP 205-264: **PBUC:** The umpire is to declare an infield fly based on the ordinary effort of the fielder, "not by some arbitrary limitation such as the grass or the base lines." {9.5} ✠

❀ Note 228: You will know, of course, that the OFF INTERP above applies most specifically to professional play. In a 10u contest, you would be wise to set the limitation as the base lines. As you travel up the age groups, etc ....

★ 265 INFIELD FLY: ORDINARY EFFORT: DEFINITION ✪
(See § 264.)

FED: No provision.

NCAA: Point not covered.

> *(ADDED)* OFF INTERP 206-265: **PARONTO:** Same as OBR. (email to cc, 12/20/11) ✠

OBR: Ordinary effort is the "average skill" that a position player should demonstrate "in that league ... with due consideration" of the weather and field conditions. (2.00 Ordinary Effort)

❀ Note 229: The OBR strikes again — for the good. Heretofore, umpires simply guessed at the meaning of this important term. Now, the pros have set in concrete that the age and skill of the players as well as the condition of the field must be considered when determining ordinary effort. Bravo! The BRD expects the other books to follow shortly.

★ 266 INFIELD FLY: UMPIRES ERR ✪

FED: (● 1) UMPIRES WRONGLY DECLARE AN INFIELD FLY: If a pop-up in the infield **IS NOT AN INFIELD FLY** (by definition because, for example, first base is not occupied) but the umpires erroneously declare out the batter, **IT IS NOT AN INFIELD FLY** and any action that occurs will stand. Both teams have the responsibility for knowing whether conditions exist for an infield fly. (10.2.3f)
(● 2) UMPIRES FAIL TO DECLARE AN INFIELD FLY: If a pop-up in the infield **IS AN INFIELD FLY** by rule but the umpires fail to call it, **THE BATTER IS OUT ANYWAY** since both teams "have the responsibility to know when conditions exist for an infield fly." (10.2.3g) "The situation determines the out, not the declaration." (7.4.1g) (See § 264.)

> **275. ALSO:** OFF INTERP 207-266: **RUMBLE:** When an infield fly occurs but is not declared, if any other runner is put out, that out will also stand. (*News* #7, 3/92) (See also 7.4.1g.) ✠

❀ Note 230: The huge problem with 10.2.3g and OFF INTERP 207 above is that the umpire must subsequently agree that the batted ball **WAS** an infield fly and not a hump-backed, soft line drive. Some umpires don't like to admit mistakes, so they make a bigger one trying to cover up the first.

NCAA: Point not covered.

> OFF INTERP 208-266: **THURSTON:** If the umpires err in not calling an infield fly, when the play is over, they must "get the play right": (1) The batter is out; (2) runners keep any bases they made on their own; and (3) if the defense puts out any baserunner, that out is canceled. Thurston agreed with Fitzpatrick: "Under no circumstances should the defense get a double play because the umpire failed to declare the infield fly." (phone call to cc, 2/29/00) ✠

OBR: Point not covered.

> OFF INTERP 209-266: **FITZPATRICK:** The umpires must ensure the intent of the rule is enforced: They must protect the offensive team from an "undeserved" double play. That could require a belated "infield fly" ruling and revocation of subsequent action: "Above all, do not allow a double play that should not occur." (email to cc, 11/15/00) ✠

❀ Note 231: In NCAA/OBR, if an umpire fails to declare properly an infield fly, then there was no infield fly unless a double play occurred. After the double play, the umpires must rely on NCAA 3-6b and OBR 9.01c to get it right. Additionally, if the umpire declares an infield pop-up to be an infield fly **WHEN IT IS NOT**, no infield fly occurred: What happens, happens. That would harmonize with the FED ruling in such cases.

⁎ *Play 112-266*: R1, R2, 0 out. B1 hits a towering pop fly on the infield. F4 moves only a step or two before settling under the ball. Inexplicably, the umpires fail to declare the infield fly. At the last moment F4 steps back, and the ball falls to the ground untouched; both R1 and R2 attempt to advance. F4 recovers the ball on one bounce, tags R1, and throws to third in time for a tag of R2 sliding in. *Ruling:* In FED, the defense has secured a triple play. In NCAA / OBR, because the umpires failed to declare the infield fly, the defense has recorded an "undeserved" double play. Therefore, the umpires must declare a dead ball, rule B1 out on the infield fly, and return R1 and R2 to TOP.

❀ Note 232: On obvious plays that is easy. The coach will yell: "The batter's out, stay where you are," and that will wake up the umpires. But in other situations, the case may not be so plain. Was it an infield fly or a soft, looping line drive? BRD recommends: Since the FED umpires can protect either team put at a disadvantage when an umpire's call is changed (§ 506), the umpires must be sure their failure to call an infield fly did not unfairly penalize the offense. In Play 112, the triple play should probably stand: There could be little doubt the popup conformed to the conditions for an infield fly. But if the umpires in another situation simply change their minds (it **WAS** an infield fly they should have called but didn't), then the BRD recommends they should simply call out B1 and leave the other runners on the bases occupied at TOP.

⁎ *Play 113-266:* R1, R2, 0 out. B1 lifts an easy pop fly to the pitcher. The umpires fail to call infield fly, and F1 does not make the catch. He retrieves the ball in time to throw to third for a tag out of R2 sliding in as R1 goes to second and B1 stops on first. *Ruling:* In FED, both B1 and R2 are out. In NCAA / OBR, because the defense did not record a double play, the play stands: one out, runners on first and second.

⁎ *Play 114-266:* Bases loaded, one out. B1 hits a high pop-up toward the third baseman who is quickly able to get under the ball. Even though the batted ball meets all the conditions of an infield fly, neither umpire so declares. While over fair territory, the ball hits the heel of F5's glove and falls to the ground. The runners, not hearing "infield fly," take off. F5 recovers in time to tag R2. *Ruling:* In FED, both B1 and R2 are out: 3 outs. R3's run counts if he scored before F5 tagged out R2. In NCAA, when the umpires admit their error, they will cancel R2's out. Instead, B1 is out, R2 is on second, and R3 scores. In OBR, since the defense put out only one runner, the play stands.

❀ Note 233: It is true that the NCAA interpretation means the umpires' error costs the defense an out and a run, which does not appear fair. But the defensive player had an easy chance, and he blew it. The batter is out on the infield fly; the runner advances on F5's error.

❀ Note 234: George Demetriou, a writer friend of mine, emailed to ask: "In BRD, you say that an improperly declared infield fly is treated differently by the three codes. Do you have a situation where there are three different rulings on the same play?" I replied that Play 114-266 was such a play: three books, three different rulings. George demurred: "I don't mean to be picky, but what threw me off is you say in Note 235 that one of the seven [now eight] situations is an 'improperly declared infield fly.' Play 114 is a play where the "umpires **FAIL** to declare an infield fly." So I made one last try: "An 'improperly declared infield fly' is one that is declared an infield fly (but isn't) or one that is **NOT DECLARED** an infield fly (but is)." George: "Thanks. I'm very anal sometimes." Umpires often are.

⁜ *Play 115-266:* R1, R2. The pitcher uncorks a wild pitch and each runner advances. B1 then lifts an easy fly to the infield with the first baseman getting ready for the catch. The field umpire erroneously calls: "Infield fly; the batter is out." The first baseman drops the ball but recovers in time to throw out R3 at home as B1 stops on first and R2 takes third. *Ruling:* The declaration of "infield fly" does not an infield fly make: "The situation determines the out, not the declaration." The play stands.

❀ Note 235: ***(EDITED)*** An improperly declared infield fly is one of nine major rules situations **WHERE EACH LEVEL TREATS THE PLAY DIFFERENTLY**. The other eight are: § 50 (designated hitter); § 83 illegal bat); § 124 (throw from dead-ball territory); § 144 (conferences / trips to the mound); § 245 (positions occupied at time of pitch or play); § 246 (fighting); § 378 (hidden ball play); § 488 (illegal substitutes).

267 INFIELDER: DEFINITION ✪

FED: The catcher is an infielder. (2-13-3)

> **276. ALSO:** OFF INTERP 210-267: **HOPKINS:** A player throws a ball to dead ball territory. He is: (1) an outfielder stationed in the infield; or (2) an infielder stationed in the outfield. In (1), award two bases from the time of the pitch. In (2), award two bases from the time of the throw. (Website 2009, #19 and #20) ✠

> **277. ALSO:** OFF INTERP 211-267: **HOPKINS:** Nobody out, R3: B1 pops up in front of the plate. The catcher does not touch the ball, which takes backspin, passes by the catcher, and strikes R3 in fair territory. R3 is out. [In] this situation [the ball] is "not considered to be 'passing' an infielder."
> (Website 2010, #14) (See § 316.] ✠

❀ Note 236: Of course, the OFF INTERP fills a hole in the FED lexicon. But if I'm the AD at that school, the coach at third is fired. Nobody out, pop up in front of the plate — and he sends R3!? Amazing!

NCAA: The catcher is **NOT** an infielder. Any fielder, occupying a position in the infield, is an infielder. (2-48)

OBR: Same as NCAA. (2.00 Infielder)

⁂ *Play 116-267:* R2. The defense brings **F8** to the left side of the infield (pinching the wing outfielders), so that the defensive lineup around the periphery of the infield is: F5, F8 (where the shortstop would play, on the skin of the outfield grass), F6 (up the middle behind second), F4 and F3. The ball is slapped deep to F8, who holds R2, then fires wildly to first. At the time of the throw, B1 had already touched first.
Ruling: The award is two from the pitch: First play by an "infielder." B1 goes to second.

⁂ *Play 117-267:* R2, R3. B1 bunts toward third on the suicide squeeze. The ball is rolling near the line when suddenly it takes backspin, passes through the trailing catcher's legs without touching him, and hits the runner from third in fair territory. *Ruling:* In FED, the ball is dead and the runner is out as per OFF INTERP 211 [this section] because it had not PASSED an infielder. In NCAA, the ball is alive because the ball had passed a FIELDER. In OBR, the ball is dead and the runner is out because he was hit by a batted ball that had not passed an INFIELDER. Also in OBR, the batter-runner is credited with a single (10.05e), and the runners remain at first and second.

❀ Note 237: For purposes of declaring an infield fly or determining the first play by an infielder, however, the umpire treats the catcher as an infielder. At all levels the catcher is also considered an infielder for purposes of appeals when a half inning is ending.

★ 268 INTERFERENCE: BATTER: ACTS DEFINED ✪

FED: It is batter interference when he hinders the catcher's throwing or fielding by: (● 1) leaning over home plate;
(● 2) stepping out of the batter's box;
(● 3) making any other movement that impedes actions at home plate or the catcher's attempt to play on a runner; or
(● 4) failing to make a reasonable effort to vacate a congested area when there is a throw to home and there is time for the batter to move away. (7-3-5 a through d) (See § 274 for the penalty.)

> **278. ALSO:** OFF INTERP 212-268: **RUMBLE:** If the batter interferes as he "unwinds" from his swing, that would constitute interference: **PENALTY:** The ball is dead, the batter is out, and runners remain TOI. (*News* #35, 4/90) (See § 272.) ✠

NCAA: Point not covered.

> ***(ADDED)*** OFF INTERP 213-268: **PARONTO:** Same as FED. Same as OBR. (email to cc, 12/20/11) ✠

(ADDED) ❀ Note: 238: Committees at all levels of amateur play have decided that "protect the runner" is just as bad for baseball as "break double play." Now the NCAA has joined the chorus – loudly. Jim Paronto believes the language of FED and OBR describes this act. I predict the interp will be written into the rules for the 2012-2013 NCAA book.

OBR: (● 1) **PLAY AT A BASE:** "The batter is obligated to avoid making **ANY MOVEMENT** which obstructs, impedes, or hinders the catcher's play in any way. A swing which carries the batter over home plate and subsequently complicates the catcher's play or attempted play should be ruled interference. Contact between the batter and catcher does not necessarily have to occur for interference to be ruled. Merely blocking the catcher's vision to second base may very possibly be interference." (PI, 6:46) (● 2) **PLAY AT THE PLATE:** Interference is any movement by the batter that "complicates" the catcher's play. But the batter is not guilty of interference if he remains in the box "unless he makes some movement to intentionally interfere." (PI 7:66)

❀ Note 239: Do not confuse batter hindrance at the plate (steal of home), when the batter may remain in the box, with a passed ball, pitcher covering, when the batter must vacate the box. (See § 307.)

❀ Note 240: FED rules and authoritative opinion hold that the batter's box is the safest place for a batter to be when the catcher attempts a throw. But that doesn't mean B1 has a pass. The batter may not with impunity make any extraordinary movements inside the box. When the play is over, the umpire must be able to say that the batter was where he was supposed to be and doing what he was supposed to be doing. Otherwise, the umpire will penalize B1 for batter interference.

❀ Note 241: The FED is the only book to write batter interference guidelines directly into the rules.

★ 269 INTERFERENCE: DEFINITION ✪

FED: Interference is any act (physical [including visual] or verbal) that impedes, hinders, or confuses the defense. (2-21-1a; 2.21.1a) (See § 331.)

NCAA: Same as FED. (2-50)

OBR: Same as FED. **EXCEPT:** Interference may not be a verbal act. (2.00 Interference a)

⁕ *Play 118-269:* B1 pops up in foul territory between home and first. The ball drifts slightly foul as the first baseman sets up to make the catch. F1, as he passes the fielder, yells: "Drop it!" The first baseman is clearly startled and drops the ball. *Ruling:* In FED / NCAA, B1 is out: no question about it. In OBR, it's simply a foul ball

⁕ *Play 119-269:* Yankees v Blue Jays, 2 out, Alex Rodriguez on second. B1 pops up between short and third. As A-Rod runs between the

fielders, he yells at them. The ball falls to the ground.
Ruling: In FED / NCAA, A-Rod is out. In OBR, there is no interference.

270 INTERFERENCE: TOUCH: DEFINITION ✪

FED: A touch or touching is "contact with," and the rule specifies that there is no difference between touching and being touched by. (2-40) (See § 332 and 336.)

NCAA: A "touch" is contact with any part of an opposing player's or umpire's body, clothing, or equipment. (2-79)

OBR: Same as NCAA. (2.00 Touch)

❀ Note 242: The implication throughout the codes is that unlike FED, in NCAA / OBR a distinction should be made. At the upper levels: If a spectator **TOUCHES THE BALL** (active), the umpire calls interference. If a spectator is **TOUCHED BY THE BALL** (passive), play continues unless other actions by the spectator warrant an interference call. (See § 321.)

271 INTERFERENCE BY: BATTER: w/CATCHER: ATTEMPTS TO CREATE CATCHER INTERFERENCE ✪

FED: No provision.

NCAA: A batter may not move back in the box and deliberately attempt to create a catcher's-interference call. **PENALTY:** (● 1) strike; or (● 2) if the batter hits the catcher, he is out and runners return TOP. (7 4h)

OBR: Point not covered.

OFF INTERP 214-271: **FITZPATRICK:** The batter may not deliberately attempt to create a catcher's interference call. **PENALTY:** The ball is dead, strike, and runners do not advance. If the swing hits the catcher, the umpire shall eject the batter. No out is charged unless the batter has two strikes. Fitzpatrick: "The umpire must be ABSOLUTELY certain that the batter was attempting to create the catcher's interference and not attempting to swing at the pitched ball." (email to cc, 11/15/00) (See § 272.) ✠

272 INTERFERENCE BY: BATTER: w/CATCHER: FOLLOW THROUGH / BACKSWING ✪

FED: If a batter's follow-through hinders the catcher attempt to "**FIELD A BALL**" or **MAKE A THROW**, the batter is guilty of interference. **PENALTY:** The ball is dead, B1 is out, and runners remain TOI. (7.3.5f; 8.4.1h; Website 2007, #20, affirmed 2010, #17) (See § 275.) **EXCEPT:** If the interference occurs during a steal of home, with fewer than two out, the runner is out. (7-3-5 Pen)

NCAA: If a batter's follow-through hits the catcher "as the pitch is caught," it is a strike, the ball is dead, and no runners advance. It is not interference. (6-2d) If the batter's follow-through accidentally hits the catcher "while the catcher is in the act of throwing," it is a strike (but not interference) and the ball is dead unless the catcher's throw retires a runner. (6-2d-2) On a third strike, the ball is dead; the batter is out. (6-2d-1)

❀ Note 243: The NCAA statute is the same as OFF INTERP 216 [this section].

OBR: The umpire declares interference on the backswing if the bat contacts the catcher before he has "**SECURELY HELD THE BALL**." (6.06c CMT ¶ 3) (See § 271.)

279. ALSO: OFF INTERP 215-272: **PBUC:** Following interference by a backswing, after a third strike, the ball is dead and the batter is out. {7.13} ✠

280. ALSO: OFF INTERP 216-272: **PBUC:** "If a batter strikes at a ball and misses and in the umpire's judgment unintentionally hits the catcher or the ball in back of the batter on the follow-through or backswing while the batter is still in the batter's box, it shall be called a strike only (no interference). If this infraction should occur in a situation where the batter would normally become a runner because of a third strike not caught, the ball shall be dead and the batter declared out." {7.13} ✠

❀ Note 244-272: PBUC even delineates the correct mechanics for the umpire. (See § 341.)

❀ Note 245: This is **HALF** of the OBR interpretations that deal with what rules experts call "weak interference." For the other half, see § 276.

∞ 273 INTERFERENCE BY: BATTER: w/CATCHER: PLAY AT THE PLATE: BATTER HITS THROW ✪

FED: If the batter hits a **THROW**, made by the pitcher while off the pitcher's plate in an attempt to retire a runner stealing home, it is batter interference and an immediate-dead ball. **PENALTY:** With two out the batter is out; with fewer than two out, the runner is out. (Dead Ball Table #25; 7.3.5g)

NCAA: Same as FED. (7-11v; 7-11v Pen)

OBR: Point not covered.

OFF INTERP 217-273: **FITZPATRICK:** Same as FED 7.3.5g. (phone call to cc, 11/8/01) ✠

★ 274 INTERFERENCE BY: BATTER: w/CATCHER: THROW TO: BASE: BATTER NOT RETIRED ✪

FED: POE 1983, 1984, 1985: When a batter interferes with the catcher's throw: **PENALTY:** (● 1) **PLAY AT A BASE:** The batter is always out; runners return TOP. (● 2) **PLAY AT THE PLATE:** with two outs, the batter is out; with fewer than two outs, the runner is out. (7-3-5 Pen) (See § 291.)
281. ALSO: During a steal of third, the [right-handed] batter is not guilty of interference unless he "moves or re-establishes his position **AFTER** F2 receives the pitch" and that movement hinders the catcher's play on R2 at third. (7.3.5e)
282. ALSO: If the runner being played on is not out because of a direct throw by the catcher: "When **AN ATTEMPT** to put out a runner [at first, second, or third] is unsuccessful, the batter is out and all runners must return TOP." (7-3-5 Pen)

NCAA: Batter interference with the catcher's play at second or third: Same as FED. (6-3b; 6-3b Pen 1) At home: If **ANY** runner is retired, the interference is disregarded. (7-11f Pen Ex 2) Otherwise: same as FED. (7-11f Pen Ex 1)
283. ALSO: "If there is an attempt by the catcher to throw and the attempt is aborted due to an action by the offense, the ball becomes dead immediately, the batter is out, and runners return to the base[s] occupied at ... TOP." (6-3b Pen 3)
284. ALSO: On a play at second or third, the interference is disregarded if the catcher's direct throw retires the runner. (6-2d-2; 6-3b Pen 3)

❀ Note 246: The NCAA is the lone book to state that guideline explicitly.

OBR: Same as NCAA. (6.06c; 6.06c CMT; 6.06c CMT ¶ 2))

285. ALSO: OFF INTERP 218-274: **PBUC:** ***(EDITED)*** Following batter interference, the batter is not out if the catcher's initial throw retires the runner, or if the runner trying to score is called out for the batter's interference. {7.10} ✠

⁜ *Play 120-274:* R1, R3, 0 outs. R1 attempts to steal, and the batter interferes with the catcher's throw. R3 scores as the ball goes into centerfield. R1 next attempts to advance to third and is thrown out. *Ruling:* In FED, the play stands. In NCAA / OBR, when the catcher's throw does not directly retire R1, the ball is dead. The batter is out, and R3 returns to third.

275 INTERFERENCE BY: BATTER: w/CATCHER: THROW TO: BASE: BATTER RETIRED ✪ (See § 268.)

FED: (● 1) When a **RETIRED BATTER** interferes with the catcher's attempt to play on a runner, if the umpire believes the runner would have been out without the interference, the **PENALTY** is: The umpire will declare out the runner on whom the defense was playing; other runners return TOP. (Website 2011, #4) (● 2) If the umpire judges the catcher had no chance for an out, interference or no, the only **PENALTY** is: Runners return TOP. (7-3-5 Pen; 7.3.5c; 8.4.2k; Website 2011, #5) (See § 291.)

286. ALSO: A sequence:

- (a) When the catcher because of "the nature of the interference" makes no play ...
- (b) if the umpire cannot determine on whom the catcher would have played ...
- (c) the umpire will call out the runner who has advanced nearest to home ...
- (d) if he is convinced the catcher could have registered an out anywhere. (8-4-2g; 7.3.5d) (See Note 250 [this section] for a **MUCH DIFFERENT RULE** in effect for NCAA / OBR.)

❀ Note 247 -275: Be certain you do not confuse this ruling (§ 275) with § 280. (● 1) In § 275 in a double play situation the runner closest to home is called out if the umpire cannot determine on whom the catcher would have played but for the interference. (● 2) In § 280 in a double play situation when the batter-runner interferes before touching first, he is called out and so is the other runner on whom the defense would have played. The rule outlined in (2) is a significant departure from NCAA / OBR play. (See § 324. Please study also Note 255-280.)

❀ Note 248: The penalty for interference at 7-3-5 Pen (runners return TOP) contradicts the penalty at 8-2-9 (runners remain TOI). But because it is virtually impossible for a runner to advance a base before the batter interferes with the catcher, the conflict will rarely (never?) be a factor in your games. If Murphy's Law strikes, BRD recommends: The runner remains TOI. That's the most recent and the most frequently confirmed interpretation.

❀ Note 249: Some point out that 8.4.2 CMT is sharply at odds with the language of 8-4-2g. Easily explained. In 1993 FED, without comment, dropped the language that interference with a double play by a batter-runner before reaching first **ALWAYS** resulted in the runner closest to home being declared out. Meanwhile, the 1992 case book play, then styled 8.4.2f CMT, remained unchanged in 1993. It reached its current spot (8.4.2 CMT) in 1994, where it has **ERRONEOUSLY** remained ever since.

NCAA: A retired batter may not interfere with the catcher's attempt to throw to a base. (7-11f Ex 3) **PENALTY:** The runner is out; other runners return TOP. (7-11f Pen)

OBR: Same as NCAA. (7.09f) (See § 362 for comment on the OBR notion of "delayed dead ball.")

❀ Note 250-275: In NCAA/OBR, if, because of the interference, the catcher can make no play, the umpire should call out the runner on whom he judges the defense would have played.

✻ *Play 121-275:* R1, 1 out, full count. R1 is moving on the pitch. B1 strikes out and interferes with the catcher's attempt to throw out R1, who slides in safely at second. *Ruling:* In FED, if the catcher without the interference had a chance to retire R1, R1 is out. But if the catcher had no chance for the out, R1 returns to first. In NCAA / OBR, R1 is automatically out.

★ ∞ 276 INTERFERENCE BY: BATTER: w/CATCHER: RETURN TOSS TO: PITCHER ✪

FED: No provision. Treat as in OBR.

NCAA: Point not covered.

> *(ADDED)* OFF INTERP 219-276: **PARONTO:** Same as OBR OFF INTERP 220 [this section]. (email to cc, 12/20/11) ✠

OBR: Point not covered.

> OFF INTERP 220-276: **PBUC:** If the batter interferes with the catcher's return toss to the pitcher by stepping out of the batter's box, it is not interference unless it is intentional or runners are attempting to advance, in which case the batter is out. **PENALTY:** For unintended interference: The ball is dead. Runners may not advance. {7.14} ✠

❀ Note 251: PBUC further states the ruling is not a license for the batter to interfere. Intentional interference is an out. This is **HALF** of the OBR interpretations that deal with what rules experts call "weak interference." For the other half, see § 272.

∞ 277 INTERFERENCE BY: BATTER-RUNNER: w/CATCHER AFTER: COLLISION AT PLATE: UNPENALIZED ✪

FED: No provision. Treat as in NCAA. (See § 279.)

NCAA: If the batter-runner and the catcher fielding the ball make contact, it is neither interference nor obstruction unless "either player attempts to alter the play." (7-11f Ex 4)

OBR: Same as NCAA. (7.09j CMT) (See § 279.)

Play 122-277: Carlton Fisk catches; Ed Armbrister bats. Armbrister bunts in front of the plate and breaks for first. Fisk goes for the ball. Contact occurs between the two. *Ruling:* It is a collision, and the play stands: no obstruction, no interference.

Note 252: Larry Barnett made that no-call in the 1975 World Series. Great series, great call. The key: Each player was where he was supposed to be and doing what he was supposed to do. Barnett knew the "case book" ruling, but the talking heads in the TV booth did not: "That's interference!" they ignorantly screamed. In 1975 all case book material, which the BRD calls "CMT," was housed in a single section following the main text of the rules. In 1977 the case book was integrated with the rules. That change, coming as it did at the first opportunity after "The Call," could not be a coincidence.

Play 123-277: Don Slaught catches; Brian Hunter bats. Hunter taps a little roller in front of the plate; then he hesitates, "confused," before starting for first. Slaught has already charged for the ball. Contact occurs between the two. *Ruling:* The ball is dead, and Hunter is out for interference.

Note 253: Bob Davidson made that call in the 1991 NLCS. Bad series, great call. But, some would ask, doesn't Davidson's decision contradict Barnett's? BRD would answer: No. The key difference between the two plays is: When Hunter **DID NOT START AT ONCE FOR FIRST**, he was not doing what he was supposed to do.

★ 278 INTERFERENCE BY: BATTER-RUNNER w/CATCHER AFTER: DROPPED FOURTH BALL ✪ (See § 279.)

FED: No provision Treat as in OBR.

NCAA: Point not covered.

> *(ADDED)* OFF INTERP 221-278: **PARONTO:** Same as OBR OFF INTERP 222 [this section]. (email to cc, 12/20/11) ✠

OBR: Point not covered.

> OFF INTERP 222-278: **FITZPATRICK:** Treat unintentional hindrance by the batter with the catcher's attempt to field a dropped fourth ball the same as you would a dropped third strike. (phone call to cc, 11/8/01) ✠

★ 279 INTERFERENCE BY: BATTER-RUNNER: w/CATCHER AFTER: DROPPED THIRD STRIKE ✪ (See § 278.)

FED: The batter-runner shall not **DELIBERATELY** interfere with the catcher's attempt to field a third strike. **PENALTY:** The batter-runner is out. (8-4-1a; 2.21.1c; 8.4.1i) (See § 98; 272; 275; 281.)

EXCEPT: OFF INTERP 223-279: **RUMBLE:** If the batter as he "unwinds" from his swing hinders the catcher, that would constitute interference. (*News* #35, 4/90) (See OFF INTERP 212-268.) ❀

❀ Note 254: The rulings are not contradictory. If the batter inside the box hinders the catcher, interference is the call; if he is outside the box, the interference must be deliberate before it is penalized. See also PBUC's OFF INTERP 224 [this section], which affirms the correctness of the FED's rule and Rumble's interpretation.

NCAA: If while advancing to first the batter-runner **INTENTIONALLY** deflects the ball, the ball is dead. **PENALTY:** The batter is out and runners return. (7-11h AR 1; 7-11o) If the batter-runner unintentionally deflects the ball, the ball is alive and in play. **EXCEPTION:** ***(EDITED)*** If there are fewer than two outs and first base is occupied, the ball is dead and runners return **UNLESS** the runners are stealing on the pitch.
(7-11h AR2) (See § 98.)

IMPORTANT NOTE: UNDERSTAND THAT IN ALL THREE PLAYS BELOW, B1 IS OUT—BEFORE HE BEGINS TO RUN. THE UMPIRE'S ONLY ISSUE IS HOW TO DEAL WITH THE RUNNERS.

❊ *Play 124-279:* **NCAA only.** R1 not moving on the pitch, 0 outs. B1 strikes out. The ball gets away from the catcher, and B1 unintentionally kicks it when he erroneously begins to run to first. *Ruling:* The ball is dead, and R1 must remain on first.

❊ *Play 125-279:* **NCAA only.** R1, R2, 0 outs, 3-2 count. B1 strikes out and erroneously starts for first. Just outside the box he unintentionally kicks the ball, and the umpire calls: "Time! Dead ball." (a) Both runners were stealing; (b) neither runner was stealing. (c) R1 was stealing, but R2 was not; (d) R2 was stealing, but R1 was not. *Ruling:* In (a), runners get second and third; in (b) and (c), they remain at first and second.
In (d), R2 keeps third, but R1 remains at first.
(Paronto, San Antonio MTG, 1/3/04)

❊ *Play 126-279:* **NCAA only.** R1 stealing on the pitch, 0 outs. B1 strikes out. The ball gets away from the catcher, and B1 unintentionally kicks it when he begins to run to first.
Ruling: The ball is dead and R1 stays at second.

OBR: After a third strike the batter shall not hinder the catcher's attempt to field the ball. (7.09a)

EXCEPT: OFF INTERP 224-279: ***(EDITED)*** **WENDELSTEDT:** "If the ball is deflected off the catcher and immediately contacts the batter-runner as he starts toward first base, no penalty shall apply." (HW/231) ✠

287. ALSO: OFF INTERP 225-279: ***(EDITED)*** **WENDELSTEDT**: "If the batter-runner's contact with the ball occurs up the baseline (not in the immediate vicinity of home plate) and **WAS AVOIDABLE**, then the contact is to be considered intentional. (HW/231) ✠

✻ *Play 127-279:* B1 swings and misses for strike three. The ball ricochets from the catcher's mitt and rolls several feet down the foul line in fair (or foul) territory. As the catcher goes for the ball, the batter-runner steps on it. The umpire is certain B1 did not willfully deflect the ball. *Ruling:* In FED / NCAA, no interference is called, and the result of the play will stand. In OBR, because of the egregiousness of the interference, the umpire "might" declare a dead ball, call out the batter-runner, and return other runners TOP. (There was no intervening play: See § 291.) But "most of the time" he would rule as in FED / NCAA. (See § 278 for what to do after a dropped fourth ball.)

★ 280 INTERFERENCE BY: BATTER-RUNNER: w/DOUBLE PLAY: WHO IS OUT? ✪

FED: If the batter-runner interferes with a double play ***(EDITED)*** **ANYWHERE**, the batter-runner is out and so is the "**OTHER RUNNER INVOLVED.**" (8-4-2g). (See § 275.)

❀ Note 255-280: The FED statute until 1993 matched NCAA/OBR. But in that year the following sentence from the 1992 book was dropped without comment (an unannounced change) from 8-2-4g: "If the batter-runner interferes, the umpire shall call him out and the runner who has also advanced the nearest to home base." At the core of the change was a 1992 revision that directed the UIC to call out "the runner closest to home" if – following interference by the batter-runner with a double play possible – the UIC **DID NOT KNOW ON WHOM THE DEFENSE WOULD HAVE PLAYED.** The rules committee may have felt that two chances to "hit 'em where it hurts the most" were one too many. (See especially § 275 for further discussion of "the runner nearest home.")

NCAA: ***(EDITED)*** If the batter runner interferes with a fielder, whether intentionally or deliberately, with a double play "**LIKELY**," the batter-runner is out and so is the runner who has advanced nearest to home, regardless of where the double play might have taken place. (8-5e)

OBR: Same as NCAA.0 (7.09g)

⁜ *Play 128-280:* R1, R3. B1 attempts to bunt. R1 is off with the pitch, but R3 is holding. As F1 prepares to glove the ball in flight, B1 DELIBERATELY (but not maliciously) bumps him. The umpire is certain that F1 would have caught the ball and then thrown to first to double up R1. *Ruling:* B1 is out at all levels. In FED, R1 (the other runner involved) is out, and R3 remains on third. In NCAA / OBR, R3 (nearest home) is out, and R1 returns to first.

★ 281 INTERFERENCE BY: BATTER-RUNNER: w/FOUL BALL ✪

FED: After hitting or bunting a ball, the batter-runner is out if he "INTENTIONALLY CONTACTS" the ball with the bat a second time in fair or foul territory. (8-4-1d) (IMPORTANT: See § 103.)

288. ALSO: If the ball is on or over foul ground, the rule applies only if the umpire judges the ball had a chance to become fair. (8-4-1d-1) (See § 317)

NCAA: If the batter-runner intentionally interferes with a foul ball, the ball is dead, the batter-runner is out, ***(ADDED)*** and no runner may advance. (7-11o)

OBR: Same as NCAA. (6.05i) (See § 317.)

❀ Note 256: In 1983 Harry Wendelstedt wrote that common sense prevails: The penalty is assessed only when the umpire judges the ball had a chance to roll fair, so touching or picking up an unquestionably and permanently foul ball is not an infraction. (See Note 295-317.)

⁜ *Play 129-281:* **OBR only.** A batter hits a little roller down the first-base line. The pitcher goes to field it. B1 bumps into the pitcher while he's trying to knock the ball farther into foul territory. After the contact, the ball, untouched, does roll fair, and B1 is safe at first. *Ruling:* ***(EDITED)*** The play stands. (See OFF INTERP 259-317.)

★ 282 INTERFERENCE BY: BATTER-RUNNER: NOT IN RUNNING LANE: DEFINITION ✪

FED: POE 2010: The batter-runner must be in the running lane the last half of the distance to first. (8-4-1g; 8.4.1c) The runner is not in the lane if either foot is outside either line. (8-4-1g-2) If he is not in the lane and interferes: **PENALTY:** The batter-runner is out and the ball is dead. (8-4-1g) Other runners remain TOI. (8-2-9)

❀ Note 257: In *The Umpire's Answer Book*, published 1988 by Referee Enterprises, I wrote: "Let's get this point clear: What I'm about to say is not in any rulebook, but it's a 'rule provision' nonetheless because it has been codified via the decisions of thousands of umpires in tens of thousands of games played all over the world. The running lane should enter an umpire's decision-making process only when the ball is being fielded to first from behind the runner. For example, when the third baseman throws off line to first and the first baseman goes for the ball, if contact occurs, don't look down to see where the BR's feet are; if you do, you're on your way to blowing the call. The intent of the rule is to keep the BR from screening the fielder behind him from the first baseman in front. Keep it that way in your games and you'll never get into trouble." Well, finally, after 22 years, someone agreed! See the next OFF INTERP.

OFF INTERP 226-282: **HOPKINS:** B1 lays down a bunt that is fielded by F2 in fair territory a few feet in front of home plate. As B1 is 60 feet from home base, he is running outside the running lane with one foot completely in fair ground and not touching the lines of the running lane. RULING: B1 is required to be in the running lane the last 45 feet to first base when the ball is fielded and thrown **FROM AN AREA BEHIND HIM**. (Website 2010, #7) ✠

289. ALSO: The running lane has no significance if the batter-runner establishes his base path away from the plate. (8.4.1j, 2006 ed)

⁕ *Play 130*-282: B1 swings and misses for strike three. The ball rolls to the backstop. B1 is near his third-base dugout when he realizes he is not yet out. He streaks directly toward first. As he nears the base, F2's throw hits him in the back. *Ruling:* Not interference.

290. ALSO: OFF INTERP 227-282: **HOPKINS:** After a dropped third strike, when the batter-runner is not in the lane, the catcher's throw does not have to hit the batter-runner to create interference. But the umpire may not call interference if the catcher does not throw. (Website 2002, #11; affirmed, Website 2010, #7) ✠

NCAA: Same as FED. (7-11p AR 1) **POE 1998: EXCEPT:** Runners return TOP unless there has been an intervening play. (2-50 AR2) (See OFF INTERP 236 and Play 139 in § 291.)

291. ALSO: If the batter-runner interferes with the attempted catch of the thrown ball or is hit by the throw, he shall be called out "**EVEN IF HE IS IN HIS APPROACH TO THE BASE.**" (7-11p AR 1)

❀ Note 258: The above statute might be called the "Take-that-Ted-and-Jim" rule. That's because this rule entered the NCAA lexicon in 2000, the first opportunity the editor had after Play 131 [this section] occurred.

OBR: The lines are part of the lane, and the batter-runner must have both feet in the lane. **EXCEPT:** The batter-runner may exit the lane "by means of a step, stride, reach, or slide in the immediate vicinity of first for the sole purpose of reaching the base." (6.05k CMT) (See § 291.)

❀ Note 259: The above statute might be called the "Take that-Joe-and-the-NCAA" rule. Of course, it took the OBR seven years (!) to decide to publish their thoughts, which likely grew out of Jim Evans' two-sentence account (JEA, 1991) of the rule. (See AO 16 below.)

AO 16-282: EVANS: An allowance should be made for the batter-runner to step inside the foul line as he reaches the immediate vicinity of first base; otherwise, the base is not readily accessible for him to touch since the runner's lane runs adjacent and past the base in foul territory. (6-32)

❀ Note 260: **THE POINT:** When the batter-runner reaches the end of the running lane, NCAA and OBR provide diametrically opposite rules.

✻Play 131-282: Game 2, ALCS, 1998, Cleveland v New York. Pinch runner Enrique Wilson on first. Travis Fryman sacrifices Wilson to second. Tino Martinez (F1) fields the bunt and throws to Chuck Knoblauch (F4) covering first. Fryman is not in the lane, and the ball hits him in the back and rolls away. After arguing with Umpire Ted Hendry for interference, Knoblauch retrieves the ball. But it's too late to get Wilson — **at home**. *Ruling:* Hendry at the plate makes no call, ruling in effect that Fryman did not interfere. Crew chief and right field umpire Jim Evans says after the game: "The umpire has to decide if it was a quality throw that would retire the runner and how close to the base the runner is. He has the right to be there that close to the base. If the runner is in fair territory, he can be called out if he interferes with the throw. This case probably happened right at the base. That's what Hendry based his ruling on. The fact that he was at the base makes it a tough judgment call. I thought it could go either way. [But] I thought it was the proper call in that situation." *Ruling:* The 2007 OBR rule change sanctified Hendry's ruling. In FED (probably) and NCAA (certainly) Fryman would be out.

292. ALSO: ***(EDITED)*** OFF INTERP 228-282: **FITZPATRICK:** (a) As long as he does not interfere, the batter-runner may run anywhere he likes. (b) He must not interfere by crashing the fielder at first. (c) The throw need not come from behind. (d) Whether the batter-runner is safe is also irrelevant: If the umpire judges the batter-runner's position outside the lane screened the fielder from the throw, he is guilty of interference even if he reaches first safely before being hit by the throw. (phone call to cc, 11/8/01) ✠

✻Play 132-282: ALDS, Oct 10, 2000. Oakland at New York, Game 1, ALDS. David Justice runs the entire distance from home to first in fair territory on the grass, with both feet well outside the running lane.

At the moment he reaches first, he crosses from fair territory to reach the base. *After* he steps safely onto first, the throw hits him from behind. *Ruling:* Justice is out. Dana Demuth, the home plate umpire, ruled that while Justice was on the base when hit, he was outside the lane at the time of the throw and hence was guilty of interference. "It's a rule in the book," DeMuth explained after the game.

AO 17-282: EVANS: "A runner who has **ADVANCED THE ENTIRE DISTANCE** from home plate to first in fair territory making no effort to run within the lane is not extended the same leniency as the runner who runs in the lane as required and then cuts into fair territory near the base to touch it. (7:94)

❀ Note 261-282-: A few seasons ago a major dispute erupted at the newsgroup rec.sport.officiating over the following play:

Bogus play -282: R3: B1 hits deep to the first baseman, who throws home to put out R3 advancing. The throw strikes B1, who is not in the running lane. Ruling: The resident baseball "expert" at rec.sport.officiating argued venomously that B1 should be out. I argued (just as venomously, he would say) that B1 should not be out.

Note 261 continued: FED 8.4.1c, which entered the case book in 2005, has put the quietus to such nonsense: "Since no play is made on [the batter-runner] at first base, 8-4-2g does not apply."

283 INTERFERENCE BY: BATTER-RUNNER OR RUNNER: CONTINUES TO ADVANCE AFTER OUT ✪

FED: A batter-runner or runner is not guilty of interference if he continues to advance, even when he knows he is out, even if that advance allows other runners to make additional bases. (8.3.3i)

✲ *Play 133-283*: R1. B1 hits to right field, where the ball is caught for an out. R1 holds at first, but B1 passes him and makes a dash for second. F9, confused, fires to second, but the ball is wildly overthrown and goes into DBT behind third. *Ruling:* In FED, R1 is awarded third! (Note: B1 is congratulated for a legal decoy, and you'll have to eject somebody [your partner?). In NCAA / OBR, call out R1. (Note: You can keep your partner in the game, but the offensive coach may have to hit the showers.)

NCAA: A retired runner may not continue to advance if such action "hinders or impedes" the defense. **PENALTY:** The umpire shall call time and declare out the runner affected by the retired runner's actions. (5-3 Pen 2) A batter-runner or runner advancing shall not by that act alone be construed as "confusing, hindering or impeding" the defense. (5-3 AR 1)

293. ALSO: An obstructed runner is not immune from "team offensive interference penalties." (5-3 Pen 2 AR 2)

294. ALSO: OFF INTERP 229-283: **THURSTON:** If a retired runner continuing to advance hinders a following play, the umpire must judge whether the hindrance was **INTENTIONAL**; if unintentional, the runner is not guilty of interference. (phone call to se, 11/19/90) ✠

OBR: Same as NCAA. (2.00 Interference-a; 7.09e CMT)

295. ALSO: OFF INTERP 230-283: **FITZPATRICK:** Same as NCAA 5-2 Pen 2 and OFF INTERP 229-283. (email to cc, 11/15/00) ✠

✻ Play 134-283: R1. B1 grounds to the shortstop. R1 is forced out at second, but the relay throw is not in time at first. Next, retired R1 gets into a rundown between second and third and is tagged "out" again as B1 takes second. *Ruling:* In FED, B1 remains at second. In NCAA / OBR, B1 is out for R1's interference.

❀ Note 262: In those upper-level games if B1 remains on first during the "rundown," do not assess a penalty.

✻ Play 135-283: R1. The runner is moving on the pitch when B1's attempted bunt is a pop-up behind the plate. B1 heads for first as the foul is caught. The catcher throws to F3 to double up R1, but his throw hits B1 in the running lane and goes into the dugout. *Ruling:* R1 is awarded third. B1 was in the running lane; that he continued to run is not sufficient to create interference.

❀ Note 263: If B1 had been to the left or right of the lane, the umpire would properly call out R1 because of interference by a retired batter-runner. Note to the note: If R1 does not retouch first before he touches second on the award, on proper appeal he will be out. (See § 434.)

✻ Play 136-283: R3. The runner retouches on B1's short fly to right. B1 begins to run out his hit, which is caught by the right fielder. But F9's throw to the plate glances off B1 as he nears first, and R3 scores easily. The umpire determines the retired batter-runner did not intentionally interfere with the throw. *Ruling:* In FED, nothing untoward has happened. In NCAA / OBR because B1's "interference" is accidental, it is ignored. The run counts — at all levels.

284 INTERFERENCE BY: BATTER-RUNNER OR RUNNER: W/HELMET: ACCIDENTAL SEE § 301.

285 INTERFERENCE BY: BATTER-RUNNER OR RUNNER: W/HELMET: DELIBERATE SEE § 301.

286 INTERFERENCE BY: BATTER-RUNNER OR RUNNER: DIVING OVER FIELDER ✪

FED: It is illegal to dive over a fielder. (8-4-2d; 8.4.2s and u; 3.3.1u 2010 ed) **PENALTY** for diving over a fielder: The ball remains alive, but the runner is out. (8-4-2d Pen) **EXCEPT:** If the umpire declares interference, the ball is dead. **PENALTY** for offensive interference by

diving over a fielder: The offender is out, and runners return TOI. The umpire may declare a double play. (See § 289.)
296. ALSO: A runner may legally hurdle a fielder's outstretched arm. (8.2.1d) (See § 290.)

NCAA: No provision.

OBR: No provision.

★ ∞ 287 INTERFERENCE BY: BATTER-RUNNER OR RUNNER: KNOCKS BALL FROM FIELDER'S HAND ✪

FED: A baserunner may not deliberately knock the ball from a fielder's hand. **PENALTY:** The baserunner is out. (8-4-2r)

(ADDED) ❀ Note 264: FED does not complete the statute. Presumably the ball is immediately dead (5-1-1e). But that citation DOES NOT list coverage for 8-4-2r . BRD recommends: Treat as in NCAA OFF INTERP 231 [this section].

NCAA: Point not covered.

> ***(ADDED)*** OFF INTERP 231-287: **PARONTO:** Same as FED: "The ball is dead immediately. Runners return to the bases occupied at the time of the interference. See 6-2g A.R." (email to cc, 12/21/11) ✠

OBR: Point not covered.

> OFF INTERP 232-287: **PBUC:** Same as FED. {7.1} ✠

⁎ *Play 137-287:* ALCS, 19 Oct, 2004. With Derek Jeter on first and one out, Alex Rodriguez hits a slow roller up the first-base line. Red Sox pitcher Bronson Arroyo fields the ball and goes to tag A-Rod, stepping in front of him as he runs up the line. Rodriguez sticks out his left hand and slaps the ball out of Arroyo's glove, allowing Jeter to run all the way around to score while Rodriguez scampers to second.
Ruling: Rodriguez is out for interference; Jeter must return to first.

❀ Note 265: The text of the play is adapted from Sam Borden's account in the *New York Daily News*.

∞ 288 INTERFERENCE BY: BATTER-RUNNER OR RUNNER: RUNS BASES IN REVERSE ORDER ✪

FED: If a runner is called out for running the bases in reverse order, the ball is dead. (5-1-1d **1994ED**) Runners return TOP. (8-2-9) (See § 436.)

❀ Note 266: It's true. If high schooler R2 starts back to first in a game where his team leads by 20 runs, just to see what will happen, you have no **CURRENT** authority to kill the ball. In 1995, FED restructured 5-1-1 and inadvertently left out the status of the ball for that situation. You don't believe me? Get a magnifying glass and read through the Dead Ball and Delayed Dead Ball Table. It's printed in 7pt type. Sample: Pitch touches runner 5-1-1a

NCAA: For running the bases in reverse order: The runner is out and the ball is dead. Runners return TOP. (8-5n; 8-5n Pen)

OBR: Same as NCAA. **EXCEPT:** The placement of other runners is not covered in the rule. (7.08i)

★ 289 INTERFERENCE BY: BATTER-RUNNER OR RUNNER: SLIDE: DEFINITION: LEGAL / ILLEGAL ✪

(See § 324.)

FED: POE 1982, 1983, 1984, 1985, 1986, 1997: LEGAL SLIDE: A legal slide is: (● 1) a foot-first slide with one leg extended and buttocks on the ground; or (● 2) a head-first slide with arms extended. (2-32-1) (See § 286.)

297. ALSO: If a runner slides, he must be within reach of the base with his hand or foot. (2-32-1; casebook New Play 9, 1992 ed)

❀ Note 267: The stipulation that the runner must slide within reach of the base is at best archaic; at worst, slipshod. It is borrowed from the OBR practice. Its purpose was to ensure that the runner did not go into the outfield grass trying to break up a double play. In 1998 FED added the requirement that on a force play runners must slide in a direct line between bases. Obviously, that made 2-32-1 obsolete, for no runner **STEALING** will fail to slide within arm's reach of the base.

ILLEGAL SLIDE: An illegal slide is: (● 1) The runner uses a roll block, pop-up slide, football cross-body block, or slashes his legs; (● 2) the runner's leg is higher than the fielder's knee when the fielder is standing; (● 3) the runner goes beyond the base and contacts the fielder or alters the fielder's play; (● 4) the runner tries to injure the fielder; or (● 5) the runner does not slide in a direct line between bases on a force play. (2-32-2; 8-4-2b) (See § 330, especially OFF INTERP 269 in that section.)

NCAA: Same as FED. (8-4; 8-4c; 8-4c Pen 1, 2 and 3) (See § 290.)

298. ALSO: If a runner makes a legal slide "directly to the base or the baseline extended," there is no interference. (8-4b) "If contact occurs on top of the base as a result of a pop-up slide, the contact is legal." (8-4b AR)

❀ Note 268: Back in the day, I called out a lot of runners because of this slide. How times change!

OBR: Point not covered.

OFF INTERP 233-289: **PBUC:** To avoid interference a sliding runner must be near enough to reach the bag with his hand or foot. {7.3} ✠

OFF INTERP 234-289: **PBUC:** If a runner contacts the ground and then slides and rolls into the defense player, that is NOT a roll block. If the initial contact is with a fielder instead of the ground for the purpose of breaking up a double play, it is a roll block. {7.3} ✠

❀ Note 269: And thereby hangs a tale, told in the Play and Note below.

✻ *Play 138-289:* 2007 NLCS, Rockies at Diamondbacks, Game 1, bottom of the seventh. Chris Snyder (R2), Juston Upton (R1), 0 outs. Augie Ojeda (B1) grounds to third. The throw goes to Kaz Matsui (F4) as Upton, already out, slides high into Matsui. *Ruling:* Umpire Larry Vanover calls out Upton and immediately signals that Ojeda is also out for the interference. Snyder returns to second.

❀ Note 270: There's more to the story. After giving up a double, Rockies' pitcher Jeff Francis hit Upton. Some thought Upton's hard slide at second might have been payback. Instead, Vanover applied what's known as the "Hal McRae Rule." His slide into Willie Randolph in the 1977 ALCS led to MLB banning the act in 1978. To those who argue that after a double, you don't intentionally hit the next batter, I say it's important to remember that Colorado was up, 5-1, at the time. Arizona's fans didn't like the call. They pelted the field with debris, and the Rockies temporarily left the field.

290 INTERFERENCE BY: BATTER-RUNNER OR RUNNER: SLIDE: TAG PLAY ✪

FED: A runner must "legally" slide or "legally" attempt to avoid a fielder. (8-4-2b; 2.32.2a) **PENALTY:** The umpire calls interference, the ball is dead, and the runner is out. (8-4-2b Pen) (See § 286, 329 and 330.) **299. ALSO:** "**RUNNERS ARE NEVER REQUIRED TO SLIDE.**" (8-4-2b-2)

Collisions may be malicious. See § 329.

NCAA: After a collision between a runner and a fielder with "clear possession of the ball," the umpire will judge whether the runner was: (● 1) attempting to reach the base / plate; (● 2) not attempting to dislodge the ball; (● 3) trying to avoid a collision. If the runner's path to the base is blocked and (1), (2), and (3) are fulfilled, it is considered unavoidable contact. (8-7 1/2/3]) **PENALTY:** If the runner tries to dislodge the ball or initiates an avoidable collision, he is out, regardless of whether the fielder maintains control of the ball. The ball is dead; other runners return TOI. (8-7 1 Pen)

300. ALSO: "Contact **ABOVE THE WAIST** that was initiated by the base runner shall **NOT** be judged as an attempt to reach the base or plate." It shall be deemed an attempt to dislodge the ball. (8-7-2)

❀ Note 271: Umpires must apply the same standards at all bases, not only to runners who might be attempting to score.

Collisions may be malicious. See § 329.

OBR: No provision.

❀ Note 272: What you see is what you get. Ask Ray Fosse.

291 INTERFERENCE BY: BATTER-RUNNER OR RUNNER: w/THROWN BALL: RUNNERS RETURN TO BASES ✪

FED: When a batter-runner or runner interferes with a thrown ball, other runners remain TOI unless they have scored. (8-2-9) (See § 30 and 345. Pay particular attention to § 274, 275 and 282.)

OFF INTERP 235-291: **HOPKINS:** If a runner scores before the batter-runner interferes with a thrown ball, the run counts. (Website 2007, #5) ✠

❀ Note 273: This OFF INTERP is not needed, of course, because in FED the runners always return to the bases occupied at the time of the interference. I suppose there was pressure from NCAA or OBR umpires who were worried about the "intervening play." (See NCAA below.)

✻ *Play 139-291:* 1 out. R3 scores on a suicide squeeze, after which F2's throw hits B1 not in the running lane. *Ruling:* The run counts at all levels.

❀ Note 274: Ah, ha! you say: The intervening play has reached FED. Sorry, but FED runners **ALWAYS** remain TOI. Still, this spells out an important ruling, which might save your cookies some day.

NCAA: (● 1) When a runner interferes with a thrown ball, other runners return TOI. (2-50 AR 1) (● 2) When the batter-runner interferes, runners return TOP unless there was an intervening play, when runners remain TOI. (2-50 AR 2)

301. ALSO: If offensive interference occurs, and all runners, including the batter-runner, have advanced one base, penalties will be measured from the bases touched at the time of the interference. (6-2g AR) (See Play 142 [this section].)

OBR: When a runner interferes with a thrown ball, other runners return TOI. (2.00 Interference a)

302. ALSO: OFF INTERP 236-291: **PBUC:** Same as NCAA 2-50 AR 2 (intervening play). {7.2} ✠

❀ Note 275: Ignore 2.00 Interference-a CMT, which says runners return to the bases occupied at the time of the pitch if the batter-runner interferes before he touches first. That rule is no longer enforced. (See Play 142 [this section].)

303. ALSO: If a runner interferes during a rundown, a succeeding runner cannot advance to one of the rundown bases. (7.08b CMT ¶ 3) (See Play 142 [this section].)

❀ Note 276: At all levels: The umpire must judge an offensive participant **DELIBERATELY** interfered with a throw or **THROWN** ball before he can declare interference. (See Play 162-325.) **UNINTENTIONAL** interference can occur with a **BATTED** ball.

⁂ *Play 140-291:* R2, R3. B1 attempts a suicide squeeze, which the defense is prepared for. When the ball is bunted, the charging third baseman fields it and throws to the plate: (a) in time, or (b) not in time to retire advancing R3. The catcher's throw to first (second play) plunks B1 in the back. B1 is not in the running lane and is therefore guilty of interference. Also, at the time of the catcher's throw R2 has already rounded third. *Ruling:* In (a) or (b) at all levels, B1 is out, and R2 remains on third: In FED, the runner always returns to the base occupied at the time of interference, which in this play is third. In OBR and NCAA, the runner also returns, but only because interference occurred on a second play: The throw to the plate was the "intervening" play.

⁂ *Play 141-291:* R3. The suicide squeeze is on. B1 bunts the ball up the first-base line, and there is no throw to the plate. R3 scores easily, after which F1's throw toward first (first play) hits B1 in the back. B1 is not in the running lane. *Ruling:* B1 is out for interference. In FED, the run counts. In NCAA / OBR, R3 must return to third.

⁂ *Play 142-291:* R1. B1 hits for extra bases. R1 rounds third, sees he cannot make it safely home, and gets in a rundown. During the hotbox, B1 advances to and is standing on third when R1 slaps the ball out of the third baseman's hand and makes it safely to home. *Ruling:* R1 is out for interference. (See § 287.) In FED / NCAA, B1 may remain on third. In OBR, B1 must return to second, for he cannot advance to a "rundown" base following interference.

292 BY: CATCHER: w/BATTER: BEFORE SWING✪

FED: If the catcher extends his mitt over the plate before F1 has begun his initial movements to deliver, there is no penalty. After the pitcher has started his "preliminary motions" in either the windup or set positions, if the catcher "reaches out over home base": **PENALTY:** The umpire will call a delayed-dead ball and catcher obstruction. (8.1.1f)

NCAA: If the catcher interferes with the batter during a practice swing, the umpire is to call time and start over from scratch. (8-2e AR)

OBR: Same as NCAA. (6.08c CMT ¶ 6)

★ 293 INTERFERENCE BY: CATCHER: w/BATTER: DURING SWING: TIME FRAME FOR OPTION ✪

FED: If a play follows catcher obstruction, the offense may take the result of the play or the penalty. The offense must exercise its option before the next pitch (legal or illegal), before an intentional walk, or before the infielders leave the diamond when a half inning is ending. (8.1.1h, I, n, o, and p) (See § 15 and 294.)

NCAA: Same as FED. (8-2e-1) **EXCEPT:** No time frame is listed for exercising the option. BRD suggests: Follow the usual time frame for making appeals, outlined in § 15.

OBR: Same as FED. **EXCEPT:** The "election [of play or penalty] shall be made immediately at the end of the play." (6.08c) (See § 362 for comment on the OBR notion of "delayed dead ball.") **304. ALSO:** In the event of a steal or squeeze at home, the umpire must enforce the additional **PENALTY** at 7.07. (6.08c CMT)

> ❀ Note 277: This language, added in 2007, puts to rest a long-standing argument between experts. Play: R2, R3 stealing, catcher's interference. R2 remains at second. Ruling: Harry Wendelstedt told me if R2 stayed for that pitch, that's where he'd be for the next pitch. Not these days: R2 is awarded third on the balk.

⁂ *Play 143-293:* R1 stealing. B1 swings and misses, but the catcher tips his bat on the swing. The umpire calls: "That's catcher's interference / obstruction." The catcher's throw goes into centerfield, and R1 makes third safely. *Ruling:* At all levels, return R1 to second and send B1 to first.

⁂ *Play 144-293:* R3. The catcher interferes with B1's attempt to bunt. R3 is: (a) moving on the pitch (suicide squeeze), or (b) holding until the bunt is down (safety squeeze). In either case, B1 is thrown out at first as R3 scores. *Ruling:* In (a), there are no options: R3 scores and B1 is awarded first. But in (b), the coach must decide: He may have runners on the corners (penalty) or one run in and B1 out (play).

❀ Note 278-293: Mechanics are not often a subject for the BRD. This is an exception. ***(EDITED)*** Both JEA (6:64) and HW (P234/171) indicate the correct procedure is for the umpire to enforce the penalty for catcher interference, willy-nilly. Then, if the offensive coach requests the option, the ruling will be changed. I believe that's wrong for amateur umpires, and I am joined in that assessment by senior NCAA Division I umpires Jon Bible and Ken Allen. Simply: When an option exists, offer it to the coach. (See § 341.)

294 INTERFERENCE BY: CATCHER: CREATES BALK DURING: PITCH OR INTENTIONAL BASE ON BALLS ✪

FED: At TOP, the catcher must have both feet in the catcher's box. (1-1-4; 6-1-1) **PENALTY:** ball / balk. (6-1-1 Pen) (See § 406.)

NCAA: The catcher must remain in the box until the ball leaves the pitcher's hand. (5-4a; 9-3i) **PENALTY:** ball / balk. (5-4a Pen)

OBR: The catcher must remain in the catcher's box when the pitcher delivers only when the defense is giving an intentional base on balls. (8.05L) The catcher may leave his position at the time of the pitch. **EXCEPT:** During an intentional walk, the catcher may not leave his box until the pitch leaves the pitcher's hand. (4.03a) **PENALTY:** balk. (4.03a Pen)

EXCEPT: OFF INTERP 237-294: **DEARY:** During an intentional walk the catcher may jump from his box as soon as the pitcher begins his preliminary motions in either legal position; *i.e.*, at the time of the pitch. (*REF* 6/87) ❀

❀ Note 279: This is an excellent example of authorities saying one thing and meaning another. The OBR and Wendelstedt (HW/72) hold that during an intentional walk, the catcher must remain in the box until the ball leaves the pitcher's hand; otherwise the umpire will assess a balk. Deary has no such illusions, Anybody who watches professional baseball knows that Barney's interpretation reigns supreme.

❀ Note 280: During a pitch-out the catcher may jump from his box at any time, regardless of whether the pitcher has started his preliminary motion.

★ 295 INTERFERENCE BY: CATCHER: CREATES BALK DURING: SQUEEZE OR STEAL OF HOME ✪

FED: Whenever the catcher ***(ADDED)*** (or any other defensive player) obstructs the batter, if the penalty is not ignored, the batter is awarded first, and runners advancing on the pitch or forced also receive one base. (8-1-1e; 8-1-1e-1; 8.1.1L; 8.3.1 b and c) (See § 293.)

NCAA: When ~~the catcher~~ ***(EDITED)*** any defensive player interferes with the batter during a squeeze or steal of home, the pitcher is charged with a balk and the catcher with interference. The runner scores, the batter is awarded first, and all other runners advance one base. (8-2e-2; 8-3p)

OBR: Same as NCAA 8-2e: The umpire must enforce 7.07 rather than 6.08c. (6.08c CMT ¶ 5) (See § 266.)

∞296 INTERFERENCE BY: CATCHER: DEFINITION ✪

FED: Catcher obstruction (interference) occurs when the catcher: (● 1) touches the batter's bat; (● 2) pushes the batter to reach the pitch; or (● 3) steps on or across home plate to reach the pitch. (8-3-1c)

NCAA: Same as FED. (8-2e) **EXCEPT:** Pushing the batter or stepping on / across the plate is listed as an infraction only on a steal / squeeze play at home. (8-3p)

❀ Note 281: The NCAA figures that on a pitch where a runner is not sprinting for home, the catcher will not push the batter or jump in front of the plate. These college boys aren't dumb.

OBR: Same as NCAA. (7.07)

★ ∞297 INTERFERENCE BY: COACH: ASSISTS RUNNER DURING: DEAD BALL ✪

FED: Contact, even physical assistance, by a coach with a home run hitter who is advancing on a four-base award is legal. (3.2.2a) (See § 298.)

NCAA: Point not covered.

> ***(ADDED)*** OFF INTERP 238-297: **PARONTO:** "There is no coach's interference during a dead ball unless the coach's actions provide an advantage for the offensive team." (email to cc, 12/21/11) ✠

OBR: No provision. ***(ADDED)*** Treat as in NCAA.

⁎ *Play 145-297:* R1 tries for third on B1's single, but F9's throw goes dead. R1 rounds the bag (he will be awarded home) but does not touch it. The coach grabs R1 by the arm and yells: "Go back and touch third." *Ruling:* ***(REVISED)*** At all levels, there is no penalty.

★ 298 INTERFERENCE BY: COACH: ASSISTS RUNNER DURING: LIVE BALL ✪

FED: During playing action a coach may not "physically assist" a runner. (3-2-2) **PENALTY:** The ball is delayed dead (5-1-2f), and the batter-runner or runner is out. Any other outs made on the play stand, and runners remain TOI. (3-2-2 Pen)
305. ALSO: If the interference occurs during a fly ball, the delayed-dead ball provision allows a fielder the "opportunity to make a catch." If the ball

is caught, the batter is out. If it is not caught, the batter is awarded first. In every case, the "assisted" runner is out. (3.2.2b)

306. ALSO: A coach's interference would deprive the hitter of a home run if two were out when the interference occurred but not if none or one was out. (3.2.2a)

> **307. ALSO:** OFF INTERP 239-298: **RUMBLE:** If a coach celebrates a good play during live action by slapping hands with a runner as he rounds a base, that is not "aiding" the runner. (*News*#30, 4/89) (See § 297.) ✠

> **308. ALSO:** OFF INTERP 240-298: **RUMBLE:** If a runner collides with a coach in the box, no interference is called and the ball remains alive. (*News*#30, 4/89) ✠

> **309. ALSO:** OFF INTERP 241-298: **HOPKINS:** Unless the contact is intentional, it is not interference when a runner crashes into a coach in the baseline. (Website 2001, #12) (See FED § 300, which contradicts this interpretation.) ✠

NCAA: "A base coach may not physically assist a runner in returning or leaving the base." (3-3e) **PENALTY:** The ball is delayed dead. "At the end of play, the assisted runner shall be declared out." (3-3e Pen.) **EXCEPT:** Status of ball if the ball is not caught:
Point not covered.

> ***(EDITED)*** OFF INTERP 242-298: **PARONTO:** Play continues if the ball is not caught (delayed dead ball). Runners may make outs or advance on the bases. (email to cc, 12/21/11) ✠

> **310. ALSO:** OFF INTERP 243-298: **FETCHIET:** Same as FED OFF INTERP 241 [this section]: no infraction when a runner accidentally collides with a coach outside the coaching box. (Website 4/18/01, 8-5f) ✠

OBR: The rule specifically refers only to the first base and third base coaches; they may not assist a runner in returning or leaving first or third bases. **PENALTY:** ***(EDITED)*** The runner is out. (7.09h)

> **EXCEPT:** OFF INTERP 244-298: ***(EDITED)*** **WENDELSTEDT:** Following a coach's interference the assisted runner is out, but the ball remains alive: Other runners may make bases or outs. (HW/298)) ✠

> **311. ALSO:** OFF INTERP 245-298: **FITZPATRICK:** A coach may not assist a runner in returning to touch home after crossing the plate. **PENALTY:** The runner is out, but the ball remains alive. (phone call to cc, 11/07/01) ✠

✻ *Play 146-298:* R3, R2, 0 out. B1 hits a high fly ball to right field. R3 heads home, but his coach pulls him back, yelling "Tag up!" The ball is not caught. Both R3 and R2 score, and B1 pulls up on second. *Ruling:* R3 is out at all levels. In FED, R2 goes to third and B1 is awarded first. In NCAA / OBR, R2 scores, and B1 remains on second.

✻ *Play 147-298:* Bases loaded, 0 out. B1 flies to right. The coach pulls R3 back to the bag. The ball is dropped. R3 scores, R2 scores, slow-footed R1 tries for third but is thrown out as B1 takes second. *Ruling:* In FED, R3 and R1 are out. R2 returns to second; B1, to first. (Note: The offensive coach? He probably returns as well — to the showers in the club house.) In NCAA / OBR, take the result of the play EXCEPT R3 is out.

❀ Note 282: The staff of PBUC was adamant: The OBR umpire should ignore the penalty for 7.09i: (delayed) dead ball. When I pressed the spokesman, Mike Felt replied succinctly: "Ball is alive and in play correct."

✻ *Play 148-298:* R2, 2 out, score tied, bottom of the last inning. B1 singles, and R2 scores the winning run but misses the plate. A bench coach grabs him and pushes him back to touch home.
Ruling: At all levels R2 is out, and the game continues.

❀ Note 283: The BRD urges: At all levels, define "physically assist" as any deliberate touching of a runner that is intended to communicate coaching instructions such as "Get back!" or "Go now!"

299 INTERFERENCE BY: COACH: HIT BY THROW ACCIDENTALLY ✪

FED: If a throw accidentally hits a base coach in foul territory, the ball remains alive. (3-2-3) If the ball touches the coach in fair territory, it is "automatic interference." (3.2.3) (See § 300.)

NCAA: If a thrown ball strikes a coach in foul ground, the ball is in play. There is no reference to a coach being hit in fair territory. (8-3j)

OBR: It is not interference if the base coach is accidentally hit by a throw anywhere on the field. (5.08)

300 INTERFERENCE BY: COACH: LEAVES COACHING BOX DURING LIVE ACTION ✪

FED: The coach must remain in his box at all times during a live ball. (3-3-1j) PENALTY: warning / ejection. (3-1-1j Pen)
(But see OFF INTERP 241-298, which contradicts that statute.)
(See also § 299 and 306.)

NCAA: The coach may leave his box to signal the runner to slide or to advance or return to a base as long as he does not interfere with a play. (3-3b) PENALTY: warning / ejection. (3-3b Pen) (See § 298.)

312. ALSO: The coach is required to stand with both feet in the box. (3-3b) (See § 134.)

OBR: Same as NCAA. (4.05b; 4.05b CMT)
EXCEPT: PENALTY: ejection (no warning). (4.05b Pen)
313. ALSO: "It has been common practice for many years" for the coach to stand with one foot outside and one foot inside the coaching box. The umpire will ignore the infraction until one team complains, when the umpire will require both teams to abide by the rule." (4.05b CMT)
PENALTY: ejection. (4.05b Pen)

❀ Note 284: If one team complains and you require both coaches to stay inside the box, when a coach "forgets," BRD recommends: Warn him the first time; eject, the second.

301 INTERFERENCE BY: EQUIPMENT ✪

Definition: See § 302.
Measure award: See § 303.
Throw touches: See § 304.
Touches pitch: See § 305.

DETACHED

∞ 301 A **HELMET: ACCIDENTAL**

FED: Point not covered.

OFF INTERP 246-301: **HOPKINS:** If a live ball hits an accidentally-detached helmet, it is not interference and the ball remains in play. (Website 2007, #2) ✠

NCAA: Same as OFF INTERP 220 [this section]. (6-1f)

OBR: Same as NCAA. (6.05h CMT ¶ 3)

----

301 B **HELMET: DELIBERATE**

FED: Point not covered.

OFF INTERP 247-301: **HOPKINS:** A batter-runner or runner may not deliberately throw a helmet or other personal equipment and interfere with a batted or thrown ball, or a fielder's attempt to play on that ball. **PENALTY:** The ball is dead, the interferer is out, and other runners remain TOI. The umpire may declare two outs if he judged the interference prevented a double play. (Website 2007, #2) (See § 428.) ✠

NCAA: A runner may not deliberately throw a helmet or other personal equipment and interfere with a batted or thrown ball. **PENALTY:** The ball is dead, the runner is out, and runners "in advance of the interference" return TOI. The batter-runner is awarded first. (6-2h)

OBR: Same as NCAA. (6.05h CMT ¶ 3)

❀ Note 285: An important distinction must be made: If a batted or thrown ball **ACCIDENTALLY** hits an **INTENTIONALLY DETACHED HELMET**, that is not interference, and the ball remains alive. The batter-runner or runner must deliberately throw his helmet and hit the ball before the umpire will assess any interference penalty.

----

301 C **LOOSE**

FED: Loose equipment (such as gloves, bats, helmets, or catcher's paraphernalia) of either team may not be on or near the field. (1-3-7) (See § 304.) **PENALTY:** If such loose equipment alters a play, the umpire may award bases, declare outs, or return runners based on his judgment. (1-3-7 Pen; 1.3.7 a and b)

NCAA: Loose equipment of either team may not be on or near the field. (1-16d) **PENALTY:** None provided. If a live ball touches equipment in live-ball territory, the ball remains alive. (1-16d AR)

OBR: Loose equipment of either team may not be on or near the field. (3.14) **PENALTY:** None provided.

AO 18: EVANS: Umpires should monitor the area in front of the dugouts and insure that gloves and equipment are not left lying on the playing field. Equipment lying on the "lip" of the dugout is legal, but a thrown ball that strikes it is considered "in the dugout," [hence dead]. (3-44)

★ 301 D **ROSIN BAG**

FED: No provision. Treat as in OBR.

NCAA: Point not covered.

(ADDED) OFF INTERP 248-301: **PARONTO:** Same as OBR. (email to cc, 12/21/11) ✠

OBR: "If at any time the ball hits the rosin bag," the ball remains alive and in play." (8.02a CMT 2) (See § 390.)

★ ∞ 302 INTERFERENCE BY: FIELDER: DETACHED EQUIPMENT: DEFINITION ✪

FED: A fielder using detached player equipment, including uniform items, may not deliberately interfere with a batted fair ball or a foul ball that in the opinion of the umpire might have become fair without the interference. **PENALTY:** All runners including the batter-runner are awarded three bases. The ball remains alive; if the batter-runner makes home safely or is thrown out at the plate, the play stands. (8-3-3b) (See § 303 for how to measure the awards.)

NCAA: Same as FED. (8-2h; 8-3g)

OBR: The rule speaks of interference with a fair ball only. (7.05b and c)

EXCEPT: OFF INTERP 249-302: **PBUC:** Same as FED 8-3-3b. {6.9} ✠

314. ALSO: Concerning measuring an award for interference with a batted ball: No provisions.

303 INTERFERENCE BY: FIELDER: DETACHED EQUIPMENT: MEASURE AWARD
ALL CODE NOW AGREE: TEXT DELETED, 2012

★ 304 INTERFERENCE BY: FIELDER: DETACHED EQUIPMENT: THROW TOUCHES ✪

FED: If a throw touches equipment that is legally on the field, it is not interference and the ball remains alive. (8.4.1e) (See § 213.)

NCAA: *(EDITED)* If a throw touches equipment that is in live ball territory, the ball remains alive. (1-16d AR) (See § 213, 284 and 285.)

OBR: No provision. Treat as in NCAA.

305 INTERFERENCE BY: FIELDER: DETACHED EQUIPMENT: TOUCHES PITCH ✪

FED: A defensive player may not touch a pitch with detached equipment. **PENALTY:** Each runner receives a two-base award, measured from the time of the touch. (8-3-3c-1)

NCAA: A defensive player may not touch a pitch with detached equipment, cap, or uniform. **PENALTY:** Each runner receives a one-base award, measured from the time of the touch. (8-3g-2)

OBR: Same as NCAA. (7.04e)

✻ Play 149-305: R2 B1 swings and misses a low curve ball; the pitch scoots a couple of feet away from the catcher. F2, watching the runner carefully, whips off his mask and uses it to drag the loose ball toward his glove. *Ruling:* R2 is awarded home in FED; third, in NCAA / OBR.

∞306 INTERFERENCE BY: OFFENSE: DRAWS THROW ✪

FED: No OFFENSIVE PERSONNEL may be "on or near" the baseline in such a way as to draw a throw by confusing a fielder. (3-2-3) **PENALTY:** The ball is dead immediately, and the runner [nearest the interference] is out. If the umpire judges the interference (misdirected throw) prevented a double play, he will also declare out the batter-runner or other runner involved. (3-2-3 Pen) (See § 300.)

NCAA: With a runner on third, the COACH may not run toward the plate in an attempt to draw a throw or prevent a "legitimate" play. (8-5g) **PENALTY:** The ball is dead, the runner is out, and other runners remain TOI. (2-50 AR 1; 3-3f; 3-3f Pen) (See § 300.)

OBR: Same as NCAA. (2-Interference; 7.09i)

∞307 INTERFERENCE BY: OFFENSE: PREVENTS CATCH ✪

FED: Members of the offense must vacate any area to allow a defensive player the chance to put out a batter or runner. (3-2-3) **PENALTY:** The runner is out. (The batter is out if the interference occurs on a play at home with two outs.) If the umpire judges the interference prevented a double play, the batter-runner or [other involved] runner may be declared out. (3-2-3 Pen) (See § 306.)

NCAA: If a fielder reaches into a dugout, bullpen, or dead-ball area to catch a foul fly ball and an opponent interferes with the attempted catch, the batter shall be declared out and no runners shall advance. (6-1d AR 1)

OBR: Same as FED. (7.11; 7.11 Pen)

308 INTERFERENCE BY: OFFENSE: REMARKS TO STOP PLAY OR "AID" DEFENSE
ALL CODES NOW AGREE: TEXT DELETED, 1995.

309 INTERFERENCE BY: OFFENSE: OUT OF DUGOUT FOR UNAUTHORIZED REASON OR TOUCH HOME RUN HITTER ✪

FED: POE 1992, 2005, 2008, 2009: No game personnel shall "leave the dugout during a live ball for an unauthorized purpose." (3-3-1a; 3.3.1a, b, e, f) **PENALTY:** team warning: All players leaving the dugout will be ejected on the second offense. (3-3-1a Pen; 3.3.1c and d)

❀ Note 286: The 2005 POE railed against the behavior at home plate, which "is becoming undesirable and antagonistic." They then suggested coaches remind their players to stay away from live-ball territory while the ball is alive. But apparently their POE was ineffective.

NCAA: POE 1999, 2000, 2001, 2002: After a home run, only an offensive coach may touch the hitter. Team members, except the on-deck batter, may not "leave the warning track area in front of the dugout (a recommended minimum area of 15 feet" to congratulate the "batter runner and other base runners." (5-2d) **PENALTY:** First offense: warning; second offense: ejection of one of the offending players. (5-2d Pen) (See § 298.)

❀ Note 287: The rule about players touching a home run hitter is now "more restrictive." (NCAA 2011 video, Paronto)

✻ *Play 150-309:* **FED and NCAA only.** The bases are loaded when B1: (a) homers over the fence; or (b) doubles, sending home all runners. Members of the offense leave the dugout to congratulate the runners as they score. *Ruling:* FED: In (a), there is no penalty. In (b), the umpire issues a team warning. NCAA: In (a) and (b), a warning for the first offense. On a second offense, ejection of an offender.

❀ Note 288: NCAA doesn't provide for a penalty similar to the FED's "team warning." (See ¶ 6 E-4 in the Introduction.) The penalty for this infraction, then, is a "generic" warning to the offending players: "Next time, I'll pick one of you."

OBR: No provision. *See ¶8.*

★ ∞ 310 INTERFERENCE BY: ON-DECK BATTER ✪

FED: Point not covered.

OFF INTERP 250-310: **HOPKINS:** If an on deck batter picks up a live ball: With runners not moving, the ball is simply dead; with runners moving, the ball is dead and the runner on whom the defense would have played is out. If the umpire cannot determine which runner, the one nearer home is out.
(Website 2003, #19) (See § 91.) ✠

NCAA: Point not covered.

(ADDED) OFF INTERP 251-310: **PARONTO:** Same as OFF INTERP 252 [this section] (email to cc, 12/21/11) ✠

OBR: Point not covered.

OFF INTERP 252-310: **LEPPERD:** While chasing a loose throw, the catcher runs into the on-deck batter — not in his circle: "As long as the collision was unintentional, umpires would **MOST LIKELY** invoke the concepts of OBR 3.15. ... If a throw should strike him, the ball would be alive and in play."
(Booth, eTeamz, 10/30/2001) (See § 91.) ✠

❀ Note 289: Fitzpatrick concurred with Lepperd's ruling. (phone call to cc, 11/8/01)

★ ∞ 311 INTERFERENCE BY: RUNNER: AIDS OTHER RUNNER ✪

FED: Point not covered.

OFF INTERP 253-311: **RUMBLE:** A following runner may aid another runner as long as he does not pass his teammate. (*News* #34, 4/76) ✠

NCAA: Point not covered.

(ADDED) OFF INTERP 254-311: **PARONTO:** Same as OFF INTERP 253 [this section]. (email to cc, 12/21/11) ✠

OBR: Point not covered.

OFF INTERP 255-311: **PBUC STAFF:** Same as FED OFF INTERP 253-311. (email to cc, 12/15/00) ✠

∞ 312 INTERFERENCE BY: RUNNER: AVOIDS FIELDER ✪

FED: It is not an infraction if a runner runs **BEHIND** a fielder (and hence out of the base path) to avoid interfering with a fielder's attempt to field a batted ball.
(8-4-2a-1) (See 325, 326 and 327. See REF May/June, 1977.)

NCAA: Same as FED. (8-5a Ex)

OBR: The runner may not leave the base path unless it is to "avoid interference with a fielder fielding a batted ball." (7.08a-1)

❀ Note 290: The OBR has no rules language mandating that a runner (generally the runner from second) must run "behind" a fielder. How many FED / NCAA umpires call interference on R2 when he does not?

313 INTERFERENCE BY: RUNNER: w/BATTED BALL: AFTER IT: PASSES A FIELDER
ALL CODES NOW AGREE: TEXT DELETED, 2009

★ ∞ 314 INTERFERENCE BY: RUNNER: w/BATTED BALL: AFTER IT: TOUCHES A FIELDER ✪

FED: After any infielder has touched a batted ball, interference shall not be called if the ball hits a runner, even when another fielder has a play on the ball. (8-4-2k) (See § 326, 327 and 328.)

NCAA: Same as FED. (6-1c)

OBR: Point not covered.

> **EXCEPT:** OFF INTERP 256-314: **PBUC:** ***(EDITED)*** "The concept of the runner being in jeopardy ... DOES NOT APPLY if the ball is TOUCHED or DEFLECTED by the first infielder, EVEN THOUGH ANOTHER INFIELDER HAS A CHANCE TO MAKE A PLAY ON THE BALL." {7.5} ✠

⁂ *Play 151-314:* R2. B1 squares to bunt as R2 heads for third. The third baseman has been creeping in. B1 decides to swing away and nicks a soft liner off F5's glove. The shortstop, coming to cover third, is about to grab the ball when it hits R2 and drops to the ground, leaving runners safe at both corners. *Ruling:* Unless R2 deliberately allowed himself to be hit, interference did not occur.

315 INTERFERENCE BY: RUNNER: w/BATTED BALL: BEFORE IT PASSES A FIELDER
ALL CODES NOW AGREE: TEXT DELETED, 2009

★ 316 INTERFERENCE BY: RUNNER: w/BATTED BALL: DEFINITION OF "PASSES BY FIELDER" ✪

FED: The umpire will not call interference if a runner in the base path is hit by a batted ball when the infielders are playing in front of the baseline. (8.4.2.i) **EXCEPT:** A runner on or off the base is out if he is hit by a batted ball with "a fielder in position to make a play." (5.1.1h; Website 2002, #13) (See OFF INTERP • 211-267.]

❀ Note 291: I hope I'm not paranoid, but the rulings seem to conflict. CB 8.4.2k does not require a fielder to be in position to make the play; if the ball passes a fielder, the runner is not out even if another fielder is in position to make the play. CB 5.1.1h and the latest interpretation from the Website both ignore that.

NCAA: A runner hit by the batted ball, including one in contact with his base, is not out if the ball has touched a fielder, or passed all infielders who have a chance to make a play on the ball, other than the pitcher. (8-5k)

> **315. ALSO:** OFF INTERP 257-316: **PARONTO:** When a runner is hit by a fair batted ball with infielders positioned behind him, the runner is out. If they are drawn in, as they would be to cut off a run at the plate, the runner is behind them, and if he gets hit, the ball remains alive. (San Antonio, MTG, 1/4/04) ✠

❀ Note 292: The FED / NCAA definitions match Joe Brinkman's in *The Umpire's Manual*, quiz question #31, p. 151. Joe used OBR rules.

OBR: Point not covered.

> OFF INTERP 258-316: **FITZPATRICK:** "Goes by a fielder" is defined as "within arm's reach." The fielder must have a "legitimate" chance to field the ball else the runner is out. (email to cc, 1/17/01) ✠

❀ Note 293: Someone told the NCAA rules committee that their rule now matches the OBR interpretations. That "someone" was dead wrong:

Childress: "Does the ball have to pass within arm's reach of the fielder before you will protect the runner?"

Paronto: "No. If the runner is behind the infielders, he is not out when hit."

∞317 INTERFERENCE BY: RUNNER: w/BATTED BALL: FOUL FLY ✪

FED: No coach or member of the offensive team "other than the runner(s)" may interfere, either deliberately or unintentionally, with a fielder's attempt to catch a foul fly. **PENALTY:** The batter is out. (7-4-1f; 7.4.1h) (See § 281.) If the runner interferes, the runner is out regardless of a catch / no catch since the ball is immediately dead. Since it is a foul ball, the batter is charged with a strike. (8-4-2g; 8.4.2b; Website 2010, #5 and # 6)

❀ Note 294: The 2009 rule (the batter is out when a runner interferes) entered the FED book in 1981! It took them 31 seasons to get it right again. Back in the day the FED committee argued that some coaches (probably on the left-hand coast) were teaching

their runners at third to interfere so the hard-hitting batter could remain at bat. I wrote Brad Rumble and said: "OK. But call out the batter only when there are two outs. Your rule seems strange: R2 [on third] interferes, B3 is out, and B4 singles in the winning run." They were not impressed. But now they have joined the other two books. This section, however, will remain because of the OBR OFF INTERP 259 below.
Note to the note: What seems strange to me now is the ridiculous method the FED uses to identify runners: "With R1 on third and R2 on first ...."

NCAA: Same as FED. (8-5d; 8-5q)

OBR: Same as FED. (7.08b; 7.11)

❀ Note 295: Harry Wendelstedt said that a runner's interference with a foul ball would be "nothing" unless the ball had a chance to become fair. But Claude Engberg, president of the (Rookie Advanced) Pioneer League, would not have seen eye-to-eye with Harry's CS / FP ruling. In 1957 the manager of Idaho Falls officially protested a game because the umpires would not call out a Great Falls runner on third who picked up an **OBVIOUS** foul ball and tossed it back to the pitcher. Engberg upheld their protest and ordered the game replayed from the spot of the "infraction." Of course, he'd never heard of Harry Wendelstedt in 1957. But somebody in the FED heard of Engberg's ruling because it became black-letter law for the NFHS in 1994.

> **316. ALSO:** OFF INTERP 259-317: **PBUC STAFF:** If a runner interferes with a fielder attempting to catch a declared "Infield fly if fair," the umpire will not stop play until the status of the ball is determined. (phone call to cc, 12/26/01) (See § 264.) ✠

❀ Note 296: BRD recommends you treat interference with an infield fly the same at all levels.
✲ *Play 152-317*: Bases loaded, 0 out. B1 pops up down the third-base line. The umpire calls: "Infield fly, if fair!" R3, who has been bluffing a steal, turns to go back to third and smacks into the third baseman. *Ruling:* The umpire calls "That's interference," but he does not stop play! If the ball when touched is fair, it is an infield fly and both B1 and R3 are out. If the ball is foul, only R3 is out, even if F5 catches the ball.

✲ *Play 153-317:* Bases loaded, 0 out. B1 pops up down the first-base line. The ball is fair ("That's an infield fly!" yells the umpire) when B1 interferes. *Ruling:* B1 is out and so is R3, the runner who has advanced nearest to home.

✲ *Play 154-317:* R3, 0 out. B1 lifts a pop foul fly down the third-base line, where: (a) R3 prevents the third baseman from catching the fly; or (b) the third-base coach prevents the catch. *Ruling:* In (a), R3 is out and, if B1 has fewer than two strikes, a strike is called. In (b), B1 is out.

318 INTERFERENCE BY: RUNNER: w/BATTED BALL: IN FOUL TERRITORY
ALL CODES NOW AGREE: TEXT DELETED, 1994.

★ 319 INTERFERENCE BY: RUNNER: w/BATTED BALL: ON BASE: HIT BY BALL ✪

FED: In general, the base is not a sanctuary: A runner is out when hit by an untouched batted ball even while in contact with his base if a fielder is in position to make a play. (5.1.1j; 8.4.2h) **EXCEPT:** A runner touching his base is **NOT OUT** if he is hit by a declared infield fly, but the ball becomes dead. (8-4-2k-1; 5.1.1j)
317. ALSO: A runner touching a base when hit by a batted ground ball is not out if the defense is playing "in front of the base line" though the ball is dead. (8.4.2i) (See § 316

NCAA: A runner touching a base is out unless he is hit by a declared infield fly (8-5k AR 1)

OBR: Same as NCAA. (7.08f Ex)

318. ALSO: OFF INTERP 260-319: ***(EDITED)*** **PBUC:** If defensive players have a chance to field a fair batted ball, but choose not to, and a runner is touched by the ball [while on base], the runner is not out." {7.5-12} ✠

⁎ *Play 155-319:* R2, 0 out. B1 bunts fair down the third-base line. The pitcher and third baseman back toward the base, hoping the ball will roll foul. It bounces on third and hits the runner who has advanced from second. *Ruling:* "Because the fielders had an opportunity to field the batted ball but chose not to," the runner is not out. {PBUC, p. 72}

❀ Note 297: BRD recommends adopting OFF INTERP 260-319 for all your games.

∞ 320 INTERFERENCE BY: RUNNER: w/BATTED BALL: ON BASE: PREVENTS PLAY ✪

FED: A runner need not vacate his base to permit a fielder to catch a fly ball, but he may not interfere. (8-2-8)
PENALTY: Point not covered.

OFF INTERP 261-320: **RUMBLE:** If a runner touching his base deliberately interferes with a fielder's catch: With two out, the batter is out; with fewer than two out, both the batter and the runner are out. (letter to cc, **3/9/81**) ✠

❀ Note 298: From this ruling we may deduce: (● 1) The play is rare: It hasn't happened in the last 30 years; or (● 2) FED umpires just call the play by the OBR rule, and coaches don't complain to the NFHS. The only

FED interpretation is in a private letter to me, and its only public dissemination over these three decades has been the BRD. Go figure!

NCAA: Same as FED. (8-5k AR2) **PENALTY:** Same as OFF INTERP 261 [this section]. (See also § 315.)

OBR: Same as NCAA. (7.08b CMT ¶ 2)

✻ *Play 156-320:* R2, R3. The suicide squeeze is on, but B1 pops the ball toward second. R3 oblivious to the play continues to advance, but R2 retreats and is standing on the bag when the ball comes down. R2 slaps the ball away, and the umpire calls interference. *Ruling:* B1 and R2 are out; R3 returns.

❀ Note 299: A controversy exists concerning whether 7.08b CMT ¶ 2 is in error in granting a double play when the runner interfering is on base. It is true that OBR seems to require always a "double play situation" before giving the umpire the power to call out two on a single play. But while the CMT at 7.08b might be in error, it's still in the book and – pending a revised official interpretation – should be enforced if the occasion arises.

✻ *Play 157-320:* R1, R2, R3, nobody out. B1 pops up, and the ball is coming down directly at second. The umpire declares an infield fly. The ball hits R2 on his helmet, and R3 heads for home. As F6 tries to grab the ball, he: (a) pushes into R2, who remains on the base; or (b) R2 deliberately pushes into F6. In either case, F6 cannot make the play. *Ruling:* The ball is dead, and B1 is out. R2 is not out when the ball hits him. He is also not out in (a), but he is out in (b). In either (a) or (b), R3 must return to third.

321 INTERFERENCE BY: RUNNER: w/BATTED BALL: RUNNER(S) RETURN TO BASES
ALL CODES NOW AGREE: TEXT DELETED, 2000.

∞ 322 INTERFERENCE BY: RUNNER: w/BATTED BALL: TWO HIT ✪

FED: No provision. Treat as in NCAA.

NCAA: If two runners are hit by the same fair batted ball, only the first runner is out. (8-5k)

OBR: Same as NCAA. (7.08f CMT)

323 INTERFERENCE BY: RUNNER: w/DOUBLE PLAY: UMPIRE OBSERVES CONTACT AT SECOND ✪

FED: No provision.

NCAA: On a force play in the two-umpire system, if the UIC has no play at home, he should move as near as practicable to second or third to watch for the runner making illegal contact. (8-4c Nt) (See § 329 and 330.)

OBR: No provision.

★ 324 INTERFERENCE BY: RUNNER: w/DOUBLE PLAY: WHEN TO CALL IT ✪ (See § 289.)

FED: With a double play obvious, if any runner, including the batter-runner, interferes with a fielder attempting to make a play, two may be called out. (8-1-2b; 8-4-1h; 8-4-2g). **A KEY PROVISION IS THIS:** Except for interference by an illegal slide on a force play (§ 330), the umpire must believe that the defense could have completed the double play but for the interference. If he does not, he may not call out two players, even when the interference is **DELIBERATE**. (8.4.1d; 8.4.2e)

❀ Note 300: That rule constitutes one of the **MOST SIGNIFICANT PLAYING DIFFERENCES** between FED rules on the one hand and NCAA/OBR on the other. (See Play 121-275 for a definitive game situation and ruling.)

319. ALSO: THE SECOND KEY PROVISION IS THIS: If an umpire judges that an interference prevented an obvious double play, he is to call the double out even if the interference was **ACCIDENTAL OR INADVERTENT**. (8.1.2 2002 ed; 9.3.2c) (See OFF INTERP • 262 [this section].)

✲ *Play 158-324:* While advancing to second, R1 is hit by a batted ball that prevents an obvious double play on him and the batter-runner. *Ruling:* In FED, both the runner and the batter-runner are declared out. In NCAA/OBR, only R1 is out unless the umpire rules the interference was intentional.

320. ALSO: When a runner is declared out for a **MALICIOUS CRASH**, which causes an immediate-dead ball, if the umpire judges the crash prevented a probable out, he will award that out. (3.3.1w) (See § 329.)

NCAA: Same as FED. (7-11r; 8-5d) (See § 330.)

> **321. ALSO:** OFF INTERP 262-324: **FETCHIET:** Contrary to FED 9.3.2c, where accidental interference created a double play under high school rules, the NCAA statute dictates that interference must be deliberate before the umpire may call out two. (Website 3/12/01) (8-5k) ✠

OBR: (● 1) With a double play possible, two are out if the interference is obvious, willful and deliberate {PBUC, 7.3, p.67} and designed to break up a double play, whether the umpire judges the double play could have been completed. (● 2) Merely attempting to hinder the pivot man does not constitute interference; actual interference (contact) must occur. (7.09f and g)

322. ALSO: OFF INTERP 263-324: ***(CHANGED)*** **PBUC:** A runner who is *safe* but who deliberately grabs the second baseman is guilty of interference. The runner is called out. "However, the batter is awarded first base since his intent was to reach second safely. {7.3-4} ✠

✻ *Play 159-324:* **OBR only:** R1 stealing. B1 rolls to short. R1 arrives safely at second and pushes F4 from the base just as he is about to receive the shortstop's throw. ***(REVISED)*** *Ruling:* R1 is out. B1 receives first.

✻ *Play 160-324:* R3. The runner attempts to score on a squeeze. B1, with two strikes, tries to bunt but misses, and the catcher does not hold the ball. B1 starts for first as R3 bulls across the plate, then maliciously crashes into F2, who is about to recover the ball. *Ruling:* In FED / NCAA, though R3 is automatically ejected, his run counts. If the catcher had a reasonable chance to throw out B1, B1's out is awarded. In OBR, the runner is out only if the umpire judges the runner's intent was to prevent a double play.

❀ Note 301: If it had been a force play in FED, the umpire would have canceled the run. (See § 330.)

❀ Note 302: Here is a summary of these differences. (**Interference in a force play situation is always a double play in FED / NCAA.** See § 330.)

Rulebook	Infraction	Outcome
FED, NCAA	Deliberate interference	not an automatic double play
OBR		automatic double play
FED	Accidental interference	can be a double play
NCAA, OBR		cannot be a double play

❀ Note 303: A "possible double play" is not necessarily a "likely" double play. In OBR, though, "possible" refers to the configuration of runners, as the ruling in Play 161-324 below, created by Bremigan in 1976, aptly illustrates:

✻ *Play 161-324:* R2. B1 hits a sharp grounder to short. As the fielder readies himself to make the play, R2 deliberately but not maliciously bumps F6 or allows himself to be hit. Both R2 and B1 reach base "safely." *Ruling:* In FED / NCAA, if the umpire judges the defense could have turned a double play, both R2 and B1 are out. In OBR, only R2 is out because there was no double play "possible."

❀ Note 304: Bremigan: [One cannot presume that R2 would be tagged out followed by a successful throw to first:] "If this [Play 161-324] were a line drive to short where there existed a good possibility of the shortstop catching the ball and doubling the runner up at second, then this rule [two out for interference] would and should apply." (See Note 247-275.)

325 INTERFERENCE BY: RUNNER: w/DOUBLE PLAY: WHO IS OUT? ✪

FED: With a double play possible, if a runner interferes, the one who interferes is out and so is the **OTHER RUNNER** involved.
(8-4-2g; 8.4.1d; 8.4.2d and e; 8.4.2 CMT following Situation X)
323. ALSO: If the umpire cannot determine on whom the defense would have played, he shall call out the **RUNNER CLOSEST TO HOME.** (8-4-2g)
(See § 280 and 324.)

NCAA: In such plays, the runner interfering is out and so is the **BATTER-RUNNER.** (8-4c Pen 1)

OBR: Same as NCAA. (2.00 Interference-a; 7.09f)

❋ *Play 162-325:* R1 stealing. B1 hits to F6, who races to the base, but R1 is safe. As F6 tries to throw to first, R1 deliberately interferes.
Ruling: In FED / NCAA, both B1 and R1 are out. In OBR, R1 is also out; but since no double play was possible, the batter-runner is awarded first base.

❋ *Play 163-325:* Bases loaded. B1 rolls slowly to F4. R3 gets a late start, so the second baseman decides to throw home. As F4 is about to throw, the runner from first – not maliciously but, in the umpire's judgment deliberately – bumps into him, and F4 drops the ball. Everybody is safe.
Ruling: At all levels R1 is out for interference. In FED, since the "other runner involved" is R3, if a double play was prevented, R3 is out and B1 is awarded first; R2 remains TOI. If the double play could not have been completed, only R1 is out, with R3, R2, and B1 now on base.
In NCAA / OBR, B1 is automatically out. R3 and R2 return TOP.

❋ *Play 164-325:* R2, R3. The suicide squeeze is on. B1 bunts a pop-up toward short, but before the fielder can make the play, R2 hits him (not maliciously), and the ball falls to the ground. B1 advances to first, and R3 goes home. The umpire is convinced that, following the catch, F6 had an easy toss to third for a double play on R3. *Ruling:* In FED, R3 and R2 are out. B1 gets first. In NCAA / OBR, R2 and B1 are out and R3 returns to third. Easy.

❀ Note 305: The FED ruling could cause a fight within the umpire crew. The "natural" double play – if there had been no interference – would involve B1 (caught fly ball) and R3 (doubled up at third). Some consider that the other runner involved here is the batter. After all, he hit a routine pop-up. Thus, the outcome of the play would be the same as in NCAA / OBR. After much reflection, BRD recommends: The second out, the "other runner involved," should be called against R3, with the batter receiving first as in Play 163-325.

❀ Note 306: Case book play 8.4.1d explicitly gives the umpire the authority to decide – on any given play – what **MIGHT** have resulted if interference had not occurred. If the umpire does not know on whom the fielder would have played, he is directed to call out the runner closest to home. (8-4-2g) Besides, if he follows the BRD recommendation, the umpire is upholding a long-existing tradition for penalizing interference: Hit 'em where it hurts the most.

❀ Note 307: For more discussion of the "runner closest to home," see § 275.

326 INTERFERENCE BY: RUNNER: w/FIELDER IN BASE PATH AFTER DEFLECTION OF BALL BY: FIELDER✪

(See § 327 and 328.)

FED: When a fielder muffs a batted ball and he must move to re-field it, if contact occurs in the base path, the umpire will protect the runner unless the official declares deliberate interference. (8-4-2g 1) (See § 314 and 328.)

NCAA: If a fielder misplays a batted ball, when the ball remains within his immediate reach or within "a step and a reach," the fielder is still considered in the act of fielding the ball. (2-50 AR 3; 2-54 AR 3) (See § 350.)

324. ALSO: If the fielder "must chase after the ball," a runner's contact with the fielder is obstruction. (2-50 AR4) (See § 328.)

325. ALSO: If a fielder chases after a deflected ball and is in the act of picking it up, contact between runner and fielder is interference. If the fielder is chasing the ball and contact occurs, obstruction is the call. (2-50 AR 5)

> **326. ALSO:** OFF INTERP 264-326: **PARONTO:** If contact occurs between a runner and a fielder attempting to field a batted ball, it must be either interference or obstruction: There is no "incidental contact." (San Antonio MTG, 1/3/04) (See OFF INTERP 266-327 for a radically different view of this collision.) ✠

OBR: Point not covered.

> OFF INTERP 265-326: **PBUC:** If a fielder has a chance to field a batted ball, but misplays it and while attempting to recover it, the ball is in the fielder's immediate reach and the fielder is contacted by the base runner attempting to reach a base, interference shall be called. {7.30-4} ✠

❀ Note 308: PBUC did not add "within a step and a reach," preferring to remain with "immediate reach."

❀ Note 309-326: At all levels a fielder is not protected if he must change his position on the field to reach a ball he himself poorly played (a "muffed" ball). He is sometimes protected when going for a "deflected" ball. (See § 327 and the **327. ALSO** in § 328.)

327 INTERFERENCE BY: RUNNER: w/FIELDER IN BASE PATH AFTER DEFLECTION OF BALL BY: PITCHER✪

(See § 326 and 328.)

FED: Point not covered.

> OFF INTERP 266-327: **RUMBLE:** Following the deflection of a batted ball by the pitcher, if a fielder and a runner have contact in the base path: The umpire assesses no penalty as long as he is certain the runner had **LITTLE OR NO TIME TO CHANGE DIRECTIONS**. The resulting play is a "collision," neither interference nor obstruction. If the runner could have avoided contact, interference is the call. (*News* #26, 4/90) (See § 314. See NCAA OFF INTERP 264-326 for a radically different view of this "collision.") ✠

NCAA: Following deflection by a pitcher of a batted ball, when a runner collides with a fielder: It is interference, not incidental contact, if the umpire judges the fielder has a "**LEGITIMATE PLAY TO RETIRE A RUNNER.**" (8-5d AR2) (See § 314 and OFF INTERP 264-326.)

OBR: Point not covered.

> OFF INTERP 267-327: **PBUC:** Same as NCAA. {7.30-5} (See § 326 and 461.) ✠

✻Play 165-327: R1. B1 smashes the ball off F1's glove. The ball rolls directly into the base path, and F4 races for it. B1 has neared first at the moment R1 crashes (not maliciously) into the second baseman. The umpire judges the runner could have avoided the contact. F4 has not yet reached the ball at the time of the crash. Both go down, but F4 retrieves the ball and tags R1. *Ruling:* In FED, R1 is out — regardless: It's interference or a tag out. In NCAA / OBR, it's obstruction! R1 is awarded second because F4 had no legitimate play to retire the runner.

★ 328 INTERFERENCE BY: RUNNER: w/FIELDER IN BASE PATH AFTER NO DEFLECTION OF BALL✪

(See § 326 and 327.)

FED: If two fielders try for a batted ball, the umpire shall determine which fielder will be protected from interference by the runner. (8-4-2g-1) (See § 314.)

327. ALSO: The interference statute protects the fielder on his "initial attempt" to field a ball. (8-4-2g) (See Note 309-326.)

NCAA: ***(ADDED)*** Same as FED 8-4-2g-1. (8-5d AR 1) But see OFF INTERP 264-326 for an important caveat.

OBR: Same as FED. (7.09j) (See § 326 and 327. Study PBUC 7.30-4.) **EXCEPT:** The ball must be within "one arm's reach" of the protected fielder. (See OBR OFF INTERP 258-316.)

❀ Note 310: An important consideration in understanding the historical theory of the interference statute is this: Absent deliberate hindrance by the runner, tradition has protected only the **FIRST FIELDER MAKING THE FIRST PLAY** on the ball. If the fielder should muff a slow roller, run toward the ball, and get creamed in the base path, the proper call is .... Until NCAA OFF INTERP 264-326, the call was collision or obstruction but not interference. Now, in NCAA it's interference or obstruction. FED and OBR retain the traditional approach though FED is the only group to write the "tradition" into law. (See News #26, 4/90. See also § 277 and 329.)

(ADDED) ❀ Note 311: This section is a paradigm for the problems umpires face who use three rulebooks. On the surface, the rule is the same: Two fielders go for the ball, you decide which one to protect. BUT: The book cannot (do not, anyway) agree on the **DEFINITION** of the protection.

★ 329 INTERFERENCE BY: RUNNER: MALICIOUS CONTACT / COLLISION: DEFINITION / PENALTY ✪

FED: POE 1985, 1986, 1987, 1988, 1993, 1994, 1995, 1996, 1997, 1998, 2001, 2006, 2007: A runner may not maliciously crash into a fielder, whether the fielder is in or out of the base path, or with or without the ball. The ball is immediately dead. (3-3-1n) **PENALTY:** ***(EDITED)*** The runner is out and ejected. (3-3-1n Pen; 3.3.1w through cc) (See § 324 and 330.)

328. ALSO: Umpires have the "latitude" to call malicious contact on any collision they witness: "That judgment should not be removed by rule but bolstered by education, experience, and field mechanics / location." The umpire might consider if: (● 1) the contact results from "intentional excessive force"; or (● 2) "there is intent to injure." (POE 2006)

> ❀ Note 312: The POE goes on to say that if **EXCESSIVE FORCE** or **INTENT TO INJURE** is not present, the umpire may still penalize for a malicious crash. Rather, those criteria merely provide a "starting point." Only rarely does the BRD include POE in the rules discussion, but you will agree that the FED language must rise to the level of case book interpretation. It is also important to point out that malicious contact has been a FED POE 13 times in the last 25

years. You'd think coaches, players – and umpires – would finally learn how to get it right.

329. ALSO: A malicious crash supersedes obstruction. (8-4-2e-1) (See Play 166 [this section].)

330. ALSO: If a runner crosses the plate before another runner causes malicious contact, the run counts. Other runners remain TOI. (3-3-1n Pen; 2.21.1b) (See Play 160-324.)

> **331. ALSO:** OFF INTERP 268-329: **RUMBLE:** Umpires should not use the force of the crash as the criterion for judging malicious contact: "The severity of the contact is not a gauge for determining malicious contact, because there are times... when the contact is unavoidable." (*News*#3, 3/93) (See § 290.) ⌘

IMPORTANT: SEE § 340 FOR A DISCUSSION OF MALICIOUS, DEFENSIVE CONTACT.

> * *Play 166-329:* **FED only.** R3. The runner is moving on the pitch; B1 squares around to attempt a suicide squeeze. The catcher jumps in front of the plate to grab the pitch and tag R3, who maliciously crashes into F2. *Ruling:* The outcome of the play is not relevant. F2 is guilty of obstruction. But since the "malicious-crash rule" supersedes the "catcher's-obstruction rule": R3 is out and ejected. B1 remains at the plate. Question: What about the pitch, which was neither a strike nor a ball? Answer: No pitch: It was a dead ball—retroactively because the batter could not hit the pitch. (6-1-4)

❀ Note 313-329: In the real game, the umpire did not know malicious contact supersedes obstruction. The play occurred before the rule change (1995), and the UIC had not read Rumble's OFF INTERP from 1988, which was the basis of the current rule. So he killed the play because of catcher obstruction, scored the run, ejected R3, and awarded first to B1. Though I did know about the Rumble interp, Gavino's ruling seemed sensible to me, and everyone accepted it without question. Remember, though, that if R3 had scored **BEFORE** the malicious crash, his run would have counted.

NCAA: POE 1992, 1993, 1994, 1995, 1996, 1997 [collision rule] The rules committee is "concerned" about the safety of players involved in "unnecessary and violent collisions with the catcher at home plate" and with "infielders at all bases." "The intent of the rule is to encourage base runners and defensive players to avoid such collisions whenever possible." (See § 289 and 330. Study particularly § 290.)
If illegal contact occurs **BEFORE** the runner touches the plate:
PENALTY 1: The ball is dead, and the offender is out, regardless of the outcome of the play. (8-7 Pen 1) (See § 323.)

332. ALSO: **PENALTY 2:** If the contact is flagrant or malicious, in addition to PENALTY 1, the runner is ejected. Other runners return to their TOI bases. (8-7 Pen 2) (See Note 314 below.)

> ⁎ *Play 167-329:* **NCAA only.** R2, R3, 0 outs. B1 hits a slow roller, fielded by F5, who throws to the catcher waiting to make the tag. There is a violent collision that the umpire determines was malicious. *Ruling:* R3 is out and ejected. R2 had reached third at the time of the crash, so he keeps that base — TOI.

❀ Note 314: Simple, yes? Ah, but before the rule changed in 2011, R2 would return to second, the "base ... last touched before the contact," which is almost assuredly always the TOP base. (8-7a AR 2 - 2009) The committee, probably for the sake of consistency, significantly reduced the penalty for a malicious crash. In Play 167 above, there is now a runner on third who can score on a productive out.

333. ALSO: If the "flagrant or malicious" crash occurs **AFTER** the runner has scored: **PENALTY 3:** The run counts, the runner is ejected, the ball is dead, and other runners return to the bases occupied at the time of the contact. (8-7 AR 3)

334. ALSO: "If this [crash] occurs at any base other than home, [with fewer than two outs]; **PENALTY 4:** The offending team may replace the runner." (8-7 Pen 4)

335. ALSO: The runner may not make "flagrant" contact at any base while he is attempting illegally to prevent a double play. **PENALTY:** With fewer than two outs, both the batter-runner and the offender are out. The ball is dead, an the offender is ejected. (8-4c Pen 3)

~~**336. ALSO:** If the flagrant collision occurs when the catcher does not have the ball, the umpire will call obstruction. The runner will be safe, but he will be ejected. (8-7b AR)~~ (See § 350 for the NCAA definition of "obstruction.")

> ***(ADDED)*** ❀ Note 315-329: Another of those "My bad!" moments. I missed last year that the change from 2009's collision rule had, as I believe, **INADVERTENTLY** omitted the statute discussed in **336. ALSO** above. Let me briefly make two points:
>
> 1. The 2011 Collision Rule clearly says: "When there is a collision between a runner and a fielder **WHO CLEARLY IS IN POSSESSION OF THE BALL**, the umpire shall judge ...." So, **336. ALSO** doesn't belong. But ....
>
> 2. Where else can we put it? Since the defensive infractions is "obstruction," let's insert it as 2-54 AR 5. Look for it there in 2013.
>
> ***(ADDED)*** ❀ Note 316: Don't look for it in the current book. I did an extensive search of the PDF version: 2009's 8-7a AR 2 ain't there.

⁎ *Play 168-329:* R1. The runner tries to score on B1's double. The catcher, seeing the throw from the cutoff man in the outfield is going to be up the line toward third, moves five or six steps up the line, cannot make the catch, and obstructs R1, who maliciously runs into him and manages to score. *Ruling:* In FED, the outcome of the play is not relevant. Though F2 is guilty of obstruction, that infraction is ignored: R1 is out, ejected, and his run does not count. In NCAA, since the catcher did not have the ball, he is guilty of obstruction. R1 scores and is then ejected. In OBR, the play stands.

* *Play 169-329:* R2. The runner tries to score on B1's single to right. The throw causes the catcher to leave the baseline and move two or three steps away from the plate. Gloving the throw, he runs toward the plate to tag the charging runner, who does not slide. After a violent collision, the ball is jarred free, and R2 rolls over to touch home, untagged. *Ruling:* Regardless of how rough the collision was, it is not malicious contact. Score the run.

❀ Note 317: The following table is a summary of the rules regarding a malicious crash in FED / NCAA at the plate. In every instance the offender is ejected.

Offense	Federation	NCAA
crash before scoring	out	out
crash when obstructed	out: See **329. ALSO** above.	awarded the base
crash after scoring: force play	out	run counts
crash after scoring	run counts	run counts

OBR: No provision. *See ¶8.*

330 INTERFERENCE BY: RUNNER: SLIDE: FORCE PLAY ✪

FED: POE 1993, 1995, 1997, 1999, 2001, 2006: On a force play, if a runner slides, it must be "in a direct line between the bases." (8-4-2b). The runner may slide (or run) away from the fielder to avoid altering the play. A runner who scores and then maliciously crashes a fielder is out and ejected. (2-32-1; 8-4-2b-1; 2.32.2a) A runner who slides legally into a fielder in front of the back edge of a base is not guilty of interference. (2.32.1; 5.1.1o)

❀ Note 318: The FED is eager for umpires to understand it is not interference when a runner slides into a fielder who is in front of the base. How do I know that? Easy: The two case plays cited above are the same – word for word! (Please understand that such contact is also legal in the NCAA.)

PENALTY: If illegal contact occurs **OR** the runner illegally alters the play, the umpire shall call interference and declare out that runner and the batter-runner [an automatic double play]. (2-32-2f; 8-4-2b Pen; 2.32.2b; 8.4.2o and p) (See § 290 and 324.) (See § 289 for definitions of legal and illegal slides.)

✻ *Play 170-330:* **FED only.** R1 moving on the pitch. B1 hits to the shortstop, who tries – not in time – for the out at second. The second baseman throws the ball to first, after which R1 pops-up on the base, jostling the fielder. *Ruling:* Though the contact occurred after the throw and did not alter the play, it resulted from an illegal slide: Both R1 and B1 are out.

✻ *Play 171-330:* **FED only.** Bases loaded. B1 grounds to F4, who fields the ball and throws to F6 to start the double play. F6 catches the throw and forces out R1 as F6 crosses the bag to the right field side. F6 now throws to first as retired R1 begins his slide into second. Retired R1's slide is clearly to the right side of the bag (the side F6 is now on). R1 is sliding toward F6, but he misses the shortstop by a foot or two as F6 keeps moving after the throw. F6's throw is in time to retire BR at first; meanwhile, R3 scores. *Ruling:* Even though it is obvious the runner is illegally sliding toward the fielder, it is not interference. The ball remains alive: two out, R3 in, R2 on third.

AO 19-330: McNEELY: Writing on the URC Message Board to explain his ruling for Play 171 above: "The best answer I can provide is if a baserunner commits an illegal slide, and during that illegal slide makes contact with a fielder or alters the immediate play, call the interference. If the illegal slide occurred, but it did not alter the play or no contact was made, there is no call. If the avoidance of the contact was due to action by the fielder, it still did not happen and I would not call it." (URC, 3/20/00) (See Play 174 [this section] for an opposite ruling by the NCAA.)

❀ Note 319: Though FED does not state the fact, this "force play slide" statute is a safety rule. It's just not as "safety" as the NCAA. Note carefully this significant difference between FED and NCAA. In Play 171 above: The FED runner is not out because he made no contact. The NCAA runner would be out because he **TRIED** to make contact. (See "RUNNER INTERFERES: DEFINITION," clause #5, in NCAA [this section] and OFF INTERP 269 [below].)

337. ALSO: "**RUNNERS ARE NEVER REQUIRED TO SLIDE.**" (8-4-2b-2)

> **EXCEPT:** OFF INTERP 269-330: **HOPKINS:** On a force play a runner hit by a throw between bases is NOT guilty of interference if he did not slide or [presumably] run well away from the fielder making the throw if he is in the baseline but "not even halfway to second: The runner cannot be expected to slide at that point in the base path." (Website 2007, #3) ✠

❀ Note 320: A 2006 Hopkins ruling said the runner was "less than halfway" to the force base. The 2007 OFF INTERP seems to indicate that a runner who is more than halfway had better hit the dirt.

Play 172-330:* **FED only. R1 stealing. The catcher makes no attempt to throw. R1 slides across the bag and into the second baseman. *Ruling:* R1 is out.

❀ Note 321: If you have to eject the offensive coach after that non-play, don't blame me. It first appeared on the NFHS Website (2000, #12). I point out that the play has never appeared in the case book.

NCAA: POE 1990, 1992, 1994, 1995, 1996, 2005, 2007: "The intent of the force-play-slide-rule is to ensure the safety of all players. This is a safety and an interference rule. **WHETHER THE DEFENSE COULD HAVE COMPLETED THE DOUBLE PLAY HAS NO BEARING ON THE APPLICABILITY OF THIS RULE.** This rule pertains to a force-play situation at any base, regardless of the number of outs." (8-4)

338. ALSO: The runner must slide "on the ground and in a direct line between the two bases." (8-4a) (See § 290.) **EXCEPT:** A runner need not slide if he runs away from the fielder to avoid interfering. (8-4a Ex)

❀ Note 322: So far, FED / NCAA are alike, but then they diverge, covered in **341. ALSO** and **342. ALSO** below.

339. ALSO: "On the ground" is head first or one leg and buttock on the ground. (8-4a- Ex 1)

340. ALSO: "Directly into a base" is the runner's whole body "(feet, legs, trunk, and arms)" sliding in a straight line between bases. (8-4a-Ex 2)

341. ALSO: If the runner slides legally, it is not interference if he makes contact with a fielder who is in the "baseline extended": in front of, on, over, or behind the base. The book gives a diagram (p. 96) to demonstrate visually a legal slide. (8-4b)

342. ALSO: A pop-up slide "on top of the base" is legal, regardless of whether contact occurs with the fielder while making a play. (8-4b AR)

❀ Note 323: The BRD urges you to study this rule carefully. It is a significant alteration of thinking by the NCAA and a marked difference between high school and college ball.

● ILLEGAL ATTEMPT TO BREAK UP DOUBLE PLAY: DEFINITION: Runners must avoid any conduct that impedes or hinders a fielder. (2-50) Contact outside the baseline extended is immediate cause for an interference penalty. (8-4b)

● RUNNER INTERFERES: DEFINITION: Interference results when a runner:

(● 1) slides or runs outside the baseline [extended] and changes the fielder's pattern of play;

(● 2) uses a rolling slide or cross-body block and contacts the fielder or alters his play;
(● 3) makes contact with the fielder anywhere if the runner's leg is raised "higher than the fielder's knee" when he is "in a standing position";
(● 4) slashes or kicks a fielder "with either leg"; or
(● 5) illegally slides toward the fielder or makes contact, even if the fielder makes no attempt to throw. (8-4c 1-5)

❀ Note 324: The NCAA book makes a distinction here, one that requires close examination. In clauses (2), (3), and (4) above, the slide is *a priori* illegal: The baseline extended exception does not apply. Clauses (1) and (5) require the runner to be outside the baseline extended.

PENALTY: The ball is dead. (6-2g) With fewer than two outs, both the interferer and the batter-runner are automatically out. (8-4c Pen 1) With two outs, the interferer is out, and no other runner may advance. (8-4c Pen 2). If the runner's slide is malicious, he is ejected. (8-4c Pen 3) If the bases are loaded with no outs, when a double-play resulting from interference is called, all other runners return to the bases occupied **AT THE TIME OF THE PITCH**. (See § 289 and 324.)

❀ Note 325: Generally, after interference in the NCAA, runners return to the bases last "touched legally at the time of the interference." But there is a caveat: "unless otherwise provided by these rules." (2-50 AR 1)

❀ Note 326: Whether the umpire believes the defense could have completed a double play (the FED linchpin: see § 324) is simply not relevant to the call in NCAA.

✻ *Play 173-330:* R1 stealing. B1 grounds slowly to F6, whose throw to second is **NOT IN TIME**. R1 then executes a pop-up slide while F6 is on top of the base, preventing the second baseman from throwing to first. *Ruling:* In FED / OBR, R1 is out, but B1 goes to first. In NCAA, neither R1 nor B1 is out — see **342. ALSO** above.

❀ Note 327: Since R1 beat the throw, no double play is possible. In FED/ OBR, then, only the interfering runner can be out. It's simply interference by a runner (one is out), not a retired runner (two would be out).

✻ *Play 174-330*: **FED and NCAA.** R1 slides into second on a force play. He slides to the side of the base where the pivot man is. His slide does not make contact with or alter the play of the pivot man. *Ruling:* In FED, the runner is not guilty of interference. This is similar to McNeely's Play 171 [this section]. In NCAA, R1 has interfered by **TRYING** to hinder a fielder outside the baseline extended. Two are out.

OBR: No provision. (See § 289.) *See ¶8.*

331 INTERFERENCE BY: RUNNER: VISUAL ✪

FED: A runner leading off first may not move up so far toward the plate that he screens the first baseman from the ball on an attempted pick-off throw. **PENALTY:** The runner is out. (8.4.2f) (See § 354.)

NCAA: No provision.

OBR: No provision

332 INTERFERENCE BY: SPECTATOR: GENERAL PRINCIPLE ✪ (See § 334 and 336.)

FED: When a batted or thrown ball touches or is touched by a spectator, the ball is immediately dead. (5-1-1f-3; 5-1-1g-1) **PENALTY:** awards or outs at the umpire's discretion. (8-3-3e; 8.3.3g) (See § 270, 333 and 335. See also 5.1.1k, which covers a photographer who intentionally touches a thrown ball.)

NCAA: If a thrown, batted, or pitched ball accidentally hits a spectator or any other individual or animal and remains in play, the ball is alive. (6-1h) If the touching is intentional, the ball is dead. **PENALTY:** Awards or outs at the umpire's discretion. (4-8a) (See § 270.)

OBR: Same as NCAA. (3.15; 3.16)
343. ALSO: Professional umpires consider a kick by a spectator, even if accidental, an intentional act—and penalize accordingly. (PI, 6:48)

> ✻ *Play 175-332:* R2. **OBR only:** A wild pitch eludes the catcher and bounces toward the backstop near the ball boy. While running to get away from the ball, he accidentally kicks it. The catcher cannot retrieve the ball soon enough to stop R2 from scoring. *Ruling:* The ball is dead at the moment of the kick; return R2 to third. (JEA, 3:48)

★ 333 INTERFERENCE BY: SPECTATOR: HIT BY PITCH OR THROW FROM PITCHER'S PLATE ✪

FED: If a pitch or throw by the pitcher from the pitcher's plate touches a spectator, the ball is dead and runners advance one base. (5-1-1g-1; 8-3-3d)

NCAA: Same as FED. (8-3k) (See § 329.) **EXCEPT:** A provision at 6 1h is contradictory: "If a thrown, batted or pitched ball that remains in live-ball territory accidentally hits a spectator, any other individual or animal, the ball is live."

❀ Note 328: The 6-1h provision slipped **UNANNOUNCED** into the NCAA code in 1996. But there's a more important point: 8-3k states: "Each runner is awarded one base if a pitch or any throw ... by the pitcher ... touches a spectator." Contrary statutes: What to do? BRD recommends: Enforce 6-1h (ball remains alive), for it is the more recent rule. To this point, this Note is copied from the 2008 BRD. In an email (2/13/09) I asked Paronto about the contradiction. He emailed back the same day: "I would agree, 6-1h [is the statute to enforce]. If a spectator got to the plate and touched a pitch then security is not doing their jobs or the pitcher has one hell of a change-up. We'll correct for the 2011 edition [the next publication of the NCAA rulebook]." They didn't. But .... On 1/18/11, I pointed out to Paronto that the NCAA had NOT corrected the error I had so graciously called to their attention. His reply 80 minutes later: "Carl, we'll correct it in 2013. Promise!" I told him I would warn him about the mistake in 2012. His reply: "So noted. I have it in my 'Futures' notebook." The BRD will have more for you next year.

OBR: The umpire will use the regular procedure for determining deliberate or unintentional interference by a spectator. (3.15; 3.16) (See § 332.)

★ 334 INTERFERENCE BY: SPECTATOR: MEDIA AUTHORIZED ON FIELD ✪ (See § 332 and 336.)

FED: Media personnel, even if authorized on the field, are not allowed in live-ball territory. **POE 1994, 2008**: The home management must create a "lined," dead-ball area for them before the game begins. (1-2-8; 1.2.8a and b) If a batted ball, throw, or pitch touches anything or anyone completely or partially inside that area, the ball is immediately dead. If it passes through the area without touching anyone or anything, it remains alive. **PENALTY** for interference outside the designated area: The "media" may have to leave the field.
(Comments on Rule Changes, 1993 ed)

344. ALSO: If a member of the media is hit by a thrown ball when he is completely **OUTSIDE** the designated media area (on live-ball ground), the ball remains alive. (5-1-1L)

345. ALSO: If a fielder reaches into a media area and a photographer prevents the catch, that is not interference: "The photographer is considered a spectator." (8.3.3n)

❀ Note 329: FED treats this play as if the fielder was learning into the stands. The OBR considers photographers to be "authorized spectators"; Any interference must be deliberate before the umpire stops play. (See § 336.)

NCAA: No provision. (See § 332.)

(ADDED) ❀ Note 330: The NCAA makes no distinction between a "spectator" and a non-participant authorized to be on the field. Paronto: "A long as the interference is not intentional, the ball remains live." (email to cc, 12/21/22)

OBR: Point not covered.

OFF INTERP 270-334: **EVANS:** "Today's league regulations restrict photographers to the warning track in foul territory, photographers' booths, or designated areas which minimize their distraction and possibility of interference." (PI, 3:48) ✠

★ ∞ 335 INTERFERENCE BY: SPECTATOR: PREVENTS RUNNER'S ADVANCE ✪

FED: No provision.

NCAA: No provision. ***(ADDED)*** (See § 260.)

OBR: If a crowd prevents a runner from advancing around the bases, those bases will be awarded. (4.09b CMT)

★ 336 INTERFERENCE BY: SPECTATOR: UNINTENTIONAL ✪ (See § 332 and 334.)

FED: The ball is dead when a spectator **UNINTENTIONALLY** interferes with a batted or thrown ball. The umpire may make awards or declare outs, as he sees fit. (5-1-1f-3; 5-1-1-g-1; 8-3-3e) **EXCEPT:** If a fielder reaches into a dead-ball area to make a play – that would include a designated media area – hindrance by a spectator is not interference. (8-3-3e; 8.3.3m and n) (See § 270.)

NCAA: On accidental interference by a spectator, the ball remains alive. (4-9b; 6-1h)

OBR: Same as NCAA. (3.15; 3.15 CMT and ¶ 2)

✻ *Play 176-336:* B1's pop-up is coming down near the third-base stands, which are protected by a three-foot high fence. F5 reaches for the ball: (a) across the fence and into the stands, but a spectator prevents the play; or (b) near the fence but on the playing field side of the barrier, and a spectator reaches out of the stands and prevents the catch.
Ruling: In (a), it is a foul ball. In (b), it is spectator interference, and the batter is out.

★ 337 INTERFERENCE BY: UMPIRE w/CATCHER DURING PLAY ON RUNNER
ALL CODES NOW AGREE: TEXT DELETED, 2000.

(ADDED) ❀ Note 331: The NASO (*Referee* magazine) preseason baseball guide for 2012 contains the following: "[Umpire] hindrance may also occur while the catcher is fielding a batted ball or a dropped third strike." Here's the representative play: "B1 strikes out on a pitch not caught in flight. As F2 attempts to throw out B1, the umpire interferes. The resulting throw goes into (a) the dugout, or (b) right field. Ruling: In both (a) and (b), the ball is dead and the batter is out. Any other runners may not advance." If the play comes up in your association, simply say you wish you had some of whatever they were smoking in Racine. (grin)

338 INTERFERENCE BY: UMPIRE: w/CATCHER DURING: PICKOFF PLAY
ALL CODES NOW AGREE: TEXT DELETED, 2012

339 INTERFERENCE BY: UMPIRE: W/CATCHER DURING: RETURN TOSS TO PITCHER
ALL CODES NOW AGREE: TEXT DELETED, 2012

★ 340 MALICIOUS CONTACT BY DEFENSE ✪

FED: A defensive player may not initiate malicious contact. (3-3-1n) **PENALTY:** The offender is ejected. The umpire shall rule safe or out on the play and award runners bases they would have received but for the contact. (3-3-1n Pen) **(IMPORTANT: SEE NOTE 312-329.)**

(ADDED) ❀ Note 332: A curious fact: "Defensive malicious contact" entered the FED book in 2007. The NFHS added two new "malicious contact" plays: 3.3.1v and w. Neither dealt with defensive malicious contact. In the years since, FED has posted 120 case plays on its Website. None dealt with defensive malicious contact. Fact is, the NFHS has **NEVER** illustrated this infraction. But, thanks to the BRD, the next two plays fill the void.

❊ *Play 177-340:* **FED only.** R2 heads home on B1's base hit to right. As he nears the plate, he begins his slide — but too early. He stops short of home. The catcher, with the ball, dives full force onto R2's body, tagging him out. *Ruling:* F2 is ejected for malicious contact. But R2, tagged between bases, is out.

(ADDED) ❊ *Play 178-340:* **FED only.** In the third inning, F3 Smith and Visitor B1 Jones – also a first baseman – are involved in a horrific train wreck at first. The umpire rules it was a legal collision. In the sixth, Smith walks. He takes a lead and the pitcher fires a pick-off throw. F3 Jones gloves the throw and slams a very hard tag on Smith' shoulder as he slides head first back to the bag, well ahead of the throw. *Ruling:* Defensive malicious contact. The umpire calls "Safe! Time!" He then ejects Jones and leaves Smith at first.

NCAA: Point not covered.

(ADDED) OFF INTERP 271-340: **PARONTO:** "Umpires should apply 5-16a, using common sense and an understanding of the actions that have led up to the act. The umpire might issue a warning to diffuse the situation. Requesting cooperation from the head coaches to stave off any future problems is also an option." (email to cc, 12/21/11)

(ADDED) ❀ Note 333: Paronto: "If defensive contact gets to the physical fight stage and this action is interpreted as physical abuse, the individual is subjects to an ejection for fighting and a three-game suspension." (email to cc, 12/21/11)

OBR: No provision.

★ 341 MECHANICS

❀ Note 334: Rulebooks deal only with rules. Right? Wrong. They deal **MOSTLY** with rules. But some play situations are so tricky that committees have felt obliged to include in their books or interpretation manuals the mechanics required to solve those situations. Here are those that are most relevant to amateur games. For additional comments on mechanics, see Notes 244-272 and 278-293.

FED: The umpire signals the count thus: left hand, balls; right hand, strikes. (Signals chart) (See § 93.)
346. ALSO: If the batter-runner is not entitled to run after a third strike not caught in flight, the umpire "shall forcefully announce" that he is out. The ball remains alive. (8.4.1k, 2006 ed) (See § 98.)
347. ALSO: The ball is dead when the umpire raises his hand, palm outward, toward the pitcher. (Signals chart) (See § 161.)
348. ALSO: To signal obstruction the umpire extends his left arm parallel to his shoulders with his hand in a fist. (Signals chart) (See § 355.)

NCAA: Following an alleged baserunning infraction, if the defense does not indicate which runner it is appealing, the umpire is to give no sign. (8-6b-6) (See § 11.)
349. ALSO: Concerning the "Do not pitch" signal: Same as FED. (6-5h)
EXCEPT: The ball is ready for play when the umpire "declares 'Play,' or uses some other appropriate signal such as a point toward the pitcher to indicate that the ball is alive." (6-5h) (See § 161.)
350. ALSO: Type 1: When a runner on whom the defense is playing is obstructed, the umpire shall point at the obstruction and call: "That's obstruction!" He will then signal "Time" and penalize the obstruction. Type 2: When a runner is obstructed while no play is being made on him, the umpire points and calls "That's obstruction." Play continues. (2-54) (See § 350.)

351. ALSO: POE 2009: The committee wants umpires to "adhere to a consistent mechanic" in handling conferences, reducing them in extra innings, and in consistently enforcing the mechanic used for a "smooth transition between each half inning."

❀ Note 335: Limiting the college players to one minute between half innings (which is black-letter law) might be a good start.

352. ALSO: Appendix F, "Pitch/Between Innings Clock Protocol," contains extensive directions for operating a stadium clock or keeping time on the field. The regulations pertain to a pitcher or batter delaying (§ 368) or time between half innings [last out / first pitch]. (See § 518). Salient features are: (● 1) The 90-second (between half innings) and 20-second (pitcher delivers with bases empty) time limits are not experimental or optional;
(● 2) they are used in all half innings except the first or when a new pitcher enters the game;
(● 3) umpires will alert the pitcher with 30 seconds left;
(● 4) clock starts when pitcher receives the ball and stops when he begins his windup;
(● 5) no warnings are required before penalizing;
(● 6) batters must be in the box and ready to hit at the 5-second mark; and
(● 7) the clock is operated by a base umpire. (See § 44.)

❀ Note 336: The material of the Protocol is beyond the scope of the BRD since only NCAA uses it. The first paragraph says: "To be clear, the intent of the rules committee is not to mandate a visible clock." I am not persuaded. If there is no visible clock, in a four- or six-man crew, the second-base umpire will keep the time; third-base umpire, crew of three; base umpire, crew of two. At some point, the umpires will say, in effect: "You want me to call ball or watch a clock?"

353. ALSO: Get the Call Right.
Coaches may request a conference to have the crew discuss a judgment call. In three circumstances the crew will deny the conference: (● 1) The call is catch / no catch with runners on base. (● 2) The calling umpire is 100% confident he got the call right. (● 3) The calling umpire had the best look at the play. (Appendix E)

❀ Note 337: Coaches have been requesting a conference "on most any play." Umpires are to discourage that. The point of the above change: "**UMPIRES SHOULD 'OWN' THEIR CALLS.**"
(NCAA 2011 video, Paronto)

354. ALSO: (● 1) "A partner who is 100 percent certain he has additional information unknown to the umpire making the call **SHOULD APPROACH**

UNSOLICITED and alert the other umpire to such information." [BRD emphasis] Examples: Deciding if...

(a) a home run is fair or foul;

(b) a batted ball left the field for a home run or double;

(c) a foul was caught by the catcher (foul tip) or trapped;

(d) a foul fly was caught or not;

(e) an umpire clearly erred in his judgment because he did not see the ball on the ground or juggled.

(f) a spectator did or did not interfere with a fielder.

(g) a balk was called erroneously by an umpire who did not realize the pitcher was not on the rubber.

(● 2) "When an umpire **SEEKS** help, he should do so shortly after making his original call."

(● 3) "Some calls cannot be changed or reversed without creating larger problems. An example is a 'catch / no catch' with multiple runners or a ball that is ruled foul."

> ✻ *Play 179-341*: R2, two-man crew. B1 hits to deep short, who throws to first. The throw is slightly wild and the first baseman has to come off the bag for a swipe tag. The umpire calls "He's out!" The home plate umpire is 100% certain that the call is wrong. *Ruling:* Help is not available.

❀ Note 338: They can get the call right at first base, but what will they do about R2? The defensive coach will say he went directly to the dugout. The offensive coach will say he came around to score. If the bases had been empty, the UIC could approach unsolicited and tell his partner what he saw.

> ✻ *Play 180-341:* R1, R2, 0 out, two-man crew. B1 slaps a dying quail to center. F8 speeds in to make a diving stab at the ball, twisting away from the view of the base umpire, whose call it is. Both runners advance. The base umpire rules "no catch." After an uproar from the defense, he immediately goes to the plate umpire to ask for help. The plate umpire is 100% certain the ball was caught. *Ruling:* Help is not available. The bases are loaded with 0 out. (modeled after NFHS 2011 *Preseason Guide*, "Get it Right," Play 2)

❀ Note 339: If the call is reversed to "catch," the runners who advanced are subject to appeal for leaving early. The defense would have a triple play. If they are returned to their bases, they are disadvantaged because on an initial call of "catch," they may have retouched and advanced. In this scenario, if the bases had been empty, the crew could "get the play right."

OBR: Point not covered.

> ***(EDITED)*** OFF INTERP 272-341: **PBUC:** Afer a half swing called a ball, when a wild pitch or passed ball will permit the batter to become a runner if the swing is ruled a strike, the plate umpire shall ask immediately without waiting for an appeal. { 9.8} (See § 74.) ✠

355. ALSO: "It is recommended that umpires indicate foul tips by signaling foul tip followed by a strike mechanic, particularly on check-swing foul tips and foul tips that are caught close to the ground." {PBUC 9.4}

356. ALSO: On an appeal of a half swing, the umpire is "to point assertively with the left arm directly at the appropriate base umpire while asking if the batter swung." {PBUC 9.8}

> **357. ALSO: *(EDITED)*** OFF INTERP 273-341: **PBUC:** In the situation detailed above, the appropriate umpire should immediately signal his call "IF he is going reverse the plate umpire's call. " {9.9} (See § 74.) ✠

❀ ***(EDITED)*** Note 340: The above is a VERY advanced technique. Be sure you and your partner are perfect on its execution. This is the so-called "voluntary strike."

358. ALSO: Concerning the "Do not pitch" signal: Same as FED. (Deary interpretation) (See § 161.)

359. ALSO: If the batter's backswing hits the catcher, "the proper mechanic is fo the umpire to call, 'Backswing hit the catcher' as soon as the violation occurs (while pointing at the infraction) and then to call 'Time' as the play dictates." {PBUC 7.13} (See § 272.}

360. ALSO: An umpire is to signal obstruction in the same way he signals time, "with both hands overhead." The signal does not, however, kill the play. (7.06a CMT) (See § 350.)

> ***(ADDED)*** **361. ALSO:** OFF INTERP 274-341: **PBUC:** If the batter-runner beats a play to first but just barely misses the bag and goes past it, the umpire is to signal the runner safe. The fielder can appeal for an out by touching the base or the runner." { 6.4-13} ✠

> ***(ADDED)*** **362. ALSO:** OFF INTERP 275-341: **PBUC:** "On a play at the plate, should the runner miss home plate and the fielder miss the tag on the runner, the umpire should make NO SIGNAL on the play." {6.3} ✠

(ADDED) ❀ Note 341: Compare mechanics for a runner missing first (OFF INTERP 274). These two plays seemed to drive the bloggers off their blocks when the Internet first showed up. Be clear: These mechanics are "official" at the OBR level. But trained umpires use them even in games where the players don't shave yet.

★ ∞ 342 NEW BALL PUT IN PLAY AFTER: AWARDED BASES ✪

FED: No provision. Treat as in OBR.

NCAA: Point not covered.

> ***(ADDED)*** OFF INTERP 276-342: **PARONTO:** Same as OBR. (email to cc, 12/28/11) ✠

OBR: After awarding bases, the umpire will not put the ball in play until all runners have reached their new bases. (3.01 CMT)

∞ 343 NEW BALL PUT IN PLAY AFTER: BALL GOES DEAD ✪

FED: No provision. Treat as in OBR.

NCAA: No provision. Treat as in OBR.

OBR: The umpire does not put another ball into play until the ball currently in use becomes dead. (3.01 CMT)

★ ∞ 344 NEW BALL PUT IN PLAY AFTER: HOME RUN ✪

FED: No provision. Treat as in OBR.

NCAA: Point not covered.

> ***(ADDED)*** OFF INTERP 277-344: **PARONTO:** Same as OBR. (email to cc, 12/22/11) ✠

(ADDED) ❀ Note 342: Childress: "Jim, I'm religious about this, regardless of the level." Paronto: "Carl, I agree with you, but in NCAA play it doesn't always happen."

OBR: After a home run, the umpire does not give the pitcher a new ball until the hitter has crossed the plate. (3.01 CMT)

∞ 345 NEW BALL PUT IN PLAY AFTER: NEEDED IN GAME ✪

FED: No provision (But see § 182.)

NCAA: The umpire must be ready with another ball when the ball in play is hit out of the field, or rejected by him, or the pitcher asks for a new ball. "The game should not be delayed to retrieve a particular ball that may have been fouled away from the playing area." (4-1d)

❀ Note 343: Ah, ha! You know what the committee is writing about. A pitcher gets his hands on a "lucky" ball, and he doesn't want to pitch with another. Scenario: Bases empty, wild pitch.

I give the catcher a new ball, the on-deck batter retrieves the first ball and throws it to the catcher. The pitcher throws the second ball to the catcher, and he tries to throw the first ball back to the pitcher. Before you can say "Jackie Robinson," I put a stop to that. My comment: "We don't delay the game just so you can get your favorite ball." The coach's comment: "No, we just delay it so you can show how anal you are." Lah, me!

OBR: Same as NCAA. (3.01e) **EXCEPT:** No provision for delay of game to retrieve one particular ball.

346 NEW BALL PUT IN PLAY AFTER: UNCAUGHT FOUL
ALL CODES NOW AGREE: TEXT DELETED, 1990.

★∞347 OBSTRUCTION: CAUSES BASERUNNING ERROR✪

FED: No provision. Treat as in NCAA.

NCAA: Point not covered.

OFF INTERP 278-347: **FETCHIET:** If, in the umpire's judgment, obstruction occurred near enough to a base so that it prevented the runner from conveniently touching the bag, a subsequent appeal at the missed base would be denied. (Website 4/20/01, 8-6a)✠

OBR: Point not covered.

OFF INTERP 279-347: ***(EDITED)*** **WENDELSTEDT:** If a runner misses a base or never reaches a base as a result of the obstruction by a fielder, the umpire may consider the base as touched or reached if he believes it would have taken place had the obstruction not occurred. (HW fn[179]/196)✠

**Play 181-347:* R2. B1 singles. As R2 nears third, F5 obstructs him, he misses third, and is safe on a close play at the plate. The defense then appeals he missed third. *Ruling:* Umpire judgment: But if the obstruction occurred several steps from the base, the base umpire would likely uphold the appeal.

★ 348 OBSTRUCTION: COLLISION AT FIRST BASE✪

FED: If an errant throw pulls the first baseman into the runner's base path, a collision before the fielder has possession of the ball is obstruction. (8.3.2k)

NCAA: Point not covered.

OFF INTERP 280-348: **YEAST:** While a fielder may not block the base without the ball, a fielder may move into the path of a runner if he must do so to make a play, *i.e.,* glove a throw. (San Diego MTG, 1/4/03) ✠

OBR: Point not covered.

OFF INTERP 281-348: **WENDELSTEDT:** If a fielder has possession of the ball and is attempted to make a tag on a runner, if unintentional contact occurs between the two, there is generally no violation. (HW/195) ✠

✻ *Play 182-348:* R2 tries to score on B1's short single. The right fielder's throw is errant, and the catcher moves up the line to grab it. He collides with R2 but tags him out. *Ruling:* In FED, R2 is awarded home on the obstruction. In NCAA / OBR, the play stands.

✻ *Play 183-348:* B1 hits to short. The throw pulls the first baseman off the bag and into B1's path before he touches the base. After the collision, F3 tags B1 off the base. *Ruling:* In FED, B1 is awarded first. In NCAA / OBR, B1 is out.

349 OBSTRUCTION: CONDITIONS FOR DELAYED-DEAD BALL / DEAD BALL ✪ (See § 33 and 34.)

FED: Obstruction is always a delayed-dead ball. (2-22-1; 5-1-3; 8-3-2; 8.3.2a) The ball becomes dead only after "runners have gone as far as possible," which allows the defense to record outs — or commit overthrows. (8.3.2d)

NCAA: Same as OBR. (2-54; 6-3c and d; 8-3e) (See § 352.)

OBR: If the batter-runner is obstructed before he "touches" first or if the defense is playing on the obstructed runner, the ball is immediately dead. (7.06a) (See § 352.)

❀ Note 344: The FED rule is by far the most "umpire friendly": All obstruction is Type (b). Hooray! Now if the OBR would just wake up. They won't, of course, and this year's NCAA change means they went back to sleep.

✻ *Play 184-349:* R2, R3. The catcher picks off R3, who becomes trapped in a rundown. Trying for the plate, he is obstructed and tagged out. F2 then throws to third, where R2 also gets in a hot-box. As R2 is about to be tagged out, he deliberately knocks the ball out of the fielder's glove and reaches third "safely." *Ruling:* R3 is awarded home. In FED, since the ball remained alive on the obstruction, R2 is out for deliberate interference. (See § 291.) In NCAA / OBR, since the defense is playing on R3, the ball is immediately dead when R3 is obstructed; R2 must return to second, which means the interference never "happened."

★ 350 OBSTRUCTION: DEFINITION ✪

FED: POE 2008: Obstruction is any act PHYSICAL (2.22.1b) or VERBAL (2.22.1a) that hinders a runner. (2-22-1; 8-3-2)

❀ Note 345: See Play 193-353 for an example of "verbal" obstruction.

363. ALSO: Obstruction can be "intentional or unintentional," and it can be by "any member of the defensive team or its team personnel" as long as it "changes the pattern of play." (2-22-1; 8-3-2; 2.22.1b) (See § 353.)

> **364. ALSO:** OFF INTERP 282-350: **HOPKINS:** After a single, B1 is returning to first when he "contacts the first baseman who is partially in his path." Since the runner was making no attempt to advance and F3 did not "change the pattern of play," the umpire will not call obstruction. (Website 2008, #14) ✠

365. ALSO: A first baseman (8.3.2g) or any fielder (8.3.2c) may block the base if he is in possession of the ball or if he blocks only part of the base. (See also Website 2009, #12 and #13.)

❀ Note 346: Since 1961, the "traditional" view of obstruction is: "If a fielder is about to receive a thrown ball and if the ball is in flight directly toward and near enough to the fielder so he must occupy his position to receive the ball, he may be considered 'in the act of fielding the ball.'" (2.00 Obstruction) In 2011 the NCAA returned to the OBR rules, which they had abandoned in 2004. Hence, such a fielder would not be guilty of obstruction.

NCAA: Obstruction is the act of any fielder who, while not in the possession of the ball " or not in the act of fielding the ball, impedes the progress of any runner." (2-54) (See § 345 and 352.)

❀ Note 347: The NCAA language is "borrowed," word for word, from the 1961 OBR.

366. ALSO: "If the fielder is about to receive a thrown ball and the ball is in flight directly toward and near enough to the fielder so he must occupy his position to receive the throw, he may be considered 'in the act of fielding' the ball." (2-54 AR 1) **EXCEPT:** "On a pickoff play at any base, the defensive player must CLEARLY HAVE POSSESSION of the ball before blocking the base WITH ANY PART OF THE DEFENSIVE PLAYER'S BODY. The umpire will call 'That's obstruction' and then signal and call 'Time.' The ball is dead immediately and the runner being played on is awarded one base beyond the last base he had attained prior to the obstruction." (2-54)

❀ Note 348: To the casual reader (me), AR 1 and AR 5 conflict. At midnight on 10/12/10, I wrote the following to Jim Paronto: "I must be stupid because I don't follow the changes. AR1 and AR5 don't match. A pickoff *play* is a pickoff *throw*," right? If I have to be in front of the base to take that throw, am I not there legally?"

Jim replied six hours later (I think he already had his message in the can): "Carl, the 'pickoff throw' is meant to cover the fielder (*i.e.*, the first baseman in most cases although it could happen at any base) who blocks the base with his knee on the ground and then receives the pickoff from the pitcher. ... I see your point, but the Committee wanted to make sure there is a difference between a 'throw' and a 'pickoff.'"

⁎ *Play 185-350*: R2 has been taking a huge, secondary lead. After a pitch, R2 lazily starts back to the base, and the pitcher and F6 execute a perfect pickoff. F6 reaches the bag, drops to one knee, and an instant later, the ball and R2 arrive simultaneously. R2 has no access to second and is tagged out. *Ruling:* In FED and NCAA, the umpire cancels the out and awards R2 third. In OBR, he's simply a former runner on the way back to his dugout.

367. ALSO: An obstructed runner is not immune from "team offensive interference penalties." (5-3 Pen 2 AR 2) (See Play 184-349.)

(EDITED) ~~**368. ALSO:** If a runner flagrantly bowls over a fielder guilty of obstruction, the runner shall be called "safe" on the obstruction and ejected for the "flagrant" contact. (8-7b AR)~~ (See Note 315-329.)

OBR: Obstruction is the act of any fielder who, not in possession of the ball nor in the "act of fielding the ball," impedes the progress of any runner. (2.00 Obstruction) (See § 352. For the definitions of Type (a) and Type (b) obstruction, see § 33 and 34.)

369. ALSO: OFF INTERP 283-350: **FITZPATRICK:** The definition of "act of fielding the ball" is purely umpire judgment, but the minor league guideline is the distance from the skin of the cutout at home to the plate, or about 13 feet on a properly designed field. (phone call to cc, 11/8/01) ✠

⁎ *Play 186-350:* R2. The runner tries to score on B1's short single to right. The catcher sets up in the base path, a full step toward third from home, readying himself for the throw. R2 (not maliciously) slides into the catcher and is tagged out. At the time of the contact, the throw from the outfield has reached the cutout in front of the plate. *Ruling:* In FED, since F2 was not in possession of the ball, the ruling is obstruction. In NCAA / OBR, R3 is out: no obstruction because F2 was in the process of fielding the ball.

❀ Note 349: Naturally, the distance guidelines do not apply in short-field (Youth Ball) games. On such fields, a catcher who sets up well in advance of the plate to receive a non-existent throw may indeed be guilty of unsportsmanlike conduct since youthful players are taught to slide or avoid. BRD recommends taking stern measures against catchers who attempt to intimidate young runners trying to score. While such fielders may not be guilty of obstruction *de jure*, they are obstructing *de facto* and should be penalized accordingly.

★ 351 OBSTRUCTION: FAKE TAG CREATES ✪

FED: POE 1982: It is obstruction when a fielder without the ball fakes a tag. (2-22-2; 3-3-1b; 8.3.2b and e) **PENALTY:** The affected runner is awarded bases as in any obstruction. The umpire also gives a team warning / ejection. (3-3-1b Pen)
(See § 350. See also Play 40-34 and Play 193-353.)

DEFINITION: A fake tag is an "act by a defensive player without the ball that simulates a tag." (2-22-2)

> ✻ *Play 187-351:* **FED only.** R1. The pitcher while standing off the pitcher's plate feints a throw (legal), and the first baseman fakes a tag (illegal). *Ruling:* The umpire awards R1 second, followed by a team warning / ejection.

> ✻ *Play 188-351:* **FED only.** R1. The runner attempts to steal when the second baseman fakes a tag. *Ruling:* R1 is awarded second. The umpire could award R1 third (F2's throw goes into centerfield, for example) if he believes the fake-tag prevented the runner's further advance. He also issues a team warning / ejection.

> ✻ *Play 189-351:* **FED only.** As B1 is streaking between first and second following a hit to the outfield, F4 pounds his glove as if about to receive a throw. B1 slows down and stops on second. *Ruling:* F4's action is not a fake tag but a legal decoy.

NCAA: No provision.
(ADDED) ❀ Note 350: Paronto: "Fake tags are legal, but defensive players would be highly encouraged not to employ this tactic. Faking a tag and thereby getting a runner to slide needlessly often leads 5to more serious actions later in the game."
(email to cc, 12/22/11.)

OBR: No provision. *See ¶8.*

352 OBSTRUCTION: NOT PENALIZED ON IMMEDIATE DEAD BALL ✪ (See § 33.)

FED: Not applicable. (See § 349.)

NCAA: Not applicable. (See § 34.)

OBR: Following obstruction, if a previously released throw enters DBT, the runners are awarded such bases on the wild throw as they would have been awarded had no obstruction occurred. **EXCEPT:** Runners who have not been obstructed receive two bases on the overthrow; the awards to those unobstructed runners are measured from the bases last legally touched before the teammate was obstructed. (7.06a CMT) (See § 34.)

> **370. ALSO:** OFF INTERP 284-352: **FITZPATRICK:** If the defense obstructs a runner and then throws the ball away, the award for the overthrow is measured from the base the runner would have reached at TOT if there had been no obstruction. (email to cc, 11/15/00) ✠

> ✻ *Play 190-352:* **OBR only.** B1 hits safely just over the head of F6. The batter, noting that F7 is lazily coming to the ball, decides to try for two. Hurriedly the left fielder gets the ball and in his haste fires one over everyone's head. The ball eventually winds up in DBT. Before the throw is airborne, F3, who was trailing the play, trips B1 from behind, and the batter-runner limps safely but angrily into second. *Ruling:* Penalize for the overthrow. With or without the obstruction, B1 would have been at second. After the overthrow, he goes to third.

❀ Note 351: Since the defense was playing on B1, it is Type (a) obstruction, and the ball is immediately dead. B1 would get second. OFF INTERP 284 [this section] also gives him an extra base.

> ✻ *Play 191-352:* **NCAA and OBR only.** R1. B1 lines to right field. He rounds first and makes an aggressive move toward second. F9 throws to first immediately after gloving the ball. B1, trying to return to first, is obstructed by the first baseman, who does not realize a throw is approaching. The throw gets by the first baseman and goes into the dugout. At the time of the throw, R1 had rounded second. *Ruling:* The defense is playing on B1, so the ball is immediately dead. B1 is awarded one base on the obstruction: second. Since the throw was en route before the obstruction, B1 receives third. If the throw had not gone dead, R1 would have received third. As it is, the umpire awards him home.

★ 353 OBSTRUCTION: VERBAL: DEFENSIVE ✪

FED: Verbal obstruction is treated the same as physical obstruction. **PENALTY:** The obstructed runner is awarded one base in advance of his position on base. (2-22-1; 2.22.1a) (See § 350.)

371. ALSO: OFF INTERP 285-353: **HOPKINS:** If a defensive player tries to confuse an opponent by yelling "Go!" to a runner tagging, the umpire will declare verbal obstruction **IF THE AFFECTED RUNNER REACTS TO THE OPPONENT'S ATTEMPT TO CONFUSE.** **PENALTY:** The affected runner is awarded one base, and the umpire warns the player committing the act. (Website 2004, #12) ✠

* *Play 192-353:* **FED only:** R3 tags on a fly to right. Just before the ball is touched in the outfield, a player from the visitor's dugout says "Go." The runner waits until his coach tells him, leaves legally, and is thrown out at home. *Ruling:* The runner is out. Verbal obstruction must affect the play before the umpire may penalize it. If the runner had left on the verbal command from the dugout, he would have been awarded home, regardless of the outcome of the play.

372. ALSO: OFF INTERP 286-353: **RUMBLE:** When a defensive player lies and tells a runner that a passed ball was a foul ball, the fielder is guilty of verbal obstruction. (*News* #11, 3/96; confirmed, #14, 3/99) ✠

373. ALSO: OFF INTERP 287-353: **HOPKINS:** Any *verbal* decoy, such as "I've got it," is obstruction. (Website 2001, #14) ✠

374. ALSO: OFF INTERP 288-353: **RUMBLE:** As the catcher throws a "pop fly" to F4 with a runner stealing, if a team member bangs bats together to simulate the sound of the batted ball, the umpire calls obstruction and ejects the offender. (*News* #6, 3/99) ✠

❀ Note 352: The interpretation – by inference – legitimizes the catcher's "pop fly": "Because of the clanging of bats, obstruction will be called" is the language of the ruling. But the second baseman must not augment his acting with verbal communication. (See OFF INTERPs 286 and 287 [this section].)

❀ Note 353-353: Almost all physical decoys – "dekes" as they are called – are legal: pretending to field a grounder, catch a popup, glove a throw, or throwing a "popup" into the air on a steal. The one physical decoy that's forbidden is the fake tag.

NCAA: No provision. (See § 309.)

(ADDED) ❀ Note 354: Paronto: "There is no penalty for offensive 'verbal obstruction.' Offensive players are expected to know the difference between their coaches' voices and the voices of their opponents." (email to cc, 12/22/11)

OBR: Point not covered.

OFF INTERP 289-353: **PBUC STAFF:** Do not penalize verbal decoys in games played using OBR rules. (email to cc, 12/15/00) *See ¶8.* ✠

⁎ *Play 193-353:* R1, R3. F1 pauses in the set position. From the defensive first-base dugout, someone yells "BACK!" R1 reacts by diving toward first. As R1 scrambles back, the pitcher throws wildly toward third, with the ball ricocheting off the fence and heading for the bullpen. As F5 and F7 chase the ball, R3 scores. Meanwhile, R1 gets up and advances around second but is thrown out on a close play at third with F6 covering. *Ruling:* In FED, R1 was "verbally" obstructed. The obstruction clearly made the difference in the play at third, so the out is canceled, with R1 remaining on third. In NCAA / OBR, R1 was simply gullible: He should know the difference between his coach's voice and voices of the defense. His out stands.

❀ Note 355: On the other hand, in FED if R1 had been out a long way at third, the umpire should rule that the runner tried to advance beyond the base he would have received on the obstruction, which in Play 193 above is second. (See § 33.)

❀ Note 356: Be careful not to confuse offensive verbal interference (an out results) with defensive verbal obstruction (§ 353, no penalty except in FED).

★ 354 OBSTRUCTION: VISUAL: DEFENSIVE✪

FED: No provision. Treat as in NCAA. (But see § 331 for a similar kind of visual hindrance, one where the **OFFENSE** is the villain.)

NCAA: A fielder may not intentionally move to block a runner's vision and prevent him from seeing the ball on a defensive play. (8-3f) **PENALTY:** The ball is delayed dead. At the end of playing action, the umpire will make awards as justified to nullify the obstruction. A team warning / ejection follows. (8-3f Pen)

375. ALSO: OFF INTERP 290-354: **FETCHIET:** The first baseman stations himself between the runner and the pitcher, moving back and forth to obstruct the runner's view: Legal, unless the pitcher makes a play at the moment of obstruction. **PENALTY:** The ball is dead, R1 receives second, and the umpire issues a team warning. (Website 3/12/01, 8-3f) ✠

OBR: Point not covered.

OFF INTERP 291-354: **PBUC:** Same as NCAA 8-3f: A fielder who intentionally blocks a runner's view of a catch in the outfield is guilty of Type (b) obstruction. (See § 33.) {7.30-11} ✠

(EDITED) ❀ Note 357: On 6 August 2004, MLU Paul Emmel was the third-base ump in a game with Seattle visiting Tampa Bay. In the bottom of the

10th with a tie score, Carl Crawford is on third (bases loaded, one out). Tino Martinez flies to left field, and according to the Associated Press, the Tampa Bay shortstop, Jose Lopez, "took a position between Crawford and left fielder Raul Ibañez." Emmel called obstruction and scored Crawford. Emmel showed a lot of guts in making the call. **BUT HE BLEW IT, NONETHELESS!** The play is Type (b) obstruction: It's a delayed dead ball, with the umpire making "awards, if any, in the appropriate manner." (MLBUM 6.23-11) Instead, Emmel killed the ball and "told Crawford to go home." (Associated Press) That's the Type a mechanic. We can guess the motivation, right? Emmel had been an umpire for years and knew the interpretation, but this third-world play had never happened in one of his games. So, when it did ....

⁂ *Play 194-354:* R2, R3. R3 retouches on B1's towering fly to medium-deep right field. The third baseman "accidentally" drifts to a position that screens R3 from seeing the catch. R3 shifts to another spot, and F5 likewise moves. *Ruling:* In FED / NCAA, the ball is delayed dead. After play has finished, if the umpire believes R3 had a chance for home, he will award him that base. Additionally, he warns the defensive team about such unsportsmanlike actions. In OBR, the umpire will yell: "That's obstruction!" Then: ***(EDITED)*** "After ALL PLAY HAS CEASED AND NO FURTHER ACTION IS POSSIBLE" [PBUC 7.27, p. 80], he will make awards that nullify the obstruction. Here, he could award R3 home if he didn't go or disallow an appeal if he left too early.

❀ Note 358: Play 194 above first appeared in the 1990 BRD in response to the NCAA rule change defining visual obstruction. Here's my note from that edition: "In my own game, I will follow the NCAA rule, regardless of the level of play. But I am not yet ready to advise all umpires to follow that procedure." Thus, Emmel's ruling is just a case of life imitating art — even if it did take 14 years for the painting to be born.

OFF INTERP 292-354: **PBUC:** "With a runner on first base, the first baseman, rather than holding the runner in the traditional manner, jockeys back and forth in front of the runner, several feet to the second base side of the bag. In the umpire's judgment the first baseman is doing this intentionally to block the runner's view of the pitcher. This is illegal and clearly not within the spirit of the rules. The first baseman should be warned to stop. If he persists, he is subject to ejection. {7.30-12} ✠

355 OBSTRUCTION: UMPIRE'S SIGNAL ✪ (See 341.)

FED: To signal obstruction the umpire extends his left arm parallel to his shoulders with his hand in a fist. (Signals)

NCAA: The umpire is to point and call: "That's obstruction!" (2-54; 8-3e Pen; 8-3f Pen)

OBR: To signal Type (a) obstruction, the umpire extends both hands above his head "in the same manner that he calls 'Time.'" (7.06a CMT) He uses the NCAA mechanic for Type (b). (AO 2-33)

★ 356 PITCH: END OF: DEFINITION ✪

FED: A pitch ends "when the pitched ball is secured by the catcher, comes to rest, goes out of play, becomes dead, or the batter hits the ball (other than a foul tip.)" (2-28-4)

NCAA: ***(ADDED)*** A pitch not secured by the catcher but remaining in the playing area ends when it stops rolling. (8-3-o-4 AR)

OBR: No provision.

IMPORTANT NOTE: IN FED, PITCHING RESTRICTIONS BEGIN WHEN THE PITCHER INTENTIONALLY CONTACTS THE PITCHER'S PLATE. **POE 1987, 1988, 1989, 1997, 1998, 2008, 2009**

★ 357 PITCHER: AMBIDEXTROUS: GUIDELINES FOR SWITCHING ARMS ✪

FED: When a pitcher wishes to pitch with either hand, if a switch-hitter steps into the box, the umpire will require the hurler to declare the hand he will pitch with, after which the batter may choose whichever box he pleases. (6-1-1; 6.1.1f) (See § 381 for an important ruling about the FED pitching-limitation rule and how it affects ambidextrous pitchers.)

NCAA: POE 1990 [balk]: Same as FED. (9-2k; 9-2k AR 1)
376. ALSO: The pitcher may not switch hands after delivering a pitch, but if the current batter is replaced by a pinch hitter, the pitcher may switch. (9-2k AR 2) **PENALTY:** After having declared, if the pitcher illegally switches hands it is: (● 1) a balk with runners on base; (● 2)an illegal pitch and a ball with the bases empty; (● 3) a warning; and (● 4) ejection if the offense is repeated. (9-2k Pen)

OBR: ***(ADDED)*** An ambidextrous pitcher "must indicate visually" to the umpire, batter, and any runners which hand he intends to use. He will then not be permitted to change until: (● 1) the batter is retired, (● 2) the batter becomes a runner, (● 3) a pinch hitter replaces the batter, (● 4) the inning ends, or (● 5) the pitcher is injured. (8.01f)

***(ADDED)* 377. ALSO:** If a pitcher, claiming injury, wishes to switch during an at-bat, he will not be given preparatory pitches nor will he be allowed to use the "injured" hand at any time during that game. (8.01f)

⁜ *Play 195-357:* Switch-hitter Bubba steps into the box as a right-handed hitter to face ambidextrous pitcher Perry. Perry announces he will pitch right-handed. Bubba then moves to the opposite side of the plate to bat left-handed. *Ruling:* ***(REVISED)*** Bubba can switch, but the pitcher can't.

★ 358 PITCHER: BALK: ARGUED ✪

FED: No provision. Treat as in OBR.

NCAA: Point not covered.

(ADDED) OFF INTERP 293-358: **PARONTO:** Same as OBR OFF INTERPs ? and 295 [this section]. (email to cc, 12/22/11) ✠

(ADDED) ❀ Note 359: Paronto: "A coach is entitled to understand the reason a balk was called but is subject to a warning and then a possible ejection if he remains to argue the call." (email to cc, 12/22/11)

OBR: Point not covered.

(CHANGED) OFF INTERP 294-358: **PBUC:** ":A manager may come out and question the reason for ANY type of balk call and shall not be ejected for his visit to learn why the balk was called." {8.5e} ✠

378. ALSO: ***(REVISED)*** OFF INTERP 295-358: **PBUC:** "A manager may be ejected if he continues to argue the call after an explanation." {8.5e} ✠

❀ Note 360: The BRD recommends: In amateur baseball do not permit participants to leave their positions to argue a balk — regardless of the nature of the infraction.

359 PITCHER: BALK: ENTICED BY: BATTER ✪

FED: If, in the umpire's judgment, the pitcher balks because the batter has illegally stepped out of the box: **PENALTY:** The balk is nullified and the umpire shall call a strike on the batter for stepping out of the batter's box. If the pitcher delivers after the balk, it is ruled no pitch. (6-2-4d-1; 6.2.4i) (See § 46 and 360.)
379. ALSO: If the umpire judges the batter's act is a deliberate attempt to entice a balk, he will eject the batter. (3-3-1o; 3-3-1o Pen)

NCAA: When the pitcher balks because the batter has illegally stepped out of the box: **PENALTY:** If the umpire rules the batter deliberately attempted to entice a balk, he will eject the offender immediately. Any balk is nullified. (5-15a-2; 5-15a-2 Pen; 9-3g AR) (See § 360.)

OBR: Same as NCAA.(4.06a-3; 4.06a-3 Pen; 6.02b CMT ¶ 7)

❀ Note 361: BRD recommends: Treat the status of the ball in an enticed balk as outlined in OBR OFF INTERP 253-360.

360 PITCHER: BALK: ENTICED BY: OFFENSE ✪

FED: No person connected with a team shall commit any act or make any remark designed to entice the pitcher to balk. (3-3-1o) **PENALTY:** The offender is ejected. If a **PLAY OR LEGAL PITCH** follows the violation, the ball is **DELAYED DEAD.** (3-3-1o Pen; 5-1-2d) If the pitcher balks, it is nullified. (6.2.4i) (See § 359.)

NCAA: Same as FED. **EXCEPT:** The status of the ball is not clear. (5-15a-2) Treat as in OFF INTERP 296 [this section]. (See § 359.)

OBR: Same as NCAA 5-15a-2. (4.06a-3; 4.06a-3 Pen)

> **EXCEPT:** OFF INTERP 296-360: **FITZPATRICK:** An enticed balk results in an immediate-dead ball. The balk is nullified, the offender is ejected, and the umpire orders a do-over. (email to cc, 11/15/00) ✠

✲ *Play 196-360:* R1: B1 has a count of 2-2. At TOP, as R1 breaks for second, the first-base coach screams "Balk!" and the pitcher: (a) does not or (b) does balk. In either case he immediately delivers the pitch. B1 swings and misses for strike three, and the catcher throws out R1 at second. *Ruling:* In (a), at all levels, the play stands. In (b) FED, the balk is cancelled and the resulting play also stands. In (b) NCAA / OBR, the ball is immediately dead, and the balk is cancelled. In (a) or (b) at all levels, the umpire ejects the first-base coach.

❀ Note 362: A word to the wise: Except in the most flagrant instances, when a member of the offense attempts to entice a balk, if the pitcher **DOES NOT BALK**, after the play, simply warn the offender.

★ 361 PITCHER: BALK: IGNORED ✪ (See § 362.)

FED: Not applicable: The balk may not be ignored since the ball is immediately dead on the cry of "Balk!"

NCAA: BALK FOLLOWED BY PITCH:
(● 1) If the batter and all runners advance at least one base, the balk is ignored (9-3 Pen 1); (● 2) if the batter does not advance – but all runners

do – the balk is still acknowledged by canceling the pitch. (9-3 Pen 3 AR 1 and 3)

❀ Note 363: The edict above also covers a balk followed by a wild pitch that is ball four or strike three, which is the subject of OFF INTERP 298 [this section].

BALK FOLLOWED BY THROW:

If all runners advance at least one base, the balk is ignored. (9-3 Pen 2)

380. ALSO: Regardless of whether the balk is followed by a pitch or a throw, runners may advance at their own risk. (9-3 Pen 2 AR)

381. ALSO: If the balk is followed immediately by a wild throw that permits runners to advance, the umpire does not call "Time" until all play has ceased or a fielder is in possession of the ball in the infield. The balk is still acknowledged. (9-3 Pen 2)

OBR: BALK FOLLOWED BY PITCH:

(● 1) If everyone advances: Same as NCAA. (8.05 Pen); or

(● 2) If everyone but the batter advances: **Point not covered.**

OFF INTERP 297-361: **PBUC:** Same as NCAA 9-3 Pen 2. {8.9-8} ✠

BALK FOLLOWED BY THROW:

Same as NCAA. Regardless, runners may advance at their own risk. (8.05 AR 1)

382. ALSO: OFF INTERP 298-361: **PBUC:** If balk is followed by a wild pitch that is strike three or ball four, play proceeds "without reference to the balk" if all runners (including B1) advance safely at least one base. {8.9-8} ✠

***(ADDED)* 383. ALSO:** OFF INTERP 299-361: **PBUC:** If all runners advance on a wild pitch but the batter does not, the balk penalty is not enforced. Nevertheless, the balk is acknowledged by nullifying the pitch: "The batter will resume his at bat with the count on him when the balk occurred. {8.9-8} ✠

384. ALSO: OFF INTERP 300-361: **FITZPATRICK:** When runners advance to or beyond the "balk" base, even though play proceeds "without reference to the balk," they *refer* to the balk by canceling the right of the defense to appeal a baserunning error. (phone call to cc, 11/8/01) (See Play 197 next.) ✠

⁕ *Play 197-361:* **OBR only.** R1 retouches on a fly to left field and makes second safely. The defense announces it will appeal at first. F1 in an attempt to throw from the pitcher's plate (a legal move), balks. The throw is wild, and R1 advances to third safely. The defense now wishes to appeal R1 left first too soon. *Ruling:* The umpire does not permit the appeal. (7.10d CMT ¶ 2.)

✻ *Play 198-361:* R1, 0-1 count. The pitcher balks but pitches wild for a swinging strike two. R1 advances to second but is thrown out at third. *Ruling:* In FED, R1 is awarded second; the strike on B1 is canceled. In NCAA / OBR, R1 is out, but the pitch is nullified; B1 remains at bat with a count of one strike.

✻ *Play 199-361:* R1, 0-1 count. The pitcher balks but pitches wild for a swinging strike two. R1 goes safely to third as B1 is charged with strike two on the wild pitch following the balk. *Ruling:* In FED, R1 returns to second; the strike on B1 is canceled. In NCAA / OBR, R1 remains on third; the strike is canceled.

362 PITCHER: BALK: STATUS OF BALL FOLLOWING ✪

(See § 361.)

FED: Following a balk the ball is immediately dead. (5-1-1k; 6.1.1b) (See § 380.)

NCAA: The ball is delayed dead anytime the pitcher balks. (9-3 Pen)

OBR: Same as NCAA. (5.09c; 8.05 Pen; 8.05 AR 1)

❀ Note 364-362: A fact, both curious and surprising, is that the OBR book does not mention a "delayed dead ball." The ball is either alive or dead. Still, some OBR "events" surely look as if they create a delayed dead ball: (● 1) a balk [this section]; (● 2) obstruction of a runner not played on (§ 33); and interference by a (● 3) batter (§ 275), (● 4) catcher (§ 293), or (● 5) umpire (§ 338 and 339). As the Bard of Avon so rosily said, "A rose by any other name...."

363 PITCHER: BATTERY: DEFINITION

ALL CODES NOW AGREE: TEXT DELETED, 1995.

★ 364 PITCHER: BULLPEN USED BY GAME PITCHER ✪

FED: No provision.

NCAA: Point not covered.

(ADDED) OFF INTERP 301-364: **PARONTO:** Same as OBR. (email to cc, 12/22/11) (See § 224.) ✠

OBR: Point not covered.

OFF INTERP 302-364: **PBUC:** The game pitcher may use the bullpen between half innings if he does not delay the game. {8.2} ✠

★ 365 PITCHER: DEFACED BALL BY: PITCHER ✪

FED: The pitcher shall not [pitch a defaced ball]: (● 1) apply foreign substance to the ball; (● 2) spit on the ball or glove; (● 3) rub the ball on glove, clothing, or body "if the act defaces the ball"; or (● 4) discolor the ball with dirt. (6-2-1) **PENALTY** if the ball is not pitched: warning / ejection. **PENALTY** for pitched ball: illegal pitch – ball / balk. The ball is immediately dead. (6-2-1 Pen a through d)

NCAA: The pitcher may not "do anything to deface the ball." (9-2e) **PENALTY:** warning / ejection. No ball or balk is called. (9-2e Pen)

OBR: The pitcher may not: (● 1) spit on the ball; (● 2) rub the ball on his glove, clothing, or person, even if the act does not deface the ball; (● 3) apply a foreign substance of any kind; (● 4) deface the ball in any way; or (● 5) deliver the balls that are called "shine," "spit," "mud," or "emery." (8.02a 2-6) **PENALTY:** The pitcher shall be ejected immediately. [In MLB, the pitcher is suspended; in the National Association, the suspension is for 10 ***(EDITED)*** games ~~days~~.] (8.02a 2-6 Pen a)

EXCEPT: OFF INTERP 303-365: **PBUC:** When the umpire observes the pitcher commit any of the acts listed in 8.02 2-6 (numbered above), if he judges the pitcher "did not intend to alter the characteristics of the baseball," he may warn the pitcher rather than ejecting. {8.10} ✠

385. ALSO: The ball is delayed dead. If a play follows the pitch, the manager of the offense may take the play or the penalty. **PENALTY:** ball **AND** balk with runners. (8.02 Pen d) If the batter and all runners advance one base, play continues without reference to the violation. Regardless of which option the manager selects, the umpire enforces 8.02a Pen a. (See § 366.)

386. ALSO: OFF INTERP 304-365: **MLBUM:** An umpire may ask that a player hand over any piece of equipment for inspection. "If the player refuses..., he is subject to ejection." An umpire is not required to inspect a pitcher for the possession of an altering substance or object simply because an opposing manager requests the inspection. (7.10) ✠

> ✻ *Play 200-365:* **OBR only.** Eighth inning, Fenway Park, Yankees-Red Sox, game 4 of the 2003 ALCS: Jeff Nelson's first pitch to Nomar Garciaparra is high and inside. Manager Grady Little asks home plate umpire Derryl Cousins to inspect Nelson's glove and belt buckle. *Ruling:* Crew chief Tim McClelland and Cousins go to the mound, perform their inspection, and the game continues without further incident. Boston won, 3-2.

⁂ *Play 201-365:* Bases loaded, score tied, 2 out, 2-2 count. The next pitch is fouled into the stands. But the NEXT pitch falls off the table just at the plate, and B1 strikes out swinging. The catcher tosses the ball to you, and you observe the ball is cut near the seams. *Ruling:* Since the ball was used for one pitch only, you know the pitcher scuffed the ball. In FED, you will retroactively call a balk, award all runners one base, and bring B1 back to hit with a full count. Additionally, you will eject F1. In NCAA, eject or warn the pitcher. In OBR, eject the pitcher without warning. Award ball three and assess a balk, which scores R3 and advances R2 and R1.

366 PITCHER: DEFACED BALL BY: RUBBING BALL ON CLOTHING
TEXT DELETED, 2006: REASON: DUPLICATE INFORMATION IN § 365)

★ 367 PITCHER: DEFACED BALL BY: UNIDENTIFIED PLAYER ✪

FED: No provision. (See § 365.)

NCAA: Point not covered.

> ***(ADDED)*** OFF INTERP 305-367: **PARONTO:** Rule 9-2e, which applies to a pitcher defacing a ball, shall be applied to any player who deliberately defaces or discolors a ball. **PENALTY:** Warning / ejection. (email to cc, 12/23/11) (See § 365.) ✠

OBR: No player may deliberately deface or discolor a ball by rubbing it with "soil, rosin, paraffin, licorice, sand-paper, emery-paper, or other foreign substance." (3.02) **PENALTY:** The offender is ejected and, in MLB, suspended for 10 days. (3.02 Pen) *See ¶8.*

★ 368 PITCHER: DELAYS: FAILURE TO PITCH WITH BATTER IN BOX ✪

FED: With or without runners, the pitcher must pitch or make a play or legal feint within 20 seconds after he receives the ball. (6-2-2c; 6.1.2a; 6.2.2c, e and f) **PENALTY:** ball. (6-2-2c Pen)
(ADDED) **387. ALSO:** Just before the 20-second count expires, the pitcher tries a pickoff move, which stops the count. When the pitcher again has the ball, the umpire may begin a new count. (6.2.2f)

> ❀ Note 365: Strange: FED has four case book plays covering a ruling that an umpire might make once in his career — if his name is Smitty.

NCAA: POE 2009: The 20-second count is in effect only with the bases empty. **PENALTY:** After a warning to the pitcher: a ball is awarded.

Coaches may not argue a 20-second call. After a warning to the coach, the head coach shall be ejected. (7-5e; 9-2c AR)

OBR: With the bases empty, the pitcher must pitch within 12 seconds. PENALTY: ball. (8.04)

(ADDED) ❀ Note 366: Two questions: Have you seen an MLB umpire call "Ball" for violation of the 12-second rule? Me, neither! Have you seen a pitcher violate the rule? Me, too!

369 PITCHER: DELAYS: UNNECESSARILY ✪

FED: The pitcher may not delay the game. (6-2-2) Example: The pitcher throws to aby player other than the catcher when the batter is in the box unless it is an attempt to retire a runner. (6-2-2a)
PENALTY: warning / ejection. (6-2-2 Pen)

NCAA: If the pitcher unnecessarily delays, the umpire shall call a balk. (9-3c; 9-3c Pen)

OBR: Same as NCAA. (8.05h)
388. ALSO: If a warning has been given for a violation of 8.02c (delay by throwing to a fielder other than to make a play) the penalty for 8.05h shall also apply. (8.05h CMT)

⁜ *Play 202-369:* R1. The pitcher throws to second though the runner is not attempting to advance. *Ruling:* At all levels: warning / ejection. (FED: 6-2-2a/Pen; NCAA: 9-2f/Pen; OBR: 8.02c)

⁜ *Play 203-369:* R1. The pitcher in Play 202 above now refuses to pitch. *Ruling:* In FED, he is ejected. In NCAA, charge the pitcher with a balk. In OBR, he is ejected, and R1 is awarded second on a balk.

★ 370 PITCHER: DISENGAGES PITCHER'S PLATE ✪

(See § 400.)

FED: When the pitcher disengages in the set position, he must step back at least "partially" within the 24-inch length of the pitcher's plate. (6-1-3)
389. ALSO: In the set position the pitcher may disengage the pitcher's plate at any time "prior to the start of the pitch." (6.1.1i)
390. ALSO: It is a balk if the pitcher pauses in the set position, separates his hands, and *then* steps off the pitcher's plate. (6.2.4d) (See § 387.)

NCAA: Regardless of the position chosen, the pitcher must step clearly back of the pitcher's plate and place his pivot foot on the ground before separating his hands. (9-1a-1c; 9-1b)

OBR: To disengage the pitcher's plate *(ADDED)* in the windup position, the pitcher must step back with his pivot foot and **DROP HIS HANDS TO HIS SIDES.** **PENALTY:** None listed. (8.01a CMT-3)

❀ Note 367-370: He does not have to separate (drop) his hands until he prepares to re-engage the pitcher's plate. That is one of the three OBR "Don't do that" pitching infractions. The other two are: (● 1) not having one hand on his side in the set position (§ 377); and (● 2) failing to take his sign from the pitcher's plate (§ 391). (See also § 400.)

371 PITCHER: FACES BATTER WHILE DELIVERING ✪

FED: From the windup or the set position, the pitcher shall **DELIVER** while facing the batter. (6-1-1) **PENALTY:** ball / balk. (6-1-1 Pen)

NCAA: In the windup position the pitcher shall **STAND** facing (shoulders squared to) the batter. (9-1a) **PENALTY:** warning / illegal pitch. (9-1a Pen)

OBR: In the windup position the pitcher shall **STAND** facing the batter (8.01a) and **DELIVER** from either position while facing the batter (8.05f). **PENALTY:** balk. (8.05f Pen)

★ 372 PITCHER: FEINT: NO STEP TO BASE ✪

(See § 222 and 375.)

FED: It is a balk if the pitcher from the pitcher's plate fails to step *(ADDED)* with his non-pivot foot directly toward a base (occupied or unoccupied) when throwing or legally feinting. (6-2-4b)

NCAA: POE 1990, 1992 [pickoff moves]: "While in a pitching position" the pitcher must step before he throws, *(EDITED)* but **THE STEP IS NOT REQUIRED FOR A LEGAL FEINT.** (9-3c)

OBR: Same as NCAA. (8.05c)

EXCEPT: *(EDITED)* OFF INTERP 306-372: **PBUC:** The pitcher must step toward the occupied base whether throwing or feinting. {8.5d Nt} ✠

★ 373 PITCHER: FEINTS TO FIRST: MOVES SHOULDERS ✪

FED: The pitcher may turn "his shoulders to check runners while in contact with the pitcher's plate in the set position." (6-1-1; 6.1.1g) *(EDITED)* **391. ALSO:** He may not turn his shoulders "during or after the stretch." (Website 2005, #19) (See Play 204 [this section].) **PENALTY:** balk. (6-1-1 Pen)

392. ALSO: If he has not brought his hands together, when checking a runner the pitcher may swing his shoulders "abruptly and quickly" or "casually." (6.1.1j; Website 2005, #17)
393. ALSO: In the windup position the pitcher may not move his shoulders to check a runner. (6-1-2) **PENALTY:** balk. (6-1-2 Pen; Website 2005, #18)

⁎ *Play 204-373:* R1. The pitcher is in the set position. Before bringing his hands together, the pitcher rapidly swings his shoulders toward first in an attempt to drive back the runner. *Ruling:* In FED, it's a legal move. In NCAA / OBR, it's a balk.

❀ Note 368: Veterans will remember the FED ruled that when a pitcher in the set position **BEFORE COMING TO THE STOP** moved his shoulders to check on a runner, he was guilty of a balk. The ruling first surfaced as OFF INTERP #38 in the 1989 *News*. It became a POE in 1992.

❀ Note 369: I'm sure members of the committee believed they were joining the NCAA / OBR by allowing the pitcher to swing his shoulders to check runners before coming to the stop in the set position. In the process they created two more differences: (● 1) The FED pitcher may swing his shoulders rapidly; and (● 2) he may not swing his shoulders during the stretch. My scorecard shows a net gain of one new difference.

394. ALSO: OFF INTERP 307-373: **RUMBLE:** A pitcher may adopt the open stance, but when he comes to his stop, he must remain in that stance. **PENALTY:** balk. (*News* #19, 3/99) ✠

❀ Note 370: The FED interpretation is: start closed, end closed; start open, end open. Be clear on one point of the FED statute: If the pitcher is in the open position, he may not swing his shoulders to check a runner during his stretch. In other words, he may not further open his open stance.

NCAA: Point not covered.

(ADDED) OFF INTERP 308-373: **PARONTO:** "Prior to coming to a stop in the set position, the pitcher may slowly move his shoulders to check a runner at first or third. After coming to a stop, that type of movement is a balk. (email to cc, 12/23/11) ✠

OBR: Point not covered.

OFF INTERP 309-373: **FITZPATRICK:** Prior to coming to the stop in the set position, the pitcher may move his shoulders slowly while checking a runner at first or third. After coming to the stop, such movement is a balk. (phone call to cc, 11/8/01) ✠

❀ Note 371: OFF INTERP 309 above matches the FED.
EXCEPT: The OBR pitcher is not allowed an "abrupt" swing of the shoulders while on the rubber.

***(ADDED)* 395. ALSO:** OFF INTERP 310-373: **WENDELSTEDT:** The pitcher may swing his shoulders during the stretch to check a runner. To commit a balk, the pitcher must make a feint to first. (P152/130) ✠

✳ *Play 205-373:* R1. The pitcher, using the set position and in legal and intentional contact with the pitcher's plate, leans forward, peering in at the catcher. Slowly, he turns his whole body to eye the runner. *Ruling:* At all levels, the movement of the shoulders is legal.

✳ *Play 206-373:* R1. Right-handed F1 stands in an open position. As he moves toward the stop his shoulders are open or slightly moving toward first or the plate. *Ruling:* In FED, the pitcher may not swing his shoulders while stretching: Balk. In NCAA / OBR, the movements and both final positions are legal.

(ADDED) ❀ Note 372: **TWO DEFINING DIFFERENCES:** (1) Prior to the discernible stop, the FED pitcher may swing his shoulders slowly or quickly. The NCAA and OBR pitchers must do it slowly. (2) The FED pitcher may not swing his shoulders to check a runner DURING his stretch before the pause. The NCAA and OBR pitchers may. AFTER the pause in the set position, any swing of the shoulders is a balk at any level.

374 PITCHER: FEINTS TO: SECOND ✪

FED: While in contact with the pitcher's plate in the set position, the pitcher may feint toward second.(6-2-4b; 6.2.4f)

396. ALSO: The pitcher from the set position wheels and feints a throw to second; the two middle infielders pretend to chase the throw into the outfield. That is not unsportsmanlike and hence is a legal deception. (6.2.4e) (See Note 353-353.)

397. ALSO: The pitcher steps back of the pitcher's plate and pretends to throw to first. A game participant may not supplement the pitcher's acting by throwing a practice ball against the fence. **PENALTY:** The ball is alive. After play has ended, the umpire will eject the offender's coach and award the affected runner one base. (8.3.2j) (See § 353 and 396.)

NCAA: The "spin or open move" to second is legal if the pitcher raises his non-pivot foot and immediately and in one continuous motion steps directly toward second. (9-3c-2) **PENALTY:** balk. (9-3-Pen) (See § 222.)

OBR: Same as FED: The pitcher may feint toward second. (8.05c)

AO 20-374: EVANS: The catcher may not decoy a stealing R1 by throwing a white sponge (which might make it to the mound) and then throwing out the runner when he tries for third. Penalty: Cancel the out and eject the catcher. (9:6)

★ 375 PITCHER: FEINTS TO BASE: THIRD, THEN TO FIRST ✪ (See § 222 and 372.)

FED: A pitcher working from the set position may feint to third and then turn and throw to first. (6.1.5) He may do that "with or without disengaging the pitcher's plate." (6.2.4c)

> **398. ALSO:** OFF INTERP 311-375: **HOPKINS:** The feint does not require arm motion. (Website 2002, #9) ✠

NCAA: If a pitcher feints to third, he must disengage the pitcher's plate during the feint before he will be allowed to throw (or feint) to first. (9-3b AR-1 and-2) **PENALTY:** balk. Arm motion is not required. (9-3b AR-3)

OBR: ***(EDITED)*** Same as NCAA. (8.05c CMT ¶ 2; OFF INTERP 313 this section)

> **399. ALSO:** ***(EDITED)*** OFF INTERP 312-375: **PBUC:** During the step to third, the pitcher must leave the pitcher's plate before throwing to first base. If he does not, it is a balk. {8.5g Nt} ✠

> ***(ADDED)*** **400. ALSO:** OFF INTERP 313-375: **PBUC:** During a feint to third, arm motion is not required. {8.5g Nt} ✠

★ ∞ 376 PITCHER: GOES TO MOUTH ✪

FED: POE 2008: While on the mound the pitcher may touch his pitching hand to his mouth as long as he wipes off that hand before it touches the ball. (6-2-1e; 6.2.1a; (Website 2008, #8) **PENALTY:** "A ball shall be called each time the pitcher violates this rule and subsequently engages the pitcher's plate."(6-2-1e Pen) (See § 365.)
401. ALSO: A pitcher intentionally in contact with the pitcher's plate, whether in the windup or set position, may not go to his mouth. (Website 2008, #6 and #7) **PENALTY:** ball / balk. (6.1.3o; 6.2.1aand b) (See § 387.)

> **EXCEPT:** OFF INTERP 314-376: **HOPKINS:** Whether in the wind-up or the set position, it is legal for the pitcher to adjust his cap or shake off the signal with his glove or head. (6.1.2d; affirmed, Website 2010, #8) ✠

❀ Note 373: At last the NFHS has dropped the charade that going to the mouth on the rubber is illegal because the pitcher has interrupted his pitching motion. All of the items in OFF INTERP 314 above are "interruptions of the pitching motion" — and legal. This problem was created by Brad Rumble's mistake in 1990. In the FED *News* Interps, he ruled that going to the mouth on the pitcher's plate was a ball / balk. The Southwest Officials Association issued the "clarification" on 3/23/90. Since black-letter law said the pitcher could go to his mouth **ANYWHERE** on the mound, including the pitcher's plate, something had to be done to save Rumble. "Interrupted his pitching motion" was the sacrificial lamb. They now have it right. I am reminded of Sir Walter Scott: "Oh, what a tangled web we weave, when first we practice to deceive."

OFF INTERP 315-376: **HOPKINS:** With (a) the bases empty, or (b) runners on first base and second base, the pitcher goes to his mouth with his pitching hand while off the pitcher's plate, but does not wipe it off. He next places his pitching hand on the ball. RULING: In both (a) and (b), while off the pitching plate, the pitcher may request to have a new ball from the plate umpire with no penalty. If the pitcher, without having received a new ball from the plate umpire subsequently engages the pitcher's plate, a ball would be awarded to the batter. (Website 2008, #9) ✠

❀ Note 374: In summary: (● 1) Pitcher is off the pitcher's plate and goes to his mouth: If he engages and touches the ball without wiping his hand, ball (with or without runners). (● 2) Pitcher is on the pitcher's plate and goes to his mouth: ball or balk, regardless of whether he wipes off his hand. And that's the name of that tune!

NCAA: Same as FED 6-2-1e. (9-2d; 9-2d Pen; 9-2d AR 1)
402. ALSO: In cold weather the umpire may announce that pitchers may blow on their hands whether on or off the rubber. (9-2d AR 2)
403. ALSO: The NCAA draws a distinction between a pitcher "going to his mouth" and deliberately applying any foreign substance or moisture to the ball. **PENALTY:** for applying foreign substance: warning / ejection. (9-2e Pen)

OBR: Same as FED. (8.02a-1) **EXCEPT:** If both managers agree in advance, during cold weather the pitcher may blow on his hands while on the mound or pitcher's plate. (8.02a-1 Ex) **PENALTY:** ball.
(ADDED) **404. ALSO:** If the ball is pitched and all runners, including the batter-runner advance one base. "play shall proceed without reference to the violation." (8.02a-1 Pen)

(ADDED) **405. ALSO:** OFF INTERP 316-376: **WENDELSTEDT:** Same as FED OFF INTERP 315 above. (HW/115) ✠

406. ALSO: OFF INTERP 317-376: **WENDELSTEDT:** ***(EDITED)*** "For repeated offenses by the same pitcher for the purpose of issuing an intentional walk, the umpire may eject the pitcher from the game." (HW/115) ✠

✻ *Play 207-376:* R3. The pitcher is: (a) on the pitcher's plate, or (b) on the mound, but not in intentional contact with the pitcher's plate when he touches his pitching hand to his mouth. *Ruling:* FED: In (a), it is an immediate balk and R3 scores. In (b), it is a ball only if the pitcher touches the ball without wiping off his hand and engages the pitcher's plate. NCAA: It is a ball in (a) but legal in (b) unless F1 fails to wipe off his hand, when the penalty is also a ball. OBR: In (a), it is a ball; in (b), it is a ball if the pitcher does not wipe the fingers of his pitching hand before touching the ball.

❀ Note 375: There are eight major rules situations where each level treats the play differently. The other seven are: § 50 (designated hitter); § 83 (use illegal bat); § 124 (throw from dead-ball area); § 144 (conferences / trips to the mound); § 246 (fighting); § 266 (improperly declared infield fly); § 378 (hidden ball play); § 488 (illegal substitutes).

★ 377 PITCHER: HAND AT SIDE, BEHIND BACK, OR "GORILLA" STANCE IN SET POSITION ✪

FED: When taking his sign in the set position, the pitcher must have his PITCHING HAND ***(EDITED)*** "down at his side or behind his back." (6-1-3) **PENALTY:** ball / balk. (2-18; 6-1-3 Pen) **EXCEPT:**

> OFF INTERP 318-377: **HOPKINS:** The "gorilla" stance is legal as long as the pitcher's arm is not moving. "THE BATTER, RUNNER(S) ON BASE, AND COACHES ARE ABLE TO VIEW THE PITCHER AND THE BALL AND ARE NOT PLACED AT A DISADVANTAGE." (Website 2010, #1 and #2) (See Note 377 below.) ✠

> **407. ALSO:** OFF INTERP 319-377: **HOPKINS:** The pitcher "has his pitching arm resting on his thigh and his pitching hand is at rest in his lower abdominal area. This is illegal." (Website 2010, #3) ✠

(EDITED) ❀ Note 376: The FED Website explains the OFF INTERP 319ruling : "Having his pitching hand at rest in this area gives the offense little or no visibility of the baseball and action by the pitcher." Likely, the NCAA 2008 POE quoted below inspired the case play. It took two years to work its way onto the Website, and it's not in the 2012 case book. OFF INTERP 318 isn't there, either.

⁜ *Play 208-377:* **FED only.** R1. F1 leans forward, peering in for his sign. His pitching hand swings slowly in front of his body. *Ruling:* balk.

NCAA: When taking his sign in the set position, the pitcher must have his pitching hand ***(EDITED)*** "at the side or behind the body." (9-1b-1) **PENALTY:** warning / balk. (9-1b-1 Pen) **EXCEPT:** The pitcher may bend ***(EDITED)*** "deeply at the waist and have his pitching arm hanging straight down in front of him. THE PITCHER IS NOT ATTEMPTING TO CONCEAL THE BALL FROM THE BASE RUNNER(S)." (9-1b-1 AR)

(ADDED) ❀ Note 377-377: As Boomer says on ESPN: "C'mon, man!"

408. ALSO: POE 2008: The committee is concerned that "pitchers are [illegally] deceiving runners by holding the ball in the pitching hand in front of the body and not at the hip or behind the body, as noted in this rule [9-1b]."

> ***(ADDED)*** ❀ Note 378: The "gorilla stance" (9-1b-1 AR) became legal in **2007**. **THE VERY NEXT YEAR**, the NCAA committee cried in public about pitchers deceiving runners by using the stance they had just sanctioned. As Casey said: "You could look it up."

OBR: In the set position the pitcher must have *one* hand "on" his side. (8.01b) **PENALTY:** None listed! **EXCEPT:**

> ***(ADDED)*** OFF INTERP 320-377: **WENDELSTEDT:** The pitcher in the gorilla stance "has done nothing wrong. His arm may even swing in front of him" before he goes into his stretch. (PL118/117) ✠

> ❀ Note 379: That is one of the three OBR "Don't do that" pitching infractions. The other two are: (● 1) failing to drop his hands to his sides after disengaging the pitcher's plate (§ 370); and (● 2) failing to take his sign from the pitcher's plate (§ 391). (See also § 400.)

★ 378 PITCHER: HIDDEN-BALL PLAY ✪

FED: When the defense attempts a hidden-ball play, the pitcher may not stand "on or astride" or within "approximately five feet" of the pitcher's plate without the ball. **PENALTY:** balk. (6-2-5)

NCAA: The pitcher, without the ball, may not stand with one or both feet on "any part of the dirt area" of the mound while his team is attempting the hidden-ball play. (9-3f) **PENALTY:** balk. (9-3f Pen)

OBR: The pitcher may not be "on or astride" the pitcher's plate without the ball. (8.05i) **PENALTY:** balk. (8.05i Pen)

❀ Note 380: ***(EDITED)*** Attempting the hidden ball play is one of the nine major rules or interpretations **WHERE EACH LEVEL TREATS THE SITUATION DIFFERENTLY**. The other eight are: § 50 (designated hitter); § 83 (use illegal bat); § 124 (throw from dead-ball area); § 144 (conferences or trips to the mound); § 245 (positions occupied at time of pitch or play) § 246 (fighting); § 266 (improperly declared infield fly); § 488 (illegal substitutes).

379 PITCHER: ILLEGAL PITCH: DEFINITION ✪

FED: An illegal pitch occurs when:
(● 1) the pitcher delivers when he is not in contact with the pitcher's plate (6-1-1); or
(● 2) there is a quick-return pitch (6-1-1); or

(● 3) **THE DELIVERY VIOLATES PROVISIONS OF RULE 6** (6-1-1 Pen; 6-1-2 Pen; 6-1-3 Pen; 6-2-1 Pen a through d; 6-2-4c); or
(● 4) a fielder other than the catcher is on foul ground during delivery (1-1-4 Pen; 6-1-1); or
(● 5) the pitcher balks. (6-2-4) (See OFF INTERP • 21-16.)
PENALTY: The ball is immediately dead (5-1-1k); ball / balk. (2-18-1) (See § 380.)

❀ Note 381: Number 3 (emphasized above) is one of the most significant differences in the pitching rules between FED on the one hand and NCAA / OBR on the other. If the infraction is not listed as an illegal pitch (balk) in the upper level games, it is treated as a "Don't do that," *i.e.*, no penalty.
(See Note 367-370 for the complete list.)

NCAA: An illegal pitch is a quick-return pitch or one delivered when the pitcher is not on the pitcher's plate. (9-1d) **PENALTY:** Warning: With nobody on, if the batter does not reach first, call a ball. (9-2a) The ball is delayed dead. With runners on base, it is a balk. (2-42)

OBR: Same as NCAA. (2.00 Illegal Pitch)

380 PITCHER: ILLEGAL PITCH: STATUS OF BALL ✪

FED: The ball is immediately dead if the pitcher delivers an illegal pitch. (5-1-1k; 6-1-1 Pen; 6-1-2 Pen; 6-1-3 Pen) (See § 362.)

NCAA: Following an illegal pitch the ball is delayed dead. (9-1d; 9-2a Pen)

OBR: Same as NCAA. (8.01d)

★ 381 PITCHER: LIMIT OF INNINGS PITCHED ✪

FED: POE 1988, 1992: State associations must adopt ***(EDITED)*** "a pitching restriction policy to afford pitchers a reasonable period between pitching appearances." (6-1-6)
***(ADDED)* 409. ALSO:** "It is not an official's responsibility to determine if a team has violated a state association's pitching restriction policy." (6.1.6b CMT)
410. ALSO: An ambidextrous pitcher is considered one pitcher (not two) for purposes of the pitching-limitation rule. (6.1.6a) (See § 357.)
411. ALSO: A pitcher does not violate the pitching limitation rule simply because he makes a play (*e.g.*, a throw). (6.1.6b; Website 2005, #14)

412. ALSO: OFF INTERP 321-381: **HOPKINS:** If a pitcher warms up on the mound but does not enter the game to pitch, that is not a violation of the pitching limitation rule. (Website 2005, #15) ✠

413. ALSO: OFF INTERP 322-381: **RUMBLE:** The pitching limitation restriction supersedes other pitching rules. (*News* #6, 3/91; affirmed, Website 2005, #15) ✠

✻ *Play 209-381:* **FED only.** Bubba enters to relieve and completes his warm-up tosses. The coach then discovers that if Bubba pitches, he will violate that state's pitching limitation rule. *Ruling:* Bubba may not pitch. Further, the new pitcher is entitled to a "normal" warmup. Bubba, naturally, may enter at any other position.

NCAA: No provision.

(ADDED) ❀ Note 382: Paronto: Teams should consider the health and safety of any pitcher." (email to cc, 12/22/11)

OBR: No provision. *See ¶ 8.*

❀ Note 383: The one constant in all of youth baseball is the pitching limitation rule. Be sure you know the one in your League.

382 PITCHER: NON-PIVOT FOOT POSITION: WINDUP ✪ (See § 385.)

FED: POE 2008: In the windup position the pitcher must stand with his non-pivot foot on or behind a line extending through the **FRONT EDGE** of the pitcher's plate. (6-1-2) **PENALTY:** ball / balk if a pitch is delivered. (6-1-2 Pen)

❀ Note 384: A current fad is the pitcher standing in the windup position with **THE HEELS OF BOTH FEET** touching the front edge of the pitcher's plate. At the TASO state meeting in January 2010, the BRD asked Kyle McNeely: "Is that legal?" Answer: "Yes."

NCAA: Concerning the demarcation "line" for the non-pivot (free) foot: His entire free foot shall not be in front of his pivot foot. (9-1a) **PENALTY:** First offense: warning; second and all subsequence offenses: illegal pitch (ball or balk). (9-1a Pen)

414. ALSO: In the windup position the pitcher with the heel of his non-pivot foot off the ground may not drop that heel before disengaging the pitcher's plate with his pivot foot. (9-1a-7) **PENALTY:** no pitch / balk. (9-1a-7 Pen) (See § 384.)

OBR: The pitcher is permitted to have his non-pivot [free] foot "on the rubber, in front of the rubber, behind the rubber, or off the side of the rubber." (8.01a CMT) (See § 385.)

> **415. ALSO:** OFF INTERP 323-382: **PBUC:** If the pitcher assumes his windup position with the heel of his non-pivot foot off the ground, treat as in NCAA 9-1a Pen. {8.5q} (See § 385.) ✠

⁜ *Play 210-382:* F1's pivot foot is near the left edge of the pitcher's plate with his free foot not touching and to the side. An imaginary line drawn through the middle of the pitcher's plate would slice off the last two inches of his Nikes. *Ruling:* The pitcher is legal at all levels.

★ 383 PITCHER: PERPENDICULAR PLANE ✪

FED: If the pitcher's "ENTIRE NON-PIVOT FOOT breaks the plane of the back edge of the pitcher's plate," he must pitch or throw (or make a legal feint) to second. **PENALTY:** If he throws to first or third: balk. (6-2-4f)

NCAA: Same as FED 6-2-4f. (9-1b-3; 9-1b Pen) **EXCEPT:** From the set position, if the pitcher breaks the plane with ANY PART OF HIS "STRIDE LEG," it is a balk if he does not pitch or throw (or feint) to second. (9 3L)

OBR: In the set position if the pitcher swings his NON-PIVOT FOOT past the back edge of the rubber, he must feint or throw to second. **PENALTY:** If he throws to first: balk. (8.05a CMT)

> **416. ALSO:** OFF INTERP 324-383: **WENDELSTEDT:** *(EDITED)* Unlike FED and NCAA, where the entire non-pivot foot must pass the plane of the rubber, it is a balk if the pitcher brings ANY PART OF HIS FOOT behind the back edge of the rubber. (PL143/129) ✠

> **417. ALSO:** OFF INTERP 325-383: **PBUC:** The prohibition against breaking the plane specifically applies only to the foot: "If the knee of the pitcher's free leg passes behind the back edge of the rubber but his foot does not, he may legally throw to first base with no violation." {8.5c} ✠

★ ∞ 384 PITCHER: PIVOT FOOT: DEFINITION ✪

FED: A pitcher's pivot foot is on the same side as the arm he pitches with. A left-handed pitcher's pivot foot is his left foot. (2-28-6; 6.1.3L)

❀ Note 385: Case book play 6.1.3L concerns a right-handed pitcher who illegally assumes a left-handed set position in order to make a stronger throw to second. The penalty is a balk since a right-handed pitcher's pivot foot is his right foot. And an ambidextrous pitcher's pivot foot is his ....

NCAA: The pivot foot is the foot in contact with the pitching rubber when the pitcher delivers. (2-63)

OBR: Same as NCAA. (2.00 Pivot Foot)

AO 21-384: HW: With a pitcher delivering a pitch with his right hand, his right foot is the pivot foot. Left hand? Left foot. (HW/pivot foot/8)

385 PITCHER: PIVOT-FOOT POSITION: WINDUP ✪ (See § 382.)

FED: When the pitcher delivers from the windup position, he must have his pivot foot in contact with the pitcher's plate. (2-28-6) **PENALTY:** ball / balk. (6-1-2 Pen; 6.1.1a)

NCAA: When he delivers from the windup, the pitcher's shoulders must be squared to the plate and his pivot foot must be on or in front of and touching the pitcher's plate. (9-1a) **PENALTY:** First offense, warning. Second offense, ball (9-1a Pen) or balk (9-3d Pen) (See § 382.)

OBR: The pitcher must have his pivot foot in contact with the rubber and his other foot free. (8.01a) **PENALTY:** ball / balk. (8.05e; 8.05e Pen)

★ 386 PITCHER: PUMPS LIMITED ✪

FED: The pitcher is limited to two pumps or rotations. (6-1-2; 8.3.5e) **PENALTY:** ball / balk. (6-1-2 Pen)

418. ALSO: The committee defines "pumps" and "rotations" in the case book. (6.1.2b)

NCAA: Same as FED. **EXCEPT:** The rule does not mention "rotations" nor does it define a "pump." (9-3k; 9-3k Pen)

OBR: No provision. (See § 369.) *See ¶8.*

❀ Note 386: "No provision" in this instance does not mean the OBR has neglected the issue. The OBR doesn't care. My evidence: A word-by-word search of JEA and Wendelstedt did not find either "pump" or "rotation" in the OBR portion of the text. So, give it up for the kid who pumps five times before pitching in a Pony League game. Or American Legion, for that matter. ***(EDITED)*** Of course, there is the 12-second rule in OBR, a rule no MLB umpire even comes close to enforcing. You don't believe me? Watch any game whenever Josh Beckett pitches.

387 PITCHER: REMOVES HAND FROM BALL WHILE IN PITCHING POSITION ✪

FED: (• 1) SET POSITION: The pitcher may not remove a hand from the ball unless he pitches, throws, or feints to a base.
(6-2-4e; 6.1.3d and e) **PENALTY:** ball / balk. (6-2-4)
(IMPORTANT: SEE § 406 [TIME OF THE PITCH].)
(• 2) WINDUP POSITION: (a) If the pitcher is simultaneously bringing both hands together in front of his body **AS HE STEPS ONTO THE PITCHER'S PLATE**, such movement is legal. (6.1.2c)
419. ALSO: (b) If the pitcher steps onto the pitcher's plate in the windup position with one hand at his side, he may bring his hands together and then pitch or step off. (6.1.2e and I)
420. ALSO: (c) If he steps onto the pitcher's plate with both hands at his side, he may move one hand at a time to bring them together and stop. He may then deliver or step off. (6.1.2h)
421. ALSO: (d) If he steps onto the pitcher's plate with both hands apart, when he begins to move both hands simultaneously, that is the start of a pitch. (6-1-2; 2.28.3c)
422. ALSO: (e) When he steps onto the pitcher's plate with his hands together, if he drops one hand to his side, that is a balk. (6.1.2f)
423. ALSO: When he is intentionally on the pitcher's plate, he may adjust his cap or shake off a signal with his glove or head. (6.1.2d)

NCAA: A pitcher on the rubber "with his hands together" and before making any motion that commits him to pitch, "may move his hand within his glove to adjust the ball." (9-1a AR 1)
424. ALSO: Same as FED 6-2-4e: After joining hands, if the pitcher separates his hands (other than to pitch or throw): **PENALTY:** balk. (9-3h)
For the WINDUP position: The pitcher may assume his position with his hands: (• 1) together in front of his body; (9-1a-1a)
(• 2) apart, and go directly to the windup; or (9-1a-1b)
(• 3) apart, and bring them together in a stop to adjust the ball. (9-1a 1c)
From any of those positions, the pitcher may deliver, attempt a pickoff, or disengage the pitcher's plate.

425. ALSO: OFF INTERP 326-387: **THURSTON:** When the pitcher assumes the windup position as in (2) or (3) above, he may not make a move from the moment his pitching hand begins moving toward his glove until his hand reaches his glove. The reason: Such a move is "obviously designed to illegally deceive the runner." **PENALTY:** balk. But after the hand reaches the glove, the pitcher may attempt a pickoff. That privilege ends the moment the pitcher makes any movement naturally associated with his delivery. (phone call to se, 1/14/92) ✠

❀ Note 387: Call a balk if a pitcher assumes the windup position with his hands together and separates them without making one of the three legal moves. In that respect at least, FED / NCAA match the OBR.

OBR: After assuming any legal position, defined as the "Windup Position and the Set Position," (8.01) the pitcher may not remove either hand from the ball, other than to pitch or throw to a base.
PENALTY: balk. (8.05j) **EXCEPT:**

OFF INTERP 327-387: **PBUC:** "Prior to assuming a legal pitching position (windup or set position) it is permissible for the pitcher to momentarily adjust the ball in his glove. In order for this to be allowed, the movement must be momentary in nature. If the pitcher has his hands together long enough that, in the judgment of the umpire, it appears that he has actually come to a set position or has actually assumed the windup position, then should the pitcher separate his hands, a balk shall be called under Official Rule 8.05(j). {8.5 m} ✠

426. ALSO: OFF INTERP 328-387: **PBUC:** Pitchers may assume the windup position with their hands apart and: (● 1) go directly into their delivery; or (● 2) bring their hands together and come to a stop before their delivery. {8.1} ✠

❀ Note 388: A pitcher might vary his routine between method (● 1) and method (● 2); that also would be legal. (See § 392.)

★ 388 PITCHER: RETURNS TO MOUND IN SAME GAME AFTER BEING: INJURED ✪

FED: If the pitcher is injured and the requirements of the pitching-substitution rule have not been met (§ 496), or if his replacement needs more warm-up throws than permitted by rule (§ 410 and 411), the replaced pitcher may not return to the mound in that game. (3-1-2) He may return at any other position. (3.1.2b) (See § 120.)

✻ *Play 211-388:* **FED only.** In the top of the second, Perry, having thrown four warm-up tosses, slips on the mound and receives a slight muscle strain. His coach sends Perry to the bench so the trainer may examine him, and Bubba enters to relieve.
Ruling: Bubba is replacing an injured pitcher, so he may have as many warm-up throws as the umpire deems appropriate. But if the coach hopes that Perry can return to pitch, Bubba will start the half inning with only one warm-up throw. (3.1.2c)

NCAA: Point not covered.

(ADDED) OFF INTERP 329-388: **PARONTO:** "A pitcher who is removed from the mound before finishing pitching to the first batter he faces or retiring the side (5-5b; 9-4c-1), shall not be allowed to return to the mound. (email to cc, 122311) ✠

OBR: No provision.

★ 389 PITCHER: RETURNS TO MOUND IN SAME GAME AFTER BEING: REMOVED ON FIRST CONFERENCE OR TRIP ✪

FED: Unless removed for excessive conferences, a pitcher may "be removed as pitcher and return as pitcher only **ONCE PER INNING.**" (3-1-2; Website 2002, #17)

NCAA: Any pitcher ("starter or reliever") who leaves the mound but remains in the game may return only once a game. (5-5b AR 1; 7-2c-5b-4; 9-4e) (See § 151.)

OBR: A pitcher "may change to another position only once during the same inning." (3.03 CMT); *i.e.*, "the pitcher will not be allowed to assume a position other than a pitcher more than once in the same inning." {PBUC 8.3} (See § 151.)

427. ALSO: OFF INTERP 330-389: **PBUC:** If a pitcher changes positions and then returns to the mound in the same inning, he will be given the customary eight warm-up tosses. {8.3} ✠

(ADDED) **428. ALSO:** OFF INTERP 331-389: **WENDELSTEDT:** When a pitcher assumes a defensive position during an inning, if he returns to the mound in that inning, trips are cumulative. (second trip/HW50) See Play 212 below. ✠

(ADDED) ✻ *Play 212-389:* **NCAA and OBR only.** Coach Neeley visits the mound and moves pitcher Bubba to shortstop. In the same inning, he returns to the mound to bring Bubba back to pitch. If he again visits the mound in that half inning, that will be his second trip while Bubba was a pitcher, and he must leave the game.

✻ *Play 213-389:* ***(EDITED)*** Bubba walks the first batter in the third inning. The coach goes to the mound and swaps Bubba with first baseman Perry. [Trip 1: Bubba is removed from the mound once: legal.]

Perry retires the next two batters. The skipper arrives again and brings Bubba back to the mound and sends Perry back to first. [Trip 1: Perry is removed from the mound once; Bubba is returned to the mound : legal.]

Bubba walks the next batter. Again the coach comes out to tell the umpire he wants Perry and Bubba to swap one last time. [Trip 2: Perry may return to the mound once. *Ruling:* ***(REVISED)*** Bubba must be removed from the game because his coach visited him twice on the mound in the same half inning.

❀ Note 389: Pitcher-to-fielder-to-pitcher is the plain vanilla change, which in FED and OBR can be repeated once every inning and in NCAA once every game. Umpires don't like pistachio nut: fielder-to-pitcher-to-fielder-to-pitcher, but that is also legal. ***(REVISED)*** By the way, in NCAA play, none of the visits result in a charged conference or "trip" to the mound because the coach changed pitchers each time he trudged up that hill. In OBR, because of "cumulative trips," the coach is charged with two trips to Bubba.

★ 390 PITCHER: ROSIN BAG ✪

FED: Under umpire supervision, the pitcher may dry his hands with a "cloth bag of powdered rosin." (6-2-1 Nt)

NCAA: (● 1) The home team must provide a rosin bag. (9-2e AR 3) (● 2) A ball hitting the bag remains alive. (9-2e AR 4) (● 3) ***(EDITED)*** No player may apply rosin to his glove or uniform. Same as OBR 8.02a CMT. (9-2e AR 4)
429. ALSO: A pitcher shall not put rosin on the ball, glove, or body. (9-2e)
PENALTY: warning / ejection. (9-2e Pen)

OBR: Before each game starts, the UIC will "ensure that an official rosin bag is placed on the ground behind the pitcher's plate." (3.01f)
See ¶ 8.
430. ALSO: (● 1) The umpire may instruct the pitcher to carry the bag in his hip pocket. (● 2) No player may dust the ball with the bag. (● 3) No player may apply rosin to his glove or uniform. (Same as NCAA 9-2e.) (8.02a CMT)

431. ALSO: OFF INTERP 332-390: **PBUC:** If the pitcher places the rosin bag into his glove with the intent to deceive a runner, the umpire will call a balk. {8.5-L} ✠

★ 391 PITCHER: SIGN NOT TAKEN ON PITCHER'S PLATE ✪

FED: The pitcher must take his sign from the "catcher" while on the pitcher's plate. (6-1-1) PENALTY: ball / balk. (6-1-1 Pen)

NCAA: Same as FED 6-1-1. **EXCEPT:** PENALTY: ball. (7-5d) If the batter and all runners advance following a pitch from the illegal position (pivot foot not on the pitcher's plate), ***(EDITED)*** "play proceeds without reference to the violation." (9-2j Pen) (See § 376.)

OBR: The pitcher must take his sign while on the pitcher's plate. PENALTY: None listed. (8.01)

❀ Note 390: That is one of the three OBR "Don't do that" pitching infractions. The other three are: (● 1) failing to drop his hands to his side when he disengages the pitcher's plate (§ 370); (● 2) not having one hand on his side in the set position (§ 377); and

(● 3) stepping to the side of the pitcher's plate during the windup (§ 394)

∞ 392 PITCHER: SPEEDS DELIVERY DURING STEAL ✪

FED: No provision. Treat as in NCAA.

NCAA: During a steal of home the pitcher may speed his delivery as long as he does not alter his "normal pitching sequence and arm motion." (9-3d AR) (See § 387.)

OBR: Point not covered.

> OFF INTERP 333-392: **FITZPATRICK:** Same as NCAA. (phone call to cc, 11/8/01) ✠

∞ 393 PITCHER: STEPS: FLEXES LEG ✪

FED: No provision.

NCAA: A pitcher may not prematurely flex either leg before stepping and throwing directly to first. **PENALTY:** balk. (9-3c-4)

❀ Note 391: The rule truly says "first" and only first. But the rule would be equally in effect for third.

OBR: No provision.

★ 394 PITCHER: STEPS: FORWARD / BACKWARD DURING WINDUP ✪

FED: The pitcher in the windup position with his non-pivot foot may: (● 1) take one step forward; (● 2) one step backward and one step forward; or (● 3) a step to the side. (6-1-2) **PENALTY** for excessive steps: ball / balk. (6-1-2 Pen)

NCAA: The pitcher may take one step backward or sideward and one step forward ***(ADDED)*** with the free foot. (9-1a) **PENALTY:** First offense: warning; subsequent offenses: illegal pitch (ball / balk). (2-42; 9-1a Pen)

OBR: Same as FED. (8.01a; 8.05e Pen)

∞ 395 PITCHER: STEPS: TOWARD BASE: DEFINITION ✪

(See § 370.)

FED: From the pitcher's plate, a left-handed pitcher is "stepping directly toward a base" if he steps to the first-base side of an imaginary line that marks a 45º-angle between the center of the pitcher's plate and a spot midway between home and first. (6.2.4b)

NCAA: The pitcher must step within a 45º-angle measured from the pivot foot to the base where the throw (first) or feint (third) will go. (9-1a-6)

432. ALSO: The non-pivot foot must gain ground in the step. (9-1c)

OBR: Point not covered.

OFF INTERP 334-395: **PBUC:** To step toward a base the pitcher must lift his non-pivot foot and put it down in a new location (some distance) toward the base. {8.6} (See the NCAA text of § 397 for a similar interpretation.) ✠

433. ALSO: OFF INTERP 335-395: **PBUC STAFF:** As long as the pitcher's step gains ground (a different place and toward the base), his step may be "toe first" or "heel first." (phone call to cc, 12/26/01) ✠

AO 22-395: EVANS: "For practical enforcement purposes, stepping directly means stepping within 45° of a direct, straight line to the base. In other words, the pitcher is not stepping more toward a different base than the one to which he is throwing." (8:32)

434. ALSO: The pitcher must step ahead of the throw; *i.e.*, a snap throw FOLLOWED by a step is a balk. (8.01c CMT)

★ 396 PITCHER: STEPS: TOWARD BASE: FROM WIND-UP POSITION ✪

FED: The pitcher may not attempt a pickoff from the windup position. (6-1-2) (See § 373 and 387.) **PENALTY:** balk. (6-1-2 Pen)

> ***(ADDED)*** ❀ Note 392: In 1987, FED, in an unannounced rule change, banned pick-off attempts from the windup position. Appearing at 6-1-2 were these words, still there today, a quarter century later: "With his feet in the wind-up position, the pitcher may only deliver a pitch or step backward off the pitcher's plate." There was some fanfare, though: In the Pitching Restriction POE, they made it clear that "pitch" or "disengage" were the only options. Just so you know, during those 25 years, the FED has never published a case play on this subject!

NCAA: From the windup position the pitcher may attempt a pickoff (9-1a-1b) if he steps directly with his non-pivot foot toward the base before throwing (9-1a-6), gains ground with the step (9-1c), and has not begun any "natural pitching motion" before the step. (9-1a-3)

OBR: Same as NCAA. (8.01a CMT ¶ 2) (See § 394.)

∞ 397 PITCHER: STEPS: TOWARD BASE: JUMP TURN ✪

FED: The jump-turn move to first or third is legal (6-1-3; 6.1.3i), but the pitcher's pivot foot must touch the ground before the throw. (6.1.3i CMT)

NCAA: The jump turn is legal provided the pitcher's non-pivot foot "gains ground" toward the base. (9-3c-5)

OBR: Point not covered.

> OFF INTERP 336-397: **PBUC:** "If a pitcher, while touching his plate, jumps into the air with both feet simultaneously and his non-pivot foot lands in a STEP towards first base (or third) before he throws to that base, he has made a legal move." {8.5f} (See § 395.) ✠

398 PITCHER: STEPS: TOWARD FIRST: FIELDER PLAYING OFF BAG ✪

FED: The pitcher must step "directly toward a base." (6-2-4b) PENALTY: balk. (6-2-4b Pen) **EXCEPT:** When a pitcher steps in the direction of the base and realizes his teammate is not covering, if the pitcher throws directly to the fielder, there is no balk as long as the fielder attached to that base is in the "proximity" of the base. (6.2.4j)

> OFF INTERP 337-398: R1: **HOPKINS:** A first baseman who is 20 feet away from the bag is not in "proximity of the base." If the pitcher throws to him, it is a balk. (Website 2007, #19) ✠

NCAA: Same as FED. (9-3c; 9-3c Pen) **EXCEPT:** If the pitcher throws to the first baseman "playing off the base, a balk shall not be called if the fielder moves toward first base in an attempt to retire the runner." (9-3c-1 AR)

> **435. ALSO:** OFF INTERP 338-398: **FETCHIET:** The pitcher may step and throw to occupied third or second base; however, the throw does not have to be directly to the base or directly to a teammate attempting a put out at that base. (Website 4/18/01, 9-3c) ✠

OBR: The pitcher when throwing while on the pitcher's plate must step "directly toward a base before THROWING to that base." (8.05c) PENALTY: balk. (8.05c Pen) (See § 358.)

❀ Note 393: In FED, the pitcher must step toward a base (second or third) even on a feint. The exact language of the OBR requires a step only on a throw, which is the NCAA practice. (But see § 372 for an official OBR ruling to the contrary.)

436. ALSO: OFF INTERP 339-398: **PBUC:** It is a balk if the pitcher throws to the first baseman who is either in front of or behind the base and obviously not making an attempt to retire the runner. {8.5a} ✠

437. ALSO: OFF INTERP 340-398: **PBUC:** The violation (throwing to a fielder instead of a base) can only occur on a throw to first; the pitcher may throw to the fielder at second and third, even the shortstop with a runner on second, regardless of where the fielder is stationed. {8.5-a} ✠

★ ∞ 399 PITCHER: STEPS: TOWARD SECOND: w/RUNNER ON FIRST ✪

FED: No provision. Treat as in OBR.

NCAA: Point not covered.

(ADDED) OFF INTERP 341-399: **PARONTO:** Same as OBR. (email to cc, 12/28/11) ✠

(ADDED) ❀ Note 394: Paronto: "I believe an umpire can see when a pitcher intends o throw to first when his initial leg movement is in the direction of the base. For that pitcher to then throw to second, he will have to change the direction of his lead leg from going toward first to going toward second. There will be a **STOP** or hesitation in the initial direction of the pitcher's leg. That would be a balk."

OBR: It is not a balk if the pitcher with a runner on first "makes a complete turn, without hesitating toward first, and throws to second." (8.05c CMT ¶ 2)

Play 214-399: R1. Right-handed F1 in the set position. As he separates his hands, the defense yells: "He's going!" The pitcher swings his pivot foot toward first and continues to spin to throw to second. R1 is NOT going. *Ruling:* Legal.

❀ Note 395: Though all three books say it is legal to feint to second without throwing, that would not be true for this spin move. It's not a feint to second. It's a "throw to first" that simply winds up at second.

★ ∞ 400 PITCHER: STEPS OFF PITCHER'S PLATE: WITH WRONG FOOT: WINDUP ✪

FED: The pitcher must step back from the pitcher's plate with his pivot foot first. (6-1-2) **PENALTY:** balk. (6-1-2 Pen)

NCAA: Same as FED. (9-1a-3; 9-1a-1-7 Pen)

OBR: The pitcher must step back from the pitcher's plate with his pivot foot first. (8.01a CMT ¶ 2-3) **PENALTY: NONE PROVIDED!**

EXCEPT: OFF INTERP 342-400: **PBUC:** Same as FED: balk. {8.5k} ✠

❀ Note 396-400: Umpires are always amazed when they discover that one of their cherished balks **AIN'T** a balk, according to "The Book." Just read through the list at 8.05 to understand that, before the PBUC ruling, the umpire **SHOULD** have simply told the pitcher who stepped off with the wrong foot: "Don't do that." (See Note 367-370 for the complete list of "don't do's.")
(ADDED) ❀ Note 397: Take your pick: "You can't teach an old dog a new trick" or "You're never too old to learn." I pick door two. Note 396 above entered the BRD in 2002. I was so smart. Right? Now comes Hunter Wendelstedt to say: "Carl, let me teach you a new trick." It is a balk when the pitcher steps back with his non-pivot foot **IF HE DOES NOT PITCH**. Hunter says F1 has committed a balk for "starting and stopping." (HW/129) I take some consolation in the knowledge that PBUC was also paddling along with me in my boat since they felt the need for OFF INTERP 342 [this section].

401 PITCHER STOPS IN: SET POSITION: COMPLETE AND DISCERNIBLE ✪

FED: POE 2008: The pitcher must come to a "complete stop, one that is clearly recognizable." (6.1.1h) A "change of direction is not considered an acceptable stop." (6-1-3) **PENALTY:** ball / balk. (6-1-3 Pen) (See § 402.)

438. ALSO: OFF INTERP 343-401: **RUMBLE:** The discernible stop is required with or without runners. (*News* #10, 3/89) ✠

439. ALSO: OFF INTERP 344-401: **RUMBLE:** The pitcher may not move his feet **TOWARD** the plate until he has come to his stop. (*News* #16, 3/89) ✠

440. ALSO: OFF INTERP 345-401: **RUMBLE:** The pitcher may not have his non-pivot foot in the air when he comes to his stop. (*News* #26, 4/89) ✠

NCAA: POE 1992, 2002, 2004 [set position]: Same as FED: The pitcher may deliver from the set position "after coming to a complete and discernible stop with his entire body." (9-1b-2) **PENALTY:** balk. (9-1b Pen) (See § 402.)

❀ Note 398: "[A]nd discernible" has a checkered history: 1988: OBR adopts the language, subject to approval by the players' union. (I have a mint copy of the *Sporting News* edition. It cost

$1.77.) 1989: FED adds the phrase; 1989: The MLP union votes down the proposal, so the language gets dropped from the OBR. 2003: NCAA adopts the phrase — **BUT DOESN'T TELL ANYBODY!** That's right: There was no announcement of that [startling] "editorial" change.

441. ALSO: The pitcher does not have to stop with the bases empty. (9-1b-2 AR)

OBR: When using the set position, the pitcher must come to a "complete" stop. (8.05m) **PENALTY:** balk. (8.05m Pen)

EXCEPT: The pitcher does not have to stop with the bases empty. (8.01b CMT)

442. ALSO: If the pitcher deliberately attempts to catch the batter off guard, it is a quick pitch. **PENALTY:** ball. (8.01b CMT)

> **443. ALSO:** OFF INTERP 346-401: **FITZPATRICK:** While there is no time-frame connected with the "stop," the rules committee is adamant: The stop must be *complete.* (email to cc, 11/15/00) ❀

❀ Note 399: Until 1964 the pitcher was required to stop for one full second. Believe me, life was tough for the OBR umpire in those distant days.

402 PITCHER: STOPS IN: SET POSITION: GLOVE BELOW CHIN ✪

FED: With or without runners in the set position (see OFF INTERP 343-401), the pitcher must "come to a complete and discernible stop ... with his glove at or below his chin." (6-1-3; 6.1.3m and n) **PENALTY:** ball / balk. (6-1-3 Pen) (See § 401.)

NCAA: If the pitcher adopts the set position, **WITH RUNNERS ON BASE** he must stop "in front of his body." (9-1b) (See § 401.)

OBR: Same as NCAA 9-1b. (8.01b)

★ 403 PITCHER: STOPS IN: SET POSITION: MORE THAN ONCE ✪

FED: The pitcher may pause in the set position only once. (6-1-3; 6.1.3f) **PENALTY:** ball / balk. (6-1-3 Pen)

NCAA: Same as FED 6-1-3. (9-3j) ***(ADDED)*** **PENALTY:** ball / balk. (9-3j Pen)

OBR: Point not covered. (See § 401.)

(ADDED) OFF INTERP 347-403: **WENDELSTEDT:** The pitcher may stop only once; that is, the "double set" is illegal as in FED and NCAA. (P175/134) ✠

(EDITED) ❀ Note 400: Some argue that the "double-set" is prohibited by 8.05a: When the pitcher moves after his first stop to the second "stop" of his double-set, that second movement is a "motion naturally associated with his pitch." Further, if the double-set is **REALLY** prohibited by 8.05a, why did the OBR rules committee feel the need to add such a prohibition in the proposed pitching change (voted down by the players' union) of 1988? In a phone call the summer of 2007, Jim Evans said that "The Book" states the obvious: "Carl, it says the pitcher shall come to **A** stop. Doesn't 'a' mean just one?" Hard to argue with a Texan who was on the UT debate team!

(NEW) 404 PITCHER: STOPS IN: WINDUP POSITION ✪

FED: The pitcher **MAY NOT PAUSE** in the windup position once he has moved any part of his body such as he habitually uses in his delivery. (6-2-4d) **PENALTY:** Balk. (6-2-4; Website #20, 2011)

❀ Note 401: The FED OFF INTERP simply affirmed that the rule had not changed in spite of what people see on television. Once the pitcher begins his delivery, "he must continue his motion without interruption or alteration." Compare NCAA : The pitcher must continue his motion "without interruption or alteration." (9-1a) They harmonize. Or so it seems. But ....

NCAA: A pitcher **MAY PAUSE** during his delivery from the windup position without penalty. (9-1a AR 2)

❀ Note 402: The rationale for the change explained that in "some parts of the country" when the pitcher paused during the windup, umpires were calling a balk. Interesting, for those were the umpires enforcing the rule: "From this [windup] position, any natural movement associated with the delivery of the ball to the batter commits the pitcher to pitch **WITHOUT INTERRUPTION OR ALTERATION.**" (9-1a) But, as the Jersey boys say: "Fuhgeddaboudit!"

OBR: Same as NCAA 9-1a AR 2. (8.01a)

OFF INTERP 348-404: **WENDELSTEDT:** A brief pause in the windup "is not enough to be considered a 'start and stop.'" (P150/130) ✠

❀ Note 403: Before you ignore the brief "start and stop" move in any OBR league, check with your umpire-in-chief to see whether officials want to allow the "Japanese pause."

❀ Note 404: While this is anew section, the material was covered in the 2011 edition in § 386.

★ 405 PITCHER: THROWS AT BATTER ✪

FED: The pitcher may not "intentionally **PITCH** close to a batter." (6-2-3) **PENALTY:** warning or ejection. (6-2-3 Pen)

(ADDED) ❀ Note 405: From the beginning of the FED until 2009, the emphasized word above was "throw."

NCAA: POE 1990, 1992, 1993, 1996, 1997, 1998, 1999 [pitcher throws at batter]: The pitcher may not "intentionally pitch at the batter." (9-2g) **PENALTY:** The umpire warns the pitcher and both coaches that any pitcher for either team who commits the next offense will be ejected, along with his head c coach. (9-2g Pen) (See § 141.) In unusual circumstances the umpire may: (● 1) eject the pitcher without warning; (● 2) warn both teams before the game; or (● 3) eject the coach without warning if that is "appropriate." (9-2g Pen 1; 9-2g Pen 2)

444. ALSO: A pitcher ejected for throwing at a batter is considered a "suspended" player, subject to the penalties under the provisions of the fight rule. (9-2g Pen 3) **PENALTY:** First offense: ejection and suspension from the team's next four regularly scheduled games. Second offense by the same pitcher in the same season: ejection and suspension from the team's next eight regularly scheduled games. Third offense by the same pitcher in the same season: ejection and suspension for the remainder of the season, including postseason play. (5-16d-1, -2 and -3) (See § 246.)

❀ Note 406: Suspension for eight games? Isn't that harsh? It would be for a position player. Since it's a pitcher, he's going to miss only two starts — unless he's the hard-hitting P/DH, when he will likely learn a well-deserved lesson.

445. ALSO: When a pitcher is removed from the mound but remains in the game, if he later ejected for unsportsmanlike conduct, it is for that game only. (2-25 AR 5)

446. ALSO: If a coach has been warned about a "beanball" incident, when his pitcher is judged to have violated the rule again, the coach is also ejected and suspended for the next regularly scheduled [one] game. (5-16d-4)

OBR: Same as NCAA 9-2g Pen. (8.02d) **EXCEPT:** No provision exists for an umpire suspending the pitcher or his coach. (See § 141.)

∞ 406 PITCHER: TIME OF PITCH: DEFINITION ✪

FED: The time of the pitch occurs:

(● 1) in the SET POSITION: when the pitcher separates his hands before delivering; or
(● 2) in the WINDUP POSITION: "when the pitcher
(a) first starts any movement of his arms(s) or leg(s) after stepping onto the pitcher's plate with his hands already together in front of his body;
(b) with both arms at his side, first starts any movement with both arms or leg(s) prior to the pitch; or
(c) with either hand in front of the body and the other hand at his side, after bringing his hands together, first starts any movement of his arm(s) or leg(s) prior to the pitch." (2-28-3; 2.28.3a through c; 2.28.3 CMT)
(See § 376 and 387.)

NCAA: Same as FED. (2-78) (See § 294.)

OBR: Point not covered.

> OFF INTERP 349-406: **PBUC:** Same as FED 2-28-3. {6.7} ✠

⁎ *Play 215-406:* R1, R3: As the pitcher begins his preliminary stretch in the set position, R1 breaks for second. F1, fearing either a balk or a score, makes no attempt to play on R1. Instead, he comes to his complete stop. Before he begins his motion to deliver, R1 touches second. B1 fouls off the pitch. *Ruling:* R1 may keep second, for he had touched the base before TOP.

★ 407 PITCHER: WARM-UP THROWS: EXCEED LIMIT ✪

FED: Point not covered.

> OFF INTERP 350-407: **RUMBLE:** At the beginning of an inning, the pitcher may not: (● 1) exceed the limit of five warm-up throws; or (● 2) take an extra toss after being warned. **PENALTY:** In (1), a ball; in (2), ejection. (*News* #4, 3/91) ✠

NCAA: ***(EDITED)*** At the beginning of an inning, the pitcher may have five warm-up tosses **TO THE CATCHER**. (9-2i) **PENALTY** for each toss: The umpire will award a "ball" to the batter. (9 2i Pen) (See § 408. See particularly Play 216-410 and the Note following.)

❀ Note 407: Observe that only warm-up tosses to the catcher count toward the limit of five. The catcher is on base when the half inning ends. The pitcher sprints to the mound and starts warming up with the third baseman. Those tosses don't count! (In Youth ball, though, I give the catcher / pitcher two warm-up tosses after the catcher finally gets to the plate. Reason: My Youth League games are generally timed.

OBR: Point not covered.

OFF INTERP 351-407: **FITZPATRICK:** No penalty is provided for pitchers who exceed the number of warm-up throws permitted by the rules. The umpire will warn – and then eject – any pitcher who repeatedly ignores requests to follow the regulations. (phone call to cc, 11/8/01) ✠

★ 408 PITCHER: WARM-UP THROWS: LOSS OF ✪

FED: No provision.

NCAA: After a reliever has been summoned from the bullpen, he "must proceed immediately to the mound." Any "additional pitches thrown in the bullpen will be subtracted from the eight preparatory pitches permitted on the mound." (9-4b AR 2) (See § 407 and 410.) ***(ADDED)* 447. ALSO:** If a pitcher is injured and must leave the mound, the reliever "SHALL" take all warm-up tosses from the mound. (9-4b AR 2)

OBR: Point not covered.

OFF INTERP 352-408: **MLBUM:** After a reliever has been summoned from the bullpen, any extra throws he makes while still there "may be" subtracted from the allowable eight he may make from the mound. An habitual or blatant offender is subject to ejection. (7.2) ✠

409 PITCHER: WARM-UP THROWS: TAKEN ON DIAMOND ✪

FED: No provision.

NCAA: If the bullpen mound is not regulation, the visiting coach must first ask the home team coach to correct the situation. (See § 224.) If the problem is not resolved, the coach may request the UIC to allow his starting pitcher time to warm up on the home team practice mound. The pitcher will have a maximum of 20 minutes, which shall be within the last 30 minutes before the pregame meeting. (4-3e AR) (See § 418 and 419.)

OBR: Point not covered.

OFF INTERP 353-409: **PBUC:** The home team pitcher may not warm up on the mound before the game; instead, he must use the bullpen mound, just like the visitor's hurler. {8.2} ✠

410 PITCHER: WARM-UP THROWS: TIME AND NUMBER ALLOWED: RELIEVER ✪

FED: POE 1983: A relief pitcher entering at the start of a half inning is allowed eight throws in one minute, timed from the third out of the previous half inning. (6.2.2d) A reliever who enters to pitch during the middle of a half inning may have eight throws with no time limit. (6.2.2f, 1990 ed)

❀ Note 408: The FED lists this under events that slow the [POE 2009] "pace of the game." These days, everybody wants the game over quickly so they can get home to the TV football cast.

448. ALSO: OFF INTERP 354-410: **RUMBLE:** If the new pitcher enters the game while his team is on offense, when he takes his place on the mound in the next half inning, he will have eight pitches with no time limit. (*News* #10, 3/91) ✠

❀ Note 409: Unfortunately, since projected substitutions are not allowed (§ 497), the umpire will not know when a "pitcher" enters the game on offense. The point: The umpire must be willing to recognize (and proceed accordingly) that the player came in on offense, which may have reduced his chances for warmup during the previous half-inning.

NCAA: POE 2001, 2002, 2009: Any relief pitcher has one minute to make eight throws. (9-2i) **PENALTY:** For each excess toss, the umpire shall award a ball to the batter. (9-2i Pen) (See § 408.) **EXCEPT:** Following ejection of the pitcher, a reliever must have "adequate" time to warm up, just as if the pitcher had been injured. (5-16d AR 2)

449. ALSO: During a pitching change, the umpire should pay particular attention to enforcing 5-2c. [See § 116: Players must remain inside their dugouts.] (5-2c AR)

✻ *Play 216-410:* **NCAA only.** R3, R2, 1 out. The coach brings in a reliever, and everyone expects an intentional walk to the clean-up hitter, who's 3 for 3. F1 finishes his eight tosses and throws a ninth. The umpire says: "Ball one! You get just eight." The pitcher says: "I'm not ready." He throws a tenth, an eleventh, a twelfth — and, per 9-2i, the clean-up batter is walked: Bases loaded, the double-play is in order.

❀ Note 410: The play illustrates something that's known as the law of unintended consequences. The NCAA wants to prevent the pitcher from taking extra tosses. So the batter gets a ball for each extra throw. Intended consequence: The offense benefits from the infraction. But the smart coach figured out he could intentionally walk the batter without risking a passed ball or wild pitch. Unintended consequence: The defense benefits from the infraction. (See 376 and 407.)

OBR: Same as NCAA. **EXCEPT:** A league may adopt provisions for fewer than eight. (8.03) *See ¶8.*

411 PITCHER: WARM-UP THROWS: TIME AND NUMBER ALLOWED: STARTER ✪

FED: Before the game the starting pitcher may have eight warm-up throws within one minute, timed from the first throw.
(6-2-2c Ex; 6.2.2c, 1991 ed)
450. ALSO: Between half innings the current pitcher has one minute, timed from the third out of the previous half inning, to make five warm-up throws. The umpire may extend the number of throws because of bad weather or injury. (6-2-2c Ex) (See § 388.)

❀ Note 411: BRD recommends: In the first inning allow both FED pitchers plenty of time to warmup on the mound; 10-12 throws (more on coolish days) is about right. Of course, those additional warmups are essential for the visiting pitcher, who is getting acquainted with the mound.

NCAA: A pitcher may make five throws with no time limit **AT THE BEGINNING OF AN INNING.** (9-2i) (See § 408 and 410.)

❀ Note 412: I'll bet a dollar to a penny you don't enforce this rule before the first inning. Strange, but the NCAA is the only book that doesn't set a limit (eight) for the starter.

OBR: Any pitcher has one minute to make eight throws. A league may adopt provisions for fewer than eight. (8.03) *See ¶8.*

412 PITCHER: WINDUP POSITION: MOVES TO SET POSITION WITHOUT DISENGAGING PITCHER'S PLATE ✪

FED: The pitcher may change from one pitching position to another only by first stepping clearly off the pitcher's plate with his pivot foot. He may not slide forward from the windup to the set. (6-1-2; 6.1.3k)
PENALTY: ball / balk. (6-1-2 Pen)

NCAA: POE 1992, 1993 [windup position]: The pitcher must change from the windup to the set by disengaging the rubber. (9-1a-5)
PENALTY: ***(ADDED)*** With the bases empty, "the umpire shall rule no pitch." With runners on base, balk. (9-1a-5 Pen)

OBR: Same as FED. **EXCEPT:** **PENALTY:** balk. (8.01a CMT-3)

❀ Note 413: Since OBR does not list the movement as an illegal pitch, like NCAA there is no penalty if the pitcher does it with the bases empty. It is important to note that CMT ¶ 3 describes the

ONLY violation of 8.01 that is a balk not listed in 8.05. Thus, umpires who say there are only 14 balk moves in the OBR (letter [I] has two) are short by one.

413 PREGAME MEETING: GROUND RULES ESTABLISHED ✪

FED: The "umpires" shall establish ground rules if the teams cannot agree. (4-1-2; 4.1.2a) The "UIC" must announce those rules. (1-1-2; 10-2-3a) (See § 27 and 417.)
451. ALSO: The ground rules may not supersede the printed rules. (4-1-2; 4.1.2a; 4.1.2b)
452. ALSO: Some possible ground rules and / or problems are now in the book. (4-1-2 a through e)

NCAA: If teams cannot agree, the "umpires" will determine ground rules: same as FED. (4-5) (See § 124.)
453. ALSO: It is recommended that the ground rules be posted in each dugout. (4-5)

OBR: Following disagreement between teams, the UIC establishes ground rules, which may not conflict with the *Official Baseball Rules.* (3.13)

★ 414 PREGAME MEETING: HEAD COACHES MUST ATTEND ✪

FED: POE 2008, 2009: The head coach, if available, must attend the pregame conference. (3-2-4; 1.1.2c 2010 ed.) **PENALTY:** For failure to attend the coach is restricted to the dugout. (3-2-4 Pen; 3.2.4b)

454. ALSO: OFF INTERP 355-414: **HOPKINS:** With the pregame conference ready to begin, the home team head coach is in the bullpen and refuses to attend. He sends his assistant coach and a captain to be present. The assistant coach provides his team's lineup and verifies to the umpire-in-chief that his team is properly equipped. RULING: The umpire-in-chief will accept the assistant coach's verification and conclude all needed activity at the pregame conference. The head coach will be restricted to the dugout for the remainder of the game. (Website 2008 #15) ✠

455. ALSO: A coach caught in traffic misses the meeting: no penalty. (3.2.4a; Website 2008, #16)
456. ALSO: A head coach treating an injured player on the bus is excused, but a coach who is finishing field maintenance or supervising his pitcher in the bullpen is restricted. (3.2.4c)

NCAA: "The head coach, during ***(EDITED)*** the first game of a weekend series or any non-conference game, must attend the pregame conference." (4-4)

OBR: ***(EDITED)*** The pregame meeting includes the umpires and the head coaches or their "designees." (4.01a and b) *See ¶ 8.*

415 PREGAME MEETING: LINEUP: BECOMES OFFICIAL ✪

FED: Lineups become official after they are exchanged, verified, and then accepted by the UIC during the pregame meeting. (1-1-2; 4-1-3; 3.1.1k) (See § 52.)

NCAA: Lineups are official when the umpire hands copies to each coach. (4-4a)

OBR: Same as NCAA. (4.01d)

416 PREGAME MEETING: LINEUP: ERRORS CORRECTED BY UMPIRE ✪

FED: No provision. (See § 465.)

NCAA: The umpire shall call attention to obvious errors in the lineup. Examples: Lineup does not include all nine players or the pitcher when there is no DH listed. (4-4a Nt)

OBR: Same as NCAA. Other examples: two players with the same last name but no identifying initial. (4.01 CMT) (See § 465 and 499.)

★ 417 PREGAME MEETING: SUBJECTS TO DISCUSS ✪

FED: POE 1985, 1986, 1987, 1988, 1989, 1995, 2000, 2001, 2002, 2008, 2012: The pregame "conference" shall include the exchange and examination of lineups and a discussion of the ground rules. Umpires must ***(EDITED)*** "receive verification" from both **HEAD** coaches that their players are "legally and properly equipped." (4-1-3b; 2-10-2) The game may not begin until both coaches verify the legal equipment. (4.1.3a) (See § 137, 413 and 416.)

❀ Note 414: Rule 2-10-2 still speaks about legal and proper equipment. Rule 4-1-3a mentions only proper equipment. The fact is, FED forgot to update 2-10-2 when they added massive revisions to 4-1-3. They will rectify that next year, I'm sure.

457. ALSO: POE 2005, 2006, 2007, 2008, 2009: The UIC will "emphasize to the coaches and captains that all participants are expected to exhibit good sporting behavior throughout the game(s)." (2-10-2; 4-1-3a; 4.1.3b)

(ADDED) ❀ Note 415: In your rulebook 4-1-3 a is shaded to show it's changed since last year. It hasn't.

NCAA: The umpires will remind coaches of: (• 1) the batter's box rule (§ 45); (• 2) dugout control (§ 116); (• 3) bench jockeying (§ 119); and (• 4) slide rules (§ 330). (4-4b) (See also § 179; 211; 289; 324.)

OBR: Though the book mandates no subject matter, a strict sequence of events exists for the pregame meeting: (• 1) Home team's manager gives lineup to UIC; (• 2) visiting team's manager presents his lineup; (• 3) the umpire inspects the cards and then tenders a copy to each skipper. (4.01) (See § 376, 415 and 419.)

418 PREGAME MEETING: TIME TO HOLD ✪

FED: Umpires and coaches meet "approximately five minutes" before game time. (2-10-2) (See § 116.)

NCAA: The pregame meeting is 10 minutes before game time. (4-4)

OBR: Same as FED. (4.01) (See § 419.)

★ 419 PREGAME MEETING: UMPIRES IN CHARGE OF GAME ✪

FED: Umpire jurisdiction begins when the umpires arrive inside the "confines of the field" and ends when they leave the field after the game. (10-1-2; 8.2.2j; 10.1.2a; 10.1.2b) (See Play 77-488.)

(ADDED) **IMPORTANT: SEE 254. AND 255. ALSOs, § 246.**

❀ Note 416-419: The current interpretation is that umpire jurisdiction begins when the crew goes inside the confines of the field with the **INTENTION OF REMAINING UNTIL THE GAME ENDS.**

❀ Note 417: Like his college brother, the high school umpire is required to enforce some rules before he is in charge of the game, namely, forbidding a game participant who is crouching without proper equipment from warming up a player (pitcher). (See § 194.)

NCAA: The UIC is in charge after the lineups, ***(ADDED)*** – now official – have been exchanged. (4-4a)

❀ Note 418-419: There are times when the college umpire is not in charge of the game and yet is required by the rules to enforce an edict. (See § 114, 217 and 409. See also § 415.)

458. ALSO: Jurisdiction on personal confrontations and conduct toward the officiating staff "begins when the umpires enter the game site and ends when the umpires have left the game site." (3-6k) (See § 246.)

OBR: The umpires are in charge of the field after the home team's batting order has been delivered to the UIC at home plate. (4.01e) (See § 418.)

459. ALSO: OFF INTERP 356-419: **PBUC:** The OBR umpire is in charge of the game after the batting order has been delivered, but the game does not begin until he says, "Play." {5.10} ✠

❀ Note 419: OFF INTERP 356 above has impact on a game stopped before the first pitch.

⁎ *Play 217-419:* **OBR only.** Consider the following scenario: (1) Pregame meeting occurs; (2) lineups are exchanged; (3) buckets of rain come down, but the home team manager wants to play; (4) pitcher, batter, ump are ready; (5) the UIC says, "Play. Now, play is suspended!" The question: Will the lineups tendered at that pregame meeting be official (and required) when the game is resumed?
Ruling: No. The game is not suspended; it is postponed.

420 PROTEST: ALLOWED ✪

FED: Protests are "optional" with state associations. A protested game is included in the official individual- and team-average statistics except there is no winning or losing pitcher recorded if the game is not regulation. (4-5) (See § 424.)

NCAA: For regular season contests each conference "should" adopt protest procedures. (5-13a)

OBR: Each league "shall" adopt protest procedures. (4.19) *See ¶ 8.*

∞ 421 PROTEST: JUDGMENT CALLS EXCLUDED ✪

FED: Where protests are allowed, they shall be accepted only for situations dealing with rules 1 through 9. (4-5; 4.5.1) (See § 43 and 239.)

❀ Note 420: The point of the edict: Judgment calls are excluded from protest.

460. ALSO: OFF INTERP 357-421: **RUMBLE:** A videotape of a game may not be used in deciding a protest. (*News* #6, 3/89) (See § 220.) ✠

NCAA: A protest is not allowed on a judgment call but only on the alleged misapplication of a rule. (5-13a) (See § 506.)

OBR: Same as NCAA. (4.19)

422 PROTEST: PLAY IN QUESTION AFFECTS GAME ✪

FED: Point not covered.

OFF INTERP 358-422: **NFHS:** Questions about protests must be decided by the state association. (*News* #25, 3/76) ✠

NCAA: No protest will be considered and no replay of any part of a game allowed unless the play in question "directly" affected the outcome of the contest. (5-13d)

OBR: Same as NCAA. (4.19)

423 PROTEST: PROCEDURE ✪

FED: Reports of protests must be submitted "using a prescribed procedure" (4-5) that includes reporting "all related conditions at the time of the protested play" to "an umpire." Following a protest, the umpire shall inform the coach of the other team and the official scorer. (10-2-3i)

NCAA: When a coach wishes to lodge a protest, the protest must be made to the UIC, who shall: (● 1) accept the protest; (● 2) inform each coach, the official scorer, and the public address announcer that the game is being played under protest; and (● 3 make a note of the game situation at the time of the protest. (5-13c)
461. ALSO: Protests involving non-conference teams will be decided by the NCAA rules editor. (5-13b)
462. ALSO: The resolution of a protest has no effect on any suspensions growing out of a disputed play. (2-25 AR 1) (See § 166.)

> ✻ *Play 218-423:* **NCAA only.** Eighth inning, score tied. Visiting B1 tries for an inside-the-park home run. Contact occurs as the catcher is fielding the throw. The force of the collision causes F2 to drop the ball, but he retrieves it and tags B1 before he touches the plate. The umpire judges the contact was not malicious, but he calls "That's obstruction!" and awards B1 home. F2 curses the umpire and then grabs B1, pulling him forcefully to the ground. The umpire ejects and suspends F2 for fighting. The home team coach pleads that the umpire has misapplied the obstruction rule. When the umpire sticks with his decision, the coach lodges a formal protest. Home loses the game by one run.
>
> *Ruling:* F2 was not guilty of obstruction under the 2011 statutes. Since the collision was not malicious, B1 should have been out. The protest is upheld. Since the play definitely

figured in the outcome of the game, it will be replayed from the moment of the collision, with B1's run canceled. While F2 will argue truthfully that the umpire's erroneous decision led to the fight, that is irrelevant. He's going to serve his one-game suspension.

OBR: Point not covered.

OFF INTERP 359-423: **PBUC:** Same as NCAA 5-13c. {5.14} ✠

463. ALSO: OFF INTERP 360-423: **PBUC:** After the protest is lodged, the umpires must "confer as a crew, making certain their ruling is correct." {5.14} ✠

❀ Note 421: Asking umpires to confer is popular with rules committees these days. (See § 509.)

★ 424 PROTEST: TIME TO LODGE ✪

FED: Protests must be lodged with the UIC at the time of the incident and before the next pitch to a batter of either team. (10-2-3i-1) (See § 239 and 420.)
464. ALSO: If the protest concerns a game-ending play, it must be lodged before the umpires leave the field. (10-2-3i-1; 10.2.2a and b) (See § 15.)

NCAA: A protest must be made before "play is resumed." On a game-ending play, the protest must be registered before "all fielders have left fair territory." (5-13b) (See § 423.)

OBR: A protest must be made before the next pitch, play, or attempted play. A protest on a game-ending play may be filed until 12 noon the next day. (4.19 CMT) *See ¶ 8.*

⁂ *Play 219-422:* Bases loaded, 2 out, full count. The umpire rules that B1's half swing is ball four, forcing in a run. The defense asks for an appeal, but the UIC refuses to check with his partner. The defensive coach vigorously argues and is ejected. With a live ball the pitcher now picks off R1. The teams change sides. Before the pitcher delivers, out comes the assistant coach to file an official protest. *Ruling:* In FED, if protests are permitted by the state association, it must be accepted: There has not been a pitch to a batter of either team. Such a protest will be denied because the FED umpire is not required to seek help on a half-swing (§ 74). In NCAA, play resumed, so it is too late to protest. In OBR, the defense played on a runner. It's also too late. It is likely the protests would be upheld at the upper levels.

★ 425 RUNNER: ABANDONS ATTEMPT TO RUN BASES ✪

FED: A runner is out if, **AFTER TOUCHING FIRST**, he abandons his attempt to touch the next base. The umpire must judge whether a runner heading for the dugout or his defensive position is abandoning his efforts to run the bases. No rule provides for non-removal of a force for that out. (8-4-2p; 8.4.2c)

NCAA: Same as FED: **EXCEPT:** A runner heading for his dugout or defensive position is **AUTOMATICALLY CHARGED** with abandonment. The ball remains alive. (8-5c)

OBR: Same as FED; that is, determining abandonment is left to umpire judgment. (7.08a-2) The ball remains alive. (7.08a-2 CMT)

> ⁎ *Play 220-425:* **OBR only.** R1, R3, 1 out, 2-2, top of the ninth. B1 hits weakly to the second baseman, who swipes at R1, then throws to first in time for what he thinks is an inning-ending double play. R3, running on contact, touches the plate before the "tag" of R1. The umpire calls R1 safe, but the runner, thinking he is out, heads for his position in center field. Now the umpire calls out R1. *Ruling:* ***(EDITED)*** R1 is out for abandonment. That out should be signaled by the umpire, who will also score the run. But if the defense appeals, the out at second becomes a force out, and the run will not count.

∞ 426 RUNNER: ESTABLISHES BASE PATH ✪

FED: When a play is being made on a runner, he establishes his base path as a direct line between his position and the base he is trying for. (8-4-2a-2) (See § 98.)

> **465. ALSO:** OFF INTERP 361-426: **HOPKINS:** The "skunk in the outfield" is legal: A runner may lead off any way he likes toward the next base and is not guilty of an infraction unless he uses more than three feet on either side of his base path to avoid a tag. (Website 2005, #16) ✠

NCAA: Same as FED 8-4-2a-2. (8-5a) **EXCEPT:** No NCAA provision for the "skunk in the outfield."

OBR: Same as FED 8-4-2a-2. (7.08a)

> **466. ALSO:** OFF INTERP 362-426: **FITZPATRICK:** As long as a runner has safely acquired a base, he may lead off toward the next base however he pleases. At first base, R1 might, for example, legally step 25 to 30 feet into the outfield and away from the bag. (phone call to cc, 11/8/01) ✠

❀ Note 422: The black-letter rules are now the same about establishing the baseline. But FED and OBR have official interpretations about the "skunk in the outfield." The NCAA, wisely, ignores that Youth League junk.

⁑ *Play 221-426:* R3: B1 walks. As soon as he touches first, he hustles toward the outfield, stopping a good 30 feet from first. Obviously, he hopes the defense will play on him, which will give R3 a chance to score. *Ruling:* Legal: He places himself in jeopardy, and he is not attempting to avoid a tag.

★ 427 RUNNER: HELMET: MANDATORY ✪

FED: Each batter-runner, runner, and retired runner during a live ball must wear a helmet with double-earflaps until he reaches his bench, dugout, or a dead-ball area. (1-5-1) **PENALTY:** The ball is delayed dead, followed by a team warning / ejection. (1-5-1 Pen; 5-1-2e; 1.5.1a and b; 8.4.1d, 1993 ed) (See § 78, 428 and 432.)

NCAA: The runner must obtain a proper, double-earflap helmet. (1-15a) **PENALTY** for refusal: The runner is ejected. (1-15a Pen) (See § 78.)

OBR: ***(EDITED)*** All major league players must wear a single or double ear flap helmet. (1.16c) **PENALTY:** The umpire will direct the ***(EDITED)*** player to comply with the rule. If he does not, he will be ejected. (1.16 CMT) (See § 78.) *See ¶ 8.*

★ 428 RUNNER: HELMET: REMOVED: PENALTY ✪

FED: A runner may not deliberately remove his helmet during a live ball unless the ball goes dead without being touched or, after having been touched, goes directly to a dead-ball area. (1-5-1) **PENALTY:** The ball is delayed dead (5-1-2e); team warning / ejection. (1-5-1 Pen; 1.5.1d) (See § 285 and 427.)

NCAA: Point not covered.

> ***(ADDED)*** OFF INTERP 363-428: **PARONTO:** If the player deliberately removes his helmet during live action, he should be warned that on a subsequent violation, he may be ejected. (email to cc, 12/23/11) ✠

OBR: No provision.

★ ∞ 429 RUNNER: NO BODY CONTROL ON BASE ✪

FED: No provision ***(EDITED)*** Treat as in NCAA.

NCAA: Point not covered.

(ADDED) OFF INTERP 364-429: **PARONTO:** "A legal tag that is forcefully applied to a runner can result in an out. When a runner is going into a base without body control and a forceful tag knocks him from the base, he is out." (email to cc, 12/23/11) ✠

OBR: Point not covered.

OFF INTERP 365-429: **FITZPATRICK:** If a runner going into a base does not have body control, he is out when a hard tag knocks him off the base. (phone call to cc, 11/8/01) ✠

⁂ *Play 222-429:* B1 rounds first too far and then hustles back, standing. As he reaches the base, he loses balance. The first baseman's hard swipe tag pushes the runner from the bag. *Ruling:* B1 is out.

❀ Note 423: A very similar play caused a great deal of trouble in the 1991 World Series between Minnesota and Atlanta. Here's how www.baseballlibrary.com puts it: "[Kent Hrbek's] most memorable contribution during the series came in Game Two, when he snuffed out a Braves' rally with a bit of first base chicanery. After singling Lonnie Smith to third base with two outs and Atlanta down by a run in the top of the third, Ron Gant scrambled to beat a throw back to first base. Although Gant reached the bag safely, he was struggling to keep his balance when Hrbek subtly pushed his leg off the base and applied a tag. Gant was called out, ending the inning."

Permit me to quote from my book *The Usual Suspects* (available from Officiating.com), where *I* quote from *Baseball Primer*: "[Baseball Primer's Craig] Burley points out there is no provision in the written rules that says a fielder can't bump a runner off the bag":

> I understand that it is commonly believed that there is, but there is not. It's not a rule and so there is only a general practice, [but] there is no clarity. A hard slap-tag that pushes a runner off the bag (when he had just touched it) can easily be called an out.'
>
> This is a classic example of a situation that is not covered by the *Official Baseball Rules*. ...Rather, it is an example of 'practical enforcement' – a rule that is applied in general practice — in true-to-life game situations even though it is not specifically spelled out by the rules. Such a ruling, which would allow the runner to remain safe after being pushed or bumped off the bag by the fielder's body, has been applied in a practical sense for as long as I've been watching baseball (which is since the early 1970s). And that's really the common sense approach. Otherwise, fielders would be trying to push runners off the base at every opportunity, making baseball the equivalent of bumper cars or block-and-tackle football.

First base umpire Drew Coble ruled that Gant, who didn't slide on the play, had come off the bag because of the momentum caused by his awkward stand-up return to the bag. "He lunged into the bag," Coble told Rob Rains of *USA Today Baseball Weekly*. "His momentum was carrying him toward the first base dugout. When he did that, he began to switch feet. He tried to pick up one foot and bring the other one down… In my judgment, [Gant's] momentum carried him over the top of Hrbek." In essence, Coble was saying that he would have called Gant safe if he felt that Hrbek's body had forced him off the bag, but he called him out because he felt that the natural momentum of Gant's twisting body had resulted in his separation from the base.

[Bruce Markesen, Manager of Program Presentations at the National Baseball Hall of Fame and Museum in Cooperstown, 11 April, 2003, as published in *Baseball Primer*.]

430 RUNNER: OUTS ACCIDENTAL
ALL CODES NOW AGREE: TEXT DELETED,2005.

★ 431 RUNNER: PASSES PRECEDING RUNNER IN BASE PATH ✪ (See § 474 and 479.)

FED: A runner may not pass an unobstructed preceding runner in the base path before such runner is out. **PENALTY:** The following runner is called out immediately, but the ball remains alive. (8-4-2m; 8.4.2L and m)

❀ Note 424: One runner passing another is not an appeal play; the umpire acts immediately upon witnessing the infraction. Further, the penalty is invoked even if the passing occurs while runners are advancing to awarded bases. With fewer than two out, the out removes the force on preceding runners.

467. ALSO: OFF INTERP 366-431: **HOPKINS:** When a home run hitter becomes the third out for passing a preceding runner, it is not a time play. (Website 2006, #14) ✠

❀ Note 425: The rationale: The ball is dead and all runners are awarded four bases. B1 passes the runner **AFTER** touching first, so his third out is not a force out: Count all the runs. But see OBR OFF INTERP 368 and Play 223 [this section] for a totally opposite point of view.

468. ALSO: OFF INTERP 367-431: **HOPKINS:** After a time out where all runners huddled, the umpire discovers that R1 switched places with R2. Both runners are out: R2, for running the bases in reverse order; R1, for passing a preceding runner in the base path. (Website 2003, #3) ✠

❀ Note 426: I would also eject the coach and both players for unsportsmanlike conduct.

NCAA: Same as OBR 7.08h. (8-5m) Same as OBR OFF INTERP 368. (8-5m AR)

OBR: A following runner may not pass a preceding runner before he is out. **PENALTY:** The following runner is out but the ball remains alive. (7.08h)

> **469. ALSO:** OFF INTERP 368-431: **PBUC:** With two outs, when a home run hitter passes a preceding runner, it may result in a time play: Only runs that score before the out count. {6.16} ✠

⁕*Play 223-431:* Bases loaded, 2 outs. B1 homers and passes R1 in the base path. At the time he passes the runner, only R3 has crossed the plate. The ball is dead on the home run. The umpire calls out B1 immediately. *Ruling:* In FED, all runners score. In NCAA / OBR, only R3 scores.

> **470. ALSO:** OFF INTERP 369-431: **PBUC:** A run scores in a force situation (where the scoring runner advances without liability to be put out) even if, before R3 crosses the plate, a third out is registered because a following runner passes a preceding runner. {6.14} ✠

⁕ *Play 224-431:* Bases loaded, 2 outs, full count. All runners except R2 are moving when B1 walks. Before R3 can touch the plate, R1 passes R2 on the third-base side of second, and the umpire calls out R1: 3 outs. *Ruling:* Score the run at all levels.

❀ Note 427: See 7.04b CMT ¶ 2 for an analogous play.

> ⁕ *Play 225-431:* **OBR only.** R1. B1 lifts a high fly to right field and passes R1 while the ball is still in the air. He suddenly realizes he has passed the runner and retreats behind him. F9 cannot make the catch. *Ruling:* B1 is out, and the force is removed on R1.

⁕ *Play 226-431:* Bases loaded, 1 out. B1's pop-up to shallow right field leaves all runners in doubt and therefore holding. The right fielder must play the ball on the bounce. Meanwhile, B1 passes R1 in the base path. When R3 sees the ball hit the ground, he belatedly starts for home. F9's throw beats him, but the catcher standing on the plate does not apply a tag, choosing instead to play successfully on R1 who has overrun second. *Ruling:* B1 is called out immediately, which removes the force on R3: No tag, no out: The run scores.

★ 432 RUNNER: RETIRED RUNNER: DEFINITION ✪

FED: A retired runner is an offensive player who is out or has scored a run and is still in live-ball territory. (2-30-3) (See § 427 and 428.)

❀ Note 428: The definition is of practical value in two situations: (● 1) When a helmet is removed during live action (The edict is left over from those days when the offender was to be called out); and (● 2) more importantly, when a runner who has scored interferes with or maliciously crashes into a defensive player. The point: Interference by a runner who has scored is now, by definition, interference by a **RETIRED RUNNER**. (See § 324 and especially § 480.)

NCAA: ***(REVISED)*** A retired batter or runner is an offensive player who has "been just put out." (8-5p)

OBR: No provision.

433 RUNNER: RETOUCHES AFTER CATCH
ALL CODES NOW AGREE: TEXT DELETED,2008.

★ 434 RUNNER: RETURNS TO ORIGINAL BASE AFTER: CATCH DURING LIVE ACTION ✪ (See § 35.)

FED: When a ball becomes dead, a runner who is "on or beyond" the next base during live action is not permitted to retouch his original base. (5-2-2b-1) **PENALTY:** The runner is out "on proper and successful appeal." (8-4-2q; 8.2.2c) The runner is allowed to return to the base, and if the defense does not appeal, he is awarded two bases on the overthrow. (8.2.5a; Website 2010, #11)

❀ Note 429: Let's be clear on something; the FED "return after catch" rule is **MUCH DIFFERENT** from the OBR rule. In FED, if the runner has passed a succeeding base, he is out on appeal when he returns to retouch and accept his award. In NCAA / OBR the runner is out on appeal only if he touches a succeeding base **AFTER THE BALL GOES DEAD**.

❀ Note 430: FED 8.2.5a confirms the ruling in Play 227 [this section], which first appeared in the BRD's sixth edition, 1986!

471. ALSO: A runner who missed a base or left too soon is out on appeal if, after the ball is dead, he advances to a succeeding base. (8-4-2q)

❀ Note 431: The FED provision is copied from OBR OFF INTERP 370-434.

472. ALSO: A runner who has touched a succeeding base and because of a catch must return shall not be called out on appeal if a fielder deliberately throws ***(EDITED)*** or carries a ball to DBT. Instead, the umpire will award the runner two bases. (8-3-3d) (See § 28.)

NCAA: If a runner is returning to his base following a catch, ***(EDITED)*** when a throw goes dead, the runner may retouch his original base and the award is made from his original base. (8-6a AR 3)

OBR: When a runner is forced to return to a base after a catch, he must retouch his original base before receiving his award, which is measured from his original base. (7.05i CMT ¶ 2; 7.10b AR 2) (See § 4 for a brief look at "last time by.")

473. ALSO: OFF INTERP 370-434: **PBUC:** A runner may not return to correct a baserunning infraction if, after the ball becomes dead, he advances to and touches a base. {6.12} ✠

❀ Note 432: The NCAA rule requires that the runner attempt to correct his error. He must be returning to his base at or about TOT. That is not relevant in OBR play.

474. ALSO: OFF INTERP 371-434: **PBUC:** A home run hitter, as long as he has not touched the next base, may return during a dead ball to touch a missed base. {6.12-1} ✠

⁜ *Play 227-434:* R1: B1 smashes a high fly deep to center field. R1, moving on the pitch, thinks the ball will not be caught. After rounding third, he realizes the ball was caught after all and will be relayed to first for the out. R1 retouches third and is heading for second, but he has not yet retouched that base when the ball goes dead. *Ruling:* In FED, R1 may not legally return to touch first, the base he left too soon. He will be declared out on proper appeal. In NCAA, since R1 was returning to his base at the time the defense threw away the ball, he may retouch first before advancing to third. In OBR, regardless of his actions, he may retouch first before advancing to third. (He is initially awarded home! Maybe. See Play 228 next.)

⁜ *Play 228-434:* R1 leaves too soon and is between second and third at the time of a throw that goes dead. He is not returning toward first. *Ruling:* In FED / NCAA, R1 is awarded home. (In FED, the runner cannot return legally during a dead ball if he has advanced to the next base. In NCAA, the runner cannot return because he had not reversed himself to return to first during the live ball.) In OBR, R1 is awarded third, two bases from his original base.

⁜ *Play 229-434:* B1 hits a fair ball that bounds into the stands near the right field foul line. The batter, who missed first, proceeds to second and touches it. The first-base coach convinces him to return, and B1 returns to touch first and then goes back to second. *Ruling:* At all levels: If the defense appeals, B1 is out.

❀ Note 433: Umpires sometimes confuse "time of the throw" with "time the ball goes dead."

If the umpire is to make an award, it is never measured from the moment the ball becomes dead. Example 1: B1 bunts. F5 charges, fields the ball, and fires to first. The throw hits off the first baseman's mitt and begins to roll toward a dead-ball area. B1 reaches second and is well on his way to third when the ball goes dead. B1 receives only second, two bases from the time of the pitch, not two bases from the time the ball became dead.

But in FED, whether a runner may return is entirely dependent on WHEN the ball becomes dead, not the time of the throw. Example 2: R1 leaves first on B1's fly to right. F9 catches the ball, and R1 must return to first or be in peril of an out. He has not yet retouched second at the time of F9's throw, but he is between second and first when the ball becomes dead. He may retouch first and receive his two-base award: The umpire will not uphold an appeal that R1 left early.

∞ 435 RUNNER RETURNS TO ORIGINAL BASE AFTER: FOUL BALL ✪

FED: After a foul ball the umpire will not put the ball back into play "until the runner RETURNS to the appropriate base." (8-2-2)

NCAA: After a foul ball "the umpire shall not put the ball in play until all runners have RETOUCHED their bases." (6-2a)

OBR: Same as NCAA. (5.09e)

AO 23-435: EVANS: "Professional umpires routinely put the ball back in play before runners actually retouch. As a matter of fact, many runners never actually retouch their original bases before the next pitch is delivered. This is a common and accepted practice in pro baseball. Umpires, however, are cautioned to make sure runners are back in the CLOSE VICINITY of their original bases before they put the ball in play in accordance with Rule 5.11." (5:20)

❀ Note 434: You will observe that only the FED language ("returns" as opposed to "retouches") actually reflects the current custom and practice of umpires at all levels. Hooray! (Now stop saying the BRD never compliments the NFHS.) When I played in the 40s, the rules required a runner to retouch after a foul ball or be subject to appeal. Many amateur coaches think that is still the rule.

★ 436 RUNNER: RETURNS TO ORIGINAL BASE AFTER: PITCHER HAS BALL ON PITCHER'S PLATE ✪

FED: No provision. Treat as in OBR.

NCAA: **Point not covered.**

OFF INTERP 372-436: **PARONTO:** After the pitcher has the ball on the rubber, a runner may not return to correct a baserunning error: Same as OBR OFF INTERP 373 [this section]. (question #24, NCAA national exam, 2005) ✠

OBR: "If a runner legally acquires title to a base, and the pitcher assumes his pitching position, the runner may not return to a previously occupied base." (7.01 CMT) PENALTY: **Point not covered.**

OFF INTERP 373-436: ***(EDITED)*** **WENDELSTEDT:** If a runner tries to return to a previously occupied base after the pitcher has the ball on the pitcher's plate, the umpire will warn him. If he persists, he is out. (HW/P242/175) ✠

AO 24-436: EVANS: Umpires should be alert and declare out any runner who [tries to] return to his previous base after the pitcher has assumed his position on the rubber. This could most logically happen when the runner felt that he "left too soon" on a tag-up and would attempt to return before an appeal was made on him. (7:3)

✲ *Play 230-436*: 2 outs, R1. B1 singles. R1 is safe at third on a close play as B1 takes second on the throw. The defense announces it will appeal B1 missed first. B1 (on second) starts back to first after the pitcher has the ball on the pitcher's plate. *Ruling:* B1 is out if he does not stop. The umpire will call time if necessary to prevent the pitcher from playing on B1. (The offense would hope to score the runner from third during the rundown of B1.) Further, if B1 returns to second following the warning, the defense may still appeal B1 at first.

437 RUNNER: RUNNING START: PITCH ✪

FED: A runner may not get a running start from behind the base either before or at TOP. **PENALTY:** The runner is called out immediately, and the ball remains alive. (8-4-2o) (See § 438.)

NCAA: Same as FED 8-4-2o. **EXCEPT:** **PENALTY:** The out is called only on appeal. (8-6a-2)

OBR: No provision. (See § 438.)

438 RUNNER: RUNNING START: RETOUCH ON FLY BALL ✪

FED: A runner may not get a running start from behind the base when tagging on a fly ball. **PENALTY:** The runner is called out immediately, and the ball remains alive. (8-4-2o) (See § 437.)

❀ Note 435: Do not make the mistake of thinking this is an appealable offense. It is similar to calling a trailing runner out when he is in advance of a preceding runner. (See § 431.)

NCAA: Same as FED. **EXCEPT:** **PENALTY:** The out is called only on appeal. (8-6a-2)

OBR: Same as NCAA. (7.10a CMT)

✲ *Play 231-438:* R3. The runner retreats down the left field foul line behind the bag on B1's fly ball to short right. R3 streaks forward, timing his run so that he touches third at the instant the ball is touched in the outfield. R3 is safe on a close play at home. *Ruling:* In FED, R3 is called out at once. In NCAA / OBR, R3 is out but only if the defense appeals.

439 SCORING: BASE ON BALLS: INTENTIONAL ✪

FED: No provision.

NCAA: No provision.

OBR: Records are kept of intentional walks. (10.02a-13)

440 SCORING: BASE ON BALLS OR HIT BY PITCH
ALL CODES NOW AGREE: TEXT DELETED,2000.

∞ 441 SCORING: BATTER NEVER BECOMES BATTER-RUNNER ✪

FED: A batter becomes a batter-runner when he is charged with a third strike. He is out the instant the pitch is caught. (8-1-1b-1)

> **475. ALSO:** OFF INTERP 374-441: **HOPKINS:** With two outs a run does not score even if the runner touches the plate before the batter strikes out. If the runner touches home before the time of the pitch, the run counts, regardless of what happens to the batter. (Website 2004, #18) ✠

NCAA: Point not covered.

> OFF INTERP 375-441: **FETCHIET:** Same as FED OFF INTERP 374 [this section]. (Website 4/20/01, 5-5c; phone call to cc, 11/27/01) ✠

OBR: Point not covered.

> OFF INTERP 376-441: **FITZPATRICK:** Same as FED OFF INTERP 374 [this section]. (phone call to cc, 11/8/01) ✠

✱ *Play 232-441:* R3, 2-2 count on B1. F1 in the windup peers in for his sign and does not notice the runner sneaking down the line. Suddenly, with a great burst of speed, R3 reaches home and touches the plate before F1 starts to deliver. The batter, as confused as everyone else, swings and misses: 3 outs. *Ruling:* The run counts.

❀ Note 436: Though Fetchiet was the first out of the blocks with his interpretation (later amended to match Fitzpatrick), the likelihood of such a play occurring at the NCAA level is rarer than a Democrat in Utah. On the smaller youth field, where games are typically played under OBR, the umpire might actually face this situation.

442 SCORING: CAUGHT STEALING ✪

FED: No provision.

NCAA: Records are kept of runners caught stealing. (10-11b)

476. ALSO: If a fielder catches a throw in time to tag a stealing runner but cannot (or does not) make the tag successfully, the runner is charged with caught stealing, and the fielder is charged with an error. (10-11a Ex 4)

OBR: Same as NCAA. (10.07h)

443 SCORING: DOUBLE PLAY: ON APPEAL ✪

FED: No provision. Treat as in NCAA.

NCAA: If a runner is called out on appeal after the ball has been in the possession of the pitcher, such out shall be part of a double or triple play. (10-15 Nt)

OBR: Same as NCAA. (10.11 CMT)

∞ 444 SCORING: DOUBLE PLAY: REVERSE: DEFINITION ✪

FED: No provision.

NCAA: No provision.

OBR: A reverse double play occurs when a following runner is put out first (the book says "force play") after which a preceding runner is tagged out. (2.00 Double Play-b) (See § 253 and 473.)

❀ Note 437: The book refers to the out at first on the batter-runner as a force out. It isn't, of course. It just goes to show you.

445 SCORING: ERRORS: DROPPED THIRD STRIKE: BATTER ADVANCES TO FIRST
ALL CODES NOW AGREE: TEXT DELETED, 1995.

446 SCORING: ERRORS: NOT CHARGED ✪

FED: No provision.

NCAA: If a player does not catch a foul fly that in the scorer's opinion would allow a run to score, the fielder is not charged with an error. (10-16 Ex 6)

OBR: Same as NCAA. (10.12a-1)

447 SCORING: ERRORS: TEAM ✪

FED: If two or more defensive players permit a ball to go unplayed that any of them could have fielded, the official scorer shall record a "team error." (2-12-1; 9-5-5; 9.5.5b)

NCAA: No provision.

OBR: No provision.

448 SCORING: ERRORS: WILD PITCH: BATTER ADVANCES TO FIRST
ALL CODES NOW AGREE: TEXT DELETED,2000.

449 SCORING: FORFEIT: RECORDS: NOT OFFICIAL ✪

FED: No provision. (See § 420 and 423.)

❀ Note 438: The 1984 rulebook at 4-3-2 contained language similar to NCAA / OBR. The provisions were dropped without comment from the next edition.

NCAA: Individual and team records do not count if a game is forfeited before it has reached regulation length. (10-28b) (See § 450.)

OBR: Same as NCAA. (10.03e-2)

450 SCORING: FORFEIT: RECORDS: OFFICIAL ✪

FED: No provision. (See § 420 and 423.)

NCAA: (● 1) If a regulation game is forfeited, individual and team records are included up to the time of the forfeit. (10-28b)
(● 2) If scoring during an incompleted inning has "no bearing on the outcome" of the game, individual and team records count. (10-28 AR 1)
(● 3) If the winning team is ahead, the official scorer will enter a winning and losing pitcher just as if the game had been completed.
(● 4) If the winning team is behind, the scorer will record no winning or losing pitcher. (10-28b)
(● 5) If the game is a tie, no winning or losing pitcher is designated. (10-28 AR2) (See § 449.)

OBR: Same as NCAA. (10.03e-2)

451 SCORING: FORFEIT: SCORE ✪

FED: A forfeit score is 7-0 if the offended team is behind. When the offended team is ahead, the attained score is the forfeit score if the game is regulation. (4-4-2)

NCAA: A forfeit score is 7-0 for seven-inning games; 9-0, for nine-inning games if the offended team is tied or behind at the time of the forfeit. If the offended team is ahead, the attained score is the forfeit score. (10-28 Nt) (See § 456.)

OBR: The forfeit score is 9-0. (2.00 Forfeited Game) *See ¶ 8.*

★ 452 SCORING: GAME LENGTH: REGULATION ✪

FED: Regulation games are seven innings. (2-17-1)
477. ALSO: Double headers shall be two, seven-innings games. (4-2-2b; 4.2.4b)

NAIA: ***(CHANGED)*** Teams may adopt a rule providing that one or both games shall be seven innings. In such a case, rules that apply in the ninth apply to the seventh. (Modification 5-8a)
(ADDED) **478. ALSO:** The nine-inning rule may be waived and shortened to seven innings before the game if both coaches agree. If both coaches do not agree, the nine-inning rule is in effect. This modification applies to regular season games. only. (Modification 5-8a)

NCAA: POE 2006: Games are nine innings. (5-8a) **EXCEPT:** By conference rule or mutual agreement games may be scheduled for seven innings in a double header. (5-8a-3) (See § 456.)
479. ALSO: ***(EDITED)*** The committee has written detailed rules concerning double-headers: (● 1) The first game must be completed before the second game may start (5-7a); (● 2) The second game begins 20 minutes after the first game ends, but the UIC may permit a longer interval (5-7b); (● 3) the games may be two 9's, a 7 and a 9, or two 7's (5 7c); (● 4) If a rescheduled (not halted) game is part of a double-header, the rescheduled game shall be the second game. If the rescheduled game is a halted game, it shall be the first game (5-7d).
(ADDED) **480. ALSO:** (● 1) a doubleheader must include the same two teams. (5-7 AR 1)
(● 2) A doubleheader is defined as consecutive games between the same two teams (5-7 AR 2) within 30 minutes of each other. (5-7 AR 7)
(● 3) A time limit at a facility is not an accepted reason to end a contest. (5-7 AR 6)

> ***(ADDED)*** ❀ Note 439: Rule 5-7 contains 8 approved rulings, all of them concerning what constitutes a regulation game in a two- or three-way competition where contests are played back-to-back. At the heart of everything: (1) how and when suspensions will be served; (2) what contests can be counted when invitations to post-season play are handed out; and (3) what the umpire pay will be. Ernie Banks' "Let's play two" seems an odd request in these days of corporate, collegiate competition.

481. ALSO: Rules that apply to the ninth inning in a nine-inning game apply to the seventh inning in seven-inning games. (5-8a AR)
482. ALSO: It is a regulation game when the umpires leave the field of play. (5-8e)

483. ALSO: The committee recognizes that "commercial air travel" is "an approved reason to end a game." Three Approved Rulings illustrate the change. (5-8e AR 1, 2 and 3. [p. 62])

OBR: ***(EDITED)*** A doubleheader is two regularly scheduled games or rescheduled games played in immediate succession. (4.10a) *See ¶8.*

453 SCORING: GAME LENGTH: SHORTENED: HALTED ✪

FED: No provision.

NCAA: POE 1994, 1995: By **PRIOR AGREEMENT** of the teams, conference, or tournament committee, any unfinished game may be a "halted" game. The halted-game procedure is as follows:
(● 1) Games stopped because of "inclement weather, darkness, light failure or curfew" are eligible for the procedure.
(● 2) Agreement must be reached **BEFORE** a game begins or the game cannot be halted; such "unhalted" contests would then be: (a) no game (5-11); (b) no contest (§ 457); (c) a win (§ 455); or (d) a tie (§ 459).
(● 3) Halted games are completed by picking them up always at the point of interruption and on the next day.
(● 4) If a halted game is scheduled for completion, it shall always be the first game of any games scheduled that day. (5-9)

❀ Note 440: A game where play is stopped but then resumes on the same day **CANNOT** be a halted game. "Completed ... the next day" means the game is finished at the earliest opportunity other than the original date of the contest.

⁂ *Play 233-453:* **NCAA only.** H 5, V 4, bottom of the seventh: The game is called because of darkness. *Ruling:* (1) If the game is halted, it will be completed the next day. (2) If no prior agreement was reached, the game is over, with H winning.

⁂ *Play 234-453:* **NCAA only.** H 4, V 4, bases loaded, 0 out, bottom of the sixth: Light failure makes further play impossible. *Ruling:* (1) If the game is halted, it will be completed the next day. (2) Without prior agreement, the game is a tie.

⁂ *Play 235-453:* **NCAA only.** H 4, V 3, bottom of the fourth: Rain washes out further play. *Ruling:* (1) If the game is halted, it will be completed the next day. (In effect, we have a suspended game.) (2) If no prior agreement was reached, it is no game since it did not reach regulation length.

❀ Note 441: The halted-game procedure does not supersede the traditional termination of a regulation game unless prior agreement is reached. Simply put: In the absence of agreement to use the halted-game procedure: (• 1) a non-regulation game is no game; (• 2) a regulation game is a win or a tie. (See § 455.)

OBR: No provision.

454 SCORING: GAME LENGTH: SHORTENED: INNING NOT COMPLETED: NON REGULATION GAME SUSPENDED ✪

FED: A non-regulation game called by the umpire is "no game." (4-3) **EXCEPT:** State associations may adopt game-ending procedures. In the absence of state regulations, mutual agreement between the coaches will govern the game. But mutual agreement may not supersede game-ending procedures adopted by the state association. (4-2-4; 4.2.4a) (See § 453, 455 and 459.)

NCAA: A non-regulation game that is called is "no game" (5-11) or by prior agreement, "halted" (5-9). (See § 453, 457 and 459.)

OBR: Non-regulation games are always suspended if play is terminated because of: (• 1) a curfew; (• 2) time limit; (• 3) artificial light failure or the malfunction of any other mechanical field device; (• 4) darkness, when law forbids turning on lights; (• 5) weather, if the game is suspended before an inning is completed when the visitors have scored to take the lead and the home team has not retaken the lead. (4.12a-1 through 5) (See § 455, 457 and 459.) *See ¶8.*

455 SCORING: GAME LENGTH: SHORTENED: INNING NOT COMPLETED: REGULATION GAME SUSPENDED / TIE GAME ✪ (See § 455 and 459.)

FED: If a regulation game is called for any reason when the teams have not had an equal number of turns at bat, the score shall be the score of the last completed inning. (4-2-3) (See § 454.) **EXCEPT: POE 1993**: State associations may adopt game-ending procedures. In the absence of state regulations, mutual agreement between the coaches will govern the game. (4-2-4)
484. ALSO: When a regulation game is called in an incompleted inning, if the home team has scored "a run(s) which equals or exceeds the opponent's score, the final score shall be as recorded when the game is called." (4-2-3; 4.3.1b)
485. ALSO: By state association adoption only: A regulation game called without a winner being determined may count as a half-game won and a half-game lost for each team. (4-3)

486. ALSO: Individual batting and fielding records count, but the game is not counted for the percentage of wins and losses. (4-2-2) (See § 454 and 455.)

NCAA: Regulation suspended games are no longer permitted. Instead, games will be: (a) a win (5-8); (b) halted (5-9); (c) a tie (5-10); (d) no game (5-11); or (e) no contest (5-14b). (See § 453, 455 and 457.)
487. ALSO: If a regulation game is called for any reason when the teams have not had an equal number of turns at bat, the score shall be the score of the last completed inning. (5-8b) **EXCEPT:** If home has gone ahead or tied the game in the incompleted inning, the score is the attained score when the game was called. (5-8b-3) [Same as FED 4-2-3.]
488. ALSO: If a game is tied, all individual and team averages shall count. (5-10 Nt) (See § 453 and 457.)

OBR: If a regulation game is called with the score tied, it is a suspended game. (4.10c) *See ¶ 8.*
489. ALSO: A called game ends at the moment the umpire terminates play unless it becomes a suspended game pursuant to 4.12a. (4.11d)

⁎ *Play 236-455:* H 1, V 0. In the sixth V scores two runs. H, not having scored, is batting in the sixth when rain washes out further play. *Ruling:* In FED, H wins or (by state adoption) the game is suspended. In NCAA, H wins or (by prior agreement) the game is halted. In OBR, the game is suspended and will be resumed at the point where play was stopped.

⁎ *Play 237-455:* H 1, V 0. In the sixth V scores one run while H scores two runs and is still batting when rain washes out further play.
Ruling: H wins, 3-1.

⁎ *Play 238-455:* H 0, V 1. In the fifth H ties the game. They are batting in the sixth when rain washes out further play. *Ruling:* In FED, the game is tied or (by state adoption) suspended. In NCAA, the game is tied or (by prior agreement) halted. In OBR, the game is suspended.

⁎ *Play 239-455:* H 0, V 1. In the sixth H ties the score and is still batting when rain washes out further play. *Ruling:* In FED, the game is a tie or (by state adoption) suspended. In NCAA, the game is a tie or (by prior agreement) halted. In OBR, the game is suspended.
490. ALSO: When play resumes in a suspended game, it must be at the "exact point of suspension." No player removed from the "original" game may play in the "resumed" game. But: "A player who was not with the club when the game was suspended may be used as a substitute, even if he has taken the place of a player no longer with the club" who could not have played in the resumed game. (4.12c)

456 SCORING: GAME LENGTH: SHORTENED: NINE TO SEVEN INNINGS ✪

FED: Not applicable.

NCAA: By mutual agreement or conference rule, a double header may be two, seven-inning games . (5-8a-3) (See § 452.)
491. ALSO: By mutual agreement or conference rule, double-headers may be two, nine-inning games or a seven and a nine. (5-7c)

OBR: In some leagues one or both games of a double-header may be shortened to seven innings. In such games, rules that govern play in the ninth shall apply in the seventh. (4.10a Ex) *See ¶ 8.*

457 SCORING: GAME LENGTH: SHORTENED: NO CONTEST ✪

FED: No provision.

NCAA: Since a game may not be forfeited unless the umpires are in charge: "An institution shall not, for statistical purposes, declare a forfeit for nonfulfillment of contract. Such instances shall be considered as 'no contest.'" (5-14b) (See § 419; 453; 455; 459.)

OBR: No provision.

458 SCORING: GAME LENGTH: SHORTENED: EXCESSIVE-RUN LEAD ✪

FED: By state association adoption: States **MAY** adopt a 10-run mercy rule, which ends the game after the trailing team has batted five times. (4-2-2; 4.2.2a, b, c, d and e) State associations may not adopt a mercy run-rule at numbers other than 10. (4.2.2b; 4.4.2c)

❀ Note 442: The "run-rule" statute has an interesting history. It was optional until 1996, when it became mandatory. After seven seasons, the rule is now where it once was. The more things change, the more they remain the same.

492. ALSO: State associations may adopt game ending procedures, which take precedence over mutual agreement of coaches. (4-2-4)
493. ALSO: If the state association has not adopted game-ending procedures, a game may end by mutual agreement of both coaches and the UIC. (4-2-4) Absent agreement, the game must continue until such time as the 10-run rule [if adopted by the state] takes effect. (4.2.4c)

NCAA: "By conference rule or mutual consent of both coaches prior to the beginning of the game," games end after seven innings when one team leads by 10 runs. (2-75; 5-8b-4)

> **EXCEPT:** OFF INTERP 377-458: **FETCHIET:** The 10-run rule is in effect for nine-inning games only. There is no run rule for seven-inning contests. (Website 2/20/01, 5-7b) ✠

❀ Note 443: The college boys like to hit, so the NCAA toyed (1998-2000) with a POE 1998, 12-run rule, figuring that the extra two runs might keep games from ending early. With very little fanfare, though, the number dropped to 10 in 2001.

OBR: No provision. *See ¶8.*

459 SCORING: GAME LENGTH: SHORTENED: TIE
TEXT MOVED TO § 455.

★ 460 SCORING: HALF-INNING ENDS ✪

FED: A half-inning ends when there is a third out or the winning run is scored in the last inning. Appeals that affect the half-inning may still be granted. (2-20-2)

NCAA: Point not covered.

> ***(ADDED)*** OFF INTERP 378-460: **PARONTO:** The half-inning ends when the third out has been recorded or, in the case of a possible appeal that would extend the half-inning, when the pitcher and all infielders have left fair territory. (email to cc, 12/23/11) ✠

OBR: Point not covered.

> OFF INTERP 379-460: **PBUC:** Same as FED: "An inning or half inning starts immediately after the third out is made in the preceding inning." {5.4} *See ¶8.* ✠

❀ Note 444: OFF INTERP 327-496 also affects unannounced substitutes. (See Play 257-479.)

∞ 461 SCORING: HITS: CREDITED AFTER INTERFERENCE BY RUNNER ✪

FED: No provision.

NCAA: No provision.

OBR: Following runner interference with a fielder making a play on a batted ball, a base hit shall be credited if the scorer believes that without the interference the batter would have reached base safely anyway. (10.05b-5) (See § 325 and 327.)

❀ Note 445: Remember that if a runner is hit by a batted ball, unless the interference is judged intentional or the batter-runner is called out, the batter automatically gets a base hit.

462 SCORING: HITS: EXTRA-BASE: DEFINITION
ALL CODES NOW AGREE: TEXT DELETED, 1996.

463 SCORING: HOME SCOREBOOK OFFICIAL ✪

FED: The home team scorebook is official unless the UIC decides otherwise. (9-2-2)

> **EXCEPT:** OFF INTERP 380-463: **RUMBLE:** The scorebook does not contain the official lineup. (*News* #18, 3/99) (See § 458; 465; 466; 481.) ✠

494. ALSO: Umpires need not sign the book to make the score official. (10.2.3k CMT)

NCAA: The home team, conference, or tournament director appoints the official scorer before each game. (10-1a)

OBR: The league president appoints an official scorer for each game. (10.01a) *See ¶8.*

❀ Note 446: Except there ain't no league president any more.

∞ 464 SCORING: LINEUP: BATTING OUT OF ORDER ✪

FED: No provision. Treat as in NCAA.

NCAA: Following an appeal of an improper batter after he has completed his turn at bat: (● 1) If the improper batter is put out during play, charge the proper batter with a time at bat and score the putout and assists exactly as they occurred; (● 2) if the improper batter BECOMES A RUNNER, charge the proper batter with a turn at bat, credit the catcher with the putout and ignore everything else; (● 3) if MULTIPLE PLAYERS bat out of order, score the plays as they occur. (10-3)

OBR: Same as NCAA. (10.03d)

★ 465 SCORING: LINEUP: NAMES MATCH JERSEY NUMBERS ✪

FED: The name listed on the lineup card establishes the official batting order. No penalty is provided if a player's name and number do not match in the scorebook or card. (1.1.3) (See § 463 and 466.)

495. ALSO: At the time the lineups are exchanged, all starting players listed must be at the game site. (4.4.1e)

NCAA: Point not covered.

> ***(ADDED)*** OFF INTERP 381-465: **PARONTO:** Whenever it is discovered that a player's jersey number does not match the number listed in the official lineup, the UIC will ensure that the number on all cards is changed. No penalty is assessed. (2012 NCAA test, question 65) (See § 416.) ✠

OBR: Point not covered.

> OFF INTERP 382-465: **FITZPATRICK:** If a player is listed twice on the lineup card, the first time the player bats locks him into that position in the batting order. (email to cc, 11/15/00) ✠

✻ *Play 240-465:* **OBR only.** For Milwaukee, Robin Yount is listed as the center fielder, batting third, and also as the DH, batting fifth. After Mike Young, the "real" DH bats, Detroit manager Sparky Anderson argues that Yount is ineligible: When Young batted fifth, he was an "unannounced" pinch-hitter for Yount. *Ruling:*-In the actual game, the umpire blew it by agreeing with Sparky. The umpire should have treated Young as an unreported substitute since Yount had already established his spot as third in the order. (See § 84 and 499.)

★ 466 SCORING: LINEUP: STARTERS / SUBSTITUTES LISTED: SCOREBOOK / SCORECARD ✪

FED: POE 1988, 1989: All starting players must be listed in the scorebook and on the lineup card by name, shirt number, batting order position, and fielding position. The umpire shall not accept the lineup card until all substitutes are listed. (1-1-2; 1-1-3;1.1.3; Website 2011, #2)

496. ALSO: If a coach refuses to correct his card, "the game cannot begin until the umpire has received both cards." **PENALTY:** No penalty assessed. (Website #3, 2011)

❀ Note 447: A BRD recommendation: If, after a reasonable time, a coach has not presented a properly filled-out card, the UIC should inform both coaches the game is forfeited. Let the conference sort it all out.

497. ALSO: A substitute not listed on the official lineup card may enter the game without penalty. (1.1.2a and b)

NCAA: Point not covered.

(ADDED) OFF INTERP 383-466: **PARONTO:** It is recommended that all substitutes be listed on the lineup card presented at the plate conference prior to the start of the game." (email to cc, 12/23/11) ✠

OBR: Each lineup card **SHOULD** list the fielding positions of each player in the batting order. "As a courtesy, potential substitute players should also be listed," but there is no penalty for failure to do so. (4.01c)

467 SCORING: OUTS: BATTER-RUNNER MAKES THIRD OUT AT FIRST BASE
ALL CODES NOW AGREE: TEXT DELETED, 1997.

468 SCORING: OUTS: BEST OUT CHOSEN TO END HALF INNING
ALL CODES NOW AGREE: TEXT DELETED, 1995.

469 SCORING: PITCHER: SAVE
ALL CODES NOW AGREE: TEXT DELETED, 1994.

470 SCORING: PITCHER: WIN: ALL STAR PLAY ✪

FED: No provision. Treat as in NCAA.

NCAA: If by prearrangement three or more pitchers will be used, the pitcher of record will be considered the winning pitcher. (10-25b-3)

OBR: Same as NCAA. **EXCEPT:** If the pitcher of record is knocked out after the winning team has a commanding lead, the scorer may award the win to a subsequent pitcher. (10.17e)

471 SCORING: PITCHER: W IN: LEAGUE PLAY ✪

FED: To get the win the starting pitcher must complete: three innings (game goes six or fewer innings) or four innings (game goes seven or more innings). (9-6-6)

NCAA: To get the win the starting pitcher must complete: four innings (game goes seven or fewer innings) or five innings (game goes eight or more innings). (10-25a)

OBR: To get the win the starting pitcher must complete: four innings (game goes five or fewer innings) or five innings (game goes six or more innings). (10.17b)

472 SCORING: RBI: GAME WINNER
ALL CODES NOW AGREE: TEXT DELETED, 1990.

∞ 473 SCORING: RBI: RUN SCORES DURING DOUBLE PLAY ✪

FED: Point not covered.

OFF INTERP 384-473: **RUMBLE:** A batter is credited with an RBI if he hits into a "time" double play. (*REF* 10/88) ✠

NCAA: Same as FED: "It is not a run batted in if there is a double play from a force or one in which the batter is or should have been put out at first base." (10-9 Ex)

OBR: No rbi is credited whenever the double play is a force-double play or a reverse-force-double play. (10.04b-1 (See § 444.)

✲ *Play 241-473:* R3, 1 out. R3 legally retouches and scores on B1's caught fly ball, after which R1 is doubled up at first. *Ruling:* B1 gets credit for an rbi and a sacrifice fly.

★ 474 SCORING: RUNS: AWARDED RUN WINS GAME ✪

(See § 476.)

FED: ***(EDITED)*** In the last inning of a tie game, if an award for a defensive penalty forces home multiple runners, all such runners score. (1.4.3, 1991 ed) (See § 32.)

(ADDED) ❀ Note 448-474: Jim Paronto's OFF INTERP 385 below motivated me to include the entire FED case play referenced above:

> With the bases loaded in the bottom of the seventh and the score tied, B4 hits a long fly ball that is about to clear the center field fence when F8 makes a leaping catch for the third out. Before the defense leaves the field, the coach of the team at bat notices that F8's glove is exceptionally large and immediately informs the umpire. Ruling: If the glove does not meet the rule specifications and is judged to be illegal, the umpire shall offer the coach of the offended team the result of the play or the penalty. In this case, the coach of the offended team would obviously want the penalty, which would be a three-base award for B4. It makes no difference whether it is a mitt or a glove.

It is true the case ruling **DOES NOT SPECIFY** that three runs score. But, by analogy, we score all runners when a batter homes over the fence in the same situation. Your best bet if it happens to you: Cancel the out, award B1 third, watch all runners touch all bases, and then head home. Let the teams and official scorer sort out what the final score is.

NCAA: Point not covered.

(ADDED) OFF INTERP 385-474: **PARONTO:** Same as OBR. (email to cc, 12/23/11) ✠

(ADDED) ❀ Note 449: Last year, I wrote that NCAA would treat this occurrence as in FED: Any runner awarded home would score. I guessed wrong. Correct is "Same as OBR." See revised Play 242 below.

OBR: The contest ends the moment the winning run is scored. (4.11c)

(ADDED) ❀ Note 450: On the other hand, the Approved Ruling at OBR 4.11c tends to support Paronto's OFF INTERP: A batter homes to win the game but passes a preceding runner. **BECAUSE THE HOME RUN HITTER WILL NOT SCORE**, "only those runs who score before the runner passes another runner shall count."

⁎ *Play 242-474:* R3, R2, 2 out, score 2-2 in the bottom of the last inning. B1 hits a sharp grounds to F4, who overthrows first. ***(REVISED)*** *Ruling:* In FED, the final score is H 4, V 2. In NCAA / OBR, it's H 3, V 2.

★ 475 SCORING: RUNS: HITS: QUALITY ✪

FED: If a batter hits a game-ending hit and would be awarded more bases than necessary to drive in the winning run: grant the batter the bases he would receive on the award.(1.4.3, 1991 ed)***(ADDED)*** (See Note 448-474. See also Play 243 [this section].)

NCAA: If a batter hits a game-ending hit and would be awarded more bases than necessary to drive in the winning run, "credit him with only as many bases on his hit as the runner who scores the winning run advances" and then only if he runs out his hit. (10-7)
(See Play 243 [this section].)

OBR: If a batter hits a game-ending hit and would be awarded more bases than necessary to drive in the winning run, credit the batter with only the number of bases necessary to drive in the winning run. (10.06f)
498. ALSO: Apply 10.06f even in instances where the batter-runner would be awarded an automatic number of bases. (10.06f CMT)
(See Play 243 [this section].)

⁎ *Play 243-475:* Bases loaded, 2-2 in the bottom of the last inning. B1 hits a deep fly that bounces over the outfield fence in fair territory for a double. *Ruling:* In FED, credit the batter with a double. In NCAA / OBR, he gets only a single.

476 SCORING: RUNS: HOME RUN: RUNNER PASSED IN BASE PATH (TEXT COVERED IN § 431.

477 SCORING: RUNS: HOME RUN: RUNS SCORE
ALL CODES NOW AGREE: TEXT DELETED,2003

478 SCORING: RUNS: SCORED AFTER THIRD OUT: AT PLATE: AT HOME ✪

FED: If a runner crosses the plate but fails to touch it, the run counts if the defense does not appeal. (8-2 Pen)

499. ALSO: (● 1) A runner who misses the plate is out if: (a) the defense touches the plate during continuing action on proper appeal; or (b) the defense tags the runner (required for the out) when he is trying to return. (● 2) The runner may not return if he has "touched the steps of the dugout" or if a following runner has crossed the plate.(8.2.2m) (See § 14.)

❀Note 451: A runner forced to the plate who misses it would be out when the base is tagged, even if the defense does not make an overt appeal.

NCAA: If a runner is awarded home but does not touch the plate before a following runner is put out, the run scores unless the out was a force out or the result of the batter runner's failure to reach first safely. (8-3a AR)

500. ALSO: If a third out occurs before a runner returns to touch the plate, treat as in OBR: Count the run. (OFF INTERP 1 in the Introduction, p. 7)

OBR: Point not covered.

> OFF INTERP 386-478: **FITZPATRICK:** A runner who misses the plate may return to touch it even after the defense has attained a third out during live action. (phone call to cc, 11/8/01) ✠

✻ *Play 244-478:* R2, 2 outs. The batter singles to center field. The throw to the plate is relayed to second base, and R2 misses home plate JUST BEFORE the batter-runner is tagged out. R2 returns to touch the plate after the out at second. *Ruling:* In FED, the run counts unless the defense appeals. In NCAA / OBR: The run counts.

> **501. ALSO:** OFF INTERP 387-478: **MLBUM:** A runner may not return to touch a base or the plate after he has entered the dugout. (5.3) ✠

★ ∞ 479 SCORING: RUNS: SCORED AFTER THIRD OUT: ON BASE ✪ (See § 431.)

FED: Point not covered.

> OFF INTERP 388-479: **HOPKINS:** A run scores on a bases-loaded walk even if a runner overruns or overslides a base and is tagged for the third out before the runner from third crosses the plate. (Website 2008, #4) ✠

NCAA: Point no covered.

> ***(ADDED)*** OFF INTERP 389-479: **PARONTO:** Same as FED. (email to cc, 12/23/11) ✠

OBR: Same as FED. (7.04b CMT)

✲ *Play 245-478:* Bases loaded, full count on B1. The runners go on the pitch, which is ball four. R1 is over-zealous and overruns second. The catcher fires to F4, who tags R1 out before R3 crosses the plate. *Ruling:* At all levels, score the run.

❀ Note 452: OBR says it best: "The run would score on the theory that the run was forced home by the base on balls and all the runners needed to do was proceed and touch the next base."

★ 480 SCORING: RUNS: SCORE: NULLIFIED ✪

FED: Point (almost) **not covered.**

> OFF INTERP 390-480: **RUMBLE:** Once a runner has legally scored a run, he cannot nullify the score by any legal action, such as retreating to third in the belief he had missed the base or left too soon. (*News* #31, 4/84) ✠

EXCEPT: A runner who has scored on a force play but is guilty of interference with a fielder nullifies his run. (2.32.2c; 8.4.2w)

> **502. ALSO:** OFF INTERP 391-480: **RUMBLE:** A runner who has scored but is guilty of **INTERFERENCE WITH A BATTED BALL** keeps his run but causes a teammate to be out. (*News* #8, 3/92) (See § 329. Contrast OBR OFF INTERP 392 [this section].) ✠

NCAA: A runner cannot nullify a legally scored run. (5-6c AR 1)
EXCEPT: Same as FED: A runner who scores on a force play but interferes is out and his run is canceled. (5-6c AR 1 Ex)

OBR: A runner cannot nullify a legally scored run. (5.06 CMT)

> **EXCEPT:** OFF INTERP 392-480: **DEARY:** The umpire will cancel a legally scored run if the runner who has scored is guilty of interference with a fair batted ball after crossing the plate.
> (letter to TH, 10/14/87) (Contrast FED OFF INTERP 391 [this section].) ✠

✲ *Play 246-480:* R2, R3. B1 lays down a suicide-squeeze bunt. R3 touches the plate but then slides into the untouched batted ball, which is in fair territory. *Ruling:* In FED, R3 scores but has interfered, so B1 is out; R2 returns to second unless he reached third prior to R3's interference. In NCAA / OBR, R3 is out because he has been hit by a batted ball before it passed an infielder. R2 returns, and B1 is awarded first. (See § 461.)

❀ Note 453: FED OFF INTERPs 390 and 391 [this section] are philosophically consistent. On the other hand, OBR OFF INTERP

392 above is easily explained: 7.08f (runner interference) supersedes 5.06 CMT (runner nullifies score). After all, the reason for 5.06 CMT is to ensure that a **DELIBERATE** act by a runner – heading back around the bases, for example – cannot cancel his legally scored run.

★ 481 SCORING: RUNS: SCORE: WRONG ✪

FED: If a scoring error is detected before the game ends, it should be corrected "immediately." If a final score is to be corrected – and the outcome of the game will be affected – it must be done before the umpires leave the field after the game is over. If the umpires leave the field, the score cannot be changed. (10-2-3m; 10.2.3k) (See § 463.)
503. ALSO: The scorer should inform umpires of a scoring error at the time of the mistake. (Website 2011, #1)

⁕ *Play 247-481:* R3, R1, 0 outs. B1 hits into a 6-4-3 double play. Inexplicably, the teams change sides, and the umpires go to their between-inning positions. The official scorer informs the UIC there are now only two outs. *Ruling:* The teams retake the field. If the plate umpire has definite knowledge that R3 crossed the plate du ring the double play, he will count the run. Otherwise, R3 returns to third.

❀ Note 454: The BRD provided the ruling above as far as it concerns R3's score being counted. It seems a safe "assumption." But what if there had been a pitch at the start of the new half-inning? We'll await clarification.

NCAA: Point not covered.

> ***(ADDED)*** OFF INTERP 393-481: **PARONTO:** Same as OBR. (email to cc, 12/25/110 ✠

OBR: Point not covered.

> OFF INTERP 394-481: **DEARY:** If the official scorebook does not have the correct score, WHENEVER the error is discovered, it may be changed. Deary stated that 4.11a takes precedence. (*REF* 1/83) ✠

⁕ *Play 248-481:* The official book shows the game is tied at the end of the last regular inning. In extra innings, V wins. The next day both coaches agree that a run legally scored by H was not counted, so at the end of regulation play, H was ahead. *Ruling:* In FED, V retains their victory. In NCAA / OBR, H wins.

482 SCORING: SACRIFICE ✪

FED: No provision.

NCAA: If the official scorer judges that a batter is bunting for a base hit, he shall not record the bunt as a sacrifice, even when the batter-runner is put out and another runner advances safely. (10-8 Ex)

OBR: Same as NCAA. (10.08a) **EXCEPT:** The scorer is instructed to give the batter the benefit of the doubt. (10.08a CMT)

483 SPEED-UP RULES: AFTER PUTOUTS ✪

FED: By state association adoption only: Speed-up rules, all or in part, may be used. After the first or second out: (● 1) In the outfield, the throw may go to one cutoff man and one additional infielder before being returned to the pitcher; and (● 2) in the infield, the throw must go directly to the pitcher. After the third out, the ball must be given to the nearest umpire. (2-33-1; 2.33.1; regulations after Rule 10, p. 64) (See § 484.)

NCAA: Speed-up rules are prohibited in "official NCAA contests." (5-8f)

OBR: No provision. *See ¶ 8.*

★ 484 SPEED-UP RULES: COURTESY RUNNER ✪

FED: POE 1991: By state association adoption only: Teams may use a courtesy runner at any time after the pitcher or catcher reaches base. (2-33-1; 2.33.1; Courtesy Runners 1-7) If a courtesy runner is approved, case book plays apply, pp. 92-93.
(● 1) The same player may not run for both. (CR.1) **PENALTY:** The illegal courtesy runner is out and restricted to the dugout. (CR.5)

> ⁎ *Play 249-484:* **FED only.** Bubba, the Bobcats' pitcher, singles in the second and is replaced by courtesy runner Perry. In the fifth, Bubba becomes the catcher. His next at bat results in a single, and courtesy runner Perry trots out as his replacement. *Ruling:* Not legal. The same player may not be a courtesy runner for both the pitcher and the catcher. (See OFF INTERP 396 [this section].)

(● 2) players who have entered the game may not be courtesy runners; **PENALTY:** The illegal courtesy runner is out and restricted to the dugout. (CR.7)
(● 3) a player may not be a courtesy runner and substitute for any player in that half inning; (CR.6) **PENALTY:** The illegal courtesy runner is out and restricted to the dugout. (CR.13)
(● 4) a player who has had a courtesy runner may not return for that runner in the same half-inning; (CR.3)

❀ Note 455: The above case book ruling is not supported by the black-letter law of the "Suggested Speed-up Rules."

(● 5) the UIC will record "courtesy runner participation"; (CR. 6) and (● 6) a courtesy runner who violates any of these rules is an illegal substitute. (CR. 7) (See § 499.)

504. ALSO: OFF INTERP 395- 484: **HOPKINS:** A courtesy runner is not a **DESIGNATED** runner; a coach may use courtesy runners interchangeably for the pitcher and / or catcher. (Website 2001, #7) ✠

❋ *Play 250-484:* **FED only.** During a long inning, F1 gets on base twice. CR1 runs for him the first time. CR2 reports to run for the same pitcher when he reaches base the second time. *Ruling:* As long as neither has run for the catcher, both moves are legal.

505. ALSO: OFF INTERP 396-484: **RUMBLE:** A courtesy runner, when used, is the courtesy runner for the offensive position, not the offensive player involved. (phone call to se, 10/10/90) (See § 483.) ✠

❋ *Play 251-484:* **FED only.** Abel is the catcher. Bubba courtesy runs for him. Later, Abel becomes the pitcher, and Bubba reports as his courtesy runner. *Ruling:* Not legal. Bubba ran for the "catcher," not Abel.

506. ALSO: Since projected substitutions are not allowed (§ 497), a coach may not, for example, pinch hit for his catcher and then, if he gets on base, send out a courtesy runner for the pinch hitter. (3.1.1n)

❋ *Play 252-484:* **FED only.** Perry pinch hits for catcher Bubba and will catch during the next half-inning. Perry singles and is replaced by courtesy runner Brown. *Ruling:* Not legal. Despite the presence of a pinch hitter, Bubba was the catcher at the end of the last half inning; therefore, only Bubba is entitled to a courtesy runner in that half inning.

507. ALSO: If a courtesy runner does not report, there is no penalty. (CR.8)

508. ALSO: OFF INTERP 397-484: **RUMBLE:** Any eligible substitute may replace an on-base courtesy runner and serve as a courtesy runner for the courtesy runner. (Website 2001, #5) (See § 483.) ✠

NCAA: Courtesy runners are prohibited in "official" NCAA games. (5-8f)

NAIA: Teams have the option to use a courtesy runner for the pitcher / designated hitter or catcher at any time. It is recommended that courtesy runners be used for both pitcher and catcher with two out. (Modification 5-5.1)

509. ALSO: Though the courtesy runner is never officially in the game, he will be credited with: (● 1) run scored; (● 2) stolen base; or (● 3) caught stealing. (Modification 5-5.2)

(ADDED) **510. ALSO:** The courtesy runner rule does not apply to aa pinch hitter for the catcher unless the catcher has been re-entered, when the courtesy runner may replace him. (Modification 5-5.3)

(ADDED) **511. ALSO:** A team may not use the same runner for the pitcher / designated hitter or catcher in the same inning. (Modification 5-5.4)

512. ALSO: A courtesy runner on base may not be removed from base (and replaced with a different runner) so that he may be a pinch hitter. (Modification 5-5.5)

(ADDED) **513. ALSO:** A player removed from the game may not be a courtesy runner. (Modification 5-5.6)

(ADDED) **514. ALSO:** If the courtesy runner becomes a pinch hitter or pinch runner or enters the game at any position, he may no longer be a courtesy runner. (Modification 5-5.7)

OBR: Same as NCAA: no courtesy runners. (3.04 CMT) *See ¶8.*

485 STADIUM MANAGEMENT ✪

FED: No provision.

❀ Note 456: **POE 2005, 2006, 2007, 2008**: Game management should pay close attention to: lining the field, "measuring and maintaining the correct height [10 inches] of the pitcher's mound," and correct maintenance of the area where the pitcher's free foot lands.

NCAA: The committee adopted stringent and thorough rules for dealing with scoreboards and video / audio displays. (Appendix B)

515. ALSO: POE 2005, 2009: The committee recommends strongly that institutions assign a representative to handle game management issues outside of the playing surface. The "game administrator" must make contact with the visiting coach and umpires before the game. (3-10a) (See § 229 and 243.)

516. ALSO: Game management is responsible for keeping order during the game. If it cannot, "the game will be suspended until order is restored." (3-6d AR 4 Pen)

517. ALSO: It is recommended that institutions provide dressing rooms and security for umpires. (3-10b)

OBR: Point not covered.

OFF INTERP 398-485: **PBUC:** The book offers **MINIMAL** guidelines for managing those in charge of music or displays that might distract the players or hold the umpires up to ridicule. {3.26} ✠

518. ALSO: OFF INTERP 399-485: **MLBUM:** The instructions offer **DETAILED** and very specific guidelines. {3.25} ✠

486 STUDENT ATHLETE
NCAA ALONE DEFINED "STUDENT ATHLETE." TEXT DELETED, 1991.

★ 487 SUBSTITUTES: FIELDER: NUMBER OF WARM-UP THROWS ALLOWED ✪

FED: No provision.

NCAA: Other than the pitcher, any defensive substitute for an injured player is allowed five warm-up throws. (5-5h)
519. ALSO: During a free visit by the coach to the mound, defensive players in the current lineup may warm-up in fair territory ***(ADDED)*** provided it does not delay the game. (9-4 AR 6)

OBR: A defensive substitute for an injured player is allowed five warm-up throws. (3.03 CMT ¶ 2)

★ 488 SUBSTITUTES: ILLEGAL ✪ (See § 493.)

(ADDED) ❀ Note 457: Material in this section concerning concussions was moved to § 120 for the 2012 edition.

FED: DEFINITION: An illegal substitute is:
(● 1) a player who is ineligible to participate, which includes a withdrawn substitute, a twice-withdrawn starter, and ejected or restricted players (3.1.1c); or
(● 2) any player, including the player for whom the DH is hitting, who re-enters in the wrong spot in the batting order (2-36-3d); or
(● 3) a designated hitter who enters the game on defense while the player for whom he is batting is still playing defense (2-36-3d); or
(● 4) a courtesy runner who violates the courtesy-runner rule. (2-36-3e) (See § 15 and 166.)
520. ALSO: The illegal substitute may be discovered by the umpire, the opposing team, the scorer, or a fan (3.1.1c). **PENALTY 1:** ***(EDITED)*** **ON OFFENSE:** (● 1) Whenever discovered, an illegal substitute is restricted to the dugout for the duration of the game. (3.1.1c, L, and m)
(● 2) "If a restricted player re-enters the game on offense, he shall be called out and ejected." (3.1.1p)

(● 3) A proper appeal will cancel any run the illegal sub scored or caused to score as well as nullify any advance of baserunners. (3.1.1g and I)
(● 4) Any outs made as a result of offensive action by the illegal sub will stand. (3-1-1) **PENALTY 2:** ***(EDITED)*** **ON DEFENSE:**
(● 1) The offender is *restricted* immediately upon discovery (3.1.3a).
(● 2) If a restricted player re-enters the game on defense, he shall be ejected upon discovery by an umpire or either team. (3.1.1o)
(● 3) If the illegal sub participates in a play and is properly appealed, the offense may take the result of the play or replay the pitch. (3-1-1; 8-4-1k;) (See Play 253-488 [this section].) {See § 15; 86; 489; 493; 499.}

> ❀ Note 458: For a player, unless an ejection carries with it a suspension from a future game, there is no essential difference between being restricted to the dugout and being ejected: He can't play in either instance. But for the coach, an ejection means that, like Elvis, he must "leave the building."
> (See Note 161-164 and Note 168 -167.)

521. ALSO: The penalty for illegal substitution supersedes the batting-out-of-order penalty. (3-1-1)
522. ALSO: In order for the full range of penalties to apply: The illegal substitute must be appealed – whether on offense or defense – before a pitch to a batter of either team or, on a game-ending play, before the infielders "cross the foul lines." (3-1-1)

> ✻ *Play 253-488:* **FED only.** Bubba, a non-starter, pinch runs for the shortstop in the second and becomes an ineligible player when F6 returns to the field. In the sixth with the bases loaded and no outs, Abel should bat but Bubba illegally comes to the plate and: (a) is appealed with a 1-1 count; (b) singles and is appealed before a pitch; or (c) walks and is appealed after Baker has a count of one strike. *Ruling:* In all cases, Bubba is restricted. In (a) Bubba is out (illegal sub rule) and Baker bats. In (b) Bubba is out (illegal sub rule); the two runs are canceled, and all runners return to the bases occupied at the time of the last pitch to Bubba. (Abel's place in the batting order is effectively "skipped.") Baker is now the proper batter with two outs and the bases loaded. In (c) Bubba is out (illegal sub rule), but the runs count and Baker continues to bat. The appeal came too late for the batting-out-of-order penalty.

NCAA: DEFINITION: An illegal (or ineligible) substitute is a disqualified or ejected player. **PENALTY:** The substitute may be discovered by the opposing team or the umpire. (5-5j-1) (● 1) On both offense and defense: The player is removed from the game. (5-5j-1 and -2) (● 2) On offense: If he is at bat or on base, he is out. If he has scored a run and is appealed before the next pitch to a batter of either team, he is out and his run does not count. (5-5j-1) (● 3) On defense: Same as FED. **EXCEPT:** Any player replaced by the ineligible substitute becomes ineligible to re-enter. (5-5j-3)

***(EDITED)* 523. ALSO:** A disqualified player is an ineligible substitute but one who has not been ejected. (2-21)

❀ Note 459: The point of the disqualified player definition: Such a player may coach but not play. Ejected players, of course, may not coach. (See § 131.)

OBR: An ineligible substitute is one who has already been substituted for. (● 1) If he is discovered **BEFORE** play begins, the correct player returns. There is no need for a second substitute. (● 2) If he is discovered *after* play begins, (a) remove the illegal player; (b) remove the player substituted for; (c) a third player must enter the game. (3.03)

524. ALSO: Either manager or the umpire may discover the illegal substitute. (3.03)

525. ALSO: All plays that occurred while the illegal substitute was in the game are legal. (3.03)

526. ALSO: This rule has no effect on the unreported substitute rule, OBR 3.08. (3.03)

527. ALSO: "If, in an umpire's judgment, the player re-entered the game knowing he had been removed, the umpire may eject the manager. (3.03 CMT) (See § 489, 493 and 494. See also 3.08b.) *See ¶ 8.*

❀ Note 460: Eject any illegal subs; but do not call any outs, cancel runs, send back runners, or disallow defensive plays. OBR treats an illegal sub like an illegal glove: Remove the glove, keep the play. That is by far the most umpire-friendly rule.

⁎ *Play 254-488:* Bases loaded, 0 out. Bubba, an illegal sub, enters to play first. B1 hits into a 3-6-3 double play with R3 scoring. The offense immediately appeals that Bubba is illegal. *Ruling:* In FED / NCAA, the offense may take the play (one run in, two men out) or the penalty (all runners return TOP, B1 hits again). In OBR, the play stands. At all levels Bubba is ejected.

⁎ *Play 255-488:* B1 sprains his ankle sliding into second. The coach, who earlier sent Bubba to play right field, now reports him as a pinch runner. The umpire does not catch the error. The next batter doubles, scoring Bubba. Now the defensive coach wakes up and before a pitch appeals that Bubba was an illegal sub. *Ruling:* In FED / NCAA, Bubba is out and restricted (FED) or out and ejected (NCAA). His run is also canceled, and B1 loses an rbi. In OBR, he is not out, the run and rbi count, and Bubba is ejected.

❀ Note 461: ***(EDITED)*** Illegal substitution is one of nine major rules situations **WHERE EACH LEVEL TREATS THE SITUATION DIFFERENTLY**. The other eight are: § 50-71 (designated hitter); § 83 (use illegal bat); § 124 (throw from dead-ball area); § 144 (conferences / trips to the mound); § 245 (positions occupied at time of pitch or play)und); § 246 (fighting); § 266 (improperly declared infield fly); § 378 (hidden ball play).

★ 489 SUBSTITUTES: LEGAL: DEFINITION ✪ (See § 490.)

FED: A substitute is a roster player eligible to enter. (2-36-1)

NCAA: Point not covered.

> ***(ADDED)*** OFF INTERP 400-489: **PARONTO:** "A substitute is a roster player who is not one of the nine or ten eligible players in the game." (email to cc, 12/25/11) ✠

OBR: No provision.

★ 490 SUBSTITUTES: MULTIPLE ✪ (See § 489.)

FED: Not applicable.

NCAA: A multiple substitution involving the pitcher going to defense (automatically involves also the DH) must include three players before the coach may shuffle his lineup. (5-5e AR; 7-2c-1a and b; 7-2c AR 1) **EXCEPT:** If the DH and pitcher move to defense at the same time, that constitutes a multiple substitution. (Study Play 52-64.)

❀ Note 462: The point of a multiple substitution: (● 1) The DH has been terminated and benched, and the skipper wants his pitcher to bat somewhere other than in the spot formerly occupied by the DH; or (● 2) the DH has been terminated and moved to defense, and the skipper wants his pitcher to bat somewhere other than in the spot formerly occupied by the replaced defensive player.

528. ALSO: No time frame exists for reporting multiple subs.

OBR: ***(EDITED)*** Two players entering constitute a multiple substitution. (6.10b-5)

529. ALSO: If multiple substitutions are made, the manager must designate their spots in the offensive lineup "before they take their positions [on the field]." Otherwise, the UIC will insert them into the spots vacated by the respective starters they replaced. (3.03)

> **EXCEPT:** OFF INTERP 401-490: **PBUC:** "There is no requirement that the manager or coach announce to the umpire a double-switch before crossing the foul line. However, the manager or coach must do so **BEFORE SIGNALING FOR A NEW PITCHER,** as his signal to the bullpen constitutes a substitution for the pitcher." [BRD emphasis] {4.6} ✠

❀ Note 463: In professional play the manager must report the multiple changes to the UIC before going to the mound to pull his pitcher. (See Play 52-64. See also § 497.)

∞ 491 SUBSTITUTES: PINCH HITTER: DEFINITION ✪

FED: No provision.

NCAA: A pinch hitter is a substitute player (not in the lineup) who bats for the listed player. (2-59) (See § 68 and 488.)

OBR: No provision. (See § 68.)

∞ 492 SUBSTITUTES: PINCH RUNNER: DEFINITION ✪

FED: No provision.

NCAA: A pinch runner is any player who enters to run for a lineup player. (2-60)

OBR: No provision.

493 SUBSTITUTES: PINCH RUNNER: ILLEGAL ✪ (See § 488.)

FED: No provision.

❀ Note 464: An illegal pinch runner would be one who is not eligible to enter the game (illegal substitute) with the attendant penalties outlined in § 488. (See Play 66-86.)

❀ Note 465: Unfortunately for umpires, FED does not specifically detail an illegal pinch runner as a player already in the lineup running for someone else in the lineup. (The case book has five plays where an illegal substitute **BATS** but none where he runs.)

NCAA: A player already in the lineup may not be a pinch runner. (5-5f) **PENALTY:** On proper appeal (before a pitch) after an illegal pinch runner enters the game: (● 1) If he is on base, he is out and ejected; (● 2) if he has scored a run, the run is disallowed, an out is declared, and he is ejected. Other runners return TOP. (5-5f Pen) (See § 492.)

❀ Note 466: While the text at 5-5f Pen may appear ambiguous, Thurston confirmed that if a run is disallowed, the umpires will also declare an out. (phone call to se, 2/13/95)

OBR: A player already in the lineup shall not pinch run for another member of his team. (3.04)

530. ALSO: OFF INTERP 402-493: **DEARY:** It is an illegal substitution when a player already in the lineup becomes a pinch runner. The illegal sub is ejected, but he is not out and a legal pinch runner will replace him. (*REF* 10/85) ✠

★ ∞ 494 SUBSTITUTES: PITCHER: IMPROPER PITCHER LEGALIZED ✪

FED: No provision. Treat as in OBR.

NCAA: Point not covered.

(ADDED) OFF INTERP 403-494: **PARONTO:** Same as OBR. (email to cc, 12/25/11) ✠

OBR: An improper pitcher (one who is in the game in contravention of the pitching-substitution rule) becomes a proper (legal) pitcher after one pitch or an out. Any play in which he participates is legal. (3.05c) (See § 152; 488; 496.)

❋ *Play 256-494:* Bubba, having relieved, reaches a count of 3-0 on his first batter. The coach, frustrated with Bubba's inept performance, brings Perry to pitch even though Bubba has not completed pitching to one batter. No one spots the error, and Perry toes the pitcher's plate. Noticing R1's big lead, Perry whips the ball to first, but his throw is wild and both runners advance. The UIC now wakes up and realizes Perry is an improper pitcher. *Ruling:* Bubba returns to the mound since Perry did not deliver a pitch or record an out, but the runners remain on second and third. Furthermore, Perry is still an eligible substitute because he never became a proper pitcher.

★ 495 SUBSTITUTES: PITCHER: RESTRICTIONS: RELIEVER ✪

FED: A substitute pitcher must pitch until the first batter (or any pinch hitter for that batter) to face him completes his at bat or a third out is registered. (3-1-2) (See 381 and 389.)

NCAA: Same as FED. (5-5b) **EXCEPT:** If a reliever comes into the game (but has not faced one batter or retired the side), if the game is stopped because of weather, when the game is resumed the pitcher may – but is not required to – continue pitching. (5-5b AR 3; 5-9e AR 2)

OBR: ***(EDITED)*** Same as NCAA 5-5b. (3.05b; 4.12c)

496 SUBSTITUTES: PITCHER: RESTRICTIONS: STARTER ✪

FED: Unless ill, injured, or removed for disciplinary reasons, the starting pitcher must pitch until the lead-off batter completes his at bat. (3-1-1) (See § 153, 381 and 389.)
531. ALSO: A starting pitcher replaced in the top of the first while his team is batting must be governed by all restrictions. (3-1-3) **EXCEPT:** If the pitcher does not face the requisite one batter, he is removed only from the mound, not the game. He may return at another position. (3.1.2c) (See Play 259-499.)

NCAA: Unless ill or injured, the starting pitcher must pitch until the lead-off batter completes his at bat. [Same as FED 3-1-1.] (5-5b)

❀ Note 467: Of course, you have no concern regarding a starting pitcher re-entering since it's not allowed. You must be concerned, though, if the visiting pitcher is hitting for himself, and a pinch hitter steps into the box in the first inning.

532. ALSO: If a game is halted, the lineups must be the same when the game is resumed, "subject to the rules of substitution." Anyone on the lineup card but not participating will be "ineligible for the remainder of the game." (5-9b)

OBR: Unless ill or injured, the starting pitcher must pitch until the lead-off batter completes his at bat. [Same as FED 3-1-1.] (3.05) (See § 494.) **EXCEPT:** If a game is suspended and the pitcher in the lineup at the time of suspension has not complied with the pitching substitution rule, he may still be removed from the lineup before resumption of play, but he may not participate in the game. (4.12c CMT) *See ¶8.*

★ 497 SUBSTITUTES: PROJECTED / REPORTED ✪

FED: The UIC may not accept projected substitutions: Offensive changes must be reported when the team is on offense; defensive changes, when on defense. (3-1-1; 3.1.1e) (See § 410 and 499.)
533. ALSO: Substitutes must be "announced" while the ball is dead. (3-1-1)
534. ALSO: The UIC shall record substitutions first on his lineup card and then report the changes to the opposing team. (3-1-1)

❀ Note 468: That edict (recording substitutions on the lineup card before reporting them) is borrowed from PBUC 4.5.

535. ALSO: Changes in fielding positions should be reported to the UIC and the scorer. (1-1-5) (See § 463.)

❀ Note 469: It is imperative that pitching changes be reported to both teams to insure compliance with limitation rules. (See § 381.)

NCAA: Any player other than the pitcher may be substituted for at any time when the ball is dead. (5-5c) (See § 56.)

❀ Note 470: The rationale: Make 5-5c harmonize with 7-2c.

536. ALSO: When the pitcher is removed from the pitching position, whether while on defense or offense, he may be immediately inserted as the DH, but he may not re-enter the game in any other capacity. (7-2c-2a) (See § 57.)

537. ALSO: A substitute becomes a player when he reports to the UIC and is entered on the UIC's lineup card. (5-5b AR 2)

NAIA: ***(ADDED)*** A defensive substitution may be reported only when the team is on defense. (Modification 5-5.3)

OBR: Same as NCAA 5-5c. (3.03; 3.07; 3.08a) (See § 490.)

★ 498 SUBSTITUTES: STARTERS RE-ENTER ✪

FED: Any of the 10 starters (includes the DH) may withdraw and re-enter the game once. (3-1-3; 3.1.3b; 3.1.3 CMT) **EXCEPT:** When the lineups are exchanged, all nine (or ten) starting players must be at the ball park. (4.4.1e)

❀ Note 471: The point: A coach may not list players who have not arrived as "starters" to preserve reentry privilege for them. If the players aren't there yet, they can't "start." (See § 259 to find out what happens to a team with missing players.)

NCAA: ***(EDITED)*** "A player who is removed from the game cannot re-enter in any capacity." Withdraw n players may not re-enter. (7-2c-9)

538. ALSO: A withdrawn player may sit on the bench, warmup players, or serve as a base coach. (5-5i)

539. ALSO: No player removed for a substitute before a suspension of play may return when the game resumes. (5-5b AR 4)

NAIA: ***(EDITED)*** Any starter, except the pitcher and designated hitter, may withdraw and re-enter once provided they occupy the same position in the batting order. (Modification 5-5.1)

(ADDED) **540. ALSO:** A pitcher or designated hitter who changes positions later in the game may not reenter since his original position was pitcher or designated hitter. (Modification 5-5.2)

OBR: A withdrawn player may not re-enter. (3.03) *See ¶ 8.*

499 SUBSTITUTES: UNREPORTED ✪

FED: POE 2001, 2002: An unreported substitute is a player eligible to participate but who did not report to the UIC when he entered the

game. (2-36-2; 3.1.1d) The substitute is legal "**WHEN THE BALL IS ALIVE**" and: (● 1) a runner reaches base (3-1-1a); (● 2) a pitcher intentionally contacts the pitcher's plate (3-1-1b); (● 3) a fielder reaches his position (3-1-1c; 3.1.1f); or (● 4) a batter takes his place in the batter's box. (3-1-1d; 3.1.1b) **PENALTY** for not reporting: none. (3-1-1)
(See § 86; 164; 484; 488.)

NCAA: An unreported offensive substitute becomes legal when he takes his position; an unreported pitcher, when he reaches the mound. An unreported defensive sub becomes legal when he reaches his position and play commences. (5-5g 1 through 4) **PENALTY** for failure to report: none. All plays made by unreported substitutes are legal. (5-5g AR) (See § 497.)
541. ALSO: A substitute "becomes a player" when he is reported to the UIC and the umpire enters the name on his lineup card.
(5-5b AR 2; 5-9e AR 1)

OBR: Same as NCAA. (3.03; 3.08a 1 through 4)

542. ALSO: OFF INTERP 404-499: **DEARY:** If a player goes to the mound as his team is taking the field, when the player throws a "warm-up" toss, he is now legally in the game as pitcher. (*REF* 12/82) ✠

❀ Note 472: The FED rule governing unreported substitutes is by far the better statute. The NFHS requires a live ball before a substitute is "official." Bravo for the FED.

⁎ *Play 257-499:* A relief pitcher mistakenly warms up on the mound at the start of a half-inning but before the umpire has declared the ball alive. *Ruling:* In FED, the pitcher need not pitch. In NCAA / OBR, the "relief" pitcher must pitch until the first batter to face him completes his at bat. (See OFF INTERP 379-518.)

⁎ *Play 258-499:* A properly reported relief pitcher begins to warm up on the mound while Bubba, an unreported center fielder, begins to toss fly balls back and forth with the left fielder. Before play commences, the skipper realizes that the wrong substitute is in center field.
Ruling: Bubba has not entered the game since the ball did not become alive (FED) nor did play commence (NCAA and OBR).

⁎ *Play 259-499:* Garza is listed as the pitcher for the visitors, but when his spot comes up in the top of the first inning, Garcia bats. In the bottom of the first Garcia goes to pitch. No one catches the error until the third inning. *Ruling:* At all levels, Garcia is a legal sub and the proper pitcher. In FED, Garza may re-enter (he was a starter), but since he did not comply with the pitching requirements, he may not pitch. In NCAA / OBR, Garza is ineligible. (See § 494 and 496.)

❀ Note 473: It is clear that in Play 259 the coach wrote "Garza" but meant "Garcia." If the UIC announces the battery of each team at the pregame meeting, he will prevent such inadvertent errors. (See § 416.)

★ 500 SUSPENSION: REASONS FOR / PENALTIES ✪

FED: No provisions.

❀ Note 474: Many states have mandatory suspension for coaches or players who are ejected. Umpires are not responsible for dispensing such penalties, but they should know the consequences of ejection and manage the game accordingly. (See Note 168-167.)

NCAA: Umpires have the authority to suspend a player from the next game(s) for the following reasons:
(● 1) a coach removes his team from the field (5-15b)
PENALTY: suspension: coach, **TWO** games. (5-15b Pen)
(● 2) fighting (5-16a); **PENALTY:** suspension: first offense – **THREE** games; second offense – **FIVE** games; third offense – **REMAINDER OF THE SEASON**, including post-season. (5-16a Pen -1/2/3)
(● 3) threat of physical intimidation or harm (5-16b)
PENALTY: suspension: same as for fighting. (5-16b Pen 1/2/3)
(● 4) leaving one's position to fight (5-16c) **PENALTY:** suspension: **THREE** games. (5-16c Pen 1)
(● 5) charging or pursuing the pitcher (5-16c)
PENALTY: suspension: **THREE** games. (5-16c Pen 2)
(● 6) a pitcher intentionally throws at a batter (5-16d).
PENALTY: suspension: first offense – **FOUR** games; second offense – **EIGHT** games; third offense – **REMAINDER OF THE SEASON**, including post-season. (5-16d Pen 1/2/3)
(● 7) coach, having been warned before or during the game, of a pitcher who intentionally throws at a batter (5-16d). **PENALTY:** suspension – **ONE** game. (5-16d Pen 4) and
(● 8) post game ejection of pitcher.
PENALTY: suspension – **FOUR** games.(2-25 AR 5).

OBR: Automatic suspensions apply to:
(● 1) player intentionally damages or discolors a ball by rubbing it with soil, rosin, paraffin, licorice, sand-paper, emery-paper, or other foreign substance. (3.02) **PENALTY:** ejection and suspension – **TEN *(EDITED)*** games. (3.02 Pen)
(● 2) pitcher spits on the ball; rubs the ball on his glove, person, or clothing; applies a foreign substance to the ball; defaces the ball in any manner; delivers a shine ball, spit ball, mud ball, or emery ball. (8.02a 2-6)

PENALTY: ejection / automatic suspension. National Association Leagues suspend for **TEN** games. (8.02a 2-6 Pen)
(● 3) pitcher has in his possession any foreign substance.
PENALTY: ejection / automatic suspension. (8.02b) (National Association Leagues suspend for **TEN** games.)

❀ Note 475: Of course, "*See* ¶ *8*" applies in all three instances.

❀ Note 476 It is somewhat interesting to me that all NCAA suspensions are connected with bad behavior and all OBR suspensions relate to bad pitching.

★ 501 TAG OUT ✪ (See § 502.)

FED: A tag out is a putout of a runner who is not in contact with a base when touched by a fielder with the ball or a glove holding the ball. It is not a tag if the fielder does not have secure possession of the ball: For example, he drops or juggles it after the touch. (2-24-4)

NCAA: A tag occurs when a fielder touches: (● 1) a **BASE** "with any part of his body while holding the ball securely in his hand or glove"; or (● 2) a **RUNNER** while in secure control of the ball. (2-74)
543. ALSO: "The fielder shall maintain or **REGAIN** control of his body and if he drops the ball due to his lack of body control or control of the ball, it is not a tag. A voluntary release is substantive proof of complete control." (2-74)

OBR: Same as NCAA. (2.00 Tag) **EXCEPT:** The pro book does not contain any language even remotely similar to the NCAA **543. ALSO** above.

❀ Note 477: The remaining text of this section is greatly changed, edited, and enhanced compared to the 2011 edition. Consequently, there is no attempt to indicate what has been altered. Simply, study this material carefully. After that, recall the old saying: "You pays your money and you takes your chances." Team 1: Jim Evans, Mike Fitzpatrick, Cris Jones. Team 2: Rick Roder, the NCAA, Hunter Wendelstedt.

TAG: DEFINITION

The NCAA / OBR books define touching either a **BASE** or a **RUNNER** as a tag. FED sensibly holds that a tag occurs only on the touch of a **RUNNER**. To begin with, then, the FED does not enter this discussion.

Jim Evans defines "tag" this way in the JEA:

AO 25-501: EVANS: "In establishing the validity of secure possession at the time of a tag, the umpire should determine that the player held the ball long enough and did not juggle the ball or momentarily lose possession before gaining full control and touching the runner. Unlike a catch, a legal tag is based on the status of the ball at the time the **RUNNER OR BASE** is touched and **NOT ON THE FINAL PROOF OF POSSESSION**." (2:40)

OFF INTERP 405-501: **FITZPATRICK:** "[In a footrace to the bag] when the fielder beats the runner, that's an out. A subsequent drop does not affect the outcome." (phone call to cc, 6/10/04) This confirms **CRIS JONES**' ruling on eteamz, May 2000: "I would call the runner out. The reason: F3 had possession of the ball and once he stepped on first the batter-runner is out, as long as F3 is not bobbling the ball as he steps on the bag." [Fitzpatrick's comments refer to Play 260 below. ✠

Rick Roder disagrees strongly with Team 1:

AO 26-501: J/R: "[To complete a tag successfully a fielder] must have complete control of the ball **DURING AND AFTER** the touch of the base or runner. If the fielder bobbles or drops the ball during or after the touch of the base or runner, and the bobble or drop is due to his lack of control of himself or the ball, or <u>due to contact with a runner,</u> **IT IS NOT A TAG**." (27-28)

For the NCAA position, re-read **543. ALSO** above.

I put the following play to Hunter and the staff of the umpire school:

⁂ *Play 260-501:* F3 fields a fair ball deep behind first base. He races for the bag and, in full control of the ball, tags the base in advance of BR. As F3 continues across the base, he trips, falls to the ground. The ball pops free.

Hunter didn't answer my question. Instead, he offered these four plays:

⁂ *Play 261-501:* **Tag of a runner:** Fielder dives for a player in an attempt to tag. As he slaps the tag on the runner, the fielder continues to the ground, where the ball comes out as he hits the ground. *Ruling:* No tag. The **MOMENTUM** of the tagging action includes the falling of the fielder in his tag attempt, therefore, secure possession has not been **PROVED**.

⁂ *Play 262-501:* **Tag of a runner:** R1 stealing. The throw beats the runner in plenty of time. But when the second baseman tags R1's foot as he slides in to the base, the ball is knocked out by the sliding foot. *Ruling:* No tag. When the ball was immediately knocked out by the sliding foot, secure possession has not been **PROVED**.

⁂ *Play 263-501:* **Tag of a base.** The batter hits a ground ball to the first baseman. F3 fields it and slides head first into the first-base bag in an attempt to put out BR. The tag attempt beats BR. The ball, however, comes out of the glove immediately after the touch of the base. **Ruling:** No tag. The **MOMENTUM** of the tagging action includes the slide of the fielder in his tag attempt. Therefore, secure possession has not been **PROVED**.

⁜ *Play 264-501:* **Tag of a base.** The batter hits a ground ball to the first baseman. He fields it to the covering pitcher. The pitcher has the ball securely in his glove and steps on the base as the BR runs into his back, knocking down F3. When he hits the ground, the ball out of his glove. *Ruling:* Successful tag and BR is out. The tag of the base was **PROVED** the moment that it was touched and the **MOMENTUM** of the tagging action ended. The BR caused the ball to be knocked out after the tag had already been **PROVED**.

Wendelstedt summary: **When a runner is tagged**, the momentum of the tagging action continues as long as contact with the runner continues, or any subsequent action of the fielder occurs because of contact with a runner. For instance, if a catcher (or any other fielder) attempts to tag a runner, and that fielder is "run over" by the runner, F2 must hold the ball through any subsequent action caused by the tag, including being knocked down.

Wendelstedt summary: **When a base is tagged**, the momentum of the tagging action continues as long as contact with the base is sustained or any subsequent action of the fielder occurs because of contact with the base. For instance, if a fielder attempts to tag a base by diving or sliding, the momentum of that dive or slide must end. However, if he is touched by a runner after tagging the base, and this causes the ball to be knocked out, the tag has been proven.

Hunter's final comment: "Carl,. this is much like Justice Potter's definition of pornography: You know it when you see it. Remember, though: A completed tag does not have the same requirements of a catch." (email to cc, 2/9/12)

I took some solace in the fact that Hunter did not buy into Rick's ruling that a tag dissolved even when the fielder was smacked by a runner. Still, I was moved to reply to Hunter: "OK, so in Play 260 [above] the first baseman still had contact with the base when he tripped and fell to the ground, which knocked the ball free. *Ruling:* BR is safe. Wow! There's 57 years of umpiring down the drain, including the work several thousand amateur umpires I've taught during five decades."

BRD's summary: The alteration of NCAA rules does demonstrate one stark, almost frightening reality: The Jaksa/Roder Manual, under the direction of Rick Roder, has infiltrated the NCAA rules committee. This significant change results from Rick's pervasive, persistent, and persuasive presence on the web. Amazing!

★ 502 THROW OUT ✪ (See § 501.)

FED: A throw out is a putout: (● 1) on the batter-runner at first [before he touches the base]; or (● 2) at any base where the runner is forced or required to ***(ADDED)*** retouch. (2-24-5)

NCAA: No provision!

❀ Note 478: The NCAA mentions "throw out" just — once (6-3b) and does not define it.

OBR: No provision!

❀ Note 479: The OBR mentions "throw out" just — never.

❀ Note 480: Seriously, FED's distinction between "throw out" and "tag out" is well-taken since it prevents disagreement about when a "tag" is complete.

503 TOBACCO PROHIBITED ✪

FED: POE 1994, 1995: Team personnel shall not use tobacco or "tobacco-like" products "within the confines of the field."
(3-3-1p; 3.3.1mm.)
PENALTY: Ejection. (3-3-1p Pen) (See § 529.)

❀ Note 481: Several other infractions are listed as occurring outside the "confines of the field": batting practice during a game (§ 114), illegal warm-up devices (§ 187), and wearing a bandanna (§ 521). FED does not allow the umpires to police those illegal activities until they have jurisdiction by going "inside" the confines of the field (§ 419). But umpires must ensure that a player warming up the pitcher **ANYWHERE** is wearing the prescribed protective gear (§ 194).

544. ALSO: It is unacceptable for individuals to **PRETEND** or **APPEAR** to be using tobacco by using a tobacco-like product. Such individuals shall be ejected. (3.3.1mm)

545. ALSO: A coach using tobacco outside the confines of the field is not within the jurisdiction of the umpire. (3.3.1kk)

546. ALSO: A coach on the field with a tin of smokeless tobacco (or tobacco-like product) must rid himself of the product. (3.3.1LL)

547. ALSO: Umpires are prohibited from using tobacco or tobacco-like products in the vicinity of the field. (10-1-8) **PENALTY:** Offenders shall be reported to the state association. (10.1.8a and b)

❀ Note 482: Interesting: Coaches can do it, but umpires can't.

NCAA: POE 2000, 2002, 2003, 2004, 2005, 2006: Student athletes and game personnel (coaches, umpires, trainers, etc.) may not use tobacco during "practice or competition." (3-11)

(EDITED) 548. **ALSO:** NCAA umpires are instructed to have "zero tolerance" for tobacco. (3-11)
PENALTY: Ejection of the offender from the practice or game as well as the head coach. Umpire jurisdiction begins when the umpires arrive on the field or dugout in uniform. (3-11 Pen)

> ❀ Note 483: I'm still trying to figure out who is going to "eject" a player who is smoking during practice. Perhaps they mean "pregame" practice.

OBR: Point not covered.

> OFF INTERP 406-503: **PBUC:** The minor leagues have outlawed the use of tobacco products by players, coaches, and umpires. {9.17} *See ¶ 8*✠

504 UMPIRE: ARRIVES AT GAME SITE ✪

FED: No provision.

NCAA: The umpires should arrive at the game site at least "60 minutes" before the scheduled start. (3-6a Nt)

OBR: Point not covered.

> OFF INTERP 407-504: **PBUC:** Professional umpires should arrive at the ball park at least one hour before the scheduled starting time and be in uniform at least 15 minutes before game time. {9.17} *See ¶ 8.* ✠

505 UMPIRE: CALL CHANGED: FOUL TO FAIR ✪

FED: A batted ball is foul and dead whenever an umpire "inadvertently announces 'Foul' on a ball that touches the ground," whether in fair or foul territory. That call cannot be changed. (2-16-1e; 5-1-1h; 5.1.1a, b and c (See § 506.)

> ✻ *Play 265-505:* **FED only.** B1 slaps a high drive that clears the fence down the line in left. The umpire calls "Foul ball!" After consulting with his partner, he changes the call to "Fair." *Ruling:* The ball became dead when it cleared the fence, not when the umpire called "Foul." The call may be changed.

> ✻ *Play 266-505:* **FED only.** The umpire declares "Foul ball" on a pop-up that the third baseman misplays. The ball becomes fair, and F5 drops it. *Ruling:* The ball is foul. If F5 had caught the ball in fair territory, B1 would have been out since the ball did not touch the ground.

NCAA: If a ball, other than one that cleared the outfield fence, is called foul, the call cannot be changed. (Appendix E)

OBR: Point not covered.

OFF INTERP 408-505: **FITZPATRICK:** The umpire may reverse his call if everyone concerned ignored his initial signal. Fitzpatrick: "In certain instances, *e.g.*, home run balls at the foul pole, a crew consultation may be necessary to determine the correct decision." (email to cc, 11/15/00) (See § 509.) ✠

⁂ *Play 267-505:* R1, R2. B1's line drive skips off third, bounds to the wooden fence, and rattles around in foul territory with the third baseman and left fielder giving chase. The umpire calls "Foul" and then immediately reverses himself. In spite of the first call, the runners and fielders keep moving. *Ruling:* In FED / NCAA, the ball is dead. In OBR, play continues without reference to the erroneous call.

⁂ *Play 268-505:* Without dropping his bat Bubba hunkers down to avoid an inside pitch. The ball nicks off the knob end and rolls into fair territory. The UIC erroneously calls "Foul ball!" and then quickly yells "Play it! Fair ball!" On the first call Bubba stops and starts to return; on the second call, F2 picks up the ball and throws to first for the out. *Ruling:* It's a foul ball.

❀ Note 484: You must understand, though, that reversing a call from "fair" to "foul" causes no rules problem. You'll face an argument, but the changed call will not affect the outcome of the play. That is true whether fielders or runners reacted to an initial "point" toward fair territory. If the ball is subsequently ruled foul, simply order the batter back to the box — and any runners back to bases occupied at TOP. (Of course, you might also need to order the coach back into the third-base coaching box.)

★ 506 UMPIRE: CALL CHANGED: PROTECTS EITHER TEAM PUT AT DISADVANTAGE ✪

FED: The UIC may rectify any situation in which an umpire's reversed decision put either team at a disadvantage. (10-2-3L; 10.2.3e, m and n) (See § 75 and 505.)
549. ALSO: Advances (and sometimes outs) made by runners following a reversed call will stand if the change clearly did not place them in jeopardy. (10.2.3i)

550. ALSO: OFF INTERP 409-506: **HOPKINS:** When the defensive team reacts to an erroneous statement of the number of outs ("two are out" when only one has been retired), the resulting play stands: "Both teams are responsible to know the count and the number of outs." (Website 2010, #19) (See §266 and 353.) ✠

NCAA: On appeal the UIC may correct errors in the interpretation of a rule. (3-6g) (See § 509 and 512.)

OBR: Appeals that a rule was misinterpreted may be presented only to the umpire who made the ***(EDITED)*** protested decision. If he does not seek help, his ruling stands. (9.02b) (See § 512.)

❀ Note 485: The team's only recourse, then, is to file an official protest. (See § 420 and 424.)

551. ALSO: The crew, after consultation, is explicitly empowered to take whatever steps they may deem necessary, in their discretion, to eliminate the results and consequences of an earlier call that they are reversing. (9.02c)

552. ALSO: After the changed call has been explained, "no one is permitted to argue that the umpires should have exercised their discretion in a different manner." Anyone doing so may be subject to ejection. (9.02c CMT)

⁎ *Play 269-506:* R1, 1 out, full count. The runner is moving on the pitch. The ump calls ball four, but the catcher throws to the second baseman covering. The throw is in time to nab the runner who is unaware of the batter's status. The umpire erroneously calls out the runner. The runner gets up and advances toward his dugout. Realizing the runner should have been awarded second, F4 tags him again while R1 is off the base. *Ruling:* In FED and OBR, the umpire will disallow the out and return R1 to second. In NCAA, BRD recommends the umpire follow the same course.

❀ Note 486: According to Evans: "The runner stepped off the base as a result of the umpire's improper call. This is a correctable umpire's error, and the umpire should nullify the out." (9:6)

⁎ *Play 270-506:* R1, full count. B1 checks his swing; the ump calls ball four. The catcher throws to second, meanwhile appealing the half-swing call to the field umpire. After a proper request from the UIC, the field ump grants the appeal by ruling that B1 struck at the pitch. R1 was oblivious to the changed call and was (a) out, or (b) safe at second. *Ruling:* In (a), if the FED umpire is convinced the changed call had no effect on R1, the out stands. In (b), R1 keeps second. In NCAA / OBR, the play stands — regardless. B1 is, of course, out at all levels.

❀ Note 487: In Play 269 the umpire made a mistake and corrected it; in Play 270 the runner made a mistake — and paid for it.

❀ Note 488: The OBR crew should not get into a predicament with a changed call on a half swing. There's help at § 341.

⁎ *Play 271-506:* R1. The runner steals, and the umpire calls him out. R1, though, gets up and continues to third because he believes the ball was on the ground. The defense makes no play. After reflection, the umpire agrees that the ball was dropped and now rules R1 safe. *Ruling:* In FED, R1 must return to second since the defense was placed at a disadvantage by the changed call. In NCAA / OBR, R1 will keep third because the defensive player should have r realized the ball was loose.

✻ *Play 272-506:* R3, 1 out. The plate umpire erroneously signals 2 out, and the scoreboard operator complies. B1 smashes a line drive to the pitcher, who catches it in flight and then slams it to the ground. R3 tags and crosses the plate as the defensive team heads off the diamond. *Ruling:* In FED, the run counts. In NCAA (OFF INTERP 1-4C) and OBR, the umpire can correct his error easily: Return the runner to third and resume play with two out.

❀ Note 489: I heard someone say: "And eject the assistant coach!" (grin) Either way. (another grin)

507 UMPIRE: COACH / OFFICIAL: PROFESSIONALISM ✪

FED: Point not covered.
But umpires must: (● 1) "demonstrate proper behavior and good sportsmanship" and "perform their jobs professionally" **(POE 1993)**; (● 2) refrain from "inappropriate language and behavior" **(POE 1994, 1995)**; and (● 3) consistently enforce the rules (**POE 1996, 1997, 1999, 2000, 2001, 2006, 2007**). (See § 535.)

553. ALSO: POE 2008, 2009: Coaches serve as mentors and should use play situations as "teachable" moments.

NCAA: The umpire is an "approved official" and is "obligated to conduct the game under conditions conducive to the highest standards." (3-6b)

554. ALSO: POE 2011: "For the sport to continue to thrive as it has, coaches and umpires need to continue to engage in healthy discussion and explanation of the rules without creating unneeded delays in the game and unsporting conduct."

❀ Note 490: The book points out the committee "reviewed several proposals" dealing with coach / umpire communication, and believes "the responsibility for improving this relationship lies with coaches, umpires and administrators [AD's] equally."

OBR: Umpires must keep the game moving and "exercise much patience and good judgment." As the "only representative of baseball on the ball field," the umpire must be "courteous, impartial and firm, and so compel respect from all." (General Instructions to Umpires, following 9.05)

❀ Note 491: The problem caused by regulations dealing with umpires is obvious: "Infractions" don't affect the game except indirectly. The coach can't restrict an umpire to the bench; no member of the UIC's crew can eject him. A bad umpire can't be forced to return to the base occupied at the time of his inconsistent strike zone. The point: Writing "rules" about umpires is all very interesting but all very academic, for the team's only salvation from an unethical umpire is the coach's scratch list.

★ 508 UMPIRE: CONFLICTING DECISIONS ✪ (See § 509.)

FED: If two umpires give differing decisions on the same play, the umpires in "consultation" decide which call will stand. (4.5.1)

> ✻ *Play 273-508:* **FED only.** Bases empty. B1 lifts a high fly ball just past first base. The first baseman tries for the ball but drops it. The plate umpire "signals fair," but the base umpire "signals foul." *Ruling:* "This would not be considered a double call. The foul ball call of the first base umpire would prevail and B1 would return to the plate." (adapted from FED 5.1.1b)

NCAA: The UIC resolves conflicts after consultation. (3-6i)
555. ALSO: The UIC is directed to consult with his crew before declaring a forfeit. (5-12) (See § 262.)

OBR: Same as NCAA. **EXCEPT:** In major league play the league president may sometimes designate the crew chief to make that decision. (9.04c) *See ¶ 8.*

509 UMPIRE: CONSULTS ✪

FED: High school umpires are directed to confer about: (● 1) when to suspend play in bad weather (§ 243); (● 2) conflicting decisions (§ 508); and (● 3) when to start the second game of a double-header (§514).

NCAA: College umpires confer to: (● 1) identify participants in a fight by "immediately" using video evidence (§ 220); (● 2) suspend play in bad weather (§ 243); (● 3) declare a forfeit (§ 262); and (● 4) resolve conflicting decisions (§ 508).

OBR: OBR umpires consult about: (● 1) placing runners following obstruction (§ 33); (● 2) suspending play in bad weather (§ 243); (● 3) confirming the on-field ruling after an official protest is lodged (§ 423); (● 4) changing a call on foul / fair; home run / double (§ 505); and (● 5) taking any measurers needed "to eliminate the results of an earlier call" that they reversed (§ 506).

★ 510 UMPIRE: CRUTCHES, CANES, CASTS, SPLINTS, BRACES ✪

FED: Like a player, an umpire may wear an artificial limb, and padded "casts, splints and braces" are legal. (10-1-7) An official using a cane may umpire. (10.1.7b and c) An official's dangerous prosthesis (hook for a hand, for example) "must be padded with a recommended ½-inch closed-cell, slow-recovery rubber or other material of the same minimum thickness and having similar physical properties." (10.1.7c) (See § 133 and 215.)

556. ALSO: Umpires may use "mobility devices," *i.e.*, wheelchairs. (10-1-7; 10.1.7a)

❀ Note 492: I'm as liberal as anybody. For example, I voted for John Kerry; and if I'd had the chance, I' would have happily voted for Senator Hillary Clinton. I eagerly voted for President Obama. But the ADA is being carried too far. I'd like someone to explain how an umpire in a wheelchair can get from Position A to second base on a possible double. Can the UIC chase back at an angle to the backstop to see if the catcher nabs a foul popup before it touches the screen? It began with coaches on crutches in the third-base box (an injury waiting to happen) and has devolved to some umpire-candidate threatening to sue if an association doesn't assign him games — wheelchair and all.

NCAA: Point not covered

> ***(ADDED)*** OFF INTERP 410-510: **PARONTO:** "This decision is left up to the local association." (email to cc, 12/25/11) ✠

OBR: No provision.

511 UMPIRE: HANDLES LIVE BALL ✪

FED: If an umpire handles a live ball, the ball becomes dead. (5-1-1h)

NCAA: Unless the umpire has asked specifically to examine the ball, it remains alive when touched by an umpire. (6-5g)

OBR: Same as NCAA. (5.10e)

> **557. ALSO:** OFF INTERP 411-511: **FITZPATRICK:** If an umpire handles a live ball when a play is ongoing, he should drop the ball in place the instant he realizes further play is possible. (email to cc, 11/15/00) ✠

❊ *Play 274-511:* R3, 1 out. B1 strikes out swinging. Thinking three are out, the catcher tosses the ball over his shoulder to the UIC, who catches it and watches in horror as R3 slides across the plate. *Ruling:* In FED, the ball is dead; R3 returns to third. In NCAA / OBR, the run counts.

★ 512 UMPIRE: POINTS NOT COVERED ✪

FED: The UIC has jurisdiction over points not covered by the rules (10-2-3g) and not assigned to the field umpire in 10-3. (10-2-2)

❀ Note 493: FED has no rule that prevents a fielder from creeping in toward the plate and "distracting" the batter. NCAA / OBR prohibit it. Only the UIC is permitted by the code to rule on that point. He could penalize the fielder, using precedent from the other two levels. He could ignore the situation. It's his decision alone.

(ADDED) **558. ALSO:** Any questions regarding legality of a player's equipment shall be resolved by the UIC." (1-5-10; Website 2012, #4)

NCAA: Each umpire has jurisdiction over points not covered. (3-6b)

OBR: Same as NCAA. (9.01c)

513 UMPIRE: RULEBOOK CARRIED ONTO FIELD ✪

FED: No provision. (See § 133.)

NCAA: The umpires and the home coach should have a current rulebook "available at the game site." (3-6a Nt)

OBR: Professional umpires are directed to take their rulebooks **ONTO THE FIELD:** "It is better to consult the rules and hold up the game ten minutes to decide a knotty problem than to have a game thrown out on protest and replayed." (General instructions to umpires, following9.05)

★ 514 UMPIRE: SECOND GAME OF DOUBLE-HEADER STARTED ✪ (See § 509.)

FED: The "umpires" in consultation make decisions about when to start the second game of a double-header. (4-1-1) (See § 243.)

NCAA: The UIC is solely responsible for when the second game of a double-header should begin. (4-2c)

559. ALSO: Special rules govern double-headers. (5-7)

OBR: Same as NCAA. (3.10b; 4.13) **EXCEPT:** During the closing weeks of a season, the league president makes such decisions. (3.10a) (See § 257.) *See ¶8.*

515 UMPIRE: SUSPENDS: PARTICIPANTS ✪

FED: No provision.

NCAA: "Any umpire may eject and suspend any player, coach, manager or trainer if the violation warrants a suspension." (3-6d AR 4) (See § 164, 246 and 500.)

OBR: No provision.

★ 516 UMPIRE: SUSPENDS: PLAY FOR INJURY ✪

FED: If a player or umpire is "incapacitated," the umpire shall not call "Time" "until no further advance or putout is possible." (5-2-1d) **EXCEPT:** "If there is a medical emergency or if, in the umpire's judgment, further play could jeopardize the injured player's safety," he may call "Time" at once. (5-2-1d-1)

NCAA: If a player or umpire is "injured"during a live ball, the umpire shall not call "Time" "until no further advance or putout is possible." (6-5d)

OBR: Same as NCAA 6-5d. (5.10c) *See ¶8.*

❀ Note 494: BRD recommends: If you think another player might be injured as a result of the first player's mishap, call time at once. In any game where the players don't shave, call time at once anyway.

★ 517 UMPIRE: TEAM WARNINGS RECORDED ✪

FED: The umpire shall record all team warnings on the appropriate team lineup card. (10-2-3j) If an umpire does not record such warnings, "the coach may wish to inform the state association or appropriate officials' association of the umpire's failure" to do so. (10.2.3j)

❀ Note 495: The umpire issues and records team warnings for eleven infractions: (● 1) an on-deck batter without a helmet (§ 88) or (● 2) not near his on-deck circle (§ 90); (● 3) a carelessly thrown bat (§ 94); (● 4) continued bench-jockeying (§ 119); (● 5) non-adults without helmets in a coaching box (§ 132); (● 6) players loosening up with a device other than a bat (§ 187) or (● 7) wearing jewelry (§ 200); (● 8) a fake tag (§ 351); (● 9) runners without helmets (§ 427) or (● 10) who remove helmets in live-ball territory during a live ball (§ 428); and (● 11) wearing a bandanna (§ 521).

NCAA: POE 2006: Point not covered.

> ***(ADDED)*** OFF INTERP 412-517: **PARONTO:** "All warnings shall be recorded on the umpire's lineup card and reported to the proper conference or NCAA administrator. Example: 'Name or number: arguing half swing, third inning.' In the report, the umpire should include the proper rules citation: 3-6f." (email to cc, 12/25/11) ✠

❀ Note 496: The 2006 POE is titled: Umpire warnings and procedures. It's a large umbrella: (● 1) argue balls and strikes (§ 43); (● 2) fielder distracts batter (§ 72); (● 3) bench jockeying (§ 119); (● 4) coach addresses opponents (§ 128); (● 5) coach refuses to continue play (§ 140); (● 6) coach removes team from field (§ 140); (● 7) fighting with opponents / umpires (§ 246); (● 8) suspended player participates (§ 247 (● 9) malicious contact (§ 329);

(● 10) argue balks (§ 358); (● 11) entice balks (§ 359 and § 360); and (● 12) pitcher throws at batter (§ 405).

❀ Note 497: The umpire may issue team warnings for two infractions: players not in the coaching box touch a home run hitter before he touches the plate (§ 309) and visual obstruction (§ 354).

OBR: Not applicable.

❀ Note 498: No provision provides for team warnings except in a beanball incident, and that is a solely a warning to the pitcher and his manager. (See § 405.) *See ¶ 8.*

∞ 518 UMPIRE: TIME LIMITS ENFORCED ✪

FED: No provision.

NCAA: Time between half innings: (● 1) Non-televised games: 90 seconds. (● 2) Televised games: 108 seconds, but the time may be extended by contract. (9-2i)

560. ALSO: PENALTY: When the defense violates, ball; when the offense violates, strike. (9-2i Pen) (See § 44 for handling delays caused by the batter. See also § 341.)

OBR: If a time limit has been set, the UIC shall announce the time set before the game begins. (9.04a-7) *See ¶8.*

★ 519 UNIFORM: CAP REQUIRED ✪

FED: A cap is a required part of each participant's uniform. (1-4-1; 1-4-4) (See § 196 and 530.)

NCAA: "A player or coach must wear a team hat on the field." (1-14h) (See § 135 and 520.) How the cap should be worn:
Point not covered.

***(ADDED)* 561. ALSO:** OFF INTERP 413-519: **PARONTO:** If the umpire feels a hat titled askew is distracting, he may direct the player to correct it, using NCAA 9-2h. (email to cc, 12/31/11) ⌘

(ADDED) ❀ Note 499: Finally, someone has joined me in this crusade. But don't carry this too far. Obviously, the interpretation applies only to pitchers. If the center fielders want to wear his hat backwards, that's all right with the NCAA.

OBR: No provision.

520 UNIFORM: IDENTICAL STYLE ✪

FED: Uniforms "should" be identical. (1-4-1) (See § 527.)

NCAA: Uniforms "shall" be identical (1-14) (See 519.)

OBR: Same as NCAA. (1.11a-1)

521 UNIFORM: ILLEGAL: BANDANNA PROHIBITED ✪

FED: Team personnel may not wear bandannas. (3-3-1d)
PENALTY: Team warning / ejection. (3-3-1d Pen)

❀ Note 500: At the risk of alienating the NFHS, I must point out that this is an attempt to legislate social conduct. You'll remember their ill-fated endeavor to prevent players from adding body paint (tattoos). (The BRD once covered that rule [3-3-1g, 1996 ed] in § 523.) Happily, the prohibition against "body paint" lasted just one year. Too many "inner-city" (read, student body is predominantly black) schools found they couldn't field teams.

562. ALSO: The umpires shall enforce the prohibition against bandannas within the confines of the field only. (3.3.1nn)

❀ Note 501: Several other infractions are listed as occurring outside the "confines of the field": batting practice during a game (§ 114), illegal warm-up devices (§ 187), and use of tobacco (§ 503). FED does not allow the umpire to police those illegal activities until they have jurisdiction by going "inside" the confines of the field with the intention of remaining (§ 419). **EXCEPT:** Umpires must ensure that a player warming up the pitcher anywhere is wearing the prescribed protective gear (§ 194).

NCAA: No provision.

OBR: No provision.

522 UNIFORM: ILLEGAL: BASEBALL PATTERN ✪

FED: No provision.

❀ Note 502: In theory, uniforms with a pattern similar to (imitating) a baseball would be legal. (See § 527.)

NCAA: No uniform shall have a design or pattern that imitates or suggests the shape of a baseball. (1-14d)

OBR: Same as NCAA. (1.11e)

523 UNIFORM: ILLEGAL: BODY PAINT
ALL CODES NOW AGREE: TEXT DELETED, 2001.

524 UNIFORM: ILLEGAL: IDENTICAL NUMBERS ✪

FED: No team members may have uniforms with identical numbers. (1-4-3)

❀ Note 503: If you find identical numbers on a team, wait until the opposing coach complains, then do what you can to see to it one number is changed. If you find that's not possible — play the game anyway and let the League sort it all out.

NCAA: No provision.

OBR: No provision. *See ¶8.*

525 UNIFORM: JACKET: PITCHER WEARS ✪

FED: Only the current pitcher may wear a jacket on the bases. (1.4.4a)

NCAA: A pitcher may wear a nylon jacket under his uniform top if it is the same color as his team's undershirts. (1-14e) (See § 526.)

OBR: No provision. *See ¶8.*

526 UNIFORM: JACKET: PLAYER WEARS ✪

FED: Players other than the current pitcher may not wear a jacket on the bases though the coach in the coaching box, whether adult or player, has no such prohibition. (1.4.4a)
563. ALSO: Players may not wear jackets while on defense. (1.4.4a) (See § 525.)

NCAA: A position player may wear a nylon jacket under his uniform top if it is the same color as his team's undershirts. (1-14e) (See § 135 and 525.)

OBR: No provision.

527 UNIFORM: LEGAL ✪

FED: Point not covered.

OFF INTERP 414-527: **RUMBLE:** No provision of the code requires uniforms to be of standard baseball design. Question: Is a team wearing blue jeans and Tee-shirts legal? Answer: Yes. (*News* #15, 3/90) (See §520, 522 and 528.) ✠

564. ALSO: OFF INTERP 415-527: **RUMBLE:** If a team protests that its opponents are wearing "illegal" uniforms (not presently defined), the umpire should permit the game to be played and then submit a report to the state association. (*News* #8, 3/90) ✠

NCAA: No provision.

❀ Note 504: Teams must be attired in traditional baseball clothes. (See § 135.)

OBR: No provision. Treat as in NCAA. *See ¶ 8.*

528 UNIFORM: LOGO ✪

FED: A visible manufacturer's uniform logo may not exceed 2¼ square inches with no dimension to exceed 2¼ inches and may appear only once on the uniform. (1-4-4) (See § 527.)

565. ALSO: A two- by three-inch American flag may be worn on *each* uniform item. (1-4-4)

566. ALSO: By state association adoption: A commemorative or memorial patch, with the same dimensions as a manufacturer's logo, may be worn on the jersey as long as the patch is "appropriate and dignified" and does not compromise "the integrity of the uniform." (1-4-4) Patches must be worn uniformly; *i.e.*, every team member must wear one. (1.4.4c)
Patches to honor or commemorate two events (players) may bear different designs. (1.4.4d)

567. ALSO: "There is no national rule prohibiting advertising."
State associations may adopt rules as they see fit. (1.4.4b)

NCAA: POE 2001, 2002: Any manufacturer's logo on the uniform: (● 1) must fit within a four-sided geometrical figure with an area of 2¼ square inches; (● 2) may appear on both jersey and pants; (● 3) must conform entirely to section 1 if it appears on a visible washing label; and (● 4) shall conform to the rules whether on pregame, game, or post-game uniforms. (1-14i)

OBR: Undue commercialization is not permitted. Manufacturers must use "good taste" as to the size and content of their brand names and logos. The rule applies to professional leagues only. (1.17) (See § 537.) *See ¶ 8.*

★ 529 UNIFORM: SHARP OBJECTS IN POCKETS / MOUTH ✪

FED: Point not covered.

> OFF INTERP 416-529: **RUMBLE:** Sharp objects (keys, wallet, etc.) would be illegal and removed from the player's person when discovered. A bag of sunflower seeds would be all right. (News #45, 4/88) (See § 503.) ✠

568. ALSO: OFF INTERP 417-529: **RUMBLE:** An umpire would require a player to remove a toothpick, lollipop, or sucker from his mouth. (*News* #18, 4/81) ✠

NCAA: No provision.

(ADDED) ❀ Note 505: Paronto: "It is recommended that any object that would threaten the safety pf a player shall be removed from the individual and the field of play." (email to cc, 12/25/11)

OBR: No provision.

★ 530 UNIFORM: SHIRT NUMBER: BORDER ✪

FED: The uniform number may have a ¼-inch border. (1-4-3)

NCAA: No provision.

(ADDED) ❀ Note 506: Paronto: "A border is approved as long as it does not interfere with the legibility of that number." (email to cc, 12/25.11)

OBR: No provision.

531 UNIFORM: SHIRT NUMBER: SIZE ✪

FED: Shirt numbers must be plain Arabic style, at least 8 inches high, that contrast with the jersey color. (1-4-3)

NCAA: Shirt numbers must be at least 6 inches high. (1-14a)

OBR: Same as NCAA. (1.11a-1)

532 UNIFORM: SHOES ✪

FED: Shoes are required equipment. No provisions govern the attachment of devices to them. (1-4-1)

❀ Note 507: Do not allow non-traditional devices. (See § 214.)

NCAA: No rule requires players to wear shoes. But no attachments, except the standard pitcher's toe plate, may be made to sole or heel. (1-14b)

OBR: Same as NCAA. (1.11g)

> **569. ALSO:** OFF INTERP 418-532: **PBUC:** "A player may not change shoes during his status as a runner." (3.15) ✠

> **570. ALSO:** OFF INTERP 419-532: **PBUC:** Excessive (distracting) shoe flaps, especially on pitchers, are illegal. {3.15} ✠

533 UNIFORM: TEAMS ENTER FIELD FULLY DRESSED ✪

FED: No provision.

NCAA: When the teams enter the field, it is recommended that they be fully dressed in pregame or regular game uniforms. (1-14)

OBR: No provision.

★ 534 UNIFORM: TWO SETS ✪

FED: No provision.

NCAA: POE 2003: It is required that each team have two sets of uniform jerseys of contrasting colors. The onus for "contrasting color" falls on the visitors. (1-14)

> ❀ Note 508: Logic would dictate the home team be responsible for distinctive uniforms; the visitors might have brought just one while it's likely the home team can put its hands on two. So much for logic.

OBR: Each team shall wear a distinctive uniform or have two sets of contrasting uniforms. The home uniforms must be white. (1.11b) *See ¶8.*

535 UNIFORM: UMPIRE ✪

FED: POE 1998, 1999: Umpires shall wear gray slacks. (10-1-9) (See § 507.)
571. ALSO: By state association adoption only: Umpires may wear the navy blue pullover shirt or state association adopted shirt. (10-1-9)

NCAA: It is recommended that umpires dress uniformly. Logos or insignias are not permitted unless connected to collegiate baseball. (3-6c) **PENALTY:** Umpires in violation shall be "reported to and punished by the proper disciplinary authority." (3-6c Pen)

OBR: No provision.

536 UNIFORM: UNDERSHIRT SLEEVES: PITCHER: COLOR AND LENGTH ✪

FED: The pitcher's undershirt sleeves may not be white or gray. or have "any white or gray sleeve that extends below the elbow. A vest and coordinating shirt that is worn underneath is viewed as a type of uniform top." (1-4-2; 6-2-1i; 1.4.2a) (See § 539.) **PENALTY:** The infraction must be corrected before the next pitch. (6-2-1i Pen)
(See OFF INTERPs • 420, 421 and 422 below.)

EXCEPT: OFF INTERP 420-536: **HOPKINS:** The visiting team is wearing a vest style jersey top over a white shirt with sleeves that end at the elbow. The coach of the home team complains that the pitcher's uniform is illegal since the shirt under the vest is white. RULING: The pitcher's uniform is legal. The shirt under the vest is considered to be part of the uniform and not an undergarment. If the shirt worn with the vest top is white, it is legal provided the sleeves do not extend below the elbow. (Website 2009, #1) ✠

572. ALSO: OFF INTERP 421-536: **HOPKINS:** The pitcher may wear a vest over a long sleeve black shirt that is not distracting. (Website 2009, #2) ✠

573. ALSO: OFF INTERP 422-536: **HOPKINS:** "It is permissible, if his team is wearing a long sleeve white shirt with the vest, for the pitcher to wear a short sleeve white shirt or a long sleeve shirt that is a different color from the rest of the team." (Website 2009, #3) ✠

574. ALSO:OFF INTERP 423-536: **HOPKINS:** The pitcher may wear a compression (medical type) sleeve on his non-pitching arm even when it is white (Website 2009 # 4) or has a different color design (Website 2009, #6) if it is not distracting. ✠

NCAA: All undershirt sleeves must be about the same length and of a solid color other than white. (1-14d)

575. ALSO: "Neoprene Sleeves, if worn by a pitcher, must be covered by an undershirt." (1-14d AR)

❀ Note 509: Neoprene is "an oil resistant, synthetic rubber" used to relieve pain. Use it but don't show it.

OBR: All undershirt sleeves must be of a solid color and about the same length. (1.11a-2)

576. ALSO: OFF INTERP 424-536: **FITZPATRICK:** The pitcher may wear white undershirts if everyone on the team wears the same color undershirt. (phone call to cc, 11/8/01) ✠

❀ Note 510-536: Though white undershirt sleeves are not prohibited by rule or official interpretation, most amateur players and coaches using OBR rules believe a pitcher cannot wear them. Lou Piniella in the 2001 playoffs made that complaint. BRD recommends: Short of professional play, decide that a pitcher's white sleeves are "distracting" and have them removed if the opponent's coach complains. (See § 196.)

★ 537 UNIFORM: UNDERSHIRT SLEEVES: PITCHER: INSIGNIAS ATTACHED ✪

FED: No provision.

NCAA: Point not covered.

(ADDED) OFF INTERP 425-537: **PARONTO:** "If the insignia contains a white or light color that might be distracting to the hitter or the umpire, the pitcher will be required to change to an undershirt that meets the requirements of 1-14d" (email to cc, 12/25/11) ✠

OBR: Only the pitcher is prohibited from wearing insignias (logos) on his undershirt sleeves. (1.11a-2) (See § 528.)

538 UNIFORM: UNDERSHIRT SLEEVES: PLAYER ✪

FED: The length of undershirt sleeves of individual players may vary, but each player's sleeves should be about the same length and shall not be "ragged, frayed or slit." (1-4-2)

577. ALSO: OFF INTERP 426-538: **RUMBLE:** The undershirt sleeves of team members need not be the same color. (*REF* 12/85) (See § 520 and 536.) ✠

NCAA: No player's exposed undershirt sleeves may be white. (1-14d)

578. ALSO: OFF INTERP 427-538: **THURSTON:** The sleeves of all team members must be the same color. (phone call to se, 11/9/89) ✠

OBR: The only requirement is that all undershirt sleeves must be the same solid color "for all players on a team." (1.11a-2)

★ 539 UNIFORM: WRISTBANDS ✪

FED: Point not covered.

OFF INTERP 428-539: **HOPKINS:** A team is wearing "quarterback-style" wristbands "that have defensive plays listed under a Velcro flap. The pitcher has a black wristband down near his glove." This is legal provided they are not dangerous. If the umpire believes the pitcher's band is distracting, it would be removed. (Website 2010, #10) ✠

NCAA: Point not covered.

(ADDED) OFF INTERP 429-539: **PARONTO:** "As long as its use does not delay the game or violate the 90- or 108-second rule, the wristband used by the catcher is legal." (email to cc, 12/25/11) ✠

OBR: Point not covered.

(***MOVED*** from § 201) OFF INTERP 430-539: **MLBUM:** Players may not wear white wristbands (including white bands with a colored stripe) or have white adhesive tape attached to their arms while at bat or on the field. (2.13) ✠

Childress Baseball Bibliography

Note: An asterisk (*) indicates the book is out of print. Check with the author if you're interested in acquiring a copy.

* Baseball Rule Differences, 1989-1996	Referee Enterprises, Inc.
* Baseball Rule Differences, 1999-2000	Gerry Davis Umpire Ed.
* Baseball Rule Differences, 2001-2006	Right Sports, Inc.
* Baseball Rule Differences, 2008	Right Sports, Inc.
* Baseball Rule Differences, 2009	Officiating.com, Inc.
Baseball Rule Differences, 2011	Home Run Press
Baseball Rule Differences, mid-Feb. 2012	Home Run Press
Baseball Umpires Encyclopedia, 2011	Home Run Press
* Behind the Mask, 1987	Referee Enterprises, Inc.
Calling All Umps!, 2011	Home Run Press
* Casebook Plus, 1989-1992	Referee Enterprises, Inc.
* On the Bases, 1987	Referee Enterprises, Inc.
151 Ways to Ruin a Baseball Game, spring 2012	Home Run Press
*51 Ways to Ruin a Baseball Game, 2002	Right Sports, Inc.
*50 More Ways to Ruin a Baseball Game, 2004	Right Sports, Inc
* Take Charge!, 1990	Referee Enterprises, Inc.
* The Umpire's Answer Book, 1988	Referee Enterprises, Inc.
The Usual Suspects, 2004	Right Sports, Inc.
Working the Plate, Working the Bases, 2002	Gerry Davis Umpire Ed.

ALPHABETICAL INDEX

Primary sections (1 — 539) are marked with a plus. ✚

- A section containing a Point of Emphasis (POE) is marked with a star. ✱
- CAPITAL LETTERS mark the A-Z major headings.
- ~~The strike-out attribute~~ indicates the section remains for historical interest only since the black letter law is now the same at all levels.
- ***(NEW)*** indicates a major section added for this edition.
- Each index item includes the page number of the section: Section # -Page # Example: (425-278)
- If a section number has no page number, that section also has no text.

CITATION INDEX

FEDERATION RULEBOOK

FEDERATION CASE BOOK

NCAA

OBR

PBUC

APPENDIX A

NAIA RULE MODIFICATIONS

The National Association of Intercollegiate Athletics (NAIA) conducts annual competition for nearly 300 schools involving more than 60,000 student athletes. NAIA baseball games are governed by the ***(CHANGED)*** NCAA Baseball Playing Rules with but five exceptions.

This list of rule modification is published with the prior consent and cooperation of the NAIA. Questions regarding the language and intent of these modifications should be referred to Scott McClure, NAIA baseball coordinator, smclure@naia.org. The NAIA address is 1200 Grand Blvd., Kansas City MO 64106. Phone: (816) 595-8000, ext. 112.

NCAA 2-6: Base on balls: NAIA modification: (1) On an intentional walk, the batter is waved to first base (no pitches to be thrown).
(2) A batter must be on deck when his turn at bat comes around.

NCAA 5-5: Reentry: NAIA modification: (1)Any of the starting players, with the exception of the pitcher and the designated hitter, may withdraw from the game and re-enter once, provided such players occupy the same batting position whenever they re-enter the lineup.
(2) Starting pitchers and designated hitters who change positions later in the same game are NOT eligible to re-enter because their original starting position was either pitcher or designated hitter.
(3) A defensive substitution cannot be made unless the team wanting to make the substitution is playing defense at the time.

NCAA 5-5: Courtesy runner: NAIA modification: (1) Teams have the option to use a courtesy runner for the pitcher / designated hitter or catcher at any time. For speed-up purposes, it is recommended that the courtesy runner be used with two men out in all games.
(2) The courtesy runner, although never officially in the game, will be credited with the following: A. run scored; B. stolen base; C. caught stealing.
(3) The courtesy runner rule does not apply to a pinch-hitter for the catcher unless the catcher has been re-entered. However, it is permissible to re-enter a catcher for his pinch-hitter and subsequently use the courtesy runner.

(4) A team may not use the same runner for the pitcher / designated hitter and catcher in the same inning.

(5) The courtesy runner may not be removed from a base to become a pinch hitter.

(6) A player removed from the game may not be used as a courtesy runner.

(7) Should the courtesy runner pinch hit, pinch run or enter the game at any position, he will no longer be eligible to be a courtesy runner.

NCAA 5-8a: Seven inning game option: NAIA modification: Teams may adopt a rule providing that one or both games shall be seven (7) innings in length. In such games, any of these rules applying to the ninth inning shall apply to the seventh inning. The 9-inning rule may be waived and shortened to 7 innings prior to the game if both coaches agree to the waiver. If both coaches do not agree, the 9-inning rule will be in effect. This applies to regular season games only.

NCAA 9-4: Trips to the mound: NAIA modification: Same as OBR.

Note: Within the rule changes above, I assigned the numbering of clauses to make for easy reference. They are not sanctioned by the NAIA as citations.

APPENDIX B

2012 BRD OFF INTERPS

First number: OFF INTERP # Second Number: SECTION #

1-Intro / d4	52-47	103-124	154-184	205-264	256-314
2-1	53-48	104-125	155-184	206-265	257-316
3-3	54-48	105-126	156-186	207-266	258-316
4-3	55-48	106-127	157-187	208-266	259-317
5-3	56-49	107-127	158-187	209-266	260-319
6-4	57-50	108-131	159-188	210-267	261-320
7-4	58-64	109-132	160-189	211-267	262-324
8-4	59-69	110-133	161-190	212-268	263-324
9-5	60-70	111-134	162-190	213-268	264-326
10-6	61-73	112-134	163-191	214-271	265-327
11-7	62-74	113-135	164-197	215-272	266-327
12-7	63-74	114-135	165-200	216-272	267-327
13-9	64-76	115-136	166-200	217-273	268-329
14-10	65-77	116-138	167-200	218-274	269-330
15-11	66-81	117-141	168-202	219-276	270-334
16-11	67-81	118-142	169-203	220-276	271-340
17-12	68-82	119-142	170-204	221-278	272-341
18-12	69-82	120-145	171-204	222-278	273-341
19-13	70-82	121-145	172-204	223-279	274-341
20-14	71-84	122-145	173-207	224-279	275-341
21-16	72-84	123-146	174-210	225-279	276-342
22-18	73-86	124-146	175-211	226-282	277-344
23-18	74-87	125-146	176-219	227-282	278-347
24-19	75-88	126-147	177-219	228-282	279-347
25-19	76-89	127-148	178-219	229-283	280-348
26-19	77-90	128-150	179-220	230-283	281-348
27-21	78-91	129-150	180-221	231-287	282-350
28-21	79-94	130-151	181-221	232-287	283-350
29-22	80-94	131-151	182-221	233-289	284-352
30-22	81-95	132-153	183-222	234-289	285-353
31-23	82-95	133-154	184-226	235-291	286-353
32-24	83-97	134-154	185-230	236-291	287-353
33-25	84-98	135-154	186-234	237-294	288-353
34-27	85-101	136-155	187-235	238-297	289-353
35-27	86-101	137-156	188-237	239-298	290-354
36-28	87-105	138-157	189-237	240-298	291-354
37-29	88-106	139-157	190-243	241-298	292-354
38-29	89-106	140-158	191-245	242-298	293-358
39-31	90-111	141-160	192-245	243-298	294-358
40-33	91-112	142-161	193-245	244-298	295-358
41-33	92-113	143-161	194-246	245-298	296-360
42-33	93-113	144-163	195-246	246-301	297-361
43-33	94-113	145-164	196-249	247-301	298-361
44-33	95-114	146-164	197-250	248-301	299-361
45-34	96-114	147-164	198-256	249-302	300-361
46-34	97-120	148-169	199-257	250-310	301-364
47-34	98-120	149-175	200-259	251-310	302-364
48-37	99-123	150-176	201-259	252-310	303-365
49-38	100-123	151-178	202-260	253-311	304-365
50-41	101-123	152-180	203-262	254-311	305-367
51-44	102-123	153-182	204-263	255-311	306-372

307-373	364-429	421-536
308-373	365-429	422-536
309-373	366-431	423-536
310-373	367-431	424-536
311-375	368-431	425-537
312-375	369-431	426-538
313-375	370-434	427-538
314-376	371-434	428-539
315-376	372-436	429-539
316-376	373-436	430-539
317-376	374-441	
318-377	375-441	
319-377	376-441	
320-377	377-441	
321-381	378-460	
322-381	379-460	
323-382	380-463	
324-383	381-465	
325-383	382-465	
326-387	383-466	
327-387	384-473	
328-387	385-474	
329-388	386-478	
330-389	387-478	
331-389	388-479	
332-390	389-479	
333-392	390-480	
334-395	391-480	
335-395	392-480	
336-397	393-481	
337-398	394-481	
338-398	395-484	
339-398	396-484	
340-398	397-484	
341-399	398-485	
342-400	399-485	
343-401	400-489	
344-401	401-490	
345-401	402-493	
346-401	403-494	
347-403	404-499	
348-404	405-501	
349-406	406-503	
350-407	407-504	
351-407	408-505	
352-408	409-506	
353-409	410-510	
354-410	411-511	
355-414	412-517	
356-419	413-519	
357-421	414-527	
358-422	415-527	
359-423	416-529	
360-423	417-529	
361-426	418-532	
362-426	419-532	
363-428	420-536	

11295088R00227

Made in the USA
Charleston, SC
13 February 2012